D0296802

RR

P 10     OCT 1976
WR
796.3331
xbn

√S

N.N.

# ENCYCLOPAEDIA OF
# RUGBY UNION FOOTBALL

*Encyclopedias published by Robert Hale*

ASSOCIATION FOOTBALL
by Maurice Golesworthy
ATHLETICS by Melvyn Watman
BOWLS by Ken Hawkes and Gerard Lindley
BOXING by Maurice Golesworthy
CHESS by Anne Sunnucks
CRICKET by Maurice Golesworthy
FLAT RACING by Roger Mortimer
GOLF by Webster Evans
MOTOR RACING
by Anthony Pritchard and Keith Davey
MOUNTAINEERING by Walt Unsworth
RUGBY UNION FOOTBALL by J. R. Jones
(Revised by Maurice Golesworthy)
RUGBY LEAGUE FOOTBALL by A. N. Gaulton
SHOW JUMPING by Charles Stratton
SWIMMING by Pat Besford
COLLECTOR'S ENCYCLOPEDIA OF
DOLLS by Dorothy S., Elizabeth A. and
Evelyn J. Coleman
HOYLE'S MODERN ENCYCLOPEDIA OF
CARD GAMES by Walter B. Gibson
ILLUSTRATED ENCYCLOPEDIA OF
WORLD COINS
by Burton Hobson and Robert Obojski

*Encyclopaedia of*
# RUGBY UNION FOOTBALL

*Compiled by*
**J. R. JONES**

*Revised and Edited by*
**Maurice Golesworthy**

THIRD EDITION

ROBERT HALE   LONDON

©J. R. Jones 1958
©Robert Hale Limited 1966 and 1976
*First published under the title*
*The Encyclopedia of Rugby Football 1958*
*Second edition 1966*
*Third edition under the present title 1976*

Robert Hale & Company
Clerkenwell House
45/47 Clerkenwell Green
London E.C.1.


IBSN 0 7091 5394 5

PRINTED IN GREAT BRITAIN BY
CLARKE, DOBLE & BRENDON LTD.,
PLYMOUTH

86637
796·3331

# INTRODUCTION TO THE FIRST EDITION

WHENEVER—and that in my native South Wales, is apt to be daily—I come across two or more people locked in argument on the subject of Rugby Football I never fail to be impressed by the truly international range of the average follower's interest in the game. It is not of course that the average follower of Rugby Football possesses by instinct a more cosmopolitan outlook on his chosen sport than his Soccer counterparts, rather I imagine it is a case of his horizons being widened and brought into closer focus through the constant interchange of Tours that has been taking place, and on an international scale, ever since the game of Rugby came into existence as a separate entity. Be this as it may however, one thing is certain, you will find the man on the "Tanner Bank" of almost any ground you like to mention ready and able to discuss the achievements of a George Nepia, or Benny Osler with the same facility and knowledgeability, as he will for the mere asking, revive the legend of an Adrian Stoop or Poulton-Palmer. It is of course a pleasing, indeed altogether praiseworthy state of affairs, but it is at the same time, one that complicates the already formidable task of one who like myself has been brash and presumptuous enough to respond to an invitation to compile an Encyclopaedia on the game, for even as one ploughs through the yellowing tomes of records that mirror almost a century of Rugby Football history in Britain, one is conscious, sometimes overwhelmingly so, that the archives are already bulging with the records of the game's parallel history in Australia, New Zealand, and South Africa. Each separate history in fact is both voluminous and luminous enough to merit an Encyclopaedia of its own, which of course makes the task of one who undertakes to compress the whole into one volume, a highly discriminating business indeed. If then any reader might feel disposed to quarrel with me on the score of omissions, then I can only ask him to believe that the "pruning" this volume has inevitably necessitated was every bit as distasteful to me as the omission of a favourite player might be to him.

Another major difficulty was the paucity of some of the club records, many of which were destroyed during World War II, and also that the progress of the game in some countries, notably in Scotland and Ireland is not quite so lavishly publicised and documented as in others. Within my own conception however I feel that in all its essentials, I have succeeded in supplying something that has been hitherto lacking from the sporting bookshelves, viz., a single volume that portrays at one and the same time, the Rugby game's evolution, its subsequent history, its mode of conduct in different parts of the world, and I hope, a goodly proportion of those facts and statistics that are argued over in factories and club houses the world over.

I make no secret of the fact that the compilation of this Encyclopedia was, at times a chore, but it was at the same time well worth while in the sense that it enriched my own knowledge of the game. If then it may in any of its aspects do the same for others, it will indeed have achieved its object

J. R. JONES

Swansea.

## INTRODUCTION TO THIRD EDITION

APART from the actual revision of the entire contents of this book I have paid a good deal of attention to its re-arrangement. Readers of my other sporting encyclopaedias will know how keen I am to see that all records are arranged for quick and easy reference so that no important facts become lost.

I have also placed a greater emphasis on the inclusion of record-breaking achievements. A few of the game's enthusiasts do not care for statistics, but one cannot escape the fact that there is an ever-growing demand for such information, and any book which purports to be an Encyclopaedia of the sport should include the vital records of individual and club achievements to make it a valuable source of reference. The need for economy has meant that a good deal of comment and other lists of names of clubs and officials have had to be dropped to make way for these records, but I hope you will agree that I have adopted the right policy towards helping to make this book one that will settle so many of those arguments which are continually cropping up.

This edition is based on information available to the end of season 1974-75 plus the England and Scotland tours 'down under' and France's South African tour of 1975.

MAURICE GOLESWORTHY

Strawberry Hill Cottage,
Lympstone,
Exmouth, Devon.

# ILLUSTRATIONS

### Between pages 64 and 65

### Between pages 128 and 129

### PICTURE CREDITS

Colorsport: 1, 2, 3, 4, 5, 6, 7, 8, 16, 19, 22, 35
Sport & General: 10, 14, 15, 21, 25, 26, 27, 29, 34, 36
Press Association: 20, 30
Radio Times Hulton Picture Library: 23, 24, 28, 31, 33

# ACKNOWLEDGEMENTS

My grateful thanks are due to the following for the assistance they have afforded me in the compilation of this encyclopaedia. To Mr. Desmond O'Brien, some-time Captain of Ireland, who put me straight on several matters affecting his country's Rugger, and with the same readiness and good humour with which he was wont to flatten its opponents in the actual arena. To Mr. W. M. Leleu, General Manager of *The South Wales Evening Post* for his assistance in the matter of photographs, and to Mr. Ron Griffiths and Mr. Ron Thomas of the same newspaper for access to their valuable files. Also to Mr. C. B. Jones, C.B.E., of Swansea who started me on the road as a writer on Rugby Football, to Mr. D. R. S. Baker, Editor of *The Herald of Wales,* and finally to the authorities at Twickenham for their invaluable assistance.

J. R. J.

To the above I must add my thanks to those whose assistance has proved invaluable in the preparation of this revised edition. The various Rugby Unions at home and abroad have been helpful, while the majority of club secretaries from whom I have had to seek information have willingly answered my questions. I am also grateful to Leslie Parsons of Redruth for compiling the index.

M. G.

## ABERAVON R.F.C.

Founded in 1876, Aberavon's tradition of spectacular back play has earned them the title of "Wizards of the West." Inevitably perhaps, in view of the club's location in the heart of industrial Glamorgan, and the depression that affected industry in the years between the wars, many of Aberavon's greatest players have turned to the professional game for a means of livelihood. These include four famous wing three-quarters John Ring, Alun Edwards, Syd Williams and Arthur Bassett, all of whom became renowned performers in the Rugby League. Another celebrated Aberavon player was E. M. (Ned) Jenkins who played 21 matches in the Welsh second row between 1927–32. Colours: Red and black hoops, red stockings, white shorts. Ground: The Talbot Athletic Ground, Port Talbot, Secretary: Brian Tashara, 90 Pentyla, Baglan Road, Port Talbot, Glamorgan.

## ABERTILLERY R.F.C.

Founded in 1885, Abertillery are another of the rugged hard scrummaging teams which have helped to establish a Monmouthshire reputation in this aspect of the game. The club have rarely dominated the Welsh club scene, but no side ever contemplates a visit to their picturesque ground at the foot of the mountains with complacency for they are notoriously tough and dour opponents. It is typical of the club and its background that nearly all their International representatives have been forwards, the best known being H. J. Morgan and A. E. I. Pask with 27 and 26 appearances respectively for Wales. Colours: Green and white hooped jerseys and stockings, white shorts. Ground:

Abertillery Park. Hon. Secretary: M. J. Cook, 10 York Street, Abertillery, Gwent.

## AGE
## YOUNGEST PLAYER

See also INTERNATIONALS sub section SCHOOLBOYS IN INTERNATIONAL RUGBY.

The youngest player to appear in an International match in Britain was C. Reid, who was capped for Scotland against England in 1881 just 22 days after his 17th birthday. Reid, who was a forward, was a pupil at Edinburgh Academy at the time, and went on to make 20 appearances for his country.

The youngest player to represent the other British Unions are as follows:-

*England*–F. T. Wright, who was capped against Scotland in 1881. Age 18 years 8 months.

*Ireland*–F. S. Hewitt, who was capped against Wales in 1924. Age 17 years 5 months.

*Wales*–Norman Biggs, who was capped against Ireland in 1889. Age 17 years and 4 months.

### Oldest Player

The oldest player to appear in an International match is believed to be the Gloucester forward, L.E. Saxby, who was 40 when he played for England (his only cap) against South Africa in 1932.

J. A. Nel was 36 years 1 month when he made his international debut for South Africa v New Zealand in 1970.

D. Hiddlestone, the Neath winging forward, was over 30 when he gained his first Welsh cap against England in 1922, as was Amos DuPlooy, of Eastern Province, when he played for South Africa against British Isles in 1955.

A world record however for any kind of representative Rugby is believed to have been created by the famous New Zealand full-back, George Nepia who in 1948 at the age of 43 played for the East Coast (New Zealand) Union in a first class representative match.

## ALL BLACKS

See under NEW ZEALAND and also TOURS.

# AMERICAN FOOTBALL

The early history of Rugby in America is mentioned under the heading U.S.A., but American Football is, of course, something quite different and is included in this Encyclopaedia only because both games sprung from the same family tree.

It was in 1882, when the Americans introduced rules on "downs" and "yards to gain," that this game really broke away from Rugby. These rules are still today the most significant differences between this American game and Rugby Union, for their game is stopped every time a player in possession is brought down, and the team in possession then goes into a huddle or "down" to decide their next move. Teams are allowed four "downs" to advance 10 yards and if they do not succeed with this number they must give up the ball to the other side.

Today the game is played on a field 160 ft. long and 300 ft. wide and which because of the lines marked on it at 15 ft. intervals, is referred to as "The Grid-Iron." The methods of scoring are as follows:

(1)   THE TOUCH DOWN—worth 6 points, and achieved more or less by the same methods as in orthodox Rugby Union.

(2)   PLACEMENT KICK—worth 1 point, and the equivalent of the conversion.

(3)   FIELD GOAL—worth 3 points and which is the equivalent of the Dropped Goal.

(4)   SAFETY—worth 2 points and achieved when one of the opposition is tackled behind his own goal-line.

The game is contested by 11 players on either side with up to 29 substitutes standing by. Play is highly scientific in that it contains a number of fixed tactical manoeuvres or "set pieces" which are put into operation on a given code word, and which consequently have to be practised and rehearsed to a pitch of word perfectedness. The leading Universities are the chief exponents of American Rugby, and the amount of coaching and planning preparation that precedes a big game more often than not exceeds that which is devoted to most professional sports. In addition the game is played on a professional basis in the leading cities.

## APIA RUGBY UNION

The Apia Rugby Union in Western Samoa was formed in 1927, and was granted affiliation to the Rugby Union of New Zealand in the same year. An internal competition is in operation, and the Union have played representative matches in Fiji, Tonga, and the Maoris.

## ARGENTINE

Introduced into the country in about 1880, Rugby Union football in the Argentine is virtually controlled by the River Plate Rugby Union which was affiliated to the Rugby Union in Britain for many years until 1932, Leading clubs Rosario, Buenos Aires, San Isidro, and Gimnasia y Esgrima. Before the war, the Rugby Union sponsored three tours in the Argentine, viz., 1910-11 when a team captained by R. V. Stanley won all their six matches, 1927-28 when D. J. McMyn's team won all nine, and 1935-36 when a side captained by B. C. Gadney were successful in all their ten fixtures. The South Africans too, have played their part in Rugby missionary work in the Argentine for in 1932, a Junior "Springbok" party led by Joe Nykamp of the Transvaal played eight matches winning them all.

In more recent years Wales (1968), Scotland (1969), and Ireland (1970) sent teams to the Argentine and were surprised at the strength of the opposition. Scotland was the only one of these sides to gain a victory in unofficial Tests. When the Argentine made their first European tour in 1973 they won two and drew two of their eight games in Ireland and Scotland.

## ARMY RUGBY UNION

The Army played a leading role in establishing the Rugby game abroad in 1870's, notably in South Africa, while at home the first inter-service game took place on February 13, 1878, when the Officers of the Army were defeated by their counterparts of the Royal Navy at Kennington Oval. The first Serviceman to appear for England was C. W. Sherrard of the Royal Engineers in 1871. while the man who in fact conceived the idea of the Army Rugby Union of the present day was Major J. E. C. ("Bird") Partridge, of the Welch Regiment, who had been capped for South Africa in 1903. In company with his brother officers Lieut-Colonel W. S. D. Craven, D.S.O., Major General C. G. Liddell, C.B., C.M.G., C.B.E., D.S.O., Colonel R. B. Campbell, C.B.E., D.S.O., and Lieut-Colonel J. R. Simpson, he drew up a scheme which was submitted to, and approved by the Rugby Union committee of the day who not only agreed to the formation of the Army Rugby Union, but in addition donated the Challenge Cup which has been competed for annually by Unit teams ever since. This was in 1906, which was also the date of the first official inter-Service match with the Royal Navy. Since then of course the R.A.F. (1919) have entered the field, so that the Triangular Tournament staged each year at Twickenham, has become a traditional, and not the least attractive event in the Rugby calendar. Prior to the 1914 war these matches were known as Officers of the Army, versus Officers of the Royal Navy, but with the resumption of peace time Rugby they became open to all ranks of the three Services.

### Army Record in Inter-Service Games
v. ROYAL NAVY: Played 58. Won 30. Lost 26. Drawn 2.
Record Victory: 23–3 at Twickenham, 1950.
Record Defeat: 3–25 at Twickenham, 1974.
v. ROYAL AIR FORCE: Played 50. Won 29. Lost 14. Drawn 7.
Record Victory: 41–13 at Twickenham, 1975.
Record Defeat: 3–26 at Twickenham, 1921.
In all the Army have won the Triangular Tournament outright on 22 occasions and shared it twice with the R.A.F.

## ASSOCIATION FOOTBALL
The following players have been capped at both Rugby and Association Football.
R. H. Birkett (Clapham Rovers), C. P. Wilson (Cambridge University), and J. W. Sutcliffe (Bolton Wanderers and Heckmondwike) were capped for England at both Rugby and Associaiton football. Dr. Kevin O'Flanagan (London Irish and Arsenal) and his brother Michael O'Flanagan (Landsdowne) were capped by the F.A. of Ireland and the Irish Rugby Union (1948).
H. W. Renny-Tailyour (R.E.) was capped for Scotland under both codes in 1872-73.
E. Hammett (Newport) won a Rugby Union cap for England, and an amateur Association cap for Wales.
D. Davies (Salford) played for Wales at Association football and at Rugby League football.
P. L. Hopkins (Swansea) played Rugby for Wales, and was at the same time a reserve for the Welsh Association XI.

## ATTENDANCE
### International
*World Record*–95,000, South Africa v British Isles, at Ellis Park, Johannesburg, August 6, 1955. Also Rumania v France, Bucharest, May 19, 1957.
*British Record*–104,053 Scotland v Wales at Murrayfield, March 1, 1975.

### Club Match
*British and World Record*–56,000 Cardiff v New Zealand Touring Team, at Cardiff Arms Park, November 23, 1953.

## AUCKLAND RUGBY FOOTBALL UNION
Formed in 1883, and affiliated to the New Zealand Rugby Union on its inception in 1892, Auckland were the original holders of the Ranfurly Shield and between 1905-13 virtually dominated the competition with a run of 26 successes. Among the great players who helped to establish this imposing record were several of the original All-Blacks amongst them such famous names as G. W. Smith, G. Gillett, and Charles Seeling, whilst other famous New Zealand representatives produced by the Union include, A. E. Cooke, W. Cunningham, A. H. Francis, T. H. C. Caughey, W. E. Hadley, M. M. N. Corner, P. L. Jones, R. W. H. Scott, and W. J. Whineray. The union colours are light blue and white hoops: they play at Eden Park, Auckland, North Island. Auckland have now won more Shield matches than any other Union.

## AUSTRALIA
Contrary perhaps to general belief, Australia is, next to Britain, the oldest of the major Rugby playing countries,

for the game there was being established on a properly organised basis at a time when it had hardly left the formative stages in New Zealand and South Africa. This was in 1874, a mere three years after the formation of the Rugby Union in London, and the body responsible was the "Southern Rugby Football Union," later (in 1892) renamed the "New South Wales Rugby Union," New South Wales in fact has ever since remained the principal, indeed on times, the sole, stronghold of Rugby Union in Australia, for apart from supplying the bulk of Australia's International players down the years the State has occasionally assumed the full onus of representing Australia on the Rugby field. They were of course obliged to in the beginnings, for the name Australia does not appear on the International record books until the year 1903, and in the meantime New South Wales had contested three Test series with New Zealand. In 1882, however, the formation of the Queensland Rugby Union relieved the New South Walians of part of least of the burden, and by 1908 Australian Rugby generally had aspired to a high enough standard as to enable them to embark on a major tour of the British Isles. Dr. Moran's first "Wallabies" fully vindicated the faith of their sponsors. (See TOURS AND TOURING), but the success they attained in Britain did not alas (as was then hoped) signify a new and greater era of Australian Rugby: on the contrary it signified merely the beginning of a long uphill battle for survival in face of the ever-growing strength and popularity of the rival Rugby League code which had been introduced into both Queensland and New South Wales the very year the first "Wallabies" had sailed away so blithely from Sydney. Indeed in the final analysis it has been the League code which has exerted the firmer and more lasting grip on the interest and imagination of Australian followers, and nowhere was its impact more disastrously felt than in Queensland where the Rugby Union game ceased to exist between the years 1919-29. Thus once again the State of New South Wales became the sole bastion of Rugby Union football in Australia, but they carried the banner bravely, even gloriously—never more so than when the "Waratahs" a side drawn

exclusively from New South Wales toured Great Britain and France during the winter of 1927-28 (See TOURS) to achieve a success undreamed of in the circumstances.

In 1929 Rugby Union was revived in Queensland, and Australian Rugby in consequence took on a new lease of life, and even though their meetings with South Africa, New Zealand, and the British Isles Touring teams did not bring any sweeping material success, they did at least commend to an admiring world public the swift enterprising back play and adventurous approach which has come to be regarded as the cardinal virtue of Australian Rugby.

In the 1960s the Australians proved themselves a world power in Rugby by their 18-9 win over England in 1963, their record 20-5 win over New Zealand at Wellington in 1964, and their two victories over the visiting Springboks, 18-11 and 12-8, in 1965.

But more recently there has been a decline in the standard of the Australian team. This has been blamed not only on the loss of players to the professional code but also the split in the control of the game through the formation of the Sydney R.U. out of the N.S.W.R.U. Despite problems at international level, however, Rugby Union is increasing in popularity in Australia with attendance figures going up, while there are now about 4,000 teams playing the game at all levels in New South Wales.

Oldest among the leading Sydney clubs are Sydney University (founded 1864), Parramatta (1870), Northern Suburbs (1900), Eastern Suburbs (1900), Western Suburbs (1900), and Randwick (1923).

The Australian national colours are green and gold jerseys and stockings.

## Record in Test Rugby

v   GREAT BRITAIN: Played 16. Won 2. Lost 14. Drawn 0.
    Biggest Win: Australia 13, Great Britain 3, at Sydney, 1899.
    Biggest Defeat: Australia 0, Great Britain 31, at Brisbane, 1966.
v.  NEW ZEALAND: Played 64, Won 13. Lost 47. Drawn 4.
    Biggest Win: Australia 25, New Zealand 11, at Sydney, 1934, also 20—5, at Wellington, 1964.
    Biggest Defeat: Australia 3, New

v. MAORIS: Played 9. Won 4. Lost 3. Drawn 2.
Biggest Win: Australia 31, Maoris 6, at Palmerston, North, 1936.
Biggest Defeat: Australia 0, Maoris 20, at Hamilton, 1946.

v. ENGLAND: Played 8. Won 6. Lost 2. Drawn 0.
Biggest Win: 23–11 at Twickenham, 1966.
Biggest Defeat: 3–20, at Twickenham, 1973.

v. SCOTLAND: Played 5. Won 2. Lost 3.

v. IRELAND; Played 5. Won 1 Lost 4.

v. WALES: Played 6. Won 1. Lost 5.

v. FRANCE: Played 9. Won 0. Lost 8. Drawn 1.
Biggest Defeat: 0–19, Paris, 1958.

v. FIJI: Played 7. Won 4. Lost 2. Drawn 1.
Biggest Win: Australia 24, Fiji 6, at Brisbane, 1961.
Biggest Defeat: Australia 16, Fiji 18, at Syndey, 1954.
Zealand 38, at Auckland, 1972.

v. SOUTH AFRICA: Played 28, Won 7, Lost 21. Drawn 0.
Biggest Win: Australia 21, South Africa 6, at Durban, 1933.
Biggest Defeat: Australia 11, South Africa 30, at Johannesburg, 1969.

## BALL, THE

Historians still argue over the stages of evolution that produced the oval ball as we know it today, but it is established that an oval shaped ball inflated with a pig skin bladder made by William Gilbert of Rugby was on view at the International Exhibition held in London in 1851. It is possible however that the ball at least approximated to that shape long before this, for in *Tom Brown's Schooldays* there is a description of the Bigside game which begins. "The new ball you may see lie there quite by itself, in the middle, *pointing* towards the school or island goal" and this particular match was supposed to have taken place in 1835. In 1870 however a man named Lindon, also of Rugby, produced a bladder in the making of which rubber was substituted for pig skin, and subsequent developments, including the formation of the Rugby Union in 1871 produced the standardised ball which is in use today. It has four panels and weighs (according to regulation) between 380-430 grms. Other stipulated dimensions are, length in line, 280-290 mm, circumference in width, 610-650 mm: circumference end on, 760-790 mm. There are it might be said (chiefly in overseas countries) certain permitted variations from the ball used in Britain.

## BARBARIAN R.F.C.

Founded at Bradford in 1890 by the famous Blackheath forward W. P. "Tottie" Carpmael who was at the time in process of leading a scratch XV on a tour of the Midlands and Yorkshire. The Barbarians have remained a touring club ever since, and their normal winter's programme is restricted to six matches, viz., a match against Leicester over the Christmas holidays, the "Edgar Mobbs Memorial" match with an East Midlands XV at Northampton in March, and a four match tour of South Wales during the Easter holidays when the opposition is supplied by Penarth, Cardiff, Swansea and Newport in that order. Since the last war the Barbarians have been meeting any overseas team which happens to be visiting the British Isles. It began in 1948 When they defeated the Australians in a thrilling and spectacular game at the Cardiff Arms Park, and subsequent meetings with both the South Africans of 1951, and the New Zealanders of 1953 at the same venue, ensured the event a permanent place in the Rugby calendar. In 1960-61 they were the only side to beat the visiting Springboks, but the Barbarians gave what was probably their finest display in that never-to-be-forgotten 23-11 victory over the New Zealanders in January, 1973. In the summer of 1957 the Barbarians ventured for the first time, outside their own islands—to Canada where they were enthusiastically received and wildly applauded for the quality of their football. The following year they went to South Africa.

In many ways the Barbarian club is a unique organisation of its kind. They have no ground of their own for instance, whilst its members, who can only be elected, pay no subscriptions; moreover its officials, who are all honorary, hold no meetings but conduct all their business through the post.

The club motto, "Rugby football is a game for gentlemen in all classes, but never for a bad sportsman in any class," has been faithfully adhered to right down the years, consequently the Barbarians with their great players drawn from all the Home Countries, and very often from those of France and overseas play an open and spectacular brand wherever they play. Nearly all the leading players in the British Isles have represented the club since its inception, and membership is an honour which is ranked only second to playing for one's country. The three great names in Barbarian history are those of Emile de

Lissa, H. A. Haigh-Smith, and Dr. H. L. Glyn Hughes, who between them guided the destiny of the club for over half a century.

## Record v. Overseas Touring Teams

1948 v.
AUSTRALIA at Cardiff,
won                                    9– 6
1952 v.
SOUTH AFRICA at Cardiff,
lost                                   3–17
1954 v.
NEW ZEALAND at Cardiff,
lost                                   5–19
1958 v.
AUSTRALIA at Cardiff, won   11– 6
1961 v.
SOUTH AFRICA at Cardiff,
won                                    6– 0
1964 v.
NEW ZEALAND at Cardiff,
lost                                   3–36
1967 v.
AUSTRALIA at Cardiff, lost   11–17
1968 v.
NEW ZEALAND at Twicken
ham, lost                            6–11
1970 v.
SOUTH AFRICA at Twicken-
ham, lost                           12–21
FIJI at Gosforth, lost           9–29
1973 v.
NEW ZEALAND at Cardiff,
won                                   23–11
1974 v.
NEW ZEALAND at Twicken-
ham drew                          13–13
                                  ―――――
                                  111–186

## 1956-57 Barbarians in Canada
Played 6. Won 6. Points for 227. Against 23.

## 1958 Barbarians in South Africa
Played 11. Won 4. Drawn 1. Lost 6. Points for 181. Against 165.

Colours: Black and white hoops. Hon. Secretary: G. Windsor-Lewis, 58 Cornmarket Street, Oxford.

## BARBARIAN R.F.C.
### (New Zealand)
As a member of the New Zealand touring team in Great Britain in 1935 the Wellington breakaway forward H. F. McLean was so impressed by the attitude towards Rugby football typified by the "Barbarians," that he immediately resolved to form its counterpart in his own country. This was accomplished in 1937, and the prime movers were McLean and a fellow "All-Black" R. G. Bush, whilst original members of the club included F. W. Lucas, G. Nicolson, M. M. N. Corner, W. E. Hadley, T. H. C. Caughey, G. F. Hart, C. S. Pepper, and a very famous all-round sportsman W. N. Carson. Hart, Pepper and Carson, unfortunately lost their lives in World War II, and in commemoration of their achievements and contribution to New Zealand Rugby the Barbarian club sponsor an annual competition for schoolboys in the Auckland area. Some 40-50 teams enter for this event every year, and the trophy―"The Carson-Hart-Pepper-Barba-rian Shield" is awarded not only for victories but for sportsmanship, deport-ment, dress, and the observance of those principles which are generally regarded as conforming to the true Barbarian ideal. The club colours are red jerseys with a white lamb monogram, white shorts and scarlet stockings. The club headquarters are at Auckland, and no doubt in deference to the originals in Britain, they are referred to as "The Little Ba-Bas."

## BATH R.F.C.
This club has never perhaps ranked with the game's aristocracy in the playing sense, but its history, dating as it does, from 1865, is as old as most, and indeed in parts, has been a dis-tinguished one. H. G. Fuller, who was capped in 1882, was the club's first International, and altogether 13 Bath players have worn the England jersey. Possibly the most distinguished of all was that fine and powerful centre-threequarter R. A. Gerrard, who gained 14 caps between 1932-36 before falling in action in January 1943. Inevitably of course the club have made an invaluable contribution to the Somerset county side. Club colours: Blue, white and black jerseys and stockings, Ground: Recreation Ground, Bath. Hon. Secre-tary: H. J. F. Simpkins, Bow Cottage, High Street, Norton St., Philip, Nr. Bath BA3 6LH.

## BAY OF PLENTY

Founded in 1911, the Bay of Plenty Union of New Zealand has produced International players in the persons of E. J. Anderson, A. G. T. Jennings, L. F. Cupples, A. L. McLean, and W. N. Gray who in 1956 played in all his country's Test matches against South Africa in addition to being awarded the "Tom French" Cup as the outstanding Maori player of the year. Ground: Rotorua, North Island. Colours: Royal blue and gold hoops.

## BECTIVE RANGERS R.F.C.

One of Leinster's leading clubs Bective Rangers, formed in 1881, have produced over 40 Irish Internationals. Record cap holder is J. Farrell with 29, whilst next to him (though only numerically) is the famous old time half back L. M. Magee with 27. W. A. Mulcahy, who has captained Ireland, won 35 caps, but most of these were while at University College, Dublin. Other internationally known Bectivians include W. P. Collopy, G. Norton who toured New Zealand with a British Isles team in 1950, P. J. Lawler and S. J. Deering. Colours: Red, green and white hoops. Ground: Donnybrook, Dublin 4.

## BEDFORD R.F.C.

Formed in 1886-87 by the amalgamation of Bedford Rovers (1876) and Bedford Swifts (1882), the new club very soon gained recognition as one of the best in the Midlands. By 1893-94 they were so well established that they went through a season of 28 matches unbeaten and only suffered defeat when they accepted an extra challenge match from Coventry. It was in this season that they also entertained Stade Français from Paris.

Bedford's most capped player is wing-forward D. P. Rogers who played for England 34 times, including three games as Captain. He also appeared in two Tests for the British Lions (South Africa 1962), and was awarded the O.B.E. for his services to Rugby. A former club captain, A. Marshall, was President of the R.F.U. in 1957-58. Ground: Goldington Road, Colours: Light and dark blue. Hon Secretary: L. Bridgeman, 28 High Street, Gt. Barford.

## BIRKENHEAD PARK R.F.C.

Founded in 1871 Birkenhead Park were at one period of their history one of the strongest clubs in the land, one of their finest players being J. R. Paterson who played in all of Scotland's games when they won the International Championship, performing the 'Grand slam,' in 1925, and took his total of caps to 21. Colours: Red, white and blue. Hon. Secretary: W. H. Ward, 6 Arundel Avenue, Wallasey, Cheshire.

## BLACKHEATH R.F.C.

One of the oldest rugby clubs in the world, Blackheath was formed in 1858 by former pupils of the Blackheath Preparatory School. Five years later the club broke away from an association of clubs which had appointed themselves the governing body of Football in London. The issue involved was that of "Hacking" (See HACKING), so Blackheath's defection was in effect the final cleavage between the existing game, and the new one of Rugby Football. In the same year came the first encounter with their greatest rivals Richmond, which took place on Richardson's Field, Blackheath. In 1866 the club joined Richmond in a move to abolish hacking, and were amongst the founder members of the Rugby Union in 1871. In 1882 they took over the tenancy of the Rectory Field which has remained their home ever since.

There were four Blackheath players B. H. Burns, C. A. Crompton, F. Stokes, and C. W. Sherrard, in the first ever England XV which played Scotland at Raeburn in 1871, Since then the club's total of Internationals has exceeded 220. Among them have been some of the game's most famous exponents, viz., A. E. Stoddart, H. H. Vassall, H. T. Gamlin, C. H. Pillman, C. N. Lowe, A. T. Young, A. L. Novis and C. D. Aarvold, whilst in addition many of the club's former players have achieved fame as administrators. These include F. W. Mellish, manager of the 1951 Springboks in Britain, and L. G. Brown, S. F. Cooper, B. C. Hartley, C. J. B. Marriott and J. A. Tallent who have all served as officials of the Rugby Union. The club colours which have remained unchanged for the whole of their existence are red and black hoops. Ground: Rectory Field, Blackheath, London. Hon. Sec.:

H. E. Franks, 22 Warwick Square, London S. W. 1.

## BOLAND RUGBY UNION

Founded in 1939, Boland are one of the younger South African Provincial Unions, but they have nevertheless proved themselves a force since Rugby football was resumed on a peacetime basis in 1946. Among their representatives to achieve full "Springbok" honours in this period are A. C. Koch, whose total of 22 internationals is a Boland record, F. P. Marais, B. F. Howe, A. J. van der Merwe, and M. Hanekom. Headquarters at Wellington. Union colours are, black jersey, gold collar, black shorts, black stockings, gold tops.

## BORDER RUGBY UNION

Founded in 1891, the year the Currie Cup competition was inaugurated, Border have shared the trophy twice, in 1932 and again in 1934, on each occasion with Western Province. Throughout their history they have remained one of the major forces in South African Rugby, and amongst their representatives who have gained "Springbok" colours are: Basil Kenyon, who captained the 1951 team in Britain, B. C. Reid and J. White. Headquarters are at East London. The Union colours are chocolate jersey, white collar and cuffs, white shorts, chocolate and white stockings.

## BOXERS

The best known example of an International Rugby player who was also a professional boxer was that of Jerry Shea the Newport and Wales centrethreequarters who fought regularly as a middle-weight in professional rings. Shea, who later joined the Wigan club as a professional, on one occasion fought the reigning British champion, Johnny Basham in a Welsh title bout, but was defeated. Joe Erskine, the British Heavyweight Champion in 1958, won a Schoolboy Rugby cap for Wales as an outside half.

## BRIDGEND R.F.C.

Founded in 1879, Bridgend are one of the oldest of Welsh clubs and—in the light of their experience down the years— the most ill-used and the unluckiest. Time and again during their

history they have produced really magnificent players only to see them attracted to more powerful and fashionable neighbours. In this respect prominent Internationals such as W. J. Delahay, Clem Lewis, V. J. G. Jenkins, C. W. Jones and Jack Matthews all began their careers with the club but established their lasting fame elsewhere. Even worse misfortune befell them in 1951 when the Rugby League code made one of its periodic forays into South Wales and secured the tenancy of their ground. For several seasons Bridgend were homeless, but thanks to their own enthusiasm and fighting spirit, and the goodwill of their neighbours they overcame their difficulties, and in the summer of 1957 finally re-obtained the lease of their traditional home—The Brewery Field, Bridgend. At one time a scheme to develop this ground as the headquarters of the Welsh national team was considered, but this was rejected in favour of Cardiff Arms Park. The club enjoyed a run of 70 home matches from April 1963 in which they were unbeaten before losing to Newport. Leading international is D. J. Lloyd who gained 24 caps for Wales up to 1973. Colours: Blue and white jerseys and stockings. Secretary: W. A. D. Lawrie, 9 Fairfield Road, Bridgend, Glamorgan.

## BRISTOL R.F.C.

The Bristol club was formed in 1888 and ever since they have ranked amongst the truly formidable of British club sides. Many of their players have won International honours, among them such household names as J. S. (Sam) Tucker who "hooked" for England on 27 occasions, L. J. Corbett, who was sometimes called the 'D'Artagnan' of centre-threequarters. W. R. Johnston, T. J. M. Barrington, T. W. Brown, Don Burland, G. G. Gregory, H. E. Shewring, and J. V. Pullin, who holds the England record with 40 caps. Club colours: Blue and white hooped jerseys and stockings, white shorts. Ground: The Memorial Ground, Bristol. Hon. Secretary: T. A. B. Mahoney, 2 Raymend Walk, Victoria Park, Bristol.

## BRITISH LIONS

The earliest British teams to tour abroad were not truly representative and, indeed, the first, that to Australia and

New Zealand in 1888, was not even an official side. It was not until the 4th tour (to Australia in 1899) that the team included players from each of the four home countries. Even then no real attempt to select the finest possible players from each of the four home countries was made until much later.

After the first tour the Rugby Football Union assumed responsibility for these tours, but for many years the team was generally referred to abroad as the "English team" in the same way as the R.F.U. was known as the "English R.F.U."

The R.F.U. continued as the organising body for these tours (with the co-operation of the other three home Unions from 1924) until 1949 when a Committee of the four home countries was formed to select the team and conduct the tours. Officially the side is now the British Isles Rugby Union Team, although it is more popularly known as the "British Lions", a title first given to the team in South Africa in 1924 when local journalists used the name because of the lion symbol on the players' ties.

The entire history of the British Lions (i.e. from 1888) now covers 19 tours which have produced these statistics: played 474, won 351, drawn 30, lost 93, points for 8,181, points against 3,651. These figures include 75 Tests, of which 30 have been won, 9 drawn, and 36 lost, with 748 points socred and 795 conceded.

Further details are given under TOURS, with summaries of results so far under each of the overseas countries involved, i.e. Australia, Canada, New Zealand, and South Africa. See also under SCORING RECORDS for other facts.

## BRITISH COLUMBIA

Rugby Union football was introduced to British Columbia in the 1880's by A. St. G. Hammersley of Marlborough, who had played for England in the first ever International game with Scotland in 1871. Earliest visitors to the Province were the great New Zealand side led by Dave Gallaher who called in at the Pacific Coast while homeward bound from Britain in 1905 to play two matches with the British Columbia representatives team. The visit has been repeated by all subsequent New Zealand sides visiting Britain. Club sides or local representative teams met the New Zealanders in 1924, 1935, and 1954, but fully representative British Columbian teams played them in 1963, 1967, and 1972. Two of the Provinces' most notable victories are 11–8 v. Australians in 1958 and 8–3 v. British Lions in 1966.

## BROKEN TIME

The Broken Time question, i.e., whether amateur Rugby players should be compensated for loss of wages sustained as a result of their participation in the game, has always been a highly controversial one, and it was as a direct result of a disagreement on the question that the rival code of Rugby League was formed. At a meeting held at the Westminster Palace Hotel, London, on September 20, 1893, two Yorkshire representatives of the Rugby Union (J. A. Millar and M. N. Newsome) Proposed that "Players be allowed compensation for bone-fide loss of time," whereupon W. Cail (President) proposed, and G. Rowland Hill (Hon. Sec.) seconded "That this meeting believing that the above principle is contrary to the true interest of the game and its spirit, declines to sanction the same, "The amendment was carried by 282 votes to 136, and several of the Northern clubs promptly announced their withdrawal from the Union on the issue. This led to the formation of the Northern Union which later became the professional Rugby League. Another result of the meeting was the complete recodifying of the Laws with an aim to exclude professionalism in any shape or form. This task was accomplished by the Union Treasurer, W. Cail, in 1895. Throughout the intervening years there has been considerable agitation for a revision of laws which are claimed to impose hardships on certain players, particularly those from the industrial areas who are paid on daily or hourly rates. Indeed from Wales, and certain parts of industrial England there have come reports of clubs secretly disregarding the laws against broken time payments, but in no instances has the allegations been substantiated. In 1953 for instance, the Welsh Rugby Union called upon a B.B.C. commentator, G. V. Wynne Jones, to substantiate allegations of broken time payments in Welsh Rugby, and on his failure to do so banned him from broadcasting on any ground under their jurisdiction. Several players have incurred suspensions for attempting to obtain compensation for loss of wages, the cause celebre perhaps being that of the Cardiff full back Alban Davies who was suspended *sine die* following a match at Oxford in 1937.

## BROTHERS

R. L. Aston (Blackheath) played for England twice in 1898-99, while his brother F. T. D. Aston went to the Transvaal and was capped for South Africa against the British Isles in 1896.

Other instances of brothers playing for different countries: P. F. Hancock (Blackheath) for England, and F. E. Hancock (Cardiff) for Wales; W. M. C. McEwan (Edinburgh Academicals, Transvaal) for Scotland and South Africa, M. C. McEwan (Edinburgh Academicals) for Scotland.

Richard Webb toured the British Isles with the Australians in 1966-67 and although he did not appear in an international he played against brother Rodney (an England international) when the Australians met the West Midlands at Coventry.

The only twin brothers ever to appear in a Test team—James and Stewart Boyce, who first appeared together for Australia v. New Zealand, at Dunedin, 1964.

Four Williams brothers appeared in the same Cardiff team on a number of occasions during season 1961-62. They were Tony, Cenydd, Elwyn and Lloyd.

Coventry probably hold a family record in so far as no less than eight of the Rotherham brothers have played for them at various times.

The Clarke family of New Zealand have had six brothers playing for the Keorone club, and five of them, including the world famous full-back, Don Clarke, appeared together in one game in August, 1961.

## BULLER RUGBY UNION

Founded 1894, only a small number of their players have represented New Zealand, the best known probably being K. Svenson, a member of Porter's invincible "All-Blacks" in 1924-25, who played in 34 matches, including 4 internationals. Ground: Victoria Square, Westport, South Island, New Zealand. Colours: Cardinal and blue hoops.

## CALCUTTA CUP

In 1877 the Calcutta Cup which had been formed in India (chiefly at the instigation of Old Rugbeians) five years earlier, was forced to disband mainly because of the lack of suitable opposition. On the suggestion of one of its leading administrators, G. A. J. Rothney, the club funds were used to provide a trophy for annual competition between England and Scotland. The trophy, made out of the actual rupees withdrawn from the Bank, was of exquisite Indian workmanship, and took the form of a tapered cup with three snake handles with a model elephant on the lid piece. The inscription on it reads:

"THE CALCUTTA CUP,
PRESENTED TO THE RUGBY
FOOTBALL UNION
BY THE CALCUTTA FOOTBALL
CLUB AS AN INTERNATIONAL
CHALLENGE CUP
TO BE PLAYED FOR ANNUALLY
BY ENGLAND AND SCOTLAND.
1878

## CAMBRIDGE UNIVERSITY R.F.C.

As indeed is the case, with the bulk of Rugby Football history, the history of the Cambridge University Rugby Football Club can be traced to the influence of an Old Rugbeian—in this instance Arthur Pell (later a Member of Parliament) who introduced the Rugby School version of the game to the University in the year 1839, and who after many initial difficulties succeeded in forming a club which played its matches on the famous "Parker's Piece." Much water, however was to flow past the "Backs" before the warring factions from Rugby and Marlborough, and the other great Public Schools were able to agree on the code of Football rules their University would henceforward honour. The final act of emancipation came in 1872 when at a meeting held in the rooms of a famous Cambridge athlete of the period, an undergraduate named R. P. Luscombe, it was decided to adopt the rules and bye-laws of the Rugby Union which had been formed a year earlier—and thus was formed the Cambridge University Rugby Football Club. In the same year another distinguished scholar-athlete, H. A. Hamilton, later Canon Douglas-Hamilton, journeyed to Oxford in order to make arrangements for a meeting between the two Universities, and this began the ageless vendetta that has subsequently enthralled the minds and imaginations of countless followers the country over (see UNIVERSITY MATCH). Oxford were successful in this first encounter and might indeed be said to have enjoyed the ascendancy for the first fifteen years of the series, for while Cambridge produced many fine individual players, notably H. F. Fuller, C. J. C. Touzel, J. H. Payne, and E. Temple Gurdon, their Rugby generally speaking was not co-ordinated with the same attention to minute tactical detail as that which featured Oxford's under the great Vassall. It was C. J. B. Marriott, later Secretary of the Rugby Union, who in response to a special invitation, implemented the first really serious coaching scheme at Cambridge, and his efforts, particularly in relation to the forwards, undoubtedly did much to hasten the end of Oxford's domination. Thus in season 1885-86 Cambridge won the first of four successive victories over their rivals. The side was captained by E. B. Brutton, and the strength of Cambridge Rugby during the period may be gauged from the fact that it produced no fewer than twenty International players, among them such famous names as M. M. Duncan (Scotland), J. Le Fleming, W. R. Leake, J. H. Dewhurst, G. L. Jeffrey (England), V. C. le Fanu (Ireland), and E. P. Alexander (Wales). Although they produced many other great players in the interval, S. M. J. Woods, G. McGregor, R. L. Aston, W. Wotherspoon, C. B. Nicholl, W. Neilson, R. O. Schwartz (the South African googly bowler), W. E. Tucker, R. F. Cumberledge, John Daniell, J. R. C. Greenless, the Bedel-Sivrights, L. M. and

K. G. MacLeod, J. E. Greenwood and J. G. Bruce-Lockhart, it was not until season 1912-13 that they entered upon a period of success comparable with that of the 1885-90 period, for following three successive defeats, they turned the tables completely on Oxford by winning consecutively in the seasons 1912-13, 1913-14 and 1919-20. There were of course some very fine players in the side during a period which spanned a World war, among them the great England wing C. N. Lowe, B. S. Cumberledge, the Welsh stand-off half, J. M. C. Lewis, J. E. Greenwood, G. S. Conway and R. Cove-Smith. Indeed the 'twenties were altogether vintage years for Cambridge, for out of the ten matches played between 1920-29, six were won, four of them consecutively between 1925-29. It was of course an era rich in attainment—an era that produced players whose names became household ones wherever the game was played: Wavell Wakefield, Conway, Cove-Smith, R. H. Hamilton-Wickes, D. J. MacMyn, A. T. Young, W. E. Tucker, T. G. Devitt, Rowe Harding, C. D. Aarvold, W. H. Sobey, Guy Morgan, Windsor Lewis, J. A. Tallent and R. W. Smeddle—their very names indeed, represent a cavalcade of Rugby football greatness. G. W. Parker, K. C. Fyfe, Wilfred Wooller, C. W. Jones, R. G. S. Dick, A. M. Rees, P. L. Candler, W. B. Young, T. A. Kemp, J. G. S. Forrest, Keith Geddes, M. R. Steele-Bodger, A. F. Dorward, J. Gwilliam, R. C. C. Thomas, A. R. Smith, J. V. Smith, and J. Horrocks-Taylor are other great players who have won the light blue jersey of Cambridge with the same skill and distinction as they subsequently wore the colours of their own countries.

Whereas more than 80 men have each appeared in four Varsity games only two have had the distinction of playing in more than four of these games—H. G. Fuller (1879-83) six games, and J. E. S. Greenwood (1910-19) five games. Both with Cambridge.

## CANADA

The credit for introducing Rugby Football to Canada (see also BRITISH COLUMBIA) goes to the former Marlborough and England player A. St. G. Hammersley. In 1903, some twenty years after Hammersley's pioneering work, a representative Canadian team toured in Britain winning eight of their 23 matches, losing 13, and drawing the remaining two. Toronto (Ontario) is the Union game's main stronghold together with British Columbia, and despite the difficulty of a "split season" the game has an enthusiastic following amongst British emigrants in these areas. In April, 1957, the visit of a strong Barbarian touring team (see BARBARIANS) served as a great fillip to the game out there, and in recent years it has shown remarkable progress in the East. In 1958 the Canadians actually beat the Wallabies, and in 1962-63 a team which toured Britain beat Welsh Western Counties and drew with the Barbarians. The first representative Canadian International team was fielded in September 1966 when they lost 8–19 to the British Lions in Toronto. The following year they were beaten 0–29 by England in Vancouver, and in 1973 Wales won 58-20 in Toronto. The British Lions have played 4 games in Canada, winning 3 and losing one (3-8 to British Columbia in 1966). The Canadian Rugby Union is affiliated to the Rugby Union, with headquarters in Vancouver.

## CANTERBURY RUGBY UNION

Formed in 1879, Canterbury are along with Wellington the oldest of the New Zealand Unions. The Union colours are scarlet and black, their ground is the Lancaster Park Oval, Christchurch, South Island.

Their most capped players are D.J. Graham and the hooker D. Young, who both toured Britain with the Fifth "All Blacks" 1963-64 and each appeared in 22 internationals. Those leading cap-holders K.R. Tremain and W.J. Whineray also first made their marks with Canterbury before moving elsewhere.

## CAPS

(See also INTERNATIONALS).

Originally it was the custom for each of the British Rugby Unions to award a separate cap for each appearance. This practice however was discontinued when International football was resumed at the end of the 1914 war. Nowadays the "Cap" made of velvet in the national colours and adorned with the national crest is only awarded on the occasion of the player's first appearance, and is accordingly inscribed appropriately. Thus if a Welsh player for instance made his initial appearance against England the cap's peak would be inscribed with the legend, "ENGLAND 1957-58." In Australia, New Zealand and South Africa, the crested blazer is preferred to the cap, as the memento of an International appearance.

## CARDIFF R.F.C.

Cardiff Rugby Football Club, with Newport and Swansea, comprise the original "Big Three" of Welsh Rugby. Founded as an Association football club, they turned to Rugby in 1876, four years before the formation of the Welsh Rugby Union. Among the club's greatest achievements are victories over the three major overseas touring teams to visit Great Britain, viz., South Africa (1906), Australia (1947), and New Zealand (1953). The club have themselves toured abroad, and in addition possess, what is for a Welsh club, the unique distinction of having once fielded two first class XVs with identical fixture lists throughout a complete season. It was Cardiff who in 1885-86 introduced the four three-quarters formation we know today, and another distinction possessed by the club is that they once supplied no fewer than ten members of the Welsh XV that played Scotland at Murrayfield in 1948— A British record. Many of the games greatest players have worn the Cardiff colours, including Gwyn Nicholls, dubbed "The Prince of Threequarters," R. T. Gabe, Percy Bush, Wilfred Wooller, Cliff Jones, Haydn Tanner, Bleddyn Williams, Cliff Morgan, the legendry Rugby League player Jim Sullivan, and that brilliant pair of half-backs who struck up such a remarkable partnership in the late sixties, the club's record cap holder G. O. Edwards, and the elegant Barry John. The Club play at the Cardiff Arms Park, itself a famous International venue. Their colours are Cambridge blue and black jerseys and stockings, and navy shorts. The club Secretary is A. J. Priday.

## CARRIBEAN R. F. U.

Rugby has been played in the West Indies since the 1920s and an inter-island tournament was begun in 1926 with a game between Trinidad and British Guiana (now Guyana) and this has now developed into a series held every other year and involving Barbados, Bahamas, Jamaica and Martinique, as well as the two original competitors.

The Carribean R.F.U. was formed in 1973.

## CASUALTIES

The history of International tours is a history as well of individual misfortune, for on several occasions players have travelled almost to the other end of the earth only to suffer an injury which has rendered them inactive—in some cases for the whole duration of the tour. Most tragic of all, of course, was the case of the Yorkshireman, R. L. Seddon, who led the first ever British Isles team in New Zealand and Australia in 1888, and who was drowned while bathing in the Hunter River even before the tour had got properly under way. The 1888 tour was indeed an ill-starred venture in other respects too, for another member of the party, J. P. Clowes (also of Yorkshire), was declared a professional and suspended by the Rugby Union before he had played a single match.

Other outstanding instances of unlucky tourists are: —

C. E. Murnin of the 1908 Australian team to Britain was taken seriously ill at Naples on the outward voyage and returned home without playing a single match. P. Burge, of the same team broke his leg in the first match of the tour and did not play again, whilst a similar fate befell his colleague, P. Flanagan (while acting as touch judge in the tour's third match).

C. Fletcher, of New Zealand, went to Australia with the "All-Blacks" in 1920 but did not play in a single match owing to an injury he had sustained before sailing.

C. E. Badeley, of the 1924-25 New Zealand side in Australia, was injured in the second game of the tour and took no further part in the remaining matches, nor in any of the 30 matches the New Zealanders went on to play in Britain and France. On the British part of the same itinerary, A. C. C. Robilliard and H. G. Munroe suffered injuries and only took part in four matches apiece.

C. G. Porter, captain of the New Zealand team which toured Australia in 1929, was idle for all but a couple of matches at the end of the tour owing to an injury sustained back in New Zealand.

W. H. Sobey, the British scrum-half in New Zealand and Australia in 1930, was injured in the very first match in New Zealand and took no further part.

J. van Niekerk, of the 1931-32 South African team in Britain, was hurt in the second match and did not play again.

W. H. Cerutti, of the 1936 Australian team in New Zealand, was injured in the opening match and was *hors de combat* until the last one.

W. M. McLean, captain of the 1947-48 Australian team in Britain, broke his leg in the sixth match of the tour and did not play again.

B. J. C. Piper (Australia in New Zealand, 1949) was injured in the second match of the tour and did not play again.

G. Norton, full-back of the British team in New Zealand and Australia in 1950, was injured in the fifth match and took no further part,

Basil Kenyon, captain of the 1951-52 South African side in Britain, was injured in the fifth game and did not play again.

S. A. M. Hodgson, hooker, broke a leg in the opening game of the British Lions South African tour of 1962 and took no further part in the tour.

Barry John fractured his collar-bone in the first half of the first Test at Pretoria on the British Lions tour of South Africa in 1968 and took no further part.

British Lions A. B. Carmichael, R. J. McLoughlin, and M. L. Hipwell were all injured in the "battle of Christchurch" v. Canterbury and took no further part in the 1971 New Zealand tour.

A. Old was injured in seventh game of the British Lions tour of South Africa in 1974 and did not play again.

## CENTRE THREEQUARTER

Ideally speaking, it is the centre threequarter's job to develop, and if possible widen, the half opening created by his stand-off half, and having done so, to send the wing outside him speeding for the goal line with a fifty-fifty chance of reaching that objective. The first centre threequarter to view and discharge his function in this light was the Bradford player Rawson Robertshaw who played for England in 1886, and whose assiduous attention to the wing outside him made him (in the manner of all pioneers) something of an oddity amid the rugged individualism of his age. Robertshaw's conception of centre threequarter play has however endured down the years, and amongst its practitioners are numbered many of the game's greatest names, viz., H. H. Vassall (England), E. Gwyn Nicholls, Bleddyn Williams, S.J. Dawes (Wales), F.N. Tarr, R.L. Aston, L.J Corbett, J. Butterfield (England), A.C. Wallace, G.P.S. McPherson, (Scotland), R.G. Deans (New Zealand).

The qualities demanded of a first-class centre may be listed as follows:

(1) An ability and temperament to play to his wing.
(2) A strong defender.
(3) A good handler and passer of the ball.
(4) Strong straight runner to create 2nd phase ball when tackled.
(5) A powerful physique.

Obviously many have achieved fame in International Rugby even though deficient in one or more of these qualities, but in the majority of cases will be found to have done so as a result of their "pairing" with players whose individual talents have been such as to offset the deficiencies of the other. In other words, centre threequarters, like fast bowlers in cricket, are more effective as pairs, the one acting as a foil for the other. In this respect experience has shown that the pairing of a strong, thrustful, straight-running player with one or more subtle technique is often a successful arrangement in International football.

## CIVIL SERVICE

The Civil Service representative XV which meets the three fighting Services in annual competition is a comparatively modern innovation, being established in 1922. The history of Civil Service Rugby, however, goes far further back than that; in fact Civil Service are enumerated as one of the clubs who founded the Rugby Union in 1871. They were pioneers in other directions, too, for it was they who supplied the opposition to the first French XV which visited Britain in 1885.

Colours: White jersey, navy blue shorts,
Hon. Secretary: D. L. Davies, 46 Harborough Avenue, Sidcup, Kent.

## CLONTARF R.F.C.

Since C. P. Stuart was capped against
South Africa in 1913, the Leinster club
Clontarf have had nine players in Irish
XVs. One of them, G. J. (George)
Morgan, made 19 appearances between
1934-39, and was rated as one of the
greatest scrum-halves of the period.
Another Clontarf player, F. G. Moran,
played on the wing for Ireland during the
same period and won the healthy respect
of opponents with his powerful stride
and immense determination. To Barney
Mullen, yet another Clontarf representative, went the distinction of scoring one
of the vital tries in Ireland's Triple
Crown victory over Wales in 1947-48,
whilst P. J. Lawler was a conspicuous
figure in the Irish scrum during the
1950s.

## COLOURS

(See under individual clubs and Internationals).

## CORK CONSTITUTION R.F.C.

Founded in 1894 by the staff of a
local newspaper "Cork Constitution"
which ceased publication in 1921 the
club has long been recognised as Munster's most powerful combination. They
won the Munster Senior League a record
nine successive seasons 1964-72 and have
included among their players two of
Ireland's all-time greats—T. J. Kiernan,
who captained the British Lions in South
Africa in 1968, and N. A. A. Murphy
who made 41 appearances for Ireland
1956-64 including four games as captain.
His father had also played for Ireland.
Club colours: Black, blue and white.

## COUNTIES R.F.U.

Founded as South Auckland 1926 and
affiliated to Auckland. Granted full status
1955 and changed to present name 1956.
Created a New Zealand first-class scoring
record when beating East Coast 101–7 in
September 1971. Their greatest international is hooker Bruce McLeod, capped
24 times. Colours: Red, white and black
hoops. Headquarters: Pukekhoe.

## COUNTY CHAMPIONSHIP

The English County Championship
which in the minds of authority and
general public alike, ranks second in importance only to International Rugby,
began in 1889 when Yorkshire (undefeated that season) were declared "Champions" by the Rugby Union. The same
procedure was adopted at the close of
the following season, but in 1890 there
was introduced a system of grouping
which was thereinafter referred to as the
"Second System," and which saw the
competing Counties grouped as follows:
NORTH-WEST: Lancashire, Cheshire,
   Cumberland, Westmorland.
NORTH-EAST: Yorkshire, Durham,
   Northumberland.
SOUTH-EAST: Middlesex, Kent, Surrey,
   and Sussex.
SOUTH-WEST: Somerset, Devon, Gloucestershire, Midland Counties.

The winners of each group met each
other and the title was decided upon a
points basis. In 1893 Cornwall were
admitted to the South-Western group
thereby enabling Midland Counties to
move over to the more geographically
suited South-East, which incidentally was
re-organised to cater for a Junior Section
comprised of Hampshire, Sussex and
South Midlands. The new system lasted
until 1896, when it was superceded by
the "Third System" in which the group,
ings were as follows:
NORTHERN DIVISION: All the Northern counties.
SOUTH-WESTERN DIVISION: As before.
SOUTH-EASTERN DIVISION: As before.

Winners of the South-Western and
South-Eastern Divisions were now obliged
to meet for the right to oppose the
Northern Division Champions in the
Final. This system lasted until 1921, when
it was replaced by a Fourth System.

The Divisions under the Fourth System were:
NORTHERN DIVISION: Yorkshire, Durham, Cheshire, Lancashire, Northumberland and Cumberland.
SOUTH-WESTERN DIVISION: Devon,
   Cornwall, Somerset and Gloucestershire.
SOUTH-EASTERN DIVISION: Middlesex, Eastern Counties, Surrey, Hampshire, Kent.
MIDLAND DIVISION: Leicestershire,
   Warwickshire, North Midlands, East
   Midlands.

In 1952-53 a Southern Division was introduced.

The individual Division Championships are still decided on a points basis with a "play-off" in case of a tie at the head of the table, the winners then going on to contest the semi-finals. Inasmuch as there are five Divisions an extra match (quarter-final) has to be played in order to determine the semi-finalists.

Warwickshire has enjoyed the most remarkable run of success in this competition, being winners seven times in eight years from 1958.

## Championship Records.

### FIRST SYSTEM

1889  Yorkshire undefeated and declared Champions by the Rugby Union.
1890  Yorkshire undefeated and declared Champions by the Rugby Union.

### SECOND SYSTEM

1891  Champions  Lancashire.  Group Winners—Yorkshire,  Surrey,  Gloucestershire.
1892  Champions  Yorkshire.  Group Winners—Lancashire, Kent, Midlands.
1893  Champions  Yorkshire.  Group Winners—Cumberland, Devon, Middlesex.
1894  Champions  Yorkshire.  Group Winners—Lancashire, Gloucestershire, Midlands.
1895  Champions  Yorkshire.  Group Winners—Cumberland, Devon, Middlesex.

### THIRD SYSTEM

|      | Champions | Runners Up | Played at | Divisional Winners |
|------|-----------|------------|-----------|--------------------|
| 1896 | Yorkshire | Surrey | Richmond | South-West: Devon |
| 1897 | Kent | Cumberland | Carlisle | South-West: Somerset |
| 1898 | Northumberland | Midlands | Coventry | South-West: Devon |
| 1899 | Devon | Northumberland | Newcastle | South-East: Kent |
| 1900 | Durham | Devon | Exeter | South-East: Kent |
| 1901 | Devon | Durham | West Hartlepool | South-East: East Midlands |
| 1902 | Durham | Gloucestershire | Gloucester | South-east: Middlesex |
| 1903 | Durham | Kent | West Hartlepool | South-West: Somerset |
| 1904 | Kent | Durham | Blackheath | South-West: Devon |
| 1905 | Durham | Middlesex | West Hartlepool | South-West: Devon |
| 1906 | Devon | Durham | Exeter | South-East: Midlands |

1907  Devon and Durham joint Champions after drawn games at West Hartlepool and Exeter.

| 1908 | Cornwall | Durham | Redruth | South-East: Middlesex |
|------|----------|--------|---------|-----------------------|
| 1909 | Durham | Cornwall | West Hartlepool | South-East: Midlands |
| 1910 | Gloucestershire | Yorkshire | Gloucester | South-East: Kent |
| 1911 | Devon | Yorkshire | Headingley | South-East: Midlands |

| | Champions | Runners Up | Played at | Losing Semi-finalists |
|---|---|---|---|---|
| 1912 | Devon | Northumberland | Devonport | South-East: Midlands |
| 1913 | Gloucestershire | Cumberland | Carlisle | South-East: Midlands |
| 1914 | Midlands | Durham | Leicester | South-West: Cornwall |
| 1920 | Gloucestershire | Yorkshire | Bradford | South-East: Midlands |

## FOURTH SYSTEM

| | Champions | Runners Up | Played at | Losing Semi-finalists |
|---|---|---|---|---|
| 1921 | Gloucestershire | Leicestershire | Gloucester | Surrey and Yorkshire |
| 1922 | Gloucestershire | North Midlands | Birmingham | Surrey and Cheshire |
| 1923 | Somerset | Leicestershire | Bridgwater | Kent and Cumberland |
| 1924 | Cumberland | Kent | Carlisle | Leicester and Somerset |
| 1925 | Leicestershire | Gloucestershire | Bristol | Yorkshire and Middlesex |
| 1926 | Yorkshire | Hampshire | Bradford | Leicester and Gloucestershire |
| 1927 | Kent | Leicestershire | Blackheath | Devon and Cheshire |
| 1928 | Yorkshire | Cornwall | Bradford | Warwick and Middlesex |
| 1929 | Middlesex | Lancashire | Blundellsands | Devon and Warwick |
| 1930 | Gloucestershire | Lancashire | Blundellsands | Middlesex and East Midlands |
| 1931 | Gloucestershire | Warwickshire | Gloucester | Hampshire and Lancashire |
| 1932 | Gloucestershire | Durham | Blaydon | Ha mpshire and Warwickshire |
| 1933 | Hampshire | Lancashire | Boscombe | Somerset and East Midland |
| 1934 | East Midlands | Gloucestershire | Northampton | Lancashire and Hampshire |
| 1935 | Lancashire | Somerset | Bath | Warwick and East Counties |
| 1936 | Hampshire | Northumberland | Gosforth | Cornwall and Warwick |
| 1937 | Gloucestershire | East Midlands | Bristol | Kent and Lancashire |
| 1938 | Lancashire | Surrey | Blundellsands | East Midlands and Cornwall |
| 1939 | Warwickshire | Somerset | Weston | Cheshire and Hampshire |
| 1947 | Lancashire | Gloucestershire | Gloucester | Warwick and Middlesex |
| 1948 | Lancashire | East Counties | Cambridge | N. Midlands and Gloucestershire |
| 1949 | Lancashire | Gloucestershire | Blundellsands | Warwick and Middlesex |
| 1950 | Cheshire | East Midlands | Birkenhead Park | Kent and Devon |
| 1951 | East Midlands | Middlesex | Northampton | Gloucestershire and Yorkshire |
| 1952 | Middlesex | Lancashire | Twickenham | Warwick and Somerset |

| Year | Champions | Runners-up | Venue | Semi-finalists |
|---|---|---|---|---|
| 1953 | Yorkshire | East Midlands | Bradford | Devon and Middlesex |
| 1954 | Middlesex | Lancashire | Blundellsands | E. Midlands and Gloucestershire |
| 1955 | Lancashire | Middlesex | Twickenham | Leicester and Cornwall |
| 1956 | Middlesex | Devon | Twickenham | Lancashire and Leicester |
| 1957 | Devon | Yorkshire | Plymouth | Leicester and Middlesex |
| 1958 | Warwickshire | Cornwall | Coventry | Surrey and Lancashire |
| 1959 | Warwickshire | Gloucestershire | Bristol | Middlesex and Durham |
| 1960 | Warwickshire | Surrey | Coventry | Durham and Cornwall |
| 1961 | Cheshire | Devon | Birkenhead | E. Counties and E. Midlands |
| 1962 | Warwickshire | Hampshire | Twickenham | Cornwall and Durham |
| 1963 | Warwickshire | Yorkshire | Coventry | Gloucester and Hampshire |
| 1964 | Warwickshire | Lancashire | Coventry | Hampshire and Gloucester |
| 1965 | Warwickshire | Durham | Hartlepool | Surrey and Oxfordshire |
| 1966 | Middlesex | Lancashire | Blundellsands | Oxfordshire and Leicester |
| 1967 | Surrey and Durham joint Champions after drawn games at Twickenham and Hartlepool. | | | Leicester and Cornwall |
| 1968 | Middlesex | Warwickshire | Twickenham | Gloucestershire and Durham |
| 1969 | Lancashire | Cornwall | Redruth | Surrey and East Midlands |
| 1970 | Staffordshire | Gloucestershire | Burton-on-Trent | E. Counties and Lancashire |
| 1971 | Surrey | Gloucestershire | Gloucester | Warwick and Northumberland |
| 1973 | Gloucestershire | Warwickshire | Coventry | Middlesex and Yorkshire |
| 1973 | Lancashire | Gloucestershire | Bristol | E. Counties and N. Midlands |
| 1974 | Gloucestershire | Lancashire | Blundellsands | Warwickshire and E. Counties |
| 1975 | Gloucestershire | E. Counties | Gloucester | Warwickshire and Lancashire |

## COVENTRY

Founded in 1877, three years after the formation of the Rugby Union, Coventyr have seldom in the whole long interim slipped from their rating as the leading Midland combination. If there is any single feature of their history that has captivated the imagination of the Rugby going public, it has been their great and age old vendetta with their famous Welsh counterparts Cardiff, Newport, and Swansea. Indeed when the game was resumed on a peace time basis in 1946, Coventry, along with Cardiff, were probably the two most powerful combinations in Britain, and their meetings produced thrilling rugger watched by large crowds. Since W.L. Oldham was capped in 1908 Coventry have had many representatives in England XVs, the record cap holder being wing-threequarter D. J. Duckham with more than 30 England appearances since 1969. The power of this club is amply illustrated in Warwickshire's remarkable run of seven County Championships in eight years. The County XV which carried off the trophy in 1965 included no less than 12 Coventry players. Colours: Blue and white jerseys and stockings, navy shorts. Ground: Coundon Road. Secretary: **P. A. J. Sharp**, 17 Astill Grove, Coventry.

# CRICKETERS

J. H. Anderson played centre three-quarter for South Africa against Great Britain in 1896, and for South Africa against Australia at cricket in 1902.

In 1891 H. H. Castens captained South Africa in the country's first ever International match in opposition to W. E. MacLagen's British team, and three years later was again captain (though no Tests were played) of the first South African cricket team to visit England.

G. R. Dickinson (Otago) played for New Zealand against Australia twice in 1922, and played Test Cricket for the same country against England (twice) and South Africa (once) in 1930, and 1931 respectively.

M. P. Donnelly (Oxford University) was at centre threequarter for England against Ireland in 1947, and as one of the world's leading left-hand batsmen played in seven Tests for New Zealand between 1937-49.

M. K. Elgie, capped eight times by Scotland in the 1950s, made three Test cricket appearances for South Africa against New Zealand 1961-62.

R. H. M. Hands (Oxford and Black-heath) was another South African to play Rugby football for England. He played as a forward twice, in 1910, and in 1913 appeared in a cricket Test for South Africa against England.

T. A. Harris (Transvaal) played five times as South Africa's stand-off half against New Zealand and Great Britain in 1937 and 1938 respectively, and played in two Tests against England in that country in 1947, and in one against the same opponents in South Africa in 1948.

The first man to play in both Inter-nation Rugby football and Test cricket was A. N. Hornby, of Lancashire, who played cricket for England against Aus-tralia in 1879, and who then, at the age of 30, became one of England's two threequarters in the first ever 15-a-side Rugby International between England

and Ireland at Kennington Oval in 1877.

P. S. T. Jones played for South Africa against Great Britain as a wing threequarters in 1896, and against Aus-tralia at cricket in 1902.

G. MacGregor, Cambridge University and London Scottish, is to date the only man to have played Rugby for Scotland and cricket for England. He won 13 Scottish caps as a full back between 1889-96, and played in eight Tests as England's wicket-keeper against Australia between 1890-93.

The first man to play Rugby football for one country and cricket for another was W. H. Milton (Marlborough) who won two caps for England as a half-back in 1894 when the game was played 20-a-side. Then in 1888 he played for and captained South Africa on their entry into Test cricket.

F. Mitchell, Cambridge University, Blackheath, and Yorkshire County Cricket Club, played in the England pack six times between 1895-96, and opened the England innings against South Africa in 1898. Mitchell later captained South Africa in the Triangular cricket tourna-ment staged in Britain in 1912.

O. E. Nothling (New South Wales) played ten times as a full back against New Zealand between 1921-24, and against England in Test cricket in season 1928-29.

H. G. Owen Smith (Oxford Univer-sity and St. Mary's Hospital) was Eng-land's full back on ten occasions between 1934-37, and before this had represented his native South Africa in the Test series against England in 1929.

M. L. Page (Canterbury) played once as New Zealand's scrum-half against Aus-tralia in 1928, and 14 times as a Test cricketer between 1927-37.

A. W. Powell (Griqualand West), played at threequarter for South Africa against Great Britain in 1896, and was a member of the South African XI against England in 1898.

A. Richards, of Western Province, who played at stand-off half against MacLagan's team, captained South Africa in the final game of the series. Since he also captained the cricket XI which opposed Lord Hawke's team in 1895-96, he is to date the only man who has captained South Africa in both Rugby and cricket Tests.

R. O. Schwarz (Richmond) was an

England half-back between 1899-1901, and played in 20 Tests as one of South Africa's far famed "googly" bowlers.

J. H. Sinclair (Transvaal played for) Great Britain in 1903, and played in 25 cricket Tests for the same country between 1896-1911.

M. J. K. Smith (Leicestershire, Oxford University and Warwickshire), captained England's Test cricket XI in the 1960s and played stand-off half for England against Wales in 1956.

R. H. Spooner (Marlborough Nomads, Liverpool, and Lancashire County Cricket Club) played wing threequarter for England against Wales in 1903, and in ten cricket Tests for the same country between 1905-12.

A. E. Stoddart, Blackheath, and Middlesex County Cricket Club played 11 times for England as a wing threequarter between 1885-93, and 16 times for England as a cricketer. Stoddart in fact must be the only man who has remained behind to take part in a tour of Australia and New Zealand immediately after a cricket tour. He did this in 1888 when, as a member of W. W. Read's cricket team in Australia he remained behind to assist a football side jointly captained by Albert Shaw and Arthur Shrewsbury.

E. W. Tindill (Wellington) played at five eights on the New Zealand tour of Great Britain in 1935, and appeared in five Test matches during a cricket career that spanned the years between 1937-47.

M. J. Turnbull (Cambridge University, Cardiff, and Glamorgan County Cricket Club) was the Welsh scrum-half in two Internationals in season 1933, and made nine appearances for England as a cricketer. Turnbull in fact is the only Welshman who has played Rugby for Wales and cricket for England.

C. B. Van Ryneveld (Oxford University) played at centre threequarter for England in all four International of the 1948-49 season, and has already appeared in 15 cricket Tests for his native South Africa.

In 1878 G. F. Vernon of Rugby played for England in the first ever Calcutta Cup match against Scotland, and later played in an England v Australia Test match in Australia.

A. K. Walker (New South Wales) played as a centre threequarter for Australia against England at Twickenham

in 1948, but although he toured South Africa with an Australian cricket side in 1950, did not actually play in a Test.

Australian born S. M. J. Woods, of Cambridge University and Somerset, played Test cricket for two countries, England and his native Australia, and gained 13 Rugby caps as a member of the England pack between 1890-95.

Several men have distinguished themselves at both games without getting double international honours. They include John Daniell who played seven times for England at Rugby, and who captained Somerset at cricket; K. G. MacLeod who had 10 Scottish caps as well as captaining Lancashire at cricket; Peter Cranmer who gained 16 English caps and captained Warwickshire at cricket; and Wilfred Wooller who captained Glamorgan at cricket and has 18 Welsh Rugby caps to his credit. In addition W. E. Jones (Neath, Gloucester, and Glamorgan County Cricket Club) played for Wales in a Wartime International during season 1939-40, and appeared in an English Test Trial during the summer of 1949.

## CROSS KEYS R.F.C.

Cross Keys (founded 1900) have built a formidable reputation on the verve, *élan,* and cohesive scrummaging power of their forwards. Most of their International representatives have in fact been forwards, and two of them, Steve Morris (19 caps) and F. A. Bowdler (15), were indispensable players in any Welsh scrum of their respective periods. In 1938 A. R. Taylor, a breakaway forward, earned selection in a British team visiting South Africa, and thus became the first, and to date, the only Cross Keys player to be so honoured. Colours: Black and white hooped jerseys and stockings, white shorts. Ground: Pandy Park, Cross Keys. Secretary: D. B. Evans, Glanant, 17 Caerphilly Close, Rhiwderin, Gwent NP1 4DW.

## CURRIE CUP

South Africa's premier Rugby Trophy, the golden Currie Cup, was presented by Sir Donald Currie, the founder of the Castle shipping line, to W. E. MacLagan the captain of the first British team to tour South Africa in 1891, and was intended for presentation to the South African team which played the best against the tourists. Griqualand West who ran the British team to a goal's margin were deemed the most worthy of the honour, and subsequently presented the cup to the South African Board which in turn utilised it as the trophy for an Inter-Union Competition. The first of these had already been decided in 1889 (2 years before the presentation of the cup by MacLagan), and had been won at Kimberley by Western Province, who thereby started the sequence that has given subsequent generations of Cape Town Bank managers an almost permanent responsibility for the safe keeping of this valuable and imposing trophy. The competition has in fact been won by Western Province no fewer than 20 occasions outright plus two shared. Next

to them are Northern Transvaal with seven wins including 1974. Of the provinces who now compete in the competition only five—Western Province, Griqualand West, Transvaal, Natal and Border were original competitors in 1889.

The Cup competition was changed in 1975 so that 10 provinces compete in two sections with each team playing the other four in its section at home and away on a league basis. In alternate years the teams meet those in the other section. The remaining 12 provinces who formerly competed in the Currie Cup now play for the Sport Pienaar Trophy and the top teams in the two sections of this competition each season meet the two bottom teams in the Currie Cup to decide promotion and relegation.

## DATES

The most important dates in the history and development of Rugby Football are: –

1823 – William Webb Ellis ran with the ball in his arms in direct contradiction to the rules which then governed the Bigside games at Rugby School.

1839 – A Rugby Club formed at Cambridge University by A. Pell.

1843 – A Rugby Club formed at Guy's Hospital, London

1951 – A Rugby football made by William Gilbert of Rugby on view at the International Exhibition in London.

1858 – Edinburgh Academicals Rugby Football Club formed.

1860 – A Rugby club formed in Manchester.

1861 – Richmond and Sale clubs formed.

1862 – Formation of Blackheath R.F.C.

1863 – Meetings held in London to draw up a code of rules. Blackheath withdrew on question of hacking.

1864 – First organised match in England – Blackheath v Richmond.

1866 – Blackheath and Richmond declined to play those clubs who still adhered to the practice of "Hacking".

1869 – Formation of Oxford University R.F.C.

1870 – Rugby Football introduced to New Zealand by C. J. Munroe who had learned the game at Sherborne School.

1871 – Rugby Union formed in London. First International match between England and Scotland at Edinburgh.

1872 – First University match. First club formed in France by British residents at Le Havre.

1873 – Scottish Rugby Union formed.

1874-75 – First International match between England and Ireland at Kennington Oval. London Hospital's Cup Competition inaugurated.

1876 – Rugby Football officially adopted by the provinces of Auckland, Canterbury, and Otago in New Zealand. University teams reduced from 20 to 15-a-side in England. Rugby Football first played in Cape Town, South Africa. Laws changed so that if the number of goals in a match were equal, or no goals kicked at all, the match could be decided on a majority of tries.

1877 – Players in International matches reduced from 20 to 15-a-side. Law amended so that when a goal was kicked from a try, only the goal counted.

1878 – Rugby Union accepted a Cup from the disbanded Calcutta Club in India – subsequently the "Calcutta Cup" competed for annually by England and Scotland. First Army v Navy match staged at Kennington Oval.

1879 – Irish Rugby Union formed. Canterbury (July), Wellington (October) from the first Rugby Unions in New Zealand. Rosslyn Park R.F.C. formed in London By C. H. H. Millar.

1880 – Welsh Rugby Union formed. Travelling expenses for International matches first paid by Rugby Union.

1881 – England and Wales met for the first time at Blackheath. Three threequarters played for the first time by Scotland against Ireland. G. Rowland Hill elected

Secretary of the Rugby Union. Neutral referees appointed for International matches.

1882—First visit of New South Wales side to New Zealand. Half back passing developed by Harry Vassall, and Alan Rotherham at Oxford. England and Wales adopt three threequarter formation.

1883—Referees provided with whistle and umpires with sticks. Four threequarter formation introduced by the Cardiff R.F.C., and used by the Welsh International XV in the same year.

1885—Paris F.C. who met the Civil Service at Dulwich, the first French side to play in Britain.

1886—The Prince of Wales (afterwards King Edward VII) present at a Charity Match at the Oval. The scoring rules in operation at Cheltenham College adopted. International Board formed.

1887—Prince of Wales became Patron of the Rugby Union.

1888—British team captained by R. L. Seddon and A. E. Stoddart, visited Australia and New Zealand. Maori native team visited Britain.

1889—South African Rugby Football Board formed. Scoring values again amended by Rugby Union, now read—Try=1 point. Goal=3 points except penalty goal which=2. Umpires abolished and touch judge appointed with the same limited powers as today. London Society of Referees formed. Rugby Union established a "Close Season", thereby making organised Rugby between May 1st-August 31st illegal.

1890—Re-constituted International Board formed.

1891—W. E. MacLagan took the first British side to South Africa.

1892—Formation of New Zealand Rugby Union. New South Wales Rugby Union formed out of the old "Southern Union" which had been in existence since 1875. Rugby Union decreed that *all* matches should be 15-a-side. Rosslyn Park first British side to play in France.

1893—"Broken Time" motion defeated at meeting of the Rugby Union, consequently the final cleavage between professional and amateur Rugby.

1894—William Cail appointed Treasurer of the Rugby Union, and at the same time entrusted with the task of drawing up a code of laws against professionalism.

1902-3—Visit of a Canadian touring team to Britain.

1905—Modern scoring values adopted. Visit of first New Zealand representative side to Britain. England met France for first time. First fully representative Australian side toured New Zealand.

1906—First South African side under Paul Roos visited Britain. Army Cup presented by Rugby Union.

1907—Rugby Union purchases site at Twickenham. Rugby League football gains foothold in both New South Wales and Queensland.

1908-9—Visit to Britain of first Australian team—the first "Wallabies".

1910—England beat Wales in first International played at Twickenham.

1914-18—The Great War. Rugby Football restricted to Service matches.

1919—New Zealand won Inter-Services Tournament held at Twickenham, and contested by Britain, Australia, R.A.F., South Africa, and Canada.

1920—France win first International in British Isles by defeating Ireland in Dublin.

1921—Tablet in memory of fallen Rugby players unveilled by King George V at Twickenham.

1922—Death of G. A. J. Rothney, originator of "Calcutta Cup".

1923—Rugby's Centenary Match played on the Close at Rugby School between teams representing Wales and England, and Scotland and Ireland.

1924—Second New Zealand touring team won all their 30 matches in Britain.

1925—Scotland beat England in the first International staged at their new H.Q.—Murrayfield.

1926—Harlequins won the first Middlesex Seven-a-Side competition at Twickenham. Dominions given right of separate representation on the International Board. Scotland introduce special legislation to prevent players or officials under their jurisdiction, writing for the Press. Laws of game re-drafted.

1927—International Board approves abolition of "loose head" in scrummage. England beaten for first time by France at Colombes. "Waratahs" on tour in Britain and France. G. Rowland Hill knighted for services to the game.

1928—Death of Sir Rowland Hill. France beat Wales for first time. First New Zealand tour of South Africa.

1929—Memorial to the late Sir G. Rowland Hill unveiled at Twickenham. Rugby Union join Scots in the ban on players and officials writing for the Press.

1931—The Home Unions break off relations with France owing to the unsatisfactory conduct of the game in that country. Visit to Britain of B. L. Osler's third South African "Springboks". Douglas Bader of the R.A.F., Harlequins, and Combined Services, subsequently to become Wing Commander Bader, the famous air ace, lost both limbs in a flying accident. Death of E. Carleton Holmes, one of the great figures in the formation of the Rugby Union.

1932—New Zealand abolished the wing forward as exploited at home and on previous tours of Britain. At the same time they adopted the three front row formation in the scrummage, and moreover decided (subject to the agreement of opposing captains) to permit replacements of injured players.

1934—Cambridge University undertook a short tour of the U.S.A.

1935—Special match at Twickenham between the Barbarians and a London XV in honour of the Jubilee of King George V. Third New Zealand side visit Britain.

1939—Outbreak of war. Rugby Football once again left to Service organisation.

1943—Guy's Hospital Centenary celebrations.

1945-46—Victory International played. The "Kiwis"—the New Zealand Army touring team—beat England, Wales and France, but lost to Scotland.

1946-47—International Championship resumed. France take part for the first time since 1931.

1947-48—Ireland win Triple Crown for first time since 1899. Fourth Australian "Wallabies" visit Britain and France.

1948-49—Dropped goal reduced in value from 4 to 3 points. South Africa receive visit from New Zealand.

1949-50—Wales win Triple Crown for first time since 1911. British tour of Australia and New Zealand.

1953—Lewis Jones, the Welsh threequarter, turns professional at a new record fee of £6,000.

1954—Reframing of the laws.

1956—South African team in New Zealand. "Springboks" beaten in a Test "rubber" for the first time in over 50 years.

1957—All-Black unbeaten in Australian tour.

1959—France won International Championship for first time outright. Combined England-Wales beat Scotland-Ireland 26—17 in Twickenham Jubilee match.

1960—Scotland make their first overseas tour playing three games in South Africa.

1961—France unbeaten in International Championship games. Ireland made first overseas tour with four games in South Africa and Rhodesia.

1962—Barbarians only side to beat Fifth Springboks. Visit of Canadian touring team to Britain.

1963—England made their first overseas tour, playing five matches in New Zealand and one in Australia. Newport the only side to beat Fifth All-Blacks.

1964—Laws of the game revised. Wales made first overseas tour with a visit to South Africa. South Africa celebrated 75th anniversary of formation of their Rugby Board. Fijians made first visit to Europe, playing five games in Wales.

1965—Further changes in Laws of the game.

1967—All-Blacks undefeated in tour of Britain and France.

1970—Centenary Congress attended by 43 countries at Cambridge. Centenary match at Twickenham and dinner at Guildhall.

1971—British Lions win series in New Zealand. Value of a try increased to 4 points.

1972—Scottish Rugby Union celebrate centenary.

34

## DOLPHIN R.F.C.

One of the leading clubs of the Munster Union the Dolphin club through its representatives J. S. McCarthy, J. O'Meara, and to a lesser degree B. O'Hanlon, have played a valuable part in Ireland's post war achievements in International Rugby. McCarthy, who is the club record-holder with 28 caps, played a vital role in the Triple Crown successes of 1948-49, both as a spoiling wing forward, and as a forager in support of the short punting of Kyle. O'Meara too as Kyle's partner earns a niche for himself amongst Ireland's famous players. Another Dolphin player, C. J. Hanrahan, played for his country on 20 occasions between 1926-32, and M. J. Bradley made the same number of appearances in the period immediately after World War I. Colours: Navy, yellow and white striped jerseys, navy shorts. Ground: Musgrave Park, Cork.

## DUBLIN UNIVERSITY

Dublin University, formed 1854 and, the oldest club in Ireland, have produced more Irish international players than any other club. There were for instance no fewer than 9 University players capped in 1875, the first season Ireland participated in International matches, and the strength of its Rugby may be accurately gauged from the fact that seventy-six Dublin University players wore the Irish jersey between 1875-1900. The most famous of all, even though others have won more caps, was surely R. A. (Dick) Lloyd, who played at stand-off half 19 times between 1910-20, and who in the process received special acclaim as one of the most adroit and accurate tactical kickers of all time. Famous too, especially as a seller of "dummies" on the blind side of the scrum, was Mark Sugden, who won 28 caps, most of them in association with another Dublin player, Eugene O'Davy at half back. J. C. Parke, a dominating figure at threequarter during Rugby's "Golden" era between 1900-10, played for Ireland on twenty occasions, J. D. Clinch a tearaway wing forward of the thirties on 30 (the University record), whilst C. V. Rooke (19), H. Thrift subsequently a leading administrator (18), and J. P. Quinn (15) were other particularly distinguished University representatives in International Rugby. Colours: White. Ground: Trinity College, Dublin.

## DUNFERMLINE R.F.C.

One of the foremost Rugby strongholds in Scotland, the Dunfermline club has produced several Scottish Internationals, since their formation in 1904. The two most prominent being H. Lind, a clever stand-off half who gained 16 caps between 1928-36, and J. T. Greenwood, a back row forward who was one of the strong men in the British Isles team which contested the 1955 Test series in South Africa and made 20 appearances for Scotland 1952-59. Colours: Royal blue and white. Ground: McKane Park, Dunfermline. Hon. Secretary: A. D. Lindgren, 41 East Port, Dunfermline.

## EAST COAST

Founded 1921, affiliated to New Zealand Rugby Union 1922. Headquarters, Ruatoria. Colours: Sky Blue. George Nepia, the great Maori full-back who became famous with Hawkes Bay, also played for East Coast towards the end of his career, indeed he played for them in his last representative game at the age of forty-three.

## EASTERN PROVINCE

Founded in 1888, Eastern Province are another of the redoubtable provincial teams of South Africa, and although they never have to date earned a Currie Cup victory, among their many fine achievements are victories over the British touring teams led by R. Cove-Smith and Robin Thompson in 1924 and 1955 respectively. "Springbok" representatives from the Province include J. G. Hirsch, J. D. Luyt, J. P. Michau, W. H. Delport, Amos Du Plooy, G. Carelse, and W. H. Parker. Provincial H.Q. is at Port Elizabeth, and the Union colours are: Red and black jerseys, blue knickers, black stockings with red tops.

## EASTERN TRANSVAAL

Founded in 1948, as an off-shoot of the larger and more antiquated Transvaal Union. Their first international was N. Riley, capped against Australia in 1963. Headquarters: Springs. Colours: Maroon jerseys with green and gold bands, gold collar, white shorts.

## EBBW VALE R.F.C.

Founded in 1895, Ebbw Vale failed to achieve first-class status until after World War II, but their subsequent achievements have more than justified their elevation. Indeed on several occasi-

ons during the post-war period the Vale have succeeded in upsetting the "form book" with resounding victories at the expense of powerful and old established clubs like Newport and Cardiff. In 1957 the club rejoiced in the selection of Graham Powell at centre threequarter in the Welsh team against Ireland—the first Valian to be so honoured.

Since then, of course, the club has provided Wales with one of their finest prop forwards in Denzil Williams—36 caps and 400 games for Ebbw Vale.

Colours: Red, green and white hoops and stockings, white shorts. Ground: Eugene Cross Park, Secretary: W. Hunt, Eugene Cross Park, Ebbw Vale, Gwent.

## EDINBURGH ACADEMICALS

Though both Guy's Hospital and Blackheath of England dispute the claim, in Scotland at least, Edinburgh Academicals are regarded as the oldest organised Rugby club in Britain. They were formed in 1858, and in the following year met Merchiston Castle School in the first Scottish club match on record. The club's ground at Raeburn Place was the venue for the very first England v Scotland International in 1871, and appropriately enough it was an Academical—F. J. Moncrieff—who captained the Scottish team. Since then over 100 Academicals have represented Scotland, among them famous names as J. I. Gillespie, W. E. MacLagan who captained the first British team in South Africa, J. M. B. Scott, that very great and classical centre threequarter G. P. S. McPherson, J. B. Neill, who captained Scotland, and W. I. D. Elliott, one of the dominating personalities of Scottish post-war Rugby. Elliott with 29 caps is the Academicals' record holder in this respect. Hon. Secretary: J. L. Paterson, 57 Murrayfield Gardens, Edinburgh EH12 6DH.

## EDINBURGH UNIVERSITY

As the inclusion of two of its members in the first ever Scottish International side of 1871 might suggest, Edinburgh University rank with the oldest of Scottish Rugby clubs, and they have contributed much to the history of Scottish Rugby as a whole. It was at the University that the immortal D. R. ("Darkie") Bedel-Sivright first revealed the power, fire and intensity of purpose that subsequently earned him universal acclaim as one of, if not "the" greatest forward of his era. Of the University products who have won a Scottish International jersey, none perhaps were more universally famous than E. H. (Eric) Liddell, an Olympic sprinter as well as a great wing threequarter in his own right, E. D. Simpson who earned 17 caps between 1902-06, and W. R. Logan who in the course of his 20 appearances between 1931-36 was regarded as one of the most powerful and competent scrum-halves of his period. Colours: white jerseys and shorts, red stockings. Ground: Craiglockhart.

## EDINBURGH WANDERERS

As their title implies the Edinburgh Wanderers, formed 1869, cater for those players resident in Edinburgh, but have no allegiance to the many Old Boy's organisations in the city. Indeed a famous Wanderers player was J.A. Gwilliam who captained Wales in the Triple Crown seasons of 1950 and 1952. "Guests", from other countries notwithstanding, however, the Wanderers have done most handsomely by their own national selectors, for since J. Reid was capped against England in 1874, more than 50 Wanderers have worn the Scottish jersey. Most famous of them all perhaps was 'The Flying Scotsman", I.S. (Ian) Smith, who gained 32 Scottish caps, and in the process a reputation as one of the greatest wing threequarters of his own or any other era. Other great names in club history are those of C.M. Usher, who led the Scottish pack superlatively both before and immediately after World War I, W.R. Logan, one of the outstanding International scrum-halves of the thirties, and in more distant times the legendary A.R. Don Waunchope—the elusive half-back genuis of the 1880s. Colours: Red and black. Hon. Secretary: P.A. Carson, Boghall House, Linlithglow.

## ENGLAND

See under INTERNATIONALS (England).

## EXETER R.F.C.

Maybe in the past it was Exeter's geographical position that prevented them from reaching the really top flight of first-class clubs but they are certainly one of the finest in the West country and can trace their history back further than most, having been formed in 1871-72. Their best season was 1945-46 when they were beaten only twice in 37 games (34 won) scoring 647 points and conceding only 147. In 1950-51 Exeter was one of only two sides able to defeat Newport. 13 of Exeter's players have been capped. Their headquarters at the County Ground has a capacity of 26,000 and a fine Memorial clubhouse. Hon. Secretary: L. J. B. Challenger, 54 Barley Lane, Exeter.

## EXILE CLUBS

The three great "Exile" clubs of Britain are, in order of antiquity, London Scottish (1876), London Welsh (1885), and London Irish (1898). All three have more than fulfilled their *raison d'etre*, i.e. catering for the needs of compatriots living or working in London, and in the process have earned distinction among the great Rugby clubs of Britain. Details are:

LONDON SCOTTISH. Colours: Blue with red lion on left hand breast, red stockings. Won Middlesex sevens in five out six seasons during 1960s. Ground: Richmond Athletic Ground, which they have shared with Richmond throughout much of their history. Hon. Secretary: D.F. Pappin, Church Stile House, Church Street, Cobham, Surrey.

LONDON WELSH. Colours: Scarlet jerseys, white shorts, scarlet stockings, white tops. Dominated the Middlesex Sevens during the early 1970s. Ground: Old Deer Park, Richmond. Hon. Secretary: M. O. Price, 53 Thornton Avenue, Chiswick, London W. 4.

LONDON IRISH. Colours: Green jerseys, white shorts, green stockings. Ground: Sunbury-on-Thames, Middlesex. Hon. Secretary: W. F. Whelan, 8 Dysart Street, London E.C.2.

## FIELD GOAL

Up until the year 1905 when it was abolished, a goal could be scored from any kick excepting a punt, or from a kick-off, thus it was possible for a player to kick the ball off the ground without first handling it. The ball for instance could be rolling in any direction or stationery, but as long as it was kicked over the crossbar and between the posts it was worth 4 points to the kicker. In Australia and New Zealand particularly the term is still used (erroneously) to denote the dropped goal.

## FIJI

It is believed that rugby was first played in Fiji in about 1884 when it was taken up by the Native Constabulary. For many years soccer was preferred to the handling code but the rugby men made steady progress and by 1904 there were enough clubs to form a regular competition. The Royal Navy and Colonial Policemen from Europe played a leading role in the early development of the game in these Pacific Islands but the Fijians have long since established their own traditional style of attacking rugby.

Today rugby is the principal sport of Fiji and the national Union which was formed in 1913 has a membership of around 750 clubs. A Native Rugby Union was formed in 1915 but this amalgamated with the older Union in 1945.

Close links have been forged with the New Zealand Maoris who made their first tour of Fiji in 1938, while the Fijians have themselves visited New Zealand not only to meet the Maoris but also on five other tours in which they have played almost all the leading Unions and won well over half of these games.

The Fijian's first tour abroad was to Tonga in 1924 and over the years a great rivalry has built up with more than a dozen tours but with the Fijians maintraining their superiority.

The Fijians first displayed their talent for fast open rugby in Europe in 1964 when they made their initial tour of Wales and France playing five games in each country and winning three. They came again in 1970 to tour England and Wales, and made a third visit in 1973, chalking up victories over the Barbarians (29–9) and Swansea (31–0) as well as several others.

The principal tournament in Fiji is the Farebrother-Sullivan Trophy which was presented in 1941 for competition between the sub-unions in a similar manner to New Zealand's Ranfurly Shield.

## FLANKER

It is difficult to pinpoint when exactly wing forward play commenced to make its impact on the game, but it is supposed to have been the "invention" of a New Zealand player named W. W. Robinson, who was active in the final decade of the last century. Individual names apart, however, there is ample evidence to support the contention that it was the New Zealanders who first used the term "Wing forward" as a designation for a forward who had been allocated a special function separate from the ordinary one of scrummaging. Indeed having experimented with the position on the Australian tour of 1903 the New Zealand representative team went to Great Britain in 1905 fully committed to the use of the wing forward as an indispensable part of their strategy. Controversy of course still rages over the legality or otherwise of Dave Gallaher's role on this historic tour, and indeed with ample reason, Gallaher in fact made not the slightest pretence of packing in the scrum; on the contrary his role was solely that of a "shield" for his own scrum-half, and as such he was wide open to a charge of obstructionism. By prearrangement Gallaher in his role of "wing-forward" put the ball into the scrummage while his own half-back stood behind it, and then continued to stand in the same spot (which of course made him off-side as well) after it was heeled on the New Zealand side. In this way he was able to prevent the opposing half-back from getting quickly to grips with his immediate opponent the New Zealand scrum-half who was accordingly able to clear his line with the minimum delay and interference. For several years New Zealand Rugby continued to flourish on the new found strategy of the winging forward, and indeed their scrum formation, 2-3-2, was specially adapted to cater for his "absence" on this roving commission. Eventually, in 1932, the policy was abandoned in face, partly of public opinion, and partly of the legislators, but not before thoughtful and enterprising players in other countries had become interested in the possibilities of creating new tactical functions for forwards who could ally speed of movement on the field to a study of trends and tactics off it. Thus was bred a new generation of intelligent and highly mobile forwards who could support their backs in attack, as well as negative the attacking movements of their opponents' backs. Men like C. H. Pillman (England) and Ivor Morgan (Wales) were perhaps the prototypes of the new vogue which reached a peak of what may be described as ruthless perfection with the emergence of the great England triumvirate of Wakefield, Voyce and Blakiston. The die was cast, and wing forward play was established as one of the game's major tactical weapons. Inevitably critics have arisen to deplore its stultifying effect on attacking back play, and there were many demands for legislation that would reduce its effectiveness.

In more recent times when the wing-forward changed from being the two outside men in the back row of the old 3-2-3 scrums to the two outside men in the second row of the 3-4-1 scrum they became more popularly known as flankers. They now usually play left and right rather than in earlier years where the open side wing forward would play the open side throughout the game.

The destructive element which was the most important feature of the wing-forward has been greatly limited by changes in the Laws governing both lineouts and scrums, and there is now a more constructive aspect in the winning of 2nd phase ball. Perhaps the most important feature of the modern flanker is the close support for the ball carrier.

## FLOODLIGHT RUGBY

The first Rugby match to be played under lights was probably that which took place at Broughton on October 22, 1878, when the home side met Swinton. The illumination was provided by two "Gramme's Lights" fixed to 30ft poles. In Scotland, Hawick was the first to try this innovation meeting Melrose on a snow-covered pitch, February 24, 1879.

A great deal of floodlit Rugby has been played during recent years but by and large the four Rugby Unions in Britain have never shown themselves wholeheartedly in favour of this type of entertainment, and indeed, in 1932-33 the Rugby Union flatly prohibited floodlit Rugby as "not in the best interests of the game." One of the first regular fixtures to combat some of this prejudice was the Harlequins-Cardiff match at the White City.

The formation of the Floodlit Alliance in Wales in 1964 was a major step forward in this aspect of the game and there was quite a stir the following year when Newport and Bristol were debarred by the Rugby Union (Newport are affiliated to both the Welsh and English Unions) from taking part in this competition. No doubt the R.F.U. took this line because of their traditional objection to competition Rugby, but maybe there was also some prejudice against floodlights.

Times change, however, and the R.F.U. have, so to speak, seen the light, for the club competition introduced in 1971 has proved to be tremendously popular. On the other hand, the Welsh have discarded their Floodlit Alliance because they felt it was no longer needed, although as Llanelli had won it six times in a row, the opposition may have lost heart!

## FRANCE

The first game of Rugby football ever played on French soil took place in 1872 when British residents formed a club in Le Havre. More clubs were formed in Paris before the end of that decade but the handling code spread much more quickly in the south of the country when Englishmen involved in the wine trade introduced the game. In February 1885 the Paris Club journeyed to England and met the Civil Service at

Dulwich. These visits became more frequent, and the impetus of further visits from leading English and Welsh club sides, not to mention the expert coaching their players received from famous British Internationals like Percy Bush, of Cardiff, who joined the British Consulate at Nantes at the end of his distinguished career, French Rugby made rapid progress so that by season 1905-06 the newly formed Federation Française felt justified in entering the field of International Rugby. As it turned out however their optimism was ill-founded, for at Paris in the same season their International representatives proved no match for New Zealand, who beat them 38–8, or England who won by 35 points to 8. Meetings with Wales (1907-08), Ireland (1908-09), and Scotland (1909-10), followed in due course, but defeat, for the most part overwhelming, continued to be France's portion until season 1919-20 when they shattered Hibernian complacency by winning 15–7 in Dublin. In the following winter Scotland were defeated by a solitary try at Inverleith, and Ireland again accounted for, this time in Paris. In 1926-27 came the initial defeat of England (3–0) again in Paris, and the following winter they erased the one remaining blot on their Rugby escutcheon by triumphing over the Welsh at Colombes. Any hopes, however, the French may have entertained of consolidating and improving on the progress they had already made in the field of International Rugby, were rudely dispelled in March 1931, when the Federation Secretary, C. F. Rutherford, received a copy of the following resolution which had been passed by a committee of representatives of the four Home Unions at a meeting held in London on February 13 of the same year:

"After examination of the documentary evidence furnished by the French Federation and the dissentient clubs, we are compelled to state that owing to the unsatisfactory state of the game of Rugby football in France, neither our Union, nor the clubs or Unions under its jurisdiction, will be able to arrange or fulfil fixtures with France or French clubs at home or away after the end of this season unless and until we are satisfied that the control and conduct of the game has

been placed on a satisfactory basis in all essentials."

The events leading up to this impasse are worth recording inasmuch as they throw a revealing light on the difficulties that beset those who organise Rugby on the Continent. The whole trouble arose out of the fiercely competitive nature of the French Championship competition—the main event in the Continental Rugby calendar. With the will to win predominant amongst both competing clubs and players. it was not surprising perhaps that there should be many instances of rough, and occasionally violent play, or any less surprising that the desire on the part of competing clubs to field the strongest possible XV should lead to breaches of the professional laws as laid down by the Rugby Union. It was this latter that led to the full scale inquiry on the part of the Rugby Union, for when a dozen of the most influential clubs broke away from the federation on the issue of "veiled professionalism", it was only natural that the Rugby Union—the game's governing body—should intervene. When they did, the result was inevitable, viz., the banishment of the offending country from the international competition.

Due largely to the sincere and unremitting efforts of the great French administrator, C. F. Rutherford, his country's affairs were eventually resolved to the complete satisfaction of the British Unions, but France's re-entry into the International tournament was nevertheless postponed owing to the outbreak of World War II. When however they did participate again in season 1946-47, it was quickly evident that they were destined to become a real force in the competition, for whereas speed, dexterity, and a mercurial opportunism were still the cardinal features of the French game, to them was added a new-found thoughtfulness and a readier appreciation and understanding of the game's tactical aspects.

First Guy Basquet, and then Jean Prat proved themselves inspiring leaders, and under them French International XVs began to wipe out their pre-war deficits in no uncertain manner. In 1947-48 for instance they won their first ever victory on Welsh soil with a thoroughly deserved 11–3 win at St. Helen's Swansea, and in 1954-55 surpassed all previous efforts with a magnificent victory over England at Rugby's headquarters.

There followed what may be described as the "Golden Years" of French Rugby. From 1958 to 1962. It was during this period that they first won the International Championship outright (1958-59). They shared it with England the following season, but in 1960-61 they took the title once again by virtue of an undefeated run, dropping only one point when drawing 5–5 with England at Twickenham. They retained the title the next season when only Wales was able to beat them.

After winning the championship with only one defeat (by Scotland) in 1966-67 France performed the Grand Slam in 1967-68, beating Scotland 8–6, Ireland 16–6, England 14–2, and Wales 14–9. But despite this success it is generally acknowledged that their much changed team at this time does not rank among the best of this country's free-running sides.

The French Club Championship was begun in 1891-92 and has continued ever since with the exception of a five-year break during World War I and a three-year break during World War II. In the early days this competition was dominated by Stade Français and Stade Bordelais, but in modern times the most successful clubs are F.C. Lourdes and A.S. Béziers.

France earned their individual victory over an overseas touring team by defeating New Zealand 3–0 at Colombes Stadium in 1953.

The national colours are: Light blue jerseys mounted with the cockerel crest.

See also under INTERNATIONALS (FRANCE).

## FULL-BACK

In the days of 20-a-side Rugby the line-up allowed for three full-backs in each team, but with the introduction of 15-a-side football the number was reduced to a single player occupying what is often referred to as "the last line of defence." The position invariably calls for specialist qualifications, the chief ones being positional sense, kicking and catching ability, and effective tackle. World famous players in the position include: W. J. Bancroft, H. B. Winfield, V. G. J. Jenkins, (Wales), H. T. Gamlin, H. G. Owen-Smith (England), W. E. Crawford (Ireland), D. Drysdale (Scotland), J. Bassett (Wales), Gerhardt Morkel, G. Brand (South Africa), W. J. Wallace, George Nepia, R. W. H. Scott, D. B. Clarke (New Zealand), and P. Carmichael (Australia).

## GALA R.F.C.

Another of the famous Scottish Border sides, and for years Hawick's main rivals in the Border League. Gala was formed in 1875 and their most capped player is J. N. M. Frame who appeared 23 times for Scotland, including once while at Edinburgh University. P. C. Brown made 27 appearances but nine of his earliest internationals were during the time he was a West of Scotland player. In season 1964-65 P. B. Townsend scored 327 points for the club. Hon. Secretary: F. G. Entwhistle, Northcote, Barr Road, Galashiels. Colours: Maroon, Ground: Netherdale.

## GARRYOWEN R.F.C.

A Limerick club founded in 1884, Garryowen have won the Munster premier trophy more times than any other club, and in doing so established a reputation for forward play of a high order. Indeed "The Garryowen"—the high lofted punt in support of a rampaging pack—is now part of the Rugby vocabulary universally.

The club has provided Ireland with more than 30 Internationals, the record being created by B. G. M. Wood with 29 caps.

Ground: Doorodoyle, Limerick. Colours: Sky blue.

## GLASGOW ACADEMICALS

With over 60 "caps" (a record surpassed only by their Edinburgh counterparts) the Academicals of Glasgow have long ranked as one of the great clubs of Scottish Rugby. Founded in 1886 there were no fewer than six of its members in the Scottish team which met England in the first International match in 1871, and subsequent Internationals have in-

cluded such names as W. M. Simmers (28 caps), J. B. Nelson (25), J. C. Dykes (20), J. C. Dawson (20), H. Waddell (15).

Ground: New Anniesland. Colours: Navy and white. Hon. Secretary: W. D. Calder, 48 West Regent Street, Glasgow C.2.

## GLASGOW HIGH R.F.C.

Formed 1884, as Glasgow High School Former Pupils this club has many claims to fame in Scottish Rugby, not the least of them the production of one of the country's leading cap holders. J. MacD. Bannermann, who made 37 International appearances between 1921-28, and during the course of them established his own special niche as one of the greatest forwards and pack leaders of all time. Next to Bannermann (but only numerically) is J.W.Y. Kemp with 27 appearances 1954-60, while R. Wilson Shaw who, during the course of his 19 appearances between 1934-39 came to be regarded as one of the rare geniuses of Rugby football. Stand-off half was Shaw's natural position, but such was his versatility and natural aptitude for the game, that he could play in any position with equal grace and facility. Other outstanding International players whose primary allegiance was to this club were G. M. Frew, J. C. Ireland, and Angus Cameron who as a full back, stand-off half, or centre threequarter was an indispensable force in Scottish XVs between 1948-52. Ground: Old Anniesland. Colours: Chocolate and gold. Hon. Secretary: A. W. Anderson, 38 Broomvale Drive, Newton Mearns, Glasgow.

## GLOUCESTER R.F.C.

Another of the truly Big Names in British club Rugby, the Gloucester club, was founded in 1873, and throughout the intervening years have been held in healthy respect by all their opponents. Possibly the most famous of the many famous players who have worn the club colours was A. T. (Tom) Voyce who won 27 England caps as a winging forward between the years 1920-26. Voyce, who also toured South Africa with the 1924 British side is indeed to this day regarded as one of the greatest back two specialists the game has ever produced. He was President of the R.F.U. 1960-61. Another famous Gloucester player was the Welshman D. R. (Dai) Gent who, having like many other of his era, failed to displace the 3'5 times capped R. M. Owen as the Welsh scrum-half, joined Gloucester to become in due course England's regular choice in that position. A contemporary of Gent's in both the Gloucester and England XVs of the period was the clever and resourceful wing threequarter Arthur Hudson. Other "Citizens" to earn International honours were Harold Broughton and G. W. Parker, both full backs, and wonderfully accurate place kickers, C. C. Tanner, A. D. Carpenter, M. A. McCanlis, H. Berry, C. Hall, G. Holford, W. G. Hook, P. C. Horden, W. J. Jackson, W. Johns, T. W. Price, L. E. Saxby, S. Smart, C. Smith, A. E. Wood, G. W. Hastings and D. Rutherford. International honours apart, however, there are four players occupying a special niche in both club history and the affections of its followers, they are full backs George Romans and Peter Butler, centre threequarter Don Meadows, and the Welsh stand-off half, W. E. Jones, whose deeds, especially the unerring drop kicking of the last named have become something of a Kingsholm legend. In 1973-74 Butler scored 574 points. Club colours: Red and white hooped jerseys, stockings, and white shorts. Ground: Kingsholm. Hon. Secretary: R. G. Long, The Chestnuts, Tewkesbury Road, Gloucester.

# GOSFORTH R.F.C.

One of the most successful clubs in the North of England, Gosforth were founded in 1877 when they were known as Gosforth Nomads. Some idea of the tremendous strides made by this club in recent years may be had from the fact that they won the Northumberland Cup 10 times in 12 years in the 1960s and 1970s, but won it only once before 1956. In several games since 1972 they have had two players in the same England side—Roy Uttley and Peter Dixon. Club colours: Green and white hoops. Ground: Great North Road, Gosforth. Hon. Secretary: R. C. York, 16 Glamis Avenue, Milton Park, Newcastle-on-Tyne.

# GRIQUALAND WEST

Founded in 1886, Griqualand West became the original holders of the Currie Cup (see CURRIE CUP) by merit of their outstanding display against the first British touring side ever to visit the Union—that led by W. E. MacLagan in 1891. The Griquas, however, have only won the Cup twice since they handed it over to the South African Board for Inter-Provincial competition. This however in no way affects their rating as one of the main pillars of South African Rugby, and among the Springbok representatives produced by the Province are such famous names as P. J. Visagie, A. F. W. Marsberg, F. J. Dobbin, J. W. E. Raaff, W. C. Martheze, H. G. Kipling, W. H. Barnard and R. J. Lockyear, an accurate place kicker, who scored 63 points for the Fifth Springboks in the British Isles, 1960-61. Union headquarters are at Kimberley. Colours: Pracock blue jersey with narrow white stripe, blue shorts, and stockings as jersey.

# GUY'S HOSPITAL R.F.C.

Guy's have throughout their long history stoutly defended their claim to be regarded as Britain's oldest Rugby club. Indeed in 1943, in the middle of a World War, they celebrated their "centenary" with two special matches at Honor Oak Park. In the first on September 25, 1943, the Present beat the Past by 33—3, and in the second Guy's defeated a London XV by 5—0. The second match was followed by a dinner at the Honor Oak pavilion which was attended by many of the game's notabilities including one of the most famous of all Guy's players, Dr. Teddy Morgan of Wales. Original winners of The Hospital's Cup on the inauguration of the competition in 1875, Guy's have now won the trophy on 30 occasions, and a great deal of their success in this competition may be attributed to the presence of the many fine South African players who have throughout the year plumped for Guy's as the source of their medical learning. Ground: Honor Oak Park (since 1893). Colours: Blue and gold.

## HAKA

One of the most famous and picturesque features of New Zealand Rugby is the "haka"—a war dance performed by the players as a prelude to the Big Matches such as Provincial and International games. Derived from an ancient Maori battle rite, the words of the haka,
"E ringa pakia waewae tahahia
E Kine nei haki
E ringa e ringa e torona kei waho
    motonu
Kamate! Kamate!
Kaora, Kaora!
Tenei te tangata puhuruhuru
Kana e tiki rai whaka whiti te ra
A hupane! a hupane!
Hupane, Kopane, whiti te ra."
have no literal translation from the original Maori, but the action of the dance is emphatic enough to convey its meaning, which is at one and the same time to unnerve the enemy and to invoke the support of the Gods in battle.

## HACKING
(See also under RUGBY UNION, BLACK-HEATH and RICHMOND R.F.C.)

Hacking—the practice of using the toe either to kick an opponent's shins, or else to trip him up—has had a more profound influence on the development of Rugby Football than any of its old time perpetrators could have dreamt of. It was because they objected to the Football Association's ban on hacking that the Blackheath club broke away from the parent body in 1863, and then a few years later they themselves are found joining Richmond in a move to abolish the practice. Indeed one might say that hacking, or at least its consequences, was directly responsible for the formation of the Rugby Football Union

for as a result of a player being killed in a Richmond practice match and several others badly injured in certain matches, twenty clubs, acting possibly under the stimulus of some adverse publicity in *The Times* and *The Lancet,* met and formed the Rugby Union under a code of laws that finally excluded hacking in any shape or form.

## HARLEQUINS R.F.C.

Founded in 1866, the Harlequins have become a household name wherever the game is played, and as witness to the fact they have countless namesakes both in Great Britain and overseas. When the Rugby Union, of which the club were one of the founder members, acquired the Twickenham ground as their head-quarters, it was the Harlequins who had the distinction of playing the first match there. On October 2, 1909, they defeated Richmond by 14 points to 10 and thereby began not only their uninterrupted tenure of this famous ground, but in addition an era of brilliant and spetacular Rugby football of a type which when reproduced elsewhere was automatically referred to as "the Harlequin game". The player who perhaps did most to implement and develop the theme of swift fluent back play which has subsequently remained a feature of the club's football was A. D. Stoop, a great outside half and one of the tactical geniuses of the era. Alongside him were several other great players, notably J. G. G. Birkett, D. Lambert, and H. Brougham. Other great Harlequin players, though of a later era, have been Sir Wavell Wakefield, R. H. Hamilton-Wickes, H. C. C. Laird, R. W. Poulton-Palmer, R. W. D. Marques, V. G. Roberts, C. M. Payne, and R. B. Hiller. In 1955 the club toured Rumania—the first English club to do so. Colours: Magenta, chocolate, green, black, light blue and French grey. Ground: Twickenham. Hon. Secretary: W. Cdr. J. Seldon, O. B. E., Coverdale Lodge, 45 Kings Road, Richmond, Surrey.

## HAWICK

One of the famous Border clubs of Scotland, and like the rest, universally renowned for the fire and quality of their forward play. The club has won the Border League Championship more often than any other side, and since T. M. Scott won the club's first cap in 1893, have had many of their players in Scottish International XVs. Inevitably most of them have been forwards, and very famous names they are, viz., G. D. Stevenson (24 caps), W. E. Kyle (21), J. A. Beattie (23), D. S. Davies (20), W. B. Welsh (21), W. R. Sutherland (13), and Adam Robson (13). But the most famous of them all is their own local discovery, H. F. McLeod, who won 40 consecutive Scottish caps, and, in 1963, was awarded the O.B.E. for his services to the game. The club dates back to 1873 and has its H.Q. at Mansfield Park. Colours: Green. Hon. Secretary: J. Imre, 76, Eildon Road, Hawick.

## HAWKES BAY RUGBY FOOTBALL UNION

Founded in 1884 Hawkes Bay are one of the oldest affiliated New Zealand Unions and throughout their history have remained one of that country's truly formidable combinations. Their record in the Ranfurly Shield competition (See RANFURLY SHIELD) is an imposing one, while several of their players have aspired to world wide renown with New Zealand teams both at home and overseas. These include the great full back George Nepia who created an all time record by appearing in all 30 of New Zealand's matches on their tour of Great Britain and France in 1924-25, the Brownlie brothers M. J. and C. J., J. J. Mills, A. E. Cooke, W. R. Irvine, and K. R. Tremain. The Union colours are: Black and white hoops, they play at McLean Park, Napier, North Island.

## HEIGHT

Among the tallest men ever to play rugby at International level are: P. K. Stagg (Scotland) 6 ft. 10 in., J. J. Williams (South Africa) 6ft. 6½in., P. J. Whiting (New Zealand) 6 ft. 6½in., C. W. Ralston (England) 6ft. 6in., G. Fay (Australia) 6ft. 5½in., I.R. Robinson (Wales) 6ft. 5½in.

Among the shortest—T.A. Gentles (South Africa) 5ft. 3in., W.C. Dalley, (New Zealand) 5ft. 4½in., G.E. Cromey (Ireland) 5ft. 4ins.

## HERIOTS F.P. R.F.C.

Comprised of former pupils of the famous George Heriot's School, Edinburgh, Heriots have a long and distinguished record in Scottish club football.

Of the Internationals produced by the club none have achieved more widespread fame than the two full-backs Dan Drysdale who began his career as Scotland's full back in 1923, and made the last of his 26 appearances in 1928, and K. J. F. Scotland who made 27 appearances between 1956 and 1965, some of them after leaving Heriots for Cambridge University and Leicester. Hon. Secretary: J. K. Hutchinson, C.A., 4 Queensferry Street, Edinburgh EH2 4PB.

## HIGHEST SCORES
See under SCORING FEATS.

## HISTORY OF RUGBY FOOTBALL
See RUGBY SCHOOL; RUGBY UNION; DATES; LAWS OF THE GAME; ORIGINS; REFEREES, etc.

## HOROWHENUA R.F.U.
Founded 1883, affiliated to New Zealand Rugby Union 1893, but subsequently resigned and re-affiliated 1898, and again in 1933. Headquarters: Levin, North Island. Colours: Dark blue with red and white narrow bands. Outstanding player is B. W. McLennan with a remarkable run of over 90 consecutive games for the Union from 1955.

## HOSPITALS CUP
The Hospital's Cup Competition was inaugurated in 1875 on the proposition of England half-back W. E. Collins of Old Cheltonians and St. George's. Indeed, Collins got off his sick-bed to captain St. George's in the first final in 1875 but they were beaten by Guy's by 1 goal, 1 try, to 2 tries. Guy's thereby laid the foundation of many subsequent successes. Guy's have in fact won the trophy 30 times out of the 88 occasions it has come up for competition, whilst they have contested the final on another 17 occasions.

St. Mary's, who did not win their first final until 1900, have been successful on 18 occasions, including a record run of 7 successive victories 1934-46. St. Thomas's have enjoyed 17 victories, London Hospital have won 10 finals, St. Bartholomew's 7, St. George's (unsuccessful finalists in 1875) 3, Westminster 2, and Middlesex Hospital 1. University College Hospital have contested 5 finals without ever winning the trophy, whilst

King's College Hospital were also defeated in their three final appearances.
The two remaining participants in the
competition, Charing Cross and Royal
Free have never to date reached the final.

The record victory margin achieved
in a final was that of Guy's who in
season 1922 beat London Hospital 42–3.

The Final venue is at present the
Athletic Ground, Richmond.

## INSTONIANS R.F.C.

Instonians are the Old Boys' club of the Royal Belfast Academical Institution one of Ireland's greatest public schools which has been playing Rugby since 1873 The Old Boys' club itself was not formed until 1919 but for long periods in their history they have exercised a virtual monopoly of the honours in the Ulster Senior League and Cup. The most famous of their International Players is Sam Walker who played on 16 occasions during the 'thirties besides leading the British Isles team in South Africa in 1938. Another captain of the British Lions team in South Africa provided by this club is R. H. Thompson. He went to South Africa in 1955 but turned professional on his return. Ground: Shane Park. Colours: Yellow, black and purple.

## INTERNATIONAL BOARD

The International Board, as its title implies, was formed in 1890 with the object of ensuring that International matches were played under a unified code of laws, its function as originally stated being:
(1) International matches shall be played under one code of laws.
(2) The laws presently existing of the R.F.U., except such parts of Laws 25 and 30 as impose a penalty of a free kick if the ball be knocked on when thrown in from touch, shall be the first code of laws for International matches.
(3) The International Rugby Football Board shall consist of 12 members, 6 of whom shall be elected ro represent the Rugby Union, 2 the Scottish Union, 2 the Irish Union, and 2 the Welsh Union.
(4) The International Board shall have power by a majority of not less than three-quarters of its number to alter or cancel any existing law, ot to add new laws to the International code.
(5) The International Board shall be the sole arbiters of any dispute arising from an International match.

The majority held by the R.F.U. (England) was a bone of contention for many years and in 1911 England gave up two of its seats. Thereafter the Dominions increased their agitation for membership, and considering the strength of New Zealand and South African rugby it is surprising to note that these countries, along with Australia, did not gain representation on the Board until 1948 when England gave up another two seats and the newcomers were given one seat each. This was increased to two in 1958 and its present constitution allows for 2 representatives each from England, Scotland, Wales and Ireland, South Africa, New Zealand and Australia. Although it still fulfils its original function, the Board is at the present time the framers of the laws of Rugby football universally as well as for International matches. France is still not represented. The Board made history in 1959 by holding their first-ever meeting outside Britain—at Wairakei, North Island, New Zealand.

## INTERNATIONALS
See also TOURS

On November 19, 1870, England beat Scotland in a match played under Association rules at Kennington Oval, and that oddly enough was the prelude to the 600 plus International Rugby Football matches which have been played on British soil as distinct from that of Europe, since 1871. It became such, because the Scots were annoyed that a so-called "international" had been played by men who did not represent Scotland in what they considered to be the foremost rules North of the Border, viz., Rugby Football. Thus it came about that in 1871, the same year as the Rugby Union was formed in London, the Scots having issued their challenge in *Bell's Life* were promptly taken up by the English with the result that the first ever Rugby International match took place at Raeburn Place, Edinburgh, on Monday, March 27, 1871. It was contested 20 aside. F. Stokes (Blackheath) captaining England, and F. J. Moncrieff

Scotland, the game was won by the Scots by 1 goal, 1 try to a try. A return match, won by England, was played at Kennington Oval in the following winter, and then England met Ireland in 1875, and Wales at Blackheath in 1880-8.

A special match was played between England and Scotland at Murrayfield on March 27, 1971, i.e. exactly 100 years after the first game. This was also won by the Scotts — 26–6.

Other landmarks in the development of International Rugby as contested between the Unions of Great Britain were:

1875-76  First International on Irish soil, that between Ireland and England.

1876-77  Scotland and Ireland met for first time at Belfast.

1882-83  Scotland and Wales met for first time at Edinburgh.

1882-83  First International match played in Wales—between England and Wales on the St. Helen's Ground at Swansea.

1905-06  England introduce France to International Rugby by playing them for the first time in Paris.

The development of the game in Australia, New Zealand, and South Africa together with its logical sequel—the innovation of tours abroad—served to make International Rugby as it were, really International. It is not however so called in the countries just mentioned, for all seemingly prefer the idiom of the cricket field, hence "the Test" has become as stern a reality at Twickenham or Murrayfield, as it has long been at both Lords and the Oval. Few people, one supposes, will cavil over a term, but it would seem perhaps, that in South Africa in particular, they are apt to think of "Test" Rugby and International Rugby as two separate entities.

## England

England's tally of Championship wins —16 outright and 10 shared titles is only exceeded by Wales, and in two separate periods her Rugby XVs have come near to achieving absolute domination in the field of Home Internationals. Between 1910-14 three Championships were won outright, and a fourth shared with Ireland, whilst between 1920-24 the records show three outright wins for four attempts. Both periods inevitably abound with truly famous names; in the first we have performers of the calibre of Adrian Stoop, and his Harlequin aides J. G. Birkett and H. Brougham, C. H. ("Cherry") Pillman, C. N. Lowe, R. W. Poulton-Palmer, J. A. King and L. G. Brown, whilst adorning the second are such names as R. Cove-Smith, W. W. Wakefield, A. T. Voyce, L. J. Corbett, A. F. Blakiston, and the incomparable half-back combination of W. J. A. Davies (whose career spanned the both periods) and C. A. Kershaw. Indeed during the period 1920-24 England played in 20 Home Internationals, winning 17 of them, drawing one, and losing only two.

England's best side since the war, at least from the point of view of results, was undoubtedly that which performed the Grand Slam in 1956-57 and retained the championship the following season when they were undefeated but held to draws by both Scotland and Wales. The side was captained throughout this period by hooker Eric Evans of Sale.

RECORD IN INTERNATIONAL
RUGBY

v. *Scotland*. Played 91. Won 43. Lost 34. Drawn 14.
Biggest Win. England 19, Scotland 0. at Murrayfield, 1924.
Biggest Defeat. England 6, Scotland 26, at Murrayfield, 1971.

v. *Ireland*. Played 87. Won 49. Lost 30. Drawn 8.
Biggest Win. England 36, Ireland 14, at Dublin, 1938.
Biggest Defeat. England 0, Ireland 22, at Dublin, 1947.

v. *Wales*. Played 80. Won 33. Lost 36. Drawn 11.
Biggest Win. England 18, Wales 3, at Twickenham, 1921.
Biggest Defeat. England 0, Wales 22, at Swansea, 1906 and England 6, Wales 28, at Cardiff, 1922.

v. *France*. Played 50. Won 29. Lost 15. Drawn 6.
Biggest Win. England 37, France 0, at Twickenham, 1911.
Biggest Defeat. England 12, France 37, at Paris, 1972.

## Scotland

Next to England and Wales it is Scotland who possess the most imposing record of successes in the International Championship, for they have won 12 outright titles, and shared in another 7 successes. The bulk of their success was achieved between the years 1887-1907 when they were concerned in ten Championships. It was a period renowned for the quality of Scottish forward play with players like Mark Morrison, D. R. Bedell-Sivright setting the standard that was so finely maintained by the Bannermanns, the Welshes, the Ushers, and the Elliots of the more modern times. Scotland has too produced some of the greatest backs in history, including A. R. Don Wauchope, K. G. MacLeod, G. MacGregor, and the later day Ian Smith, G. P. S. MacPherson, H. Waddell, R. W. Shaw, W. R. Logan, D. Drysdale and K. J. F. Scotland. A less enviable feature of their International history, however, has been their post-war record which amongst other mediocrities includes a losing sequence of 17 matches between February, 1951 and February, 1955. There have been no runs as bad as that in more recent years, indeed Scotland recovered sufficiently to share the Championship in 1963-64 when only Wales beat them. It was during this season that they were the only country to avoid defeat by the Fifth All-Blacks, holding them to a pointless draw.

## RECORD IN THE INTERNATIONAL CHAMPIONSHIP

v. *England.* Played 91. Won 34. Lost 43. Drawn 14.
   Biggest Win. Scotland 26, England 6, at Murrayfield, 1971.
   Biggest Defeat. Scotland 0, England 19, at Murrayfield, 1924.
v. *Ireland.* Played 85. Won 43. Lost 39. Drawn 3.
   Biggest Win. Scotland 19, Ireland 0, at Edinburgh, 1920.
   Biggest Defeat. Scotland 0, Ireland 21, at Dublin, 1950.
v. *Wales.* Played 79. Won 34. Lost 43. Drawn 2.
   Biggest Win. Scotland 33, Wales 10, at Inverleith, 1924.
   Biggest Defeat. Scotland 12, Wales 35, at Cardiff, 1972.
v. *France.* Played 45. Won 23. Lost 20. Drawn 2.
   Biggest Win. Scotland 31, France 3, at Inverleith, 1912.
   Biggest Defeat. Scotland 0, France 15, at Paris, 1955.

## Ireland

Despite their tradition of firey forward play and the long list of famous names which adorn the Record Books, Ireland's success in International Rugby has been mainly spasmodic. Winning the title for the first time in 1894, they repeated the success in 1896 and 1899, and then had to wait 36 years for their next outright win which was achieved in 1935. In the interim they shared the Championship on five occasions, but it was not until after the Second World War that Irish Rugby really lived up to its high and altogether justifiable repute when Karl Mullen's team won the title in the successive winters of 1948 and 1949 — a success which they repeated in 1951. A gap of 23 years followed before they brought their tally of outright wins to eight in 1974. Whether its back or forwards the great Irish names are bound to impinge on any discussion of Rugby Football—R. A. ("Dickie") Lloyd, Basil Maclear, J. J. Coffey, G. V. Stephenson, W. E. Crawford, the Beamish brothers G. R. and C. E., J. D. Clinch, J. A. Siggins, George Morgan, Eugene O'Davy, Mark Sugden, J. W. Kyle, Karl Mullen, D. J. O'Brien, W. J. McBride, T. J. Kiernan, C. M. H. Gibson—ancients and moderns alike their names are legion, and honoured wherever the game is played.

## RECORD IN INTERNATIONAL MATCHES

v. *England.* Played 87. Won 30. Lost 49. Drawn 8.
   Biggest Win. Ireland 22, England 0, at Dublin, 1947.
   Biggest Defeat. Ireland 14, England 36, at Dublin, 1938.
v. *Scotland.* Played 85. Won 39. Lost 43, Drawn 3.
   Biggest Win. Ireland 21, Scotland 0, at Dublin, 1950.
   Biggest Defeat. Ireland 0, Scotland 19, at Edinburgh, 1920.
v. *Wales.* Played 77. Won 26. Lost 46. Drawn 5.
   Biggest Win. Ireland 19, Wales 3, at Belfast, 1925.
   Biggest Defeat. Ireland 0, Wales 29, at Cardiff, 1907.
v. *France.* Played 48. Won 24. Lost 21. Drawn 3.
   Biggest Win. Ireland 24, France 0, at Cork, 1913.

Biggest Defeat. Ireland 6, France 27, at Paris, 1964.

## Wales

The most successful country in the International Championship Wales have won the title outright on 18 occasions, and in addition shared the honour with other competing countries on another 11 occasions. Six of these successes were obtained between the years 1900-11, a period that is still referred to as "The Golden Era" of Welsh Rugby, and certainly the quality of Welsh Rugby was at its very zenith in a period which produced such immortal names as Gwyn Nicholls, W. J. Trew, R. M. Owen, R. T. Gabe, Percy Bush, Dr. Teddy Morgan, W. Llewelyn, George Travers, A. F. Harding, and W. Joseph. It was, of course, during this period (in 1905) that Wales defeated Dave Gallacher's invincible All-Blacks in that famous and highly controversial enocunter at the Cardiff Arms Park.

Some of the glory of earlier years was recaptured by the brilliant Welsh side that performed the Grand Slam in 1970-71, a side that included a number of the world's finest players at this time, Barry John, John Williams, Gerald Davies, Gareth Edwards, and Mervyn Davies. Wales won all 4 games this season, scoring 13 tries in the process, and using only 16 players throughout.

## RECORD IN INTERNATIONAL RUGBY

v. *England.* Played 80. Won 36. Lost 33. Drawn 11.
  Biggest Win. Wales 22, England 0, at Swansea, 1906 and Wales 28, England 6, at Cardiff, 1922.
  Biggest Defeat. Wales 3, England 18, at Twickenham, 1921.

v. *Scotland.* Played 79. Won 43. Lost 34. Drawn 2.
  Biggest Win. Wales 35, Scotland 12, at Cardiff, 1972.
  Biggest Defeat. Wales 10, Scotland 35, at Inverleith, 1924.

v. *Ireland.* Played 77. Won 46. Lost 26. Drawn 5.
  Biggest Win. Wales 29, Ireland 0, at Cardiff, 1907.
  Biggest Defeat. Wales 3, Ireland 19, at Belfast, 1925.

v. *France.* Played 47. Won 31. Lost 13. Drawn 3.
  Biggest Win. Wales 47, France 5, at Paris, 1910.
  Biggest Defeat. Wales 13, France 22, at Paris, 1976 .7

## France

France did not enter the International Championship until season 1909-10, and owing to a dispute (see main section—FRANCE) with the Rugby Union in Britain did not participate during the years 1931-39. In the beginning French International XVs were understandably perhaps no match for their powerful and more experienced counterparts in other countries, but the standard of play kept on improving steadily right up until the outbreak of World War II, and then when the game was resumed on a peace-time basis in 1946, it was quickly apparent that French Rugby had well and truly arrived as a formidable power in the International field.

Under the leadership of Jean Prat of Lourdes they first shared the honours with England and Wales in 1954, and with Wales alone the following year. Better was still to come, for they were to enjoy a period of four seasons in which they were practically invincible. First under the captaincy of Mias and then under Moncla they won the championship in 1958-59, shared it with England the following season, and won it outright again in each of the next two campaigns. The first French side to perform the Grand Slam was that of 1967-68, their second successive championship win at this time. Obviously, therefore, the post-war period has produced several players of world-ranking, including men like Prat, Basquet, Dufau, Pomathios, Alvarez, Albaladejo, Domec, Romeu, Crauste, Dauga, Spanghero, but the splendid progress of Rugby in that country also owes a tremendous amount to men like Cassayet, Jaurreguy, Ribere, Gallia, Mauriat, Crauste, Celaya, and Domenech.

## RECORD IN THE INTERNATIONAL CHAMPIONSHIP

v. *England.* Played 50. Won 15. Lost 29. Drawn 6.
  Biggest Win. France 37, England 12, at Paris, 1972.
  Biggest Defeat. France 0, England 37, at Twickenham, 1911.

v. *Scotland.* Played 45. Won 20. Lost 23, Drawn 2.

Biggest Win. France 15, Scotland 0, at Paris, 1955.

Biggest Defeat. France 3, Scotland 31, at Inverleith, 1912.

v. *Ireland.* Played 48. Won 21. Lost 24. Drawn 3.

Biggest Win. France 27, Ireland 6, at Paris, 1964.

Biggest Defeat. France 0, Ireland 24, at Cork, 1913.

v. *Wales.* Played 47. Won 13. Lost 31 Drawn 3.

Biggest Win. France 27, Wales 13, at Paris, 1965.

Biggest Defeat. France 5, Wales 47, at Paris, 1910.

## Schoolboys in International Rugby

The following players won Senior International caps while still at school.

*For England*

J. G. Milton (Bedford School), 1904.

Ryder Richardson (Manchester Grammar School), 1881.

F. T. Wright (Edinburgh Academy), 1881.

*For Scotland*

T. Anderson (Merchiston), 1882.

J. A. Campbell (Merchiston), 1878.

N. J. Finlay (Edinburgh Academy), 1875.

W. St. Clair Grant (Craigmount), 1873.

D. M. Grant (Elstow Bedford), 1911.

G. Neilson (Merchiston), 1891.

W. Neilson (Merchiston), 1891.

C. Reid (Edinburgh Academy), 1881.

Marshall Reid (Loretto), 1882.

*For Ireland*

J. B. Allison (Campbell College, Belfast), 1899.

Adrian Bailey (Presentation College Bray) 1934.

F. M. W. Harvey (Portora), 1907

F. S. Hewitt (Royal Inst., Belfast), 1924

G. McAllan (Dungannon H.S.), 1896.

*For Wales*

N. H. Biggs (Cardiff College), 1889.

H. Tanner (Gowerton County School), 1935.

W. H. Thomas (Llandovery), 1885.

W. Wooller (Rydall School), 1933.

## Played for Two Countries

For Australia and Scotland: D. H. Keller, Australia 1947; Scotland 1950.

For New South Wales and Scotland: A. C. Wallace, N.S.W. 1921-26-27-28; Scotland 1923-24-25-26.

For New South Wales and Ireland: M. Barlow, Ireland 1875; N.S.W. 1882.

For New South Wales and England: C. G. Wade, England 1883-84-85-86; N.S.W. 1888. B. H. Travers, England 1947-48-49; N.S.W. 1950.

For New South Wales and Great Britain; B. I. Swannell, Britain 1899 and 1904; N.S.W. 1905-06.

For New South Wales and New Zealand: Jas. O'Donnell, N.Z. 1884; N.S.W. 1884. H. Y. Braddon, N.Z. 1884; N.S.W. 1888. F. Surman, N.S.W. 1894; N.Z. 1896. T. Pauling, N.Z. 1896; N.S.W. 1898. W. Hardcastle, N.Z. 1897; N.S.W. 1898. E. E. Booth, N.Z. 1905; N.S.W. 1908. J. Wylie, N.S.W. 1911; N.Z. 1913.

For Australia and New Zealand: Jas. O'Donnell, N.Z. 1884; Australia 1899. W. Hardcastle, N.Z. 1897; Australia 1899. J. Wylie, Australia 1912; N.Z. 1913. E. M. Jessep, N.Z. 1932; Australia 1934. D. M. Connor, Australia 1957-58-59; New Zealand 1960-61-62-63. O.G. Stephens, New Zealand 1968; Australia 1973-74.

For Australia and Great Britain: B. I. Swannell, Britain 1899 and 1904; Australia 1905. T. J. Richards, Australia 1908; Britain 1910 (in South Africa).

For Queensland and England: L. G. Brown, Queensland 1908, England 1911-13-14-21.

For South Africa and England: F. W. Mellish, England 1920; South Africa 1921-24.

For New Zealand and England: I. J. Botting, New Zealand 1949; England 1950.

For England and Scotland: J. H. Marsh, Scotland 1889; England 1892.

For New Zealand and Scotland: G. G. Aitken, New Zealand 1921; Scotland 1924-25-29. C. M. Gilray, New Zealand 1905; Scotland 1908-09-12. D. G. Macpherson, New Zealand 1905; Scotland 1910.

For Ireland and South Africa: J. H. Gage, Ireland 1926-27; South Africa 1933.

For Scotland and South Africa: W. M. C. McEwan, Scotland 1894-95-96-97-98-99-1900; South Africa 1903. A. Frew, Scotland 1901; South Africa 1903.

For Ireland and Wales: F. Purdon, Wales 1881-82-83, and H. M. Jordan, Wales 1885-89, both played for Ireland v Wales, at Cardiff, 1884, when Ireland arrived short of players.

## Colours

*England*—White with red rose crest. white shorts, black stockings with white tops.

*Scotland*—Navy blue jerseys with thistle crest, white shorts, navy stockings.

*Ireland*—Bright green jerseys and stockings with shamrock crest, white shorts.

*Wales*—Scarlet jerseys with Prince of Wales feathers crest, white shorts, scarlet stockings with white tops.

*France*—Light blue jerseys with Chanticleer crest, white shorts, light blue stockings.

*Australia*—Gold jerseys with Australian national crest and green numbers on back, green collars and shorts, green and gold stockings.

*New Zealand*—Black jerseys with silver fern crest, black shorts, black stockings with white bands on tops.

*South Africa*—Dark green jerseys with gold "Springbok" crest, white shorts, dark green stockings with two gold bands on tops.

## Caps

The brevity of the lists referring to New Zealand, Australia and South African capped players is of course explained by the infrequency with which these countries appear in International Rugby. Inevitably the British players who have the opportunity of obtaining a maximum of four caps in any season have a decided advantage here over their counterparts in the countries mentioned who have to rely entirely on tour either abroad or in their own countries. In addition, the fact that the state of New South Wales has for certain periods been virtually representative of Australia in International Rugby, has inevitably created many anomalies. In some record books for instance, an appearance against New South Wales is credited as a full cap, on which basis the New Zealand players in particular, might be credited with many more International appearances than some record books are prepared to allow them. For the purposes of this encyclopedia, however, we have only taken into account appearances for and against the main Rugby countries which are generally acknowledged as: England, Wales, Scotland, Ireland, France, British Isles, Australia, New Zealand, South Africa.

### ENGLAND (30 or more caps)

| | |
|---|---|
| J. V. Pullin | 41 |
| D. P. Rogers | 34 |
| D. J. Duckham | 33 |
| W. W. Wakefield | 31 |
| E. Evans | 30 |

### IRELAND (35 or more caps)

| | |
|---|---|
| W. J. McBride | 63 |
| T. J. Kiernan | 54 |
| C. M. H. Gibson | 52 |
| J. W. Kyle | 46 |
| K. W. Kennedy | 45 |
| G. V. Stephenson | 42 |
| N. A. A. Murphy | 41 |
| N. J. Henderson | 40 |
| R. J. McLoughlin | 40 |
| S. Millar | 37 |
| W. A. Mulcahy | 35 |
| J. R. Kavanagh | 35 |

### SCOTLAND (30 or more caps)

| | |
|---|---|
| H. F. McLeod | 40 |
| D. M. D. Rollo | 40 |
| A. B. Carmichael | 40 |
| J. MacD. Bannermann | 37 |
| A. R. Smith | 33 |
| F. A. L. Laidlaw | 32 |
| I. S. Smith | 32 |
| N. S. Bruce | 31 |
| I. H. P. Laughland | 31 |

### WALES (30 or more caps)

| | |
|---|---|
| K. J. Jones | 44 |
| G. O. Edwards | 40 |
| D. Williams | 36 |
| R. M. Owen | 35 |
| D. I. E. Bebb | 34 |
| W. D. Morris | 34 |
| B. V. Meredith | 34 |
| T. G. R. Davies | 33 |
| W. J. Bancroft | 33 |
| T. M. Davies | 33 |
| J. P. R. Williams | 32 |
| J. R. G. Stephens | 32 |
| D. Price | 32 |

### FRANCE (30 or more caps)

| | |
|---|---|
| B. Dauga | 50 |
| M. Crauste | 43 |
| W. Spanghero | 42 |
| J. P. Lux | 40 |
| J. Prat | 38 |
| M. Celaya | 35 |
| A. Boniface | 34 |
| A. Domenech | 34 |
| G. Dufau | 33 |
| E. Cester | 30 |
| M. Vannier | 30 |

AUSTRALIA (30 or more caps)
P. G. Johnson .................. 42
A. R. Millar ................... 41
G. V. Davies .................. 39
J. E. Thornett ................. 37
N. Shehadie. .................. 30

NEW ZEALAND (30 or more caps)
C. E. Meads ................... 55
K. R. Tremain ................ 38
W. J. Whineray ............... 32
D. B. Clarke .................. 31

SOUTH AFRICA (30 or more caps)
F. C. H. du Preez .............. 38
J. H. Ellis .................... 37

J.F.K. Marais .................. 35
J.L. Gainsford ................. 33
J.P. Engelbrecht ............... 33

## Longest International Careers

The record for the longest career in Test Rugby belongs to the Queensland second row forward G. M. Cooke, who was originally capped for Australia as far back as 1932, and who played his last Test Match for his country against France at Colombes, in 1948. In all Cooke made 13 appearances for Australia in a career spanning the 17 seasons between 1932-48. Below is a list of players who have played Test Rugby over a period of 12 seasons or more:

| | | | |
|---|---|---|---|
| G.M. Cooke (Queensland and Australia) | (17) | 1932-48 | Caps 13 |
| A.R. Miller (New South Wales and Australia) | (16) | 1952-67 | Caps 41 |
| A.J.F. O'Reilly (Leicester and Ireland) | (16) | 1955-70 | Caps 29 |
| H. Tanner (Swansea and Wales) | (15) | 1935-49 | Caps 25 |
| C.E. Meads (King Country and New Zealand) | (15) | 1957-71 | Caps 55 |
| E.E. Hughes (Southland and New Zealand) | (15) | 1907-21 | Caps  6 |
| W. C. Murdoch (Hillhead H.S.F.P. and Scotland) | (14) | 1935-48 | Caps  9 |
| W. J. Trew (Swansea and Wales) | (14) | 1900-13 | Caps 29 |
| T. H. Vile (Newport and Wales) | (14) | 1908-21 | Caps  8 |
| W. J. McBride (Ballymena and Ireland) | (14) | 1962-75 | Caps 62 |
| T. J. Kiernan (Cork Constitution and Ireland) | (14) | 1960-73 | Caps 54 |
| R. J. McLoughlin (Blackrock College and Ireland | (14) | 1962-75 | Caps 39 |
| B. H. Heatlie (Western Province and South Africa) | (13) | 1891-1903 | Caps  6 |
| A. Boniface (Mont de Marsan and France) | (13) | 1954-66 | Caps 34 |
| J. M. Powell (Griqualand W. and S. Africa) | (13) | 1891-1903 | Caps  4 |
| A. J. Gould (Newport and Wales) | (13) | 1885-97 | Caps 27 |
| J. Heaton (Waterloo and England) | (13) | 1935-47 | Caps  9 |
| J. P. Jones (Pontypool and Wales) | (13) | 1909-21 | Caps 14 |
| W. E. MacLagan (Edinburgh Acads. and Scotland) | (13) | 1878-90 | Caps 25 |
| T. W. Pearson (Newport and Wales) | (13) | 1891-1903 | Caps 13 |
| W. H. Travers (Newport and Wales) | (13) | 1937-49 | Caps 12 |
| P. G. Johnson (New South Wales and Australia) | (13) | 1959-72 | Caps 42 |
| S. Millar (Ballymena and Ireland) | (13) | 1958-70 | Caps 37 |
| N. A. A. Murphy (Cork Constitution and Ireland) | (12) | 1958-69 | Caps 41 |
| W. J. Bancroft (Swansea and Wales) | (12) | 1890-1901 | Caps 33 |
| C. T. Burke (New South Wales and Australia) | (12) | 1946-57 | Caps 26 |
| T. A. Kemp (Richmond and England) | (12) | 1937-48 | Caps  5 |
| J. W. Kyle (Queen's University and Ireland) | (12) | 1947-58 | Caps 46 |
| J. M. C. Lewis (Cardiff and Wales) | (12) | 1912-23 | Caps 11 |
| W. H. (Boy) Morkel (W. Province and S. Africa) | (12) | 1910-21 | Caps  9 |
| E. G. Nicholls (Newport and Wales) | (12) | 1896-1907 | Caps 24 |
| R. M. Owen (Swansea and Wales) | (12) | 1901-12 | Caps 35 |
| N. Shehadie (New South Wales and Australia) | (12) | 1947-58 | Caps 30 |
| J. Wetter (Newport and Wales) | (12) | 1914-25 | Caps 10 |
| W. B. Young (Cambridge University and Scotland) | (12) | 1937-48 | Caps 10 |

Of the above list the following players had their careers interrupted by one of the two World Wars: G. M. Cooke, H. Tanner, W. C. Murdoch, T. H. Vile, J. Heaton, J. P. Jones, W. H. Travers, T. A. Kemp, J. M. C. Lewis, W. H. (Boy) Morkel, J. Wetter, W. B. Young.
NOTE—If one takes into consideration the fact that T. H. Vile of Newport and Wales played in Australia and New Zealand for Great Britain during the summer of 1904 and *before* he was capped for Wales in 1908, four years later, then he establishes an all-time record with a Test career extending 18 seasons, viz., 1904-21.

*Although* he did not play for New Zealand after 1930 the great Hawkes Bay full back, George Nepia, who was of Maori descent, played for the Maori representative Team in matches against New South Wales as late as 1935. Therefore if one accepts these matches as of being of full Test status Nepia's Test career extended from 1924-35–12 seasons.

## International Match Results
See separate section TOURS for results of Tests.

### ENGLAND v SCOTLAND

1870-71 –Scotland. 1 goal, 1 try to 1 try, at Raeburn Place, Edinburgh.
1871-72 –England. 2 goals, 2 tries to 1 goal, at Kennington Oval.
1872-73 –Drawn, No score, at Glasgow.
1873-74 –England. 1 goal, 1 try to 0, at Kennington Oval.
1874-75 –Drawn. No score, at Raeburn Place, Edinburgh.
1875-76 –England. 1 goal, 1 try to 0, at Kennington Oval.
1876-77 –Scotland. 1 goal to 0, at Raeburn Place, Edinburgh.
1877-78 –Drawn. No score, at Kennington Oval.
1878-79 –Drawn. 1 goal each, at Raeburn Place, Edinburgh.
1879-80 –England. 2 goals, 3 tries to 1 goal, at Manchester.
1880-81 –Drawn. 1 goal, 1 try each, at Raeburn Place, Edinburgh.
1881-82 –Scotland. 2 tries to 0, at Manchester.
1882-83 –England. 2 tries to 1 try, at Raeburn Place, Edinburgh.
1883-84 –England. 1 goal to 1 try, at Blackheath.
1884-85 –No Match.
1885-86 –Drawn. No score, at Raeburn Place, Edinburgh.
1886-87 –Drawn. 1 try each, at Manchester.
1887-88 and 1888-89 –No Match.
1889-90 –England. 1 goal, 1 try to 0, at Raeburn Place, Edinburgh.
1890-91 –Scotland. 3 goals to 1 goal, at Richmond.
1891-92 –England. 1 goal to 0, at Raeburn Place, Edinburgh.
1892-93 –Scotland. 2 dropped goals to 0, at Leeds.
1893-94 –Scotland. 2 tries to 0, at Raeburn Place, Edinburgh.
1894-95 –Scotland. 1 penalty goal, 1 try to 1 penalty goal, at Richmond.
1895-96 –Scotland. 1 goal, 2 tries to 0, at Glasgow.
1896-97 –England. 1 goal, 1 dropped goal, 1 try to 1 try, at Manchester.
1897-98 –Drawn. 1 try each, at Powderhall, Edinburgh.
1898-99 –Scotland. 1 goal to 0, at Blackheath.
1899-1900 –Drawn. No score at Inverleith, Edinburgh.
1900-01 –Scotland. 3 goals, 1 try to 1 try, at Blackheath.
1901-02 –England. 2 tries to 1 try, at Inverleith.
1902-03 –Scotland. 1 dropped goal, 2 tries to 2 tries, at Richmond.
1903-04 –Scotland. 2 tries to 1 try, at Inverleith.
1904-05 –Scotland. 1 goal, 1 try to 0, at Richmond.

### MODERN SCORING VALUES ADOPTED

1905-06 –England. 3 tries (9 points) to 1 try (3 points), at Inverleith.
1906-07 –Scotland. 1 goal, 1 try (8) to 1 try (3), at Blackheath.
1907-08 –Scotland. 1 goal, 2 dropped goals, 1 try (16), to 2 goals (10), at Inverleith.
1908-09 –Scotland. 3 goals, 1 try (18) to 1 goal, 1 try (8), at Richmond.
1909-10 –England. 1 goal, 3 tries (14) to 1 goal (5), at Inverleith.
1910-11 –England. 2 goals, 1 try (13) to 1 goal, 1 try (8), at Twickenham.
1911-12 –Scotland. 1 goal, 1 try (8) to 1 try (3), at Inverleith.
1912-13 –England. 1 try (3) to 0, at Twickenham.
1913-14 –England. 2 goals, 2 tries (16) to 1 goal, 1 dropped goal, 2 tries (15), at Inverleith.
1919-20 –England. 2 goals, 1 try (13) to 1 dropped goal (4), at Twickenham.

1920-21 – England. 3 goals, 1 try (18) to 0, at Inverleith.
1921-22 – England. 1 goal, 2 tries (11) to 1 goal (5), at Twickenham.
1922-23 – England. 1 goal, 1 try (8) to 2 tries (6), at Inverleith.
1923-24 – England. 3 goals, 1 dropped goal (19) to 0, at Twickenham
1924-25 – Scotland. 2 goals, 1 dropped goal (14) to 1 goal, 1 penalty goal, 1 try (11), at Murrayfield.
1925-26 – Scotland. 2 goals, 1 dropped goal, 1 try (17) to 3 tries (9) at Twickenham.
1926-27 – Scotland. 1 goal, 1 dropped goal, 4 tries (21) to 2 goals, 1 penalty goal (13), at Murrayfield.
1927-28 – England. 2 tries (6) to 0, at Twickenham.
1928-29 – Scotland. 4 tries (12) to 2 tries (6), at Murrayfield.
1929-30 – Drawn. No score at Twickenham.
1930-31 – Scotland. 5 goals, 1 try (28) to 2 goals, 1 penalty goal, 2 tries (19), at Murrayfield.
1931-32 – England. 2 goals, 2 tries (16) to 1 try (3), at Twickenham.
1932-33 – Scotland. 1 try (3) to 0, at Murrayfield.
1933-34 – England. 2 tries (6) to 1 try (3), at Twickenham.
1934-35 – Scotland. 2 goals (10) to 1 dropped goal, 1 try (7), at Murrayfield.
1935-36 – England. 3 tries (9) to 1 goal, 1 penalty goal (8), at Twickenham.
1936-37 – England. 2 tries (6) to 1 penalty goal (3), at Murrayfield.
1937-38 – Scotland. 2 penalty goals, 5 tries (21) to 1 dropped goal, 3 penalty goals, 1 try (16), at Twickenham.
1938-39 – England. 3 penalty goals (9) to 2 tries (6), at Murrayfield.
1946-47 – England. 4 goals, 1 dropped goal (24) to 1 goal (5), at Twickenham.
1947-48 – Scotland. 2 tries (6) to 1 penalty goal (3), at Murrayfield.

## DROPPED GOAL REDUCED TO 3 POINTS

1948-49 – England. 2 goals, 3 tries (19) to 1 penalty goal (3), at Twickenham.
1949-50 – Scotland. 2 goals, 1 try (13) to 1 goal, 1 penalty goal, 1 try (11), at Murrayfield.
1950-51 – England. 1 goal (5) to 1 try (3), at Twickenham.
1951-52 – England. 2 goals, 1 dropped goal, 2 tries (19) to 1 try (3), at Murrayfield.
1952-53 – England. 4 goals, 2 tries (26) to 1 goal, 1 try (8), at Twickenham.
1953-54 – England. 2 goals, 1 try (13) to 1 try (3), at Murrayfield.
1954-55 – England. 1 penalty goal, 2 tries (9) to 1 penalty goal, 1 try (6), at Twickenham.
1955-56 – England. 1 goal, 2 penalty goals (11) to 1 penalty goal, 1 try (6), at Murrayfield.
1956-57 – England. 2 goals, 1 penalty goal, 1 try (16) to 1 penalty goal (3), at Twickenham.
1957-58 – Drawn. England 1 try (3), Scotland 1 penalty goal (3), at Murrayfield.
1958-59 – Drawn. 1 penalty goal each, at Twickenham.
1959-60 – England. 3 goals, 1 dropped goal, 1 penalty goal (21) to 3 penalty goals, 1 try (12), at Murrayfield.
1960-61 – England. 1 penalty goal, 1 try (6), to 0, at Twickenham.
1961-62 – Drawn. 1 penalty goal each, at Murrayfield.
1962-63 – England. 2 goals (10) to 1 goal, 1 dropped goal (8), at Twickenham.
1963-64 – Scotland. 3 goals (15) to 1 penalty goal, 1 try (6), at Murrayfield.
1964-65 – Drawn. England 1 try (3) Scotland 1 dropped goal (3), at Twickenham.
1965-66 – Scotland. 1 penalty goal, 1 try (6) to 1 dropped goal (3), at Murrayfield.
1966-67 – England. 3 goals, 2 penalty goals, 1 dropped goal, 1 try (27) to 1 goal, 2 penalty goals, 1 try (14), at Twickenham.
1967-68 – England. 1 goal, 1 penalty goal (8) to 1 penalty goal, 1 dropped goal (6), at Murrayfield.
1968-69 – England. 1 goal, 1 try (8) to 1 penalty goal (3), at Twickenham.
1969-70 – Scotland. 1 goal, 2 penalty goals, 1 try (14) to 1 goal (5), at Murrayfield.
1970-71 – Scotland. 2 goals, 1 dropped goal, 1 try (16) to 3 penalty goals, 2 tries (15), at Twickenham.

—Scotland. (Centenary Match. Not a championship game). 4 goals, 1 penalty goal, 1 try (26) to 1 penalty goal, 1 dropped goal (6), at Murrayfield.

## TRY INCREASED TO 4 POINTS

1971-72—Scotland. 4 penalty goals, 1 dropped goal, 2 tries (23) to 3 penalty goals (9), at Murrayfield.

1972-73—England. 2 goals, 2 tries (20) to 1 goal, 1 penalty goal, 1 try (13), at Twickenham.

1973-74—Scotland. 1 goal, 2 penalty goals, 1 try (16) to 1 dropped goal, 1 penalty goal, 2 tries (14), at Murrayfield.

1974-75—England. 1 penalty goal, 1 try (7) to 2 penalty goals (6), at Twickenham.

## ENGLAND v IRELAND

1874-75—England. 2 goals, 1 try to 0, at the Oval.
1875-76—England. 1 goal, 1 try to 0, at Dublin.
1876-77—England. 2 goals, 2 tries to 0, at the Oval.
1877-78—England. 2 goals, 1 try to 0, at Dublin.
1878-79—England. 3 goals, 2 tries to 0, at the Oval.
1879-80—England. 1 goal, 1 try to 1 try, at Dublin.
1880-81—England. 2 goals, 2 tries to 0, at Manchester.
1881-82—Drawn. 2 tries each, at Dublin.
1882-83—England. 1 goal, 3 tries to 1 try, at Manchester.
1883-84—England. 1 goal to 0, at Dublin.
1884-85—England. 2 tries to 1 try, at Manchester.
1885-86—England, 1 try to 0, at Dublin.
1886-87—Ireland. 2 goals to 0, at Dublin.
1887-88 and 1888-89—No Matches.
1889-90—England. 3 tries to 0, at Blackheath.
1890-91—England. 2 goals, 3 tries to 0, at Dublin.
1891-92—England. 1 goal, 1 try to 0, at Manchester.
1892-93—England. 2 tries to 0, at Dublin.
1893-94—Ireland. 1 dropped goal, 1 try to 1 goal, at Blackheath.
1894-95—England. 2 tries to 1 try, at Dublin.
1895-96—Ireland. 2 goals to 1 dropped goal, at Blackheath.
1896-97—Ireland. 1 goal (mark), 3 tries to 2 penalty goals, 1 try, at Dublin.
1897-98—Ireland. 1 penalty goal, 2 tries to 1 penalty goal, 1 try, at Richmond.
1898-99—Ireland. 1 penalty goal, 1 try to 0, at Dublin.
1899-1900—England. 1 goal, 1 dropped goal, 2 tries to 1 dropped goal, at Richmond.
1900-01—Ireland. 2 goals to 1 penalty goal, 1 try, at Dublin.
1901-02—England. 2 tries to 1 try, at Leicester.
1902-03—Ireland. 1 penalty goal, 1 try to 0, at Dublin.
1903-04—England. 2 goals, 3 tries to 0, at Blackheath.
1904-05—Ireland. 1 goal, 4 tries to 1 try, at Cork.

## MODERN SCORING VALUES ADOPTED

1905-06—Ireland. 2 goals, 2 tries (16) to 2 tries (6), at Leicester.
1906-07—Ireland. 2 goals (1 mark), 3 tries (17) to 1 dropped goal (4), at Dublin.
1907-08—England. 2 goals, 1 try (13) to 1 penalty goal (3), at Richmond.
1908-09—England. 1 goal, 2 tries (11) to 1 goal (5), at Dublin.
1909-10—Drawn. No score, at Twickenham.
1910-11—Ireland. 1 try (3) to 0, at Dublin.
1911-12—England. 5 tries (15) to 0, at Twickenham.
1912-13—England. 1 penalty goal, 4 tries (15) to 1 dropped goal (4), at Dublin.
1913-14—England. 1 goal, 4 tries (17) to 1 goal, 1 dropped goal, 1 try (12), at Twickenham.
1919-20—England. 1 goal, 3 tries (14) to 1 goal, 1 penalty goal, 1 try (11), at Dublin.
1920-21—England. 1 goal, 1 dropped goal, 2 tries (15) to 0, at Twickenham.

1921-22—England. 4 tries (12) to 1 try (3), at Dublin.

1922-23—England. 2 goals, 1 dropped goal, 3 tries (23) to 1 goal (5), at Leicester.'

1923-24—England. 1 goal, 3 tries (14) to 1 try (3), at Belfast.

1924-25—Drawn. 2 tries (6) each, at Twickenham.

1925-26—Ireland. 2 goals, 1 penalty goal, 2 tries (19) to 3 goals (15), at Dublin.

1926-27—England. 1 goal, 1 try (8), to 1 penalty goal, 1 try (6), at Twickenham.

1927-28—England. 1 dropped goal, 1 try (7) to 2 tries (6), at Dublin.

1928-29—Ireland. 2 tries (6) to 1 goal, (5), at Twickenham.

1929-30—Ireland. 1 dropped goal (4) to 1 try (3), at Dublin.

1930-31—Ireland. 1 penalty goal, 1 try (6) to 1 goal (5), at Twickenham.

1931-32—England. 1 goal, 2 penalty goals (11) to 1 goal, 1 penalty goal (8), at Dublin.

1932-33—England. 1 goal, 4 tries (17) to 1 penalty goal, 1 try (6), at Twickenham.

1933-34—England. 2 goals, 1 try (13) to 1 try (3), at Dublin.

1934-35—England. 1 goal, 3 penalty goals (14) to 1 try (3), at Twickenham.

1935-36—Ireland. 2 tries (6) to 1 try (3), at Dublin.

1936-37—England. 1 penalty goal, 2 tries (9) to 1 goal, 1 try (8), at Twickenham.

1937-38—England. 6 goals, 1 penalty goal, 1 try (36) to 1 goal, 3 tries (14), at Dublin.

1938-39—Ireland. 1 goal (5) to 0, at Twickenham.

1946-47—Ireland. 2 dropped goals, 1 penalty goal, 3 tries (20) to 0, at Dublin.

1947-48—Ireland. 1 goal, 2 tries (11) to 2 goals (10), at Twickenham.

## DROPPED GOAL REDUCED TO 3 POINTS

1948-49—Ireland. 1 goal, 2 penalty goals, 1 try (14) to 1 goal (5), at Dublin.

1949-50—England. 1 try (3) to 0, at Twickenham.

1950-51—Ireland. 1 penalty goal (3) to 0, at Dublin.

1951-52—England. 1 try (3) to 0, at Twickenham.

1952-53—Drawn. 2 penalty goals, 1 try (9) each, at Dublin.

1953-54—England. 1 goal, 1 penalty goal, 2 tries (14) to 1 penalty goal (3), at Twickenham.

1954-55—Drawn. Ireland. 1 penalty goal, 1 try (6), England 2 tries (6), at Dublin.

1955-56—England. 1 goal, 3 penalty goals, 2 tries (20) to 0, at Twickenham.

1956-57—England. 1 penalty goal, 1 try (6) to 0, at Dublin.

1957-58—England. 2 tries (6) to 0, at Twickenham.

1958-59—England. 1 penalty goal (3) to 0, at Dublin.

1959-60—England. 1 goal, 1 dropped goal (8) to 1 goal (5), at Twickenham.

1960-61—Ireland. 1 goal, 2 penalty goals (11) to 1 goal, 1 try (8), at Dublin.

1961-62—England. 2 goals, 1 penalty goal, 1 try (16) to 0, at Twickenham.

1962-63—Drawn. No score, at Dublin.

1963-64—Ireland. 3 goals, 1 try (18) to 1 goal (5), at Twickenham.

1964-65—Ireland. 1 goal (5) to 0, at Dublin.

1965-66—Drawn. England 1 try, 1 penalty goal (6), Ireland 1 penalty goal, 1 try (6), at Twickenham.

1966-67—England. 1 goal, 1 penalty goal (8) to 1 penalty goal (3), at Dublin.

1967-68—Drawn. England, 2 penalty goals, 1 dropped goal (9), Ireland, 3 penalty goals (9), at Twickenham.

1968-69—Ireland. 1 goal, 2 penalty goals, 1 dropped goal, 1 try (17) to 4 penalty goals, 1 try (15), at Dublin.

1969-70—England. 2 dropped goals, 1 try (9) to 1 penalty goal (3), at Twickenham.

1970-71—England. 3 penalty goals (9), to 2 tries (6), at Dublin.

## TRY INCREASED TO 4 POINTS

1971-72—Ireland. 1 goal, 1 dropped goal, 1 penalty goal, 1 try (16) to 1 goal, 2 penalty goals (12), at Twickenham.

1972-3— Ireland. 2 penalty goals, 1 goal, 1 dropped goal (18) to 1 goal, 1 penalty goal (9), at Dublin.

1973-74—Ireland. 2 goals, 1 penalty goal, 1 dropped goal, 2 ˚tries (26) to 1 goal, 5 penalty goals (21), at Twickenham.

1974-75—Ireland. 2 goals (12) to 1 goal, 1 dropped goal (9), at Dublin.

## ENGLAND v WALES

1880-81 – England. 7 goals, 1 dropped goal, 6 tries to 0, at Blackheath.
1881-81 – No Match.
1882-83 – England. 2 goals, 4 tries to 0, at Swansea.
1883-84 – England. 1 goal, 2 tries to 1 goal, at Leeds.
1884-85 – England. 1 goal, 4 tries to 1 goal, 1 try, at Swansea.
1885-86 – England. 1 goal, 2 tries to 1 goal, at Blackheath.
1886-87 – Drawn. No score, at Llanelli.
1887-88 and 1888-89 – No Matches.
1889-90 – Wales. 1 try to 0, at Dewsbury.
1890-91 – England. 2 goals, 1 try to 1 goal, at Newport.
1891-92 – England. 3 goals, 1 try to 0, at Blackheath.
1892-93 – Wales. 1 goal, 1 penalty goal, 2 tries to 1 goal, 3 tries, at Cardiff.
1893-94 – England. 5 goals (1 mark) to 1 try, at Birkenhead.
1894-95 – England. 1 goal, 3 tries to 2 tries, at Swansea.
1895-96 – England. 2 goals, 5 tries to 0, at Birkenhead.
1896-97 – Wales. 1 goal, 2 tries to 0, at Newport.
1897-98 – England. 1 goal, 3 tries to 1 dropped goal, 1 try, at Blackheath.
1898-99 – Wales. 4 goals, 2 tries to 1 try, at Swansea.
1899-1900 – Wales. 2 goals, 1 penalty goal to 1 try, at Gloucester.
1900-01 – Wales. 2 goals, 1 try to 0, at Cardiff.
1901-02 – Wales. 1 penalty goal, 2 tries to 1 goal, 1 try, at Blackheath.
1902-03 – Wales. 3 goals, 2 tries to 1 goal, at Swansea.
1903-04 – Drawn. England 1 goal, 1 penalty goal, 2 tries; Wales 3 goals (1 mark) at, Leicester.
1904-05 – Wales. 2 goals, 5 tries to 0, at Cardiff.

## MODERN SCORING VALUES ADOPTED

1905-06 – Wales, 2 goals, 2 tries (16) to 1 try (3), at Richmond.
1906-07 – Wales. 2 goals, 4 tries (22) to 0, at Swansea.
1907-08 – Wales. 3 goals, 1 dropped goal, 1 penalty goal, 2 tries (28) to 3 goals, 1 try (18), at Bristol.
1908-09 – Wales. 1 goal, 1 try (8) to 0, at Cardiff.
1909-10 – England. 1 goal, 1 penalty goal, 1 try (11) to 2 tries (6), at Twickenham.
1910-11 – Wales. 1 penalty goal, 4 tries (15) to 1 goal, 2 tries (11), at Swansea.
1911-12 – England. 1 goal, 1 try (8) to 0, at Twickenham.
1912-13 – England. 1 goal, 1 dropped goal, 1 try (12) to 0, at Cardiff.
1913-14 – England. 2 goals, (10) to 1 goal, 1 dropped goal (9), at Twickenham.
1919-20 – Wales. 1 goal, 2 dropped goals, 1 penalty goal, 1 try (19) to 1 goal (5), at Swansea.
1920-21 – England. 1 goal, 1 dropped goal, 3 tries (18) to 1 try (3), at Twickenham.
1921-22 – Wales. 2 goals, 6 tries (28) to 2 tries (6), at Cardiff.
1922-23 – England. 1 dropped goal, 1 try (7) to 1 try (3), at Twickenham.
1923-24 – England. 1 goal, 4 tries (17) to 3 tries (9), at Swansea.
1924-25 – England. 1 penalty goal, 3 tries (12) to 2 tries (6), at Twickenham.
1925-26 – Drawn. 1 try (3) each, at Cardiff.
1926-27 – England. 1 goal, 1 penalty goal, 1 goal (mark), (11) to 1 penalty goal, 2 tries (9), at Twickenham.
1927-28 – England. 2 goals (10) to 1 goal, 1 try (8), at Swansea.
1928-29 – England. 1 goal, 1 try (8) to 1 try (3), at Twickenham.
1929-30 – England. 1 goal, 1 penalty goal, 1 try (11) to 1 penalty goal, 1 try (6), at Cardiff.
1930-31 – Drawn. England 1 goal, 2 penalty goals (11); Wales 1 goal, 1 goal (mark), 1 try (11), at Twickenham.
1931-32 – Wales. 1 goal, 1 dropped goal, 1 penalty goal (12) to 1 goal (5), at Swansea.
1932-33 – Wales. 1 dropped goal, 1 try (7) to 1 try (3), at Twickenham.
1933-34 – England. 3 tries (9) to 0, at Cardiff.
1934-35 – Drawn. England. 1 penalty goal (3); Wales 1 try (3), at Twickenham.

1935-36—Drawn. No score, at Swansea.
1936-37—England. 1 dropped goal (4) to 1 try (3), at Twickenham.
1937-38—Wales. 1 goal, 2 penalty goals, 1 try (14) to 1 goal, 1 try (8), at Cardiff.
1938-39—England. 1 try (3) to 0, at Twickenham.
1946-47—England. 1 goal, 1 dropped goal (9) to 2 tries (6), at Cardiff.
1947-48—Drawn. England 1 penalty goal (3); Wales 1 try (3), at Twickenham.

## DROPPED GOAL REDUCED TO 3 POINTS

1948-49—Wales. 3 tries (9) to 1 dropped goal (3), at Cardiff.
1949-50—Wales. 1 goal, 1 penalty goal, 1 try (11) to 1 goal (5), at Twickenham.
1950-51—Wales. 4 goals, 1 try (23) to 1 goal (5), at Swansea.
1951-52—Wales. 1 goal, 1 try (8) to 2 tries (6), at Twickenham.
1952-53—England. 1 goal, 1 penalty goal (8) to 1 penalty goal (3), at Cardiff.
1953-54—England. 3 tries (9) to 1 penalty goal, 1 try (6), at Twickenham.
1954-55—Wales. 1 penalty goal (3) to 0, at Cardiff.
1955-56—Wales. 1 goal, 1 try (8) to 1 penalty goal (3), at Twickenham.
1956-57—England. 1 penalty goal (3) to 0, at Cardiff.
1957-58—Drawn. England 1 try (3); Wales 1 penalty goal (3), at Twickenham.
1958-59—Wales. 1 goal (5) to 0, at Cardiff.
1959-60—England. 1 goal, 2 penalty goals, 1 try (14) to 2 penalty goals (6), at Twick-
        enham.
1960-61—Wales. 2 tries (6) to 1 try (3), at Cardiff.
1961-62—Drawn. No score, at Twickenham.
1962-63—England. 2 goals, 1 dropped (13) to 1 penalty goal, 1 try (6), at Cardiff.
1963-64—Drawn. 2 tries each (6), at Twickenham.
1964-65—Wales. 1 goal, 1 dropped goal, 2 tries (14) to 1 penalty goal (3), at Cardiff.
1965-66—Wales, 2 penalty goals, 1 goal (11) to 2 penalty goals (6), at Twickenham.
1966-67—Wales. 5 goals, 2 penalty goals, 1 dropped goal (34) to 4 penalty goals, 3
        tries (21), at Cardiff.
1967-68—Drawn. England 1 goal, 1 penalty goal, 1 try (11), Wales 1 goal, 1 dropped
        goal, 1 try (11), at Twickenham.
1968-69—Wales. 3 goals, 1 dropped goal, 2 penalty goals, 2 tries (30), to 3 penalty
        goals (9), at Cardiff.
1969-70—Wales. 1 goal, 1 dropped goal, 3 tries (17) to 2 goals, 1 penalty goal (13) at
        Twickenham.
1970-71—Wales. 2 goals, 2 dropped goals, 1 penalty goal, 1 try (22) to 1 penalty
        goal, 1 try (6), at Cardiff.

## TRY INCREASED TO 4 POINTS

1971-72—Wales. 1 goal, 2 penalty goals (12) to 1 penalty goal (3), at Twickenham.
1972-73—Wales. 1 goal, 1 penalty goal, 4 tries (25) to 2 penalty goals, 1 dropped
        goal (9), at Cardiff.
1973-74—England. 1 goal, 2 penalty goals, 1 try (16) to 1 goal, 2 penalty goals, (12)
        at Twickenham.
1974-75—Wales. 1 goal, 2 penalty goals, 2 tries (20) to 1 try (4), at Cardiff.

## ENGLAND v FRANCE

1905-06—England. 4 goals, 5 tries (35) to 1 goal, 1 try (8), at Paris.
1906-07—England. 5 goals, 1 dropped goal, 4 tries (41) to 2 goals, 1 penalty goal,
        (13), at Richmond.
1907-08—England. 2 goals, 3 tries (19) to 0, at Paris.
1908-09—England. 2 goals, 4 tries (32) to 0, at Leicester.
1909-10—England. 1 goal, 2 tries (11) to 1 try (3), at Paris.
1910-11—England. 5 goals, 2 penalty goals, 2 tries (37) to 0, at Twickenham.
1911-12—England. 1 goal, 1 dropped goal, 3 tries (18) to 1 goal, 1 try (8), at Paris.
1912-13—England. 1 goal, 5 tries (20) to 0, at Twickenham.
1913-14—England. 6 goals, 3 tries (39) to 2 goals, 1 try (13), at Paris.
1919-20—England. 1 goal, 1 penalty goal (8) to 1 try (3), at Twickenham.
1920-21—England. 2 goals (10) to 2 penalty goals (6), at Paris.

1921-22—Drawn. England 1 goal, 2 penalty goals (11); France 1 goal, 2 tries (11), at Twickenham.
1922-23—England. 1 goal, 1 dropped goal, 1 try (12) to 1 penalty goal (3), at Paris.
1923-24—England. 2 goals, 3 tries (19) to 1 dropped goal, 1 try (7), at Twickenham.
1924-25—England. 2 goals, 1 goal (mark), (13) to 1 goal, 2 tries (11), at Paris.
1925-26—England. 1 goal, 2 tries (11) to 0, at Twickenham.
1926-27—France. 1 try (3) to 0, at Paris.
1927-28—England. 3 goals, 1 try (18) to 1 goal, 1 try (8), at Twickenham.
1928-29—England. 2 goals, 2 tries (16) to 2 tries (6), at Paris.
1929-30—England. 1 goal, 2 tries (11) to 1 goal (5), at Twickenham.
1930-31—France. 2 dropped goals, 2 tries (14) to 2 goals, 1 try (13), at Paris.
1946-47—England. 2 tries (6) to 1 penalty goal (3), at Twickenham.
1947-48—France. 1 goal, 1 dropped goal, 2 tries (15) to 0, at Paris.

## DROPPED GOAL REDUCED TO 3 POINTS

1948-49—England. 1 goal, 1 dropped goal (8) to 1 dropped goal (3), at Twickenham.
1949-50—France. 2 tries (6) to 1 try (3), at Paris.
1950-51—France. 1 goal, 1 dropped goal, 1 try (11) to 1 try (3), at Twickenham.
1951-52—England. 2 penalty goals (6) to 1 try (3), at Paris.
1952-53—England. 1 goal, 2 tries (11) to 0, at Twickenham.
1953-54—France. 1 goal, 1 dropped goal, 1 try (11) to 1 try (3), at Paris.
1954-55—France. 2 goals, 2 dropped goals (16) to 2 penalty goals, 1 try, (9), at Twickenham.
1955-56—France. 1 goal, 2 penalty goals, 1 try (14) to 2 penalty goals, 1 try (9), at Paris.
1956-57—England. 3 tries (9) to 1 goal (5), at Twickenham.
1957-58—England. 1 goal, 1 penalty goal, 2 tries (14) to 0, at Paris.
1958-59—Drawn. 1 penalty goal (3) each, at Twickenham.
1959 60—Drawn. England 1 try (3), France 1 penalty goal (3), at Paris.
1960-61—Drawn. 1 goal each (5), at Twickenham.
1961-62—France. 2 goals, 1 try (13) to 0, at Paris.
1962-63—England. 2 penalty goals (6) to 1 goal (5), at Twickenham.
1963-64—1 penalty goal, 1 try (6) to 1 try (3), at Paris.
1964-65—England. 2 penalty goals, 1 try (9) to 1 penalty goal, 1 try (6), at Twickenham.
1965-66—France. 2 goals, 1 try (13) to 0, at Paris.
1966-67—France. 2 goals, 1 dropped goal, 1 penalty goal (16) to 3 penalty goals, 1 dropped goal (12), at Twickenham.
1967-68—France. 1 goal, 2 dropped goals, 1 penalty goal (14) to 1 dropped goal, 2 penalty goals (9), at Paris.
1968-69—England. 2 goals, 3 penalty goals, 1 try (22) to 1 goal, 1 dropped goal (8), at Twickenham.
1969-70—France. 4 goals, 2 dropped goals, 1 penalty goal, 2 tries (35) to 2 goals, 1 penalty goal (13), at Paris.
1970-71—Drawn. England 1 goal, 3 penalty goals (14), France 1 goal, 1 penalty goal, 1 dropped goal, 1 try (14), at Twickenham.

## TRY INCREASED TO 4 POINTS

1971-72—France. 5 goals, 1 penalty goal, 1 try (37) to 1 goal, 2 penalty goals (12), at Paris.
1972-73—England. 2 penalty goals, 2 tries (14) to 1 goal (6), at Twickenham.
1973-74—Drawn. 1 goal, 1 penalty goal, 1 dropped goal (12) each, at Paris.
1974-75—France. 4 goals, 1 penalty goal (27) to 4 penalty goals, 2 tries (20), at Twickenham.

## SCOTLAND v IRELAND

1876-77—Scotland 6 goals, 2 tries to 0, at Belfast.
1877-78—No Match.

1878-79—Scotland. 2 goals, 1 try to 0, at Belfast.
1879-80—Scotland. 3 goals, 2 tries to 0, at Glasgow.
1880-81—Ireland. 1 goal to 1 try, at Belfast.
1881-82—Scotland. 2 tries to 0, at Glasgow.
1882-83—Scotland. 1 goal, 1 try to 0, at Belfast.
1883-84—Scotland. 2 goals, 2 tries to 1 try, at Edinburgh.
1884-85—Scotland. 1 goal, 2 tries to 0, at Edinburgh.
1885-86—Scotland. 4 goals, 2 tries to 0, at Edinburgh.
1886-87—Scotland. 2 goals, 2 tries to 0, at Belfast.
1887-88—Scotland. 1 goal to 0, at Edinburgh.
1888-89—Scotland. 1 dropped goal to 0, at Belfast.
1889-90—Scotland. 1 dropped goal, 1 try to 0, at Edinburgh.
1890-91—Scotland. 4 goals, 2 tries to 0, at Belfast.
1891-92—Scotland. 1 try to 0, at Edinburgh.
1892-93—Drawn. No score, at Belfast.
1893-94—Ireland. 1 goal to 0, at Dublin.
1894-95—Scotland. 2 tries to 0, at Edinburgh.
1895-96—Drawn. No score, at Dublin.
1896-97—Scotland. 1 goal, 1 penalty goal to 1 try, at Edinburgh.
1897-98—Scotland. 1 goal, 1 try to 0, at Belfast.
1898-99—Ireland. 3 tries to 1 penalty goal, at Edinburgh.
1899-1900—Drawn. No score, at Dublin.
1900-01—Scotland. 3 tries to 1 goal, at Edinburgh.
1901-02—Ireland. 1 goal to 0, at Belfast.
1902-03—Scotland. 1 try to 0, at Edinburgh.
1903-04—Scotland. 2 goals, 3 tries to 1 try, at Dublin.
1904-05—Ireland. 1 goal, 2 tries to 1 goal, at Edinburgh.

## MODERN SCORING VALUES ADOPTED

1905-06—Scotland. 2 goals, 1 goal (mark) (13) to 2 tries (6), at Dublin.
1906-07—Scotland. 3 goals (15) to 1 penalty goal (3), at Edinburgh.
1907-08—Ireland. 2 goals, 2 tries (16) to 1 goal, 1 penalty goal, 1 try (11), at Dublin.
1908-09—Scotland. 3 tries (9) to 1 penalty goal (3), at Edinburgh.
1909-10—Scotland. 1 goal; 3 tries (14) to 0, at Belfast.
1910-11—Ireland. 2 goals, 2 tries (16) to 1 dropped goal, 2 tries (10), at Edinburgh.
1911-12—Ireland. 1 dropped goal, 1 penalty goal, 1 try (10) to 1 goal, 1 try (8), at Dublin.
1912-13—Scotland. 4 goals, 3 tries (29) to 2 goals, 1 dropped goal, 1 try (17), at Edinburgh.
1913-14—Ireland. 2 tries (6) to 0, at Dublin.
1919-20—Scotland. 2 goals, 1 penalty goal, 2 tries (19) to 0, at Edinburgh.
1920-21—Ireland. 3 tries (9) to 1 goal, 1 try (8), at Dublin.
1921-22—Scotland. 2 tries (6) to 1 try (3), at Edinburgh.
1922-23—Scotland. 2 goals, 1 try (13) to 1 try (3), at Dublin.
1923-24—Scotland. 2 goals, 1 try (13) to 1 goal, 1 try (8), at Edinburgh.
1924-25—Scotland. 2 goals, 1 dropped goal, (14) to 1 goal, 1 penalty goal (8), at Dublin.
1925-26—Ireland. 1 try (3) to 0, at Murrayfield.
1926-37—Ireland. 2 tries (6) to 0, at Dublin.
1927-28—Ireland. 2 goals, 1 try (13) to 1 goal (5), at Murrayfield.
1928-29—Scotland. 2 goals, 2 tries (16) to 1 dropped goal, 1 try (7), at Dublin.
1929-30—Ireland. 1 goal, 3 tries (14) to 1 goal, 2 tries (11), at Murrayfield.
1930-31—Ireland. 1 goal, 1 try (8) to 1 goal, (5), at Dublin.
1931-32—Ireland. 4 goals (20) to 1 goal, 1 try (8), at Murrayfield.
1932-33—Scotland. 2 dropped goals, (8) to 2 tries (6), at Dublin.
1933-34—Scotland. 2 goals, 1 penalty goal, 1 try (16) to 3 tries (9), at Murrayfield.
1934-35—Ireland. 4 tries (12) to 1 goal (5), at Dublin.
1935-36—Ireland. 1 dropped goal, 2 tries (10) to 1 dropped goal (4), at Murrayfield.
1936-37—Ireland. 1 goal, 2 tries (11) to 1 dropped goal (4), at Dublin.

1937-38 – Scotland. 2 goals, 1 dropped goal, 1 penalty goal, 2 tries (20) to 1 goal, 3 tries (14), at Murrayfield.
1938-39 – Ireland. 1 penalty goal, 1 goal (mark), 2 tries (12) to 1 try (3), at Dublin.
1946-47 – Ireland. 1 try (3) to 0, at Murrayfield.
1947-48 – Ireland. 2 tries (6) to 0, at Dublin.

## DROPPED GOAL REDUCED TO 3 POINTS

1948-49 – Ireland. 2 goals, 1 penalty goal (13) to 1 penalty goal (3), at Murrayfield.
1949-50 – Ireland. 3 goals, 2 penalty goals (21) to 0, at Dublin.
1950-51 – Ireland. 1 dropped goal, 1 try (6) to 1 goal (5), at Murrayfield.
1951-52 – Ireland. 1 penalty goal, 3 tries (12) to 1 goal, 1 penalty goal (8), at Dublin.
1952-53 – Ireland. 4 goals, 2 tries (26) to 1 goal, 1 penalty goal (8), at Murrayfield.
1953-54 – Ireland. 2 tries (6) to 0, at Belfast.
1954-55 – Scotland. 2 penalty goals, 1 dropped goal, 1 try (12) to 1 penalty goal (3), at Murrayfield.
1955-56 – Ireland. 1 goal, 3 tries (14) to 2 goals (10), at Dublin.
1957-58 – Ireland. 1 goal (5) to 1 penalty goal (3), at Murrayfield.
1957-58 – Ireland. 2 penalty goals, 2 tries (12) to 2 tries (6), at Dublin.
1958-59 – Ireland. 1 goal, 1 penalty goal (8) to 1 penalty goal (3), at Murrayfield.
1959-60 – Scotland. 1 dropped goal, 1 try (6) to 1 goal (5), at Dublin.
1960-61 – Scotland. 2 goals, 1 penalty goal, 1 try (16) to 1 goal, 1 try (8), at Murrayfield.
1961-62 – Scotland. 1 goal, 1 dropped goal, 2 penalty goals, 2 tries (20) to 1 penalty goal, 1 try (6), at Dublin.
1962-63 – Scotland. 1 penalty goal (3) to 0, at Murrayfield.
1963-64 – Scotland. 2 penalty goals (6), to 1 penalty goal (3), at Dublin.
1964-65 – Scotland. 2 goals, 1 dropped goal, 1 try (16) to 1 dropped goal, 1 penalty goal (6), at Murrayfield.
1965-66 – Scotland. 1 goal, 2 tries (11) to 1 penalty goal (3), at Dublin.
1966-67 – Ireland. 1 goal (5) to 1 penalty goal (3), at Murrayfield.
1967-68 – Ireland. 1 goal, 1 penalty goal, 2 tries (14) to 2 penalty goals (6), at Dublin.
1968-69 – Ireland. 2 goals, 2 tries (16) to 0, at Murrayfield.
1969-70 – Ireland. 2 goals, 2 tries (16) to 1 goal, 1 dropped goal, 1 try (11), at Dublin.
1970-71 – Ireland. 1 goal, 2 penalty goals, 2 tries (17) to 1 goal (5), at Murrayfield.

## TRY INCREASED TO 4 POINTS

1971-72 – No match.
1972-73 – Scotland. 2 penalty goals, 3 dropped goals, 1 try (19) to 2 penalty goals, 2 tries (14), at Murrayfield.
1973-74 – Ireland. 1 goal, 1 penalty goal (9) to 2 penalty goals (6), at Dublin.
1974-75 – Scotland. 2 dropped goals, 2 penalty goals, 2 tries (20) to 1 goal, 1 penalty goal, 1 try (13), at Murrayfield.

## SCOTLAND v WALES

1882-83 – Scotland. 3 goals to 1 goal, at Edinburgh.
1883-84 – Scotland. 1 goal, 1 try to 0, at Newport.
1884-85 – Drawn. No score, at Glasgow.
1885-86 – Scotland. 2 goals, 1 try to 0, at Cardiff.
1886-87 – Scotland. 4 goals, 8 tries to 0, at Edinburgh.
1887-88 – Wales. 1 try to 0, at Newport.
1888-89 – Scotland. 2 tries to 0, at Edinburgh.
1889-90 – Scotland. 1 goal, 2 tries to 1 try, at Cardiff.
1890-91 – Scotland. 3 goals, 6 tries to 0, at Edinburgh.
1891-92 – Scotland. 1 goal, 1 try to 1 try, at Swansea.
1892-93 – Wales. 1 goal, 3 tries to 0, at Edinburgh.
1893-94 – Wales. 1 goal, 1 try to 0, at Newport.

1894-95—Scotland. 1 goal to 1 dropped goal, at Edinburgh.
1895-96—Wales. 2 tries to 0, at Cardiff.
1896-97 and 1897-98—No Match.
1898-99—Scotland. 1 goal (mark), 2 dropped goals, 3 tries, to 2 goals, at Edinburgh.
1899-1900—Wales. 4 tries to 1 try, at Swansea.
1900-01—Scotland. 3 goals, 1 try to 1 goal, 1 try, at Inverleith.
1901-02—Wales. 1 goal, 3 tries to 1 goal, at Cardiff.
1902-03—Scotland. 1 penalty goal, 1 try to 0, at Inverleith.
1903-04—Wales. 3 goals, 1 dropped goal, 1 try to 1 try, at Swansea.
1904-05—Wales. 2 tries to 1 try, at Inverleith.

## MODERN SCORING VALUES ADOPTED

1905-06—Wales. 3 tries (9) to 1 goal (5), at Cardiff.
1906-07—Scotland. 2 tries (6) to 1 penalty goal (3), at Inverleith.
1907-08—Wales. 2 tries (6) to 1 goal (5), at Swansea.
1908-09—Wales. 1 goal (5) to 1 penalty goal (3), at Inverleith.
1909-10—Wales. 1 goal, 3 tries (14) to 0, at Cardiff.
1910-11—Wales. 2 goals, 1 dropped goal, 6 tries (32) to 1 dropped goal, 2 tries (10), at Inverleith.
1911-12—Wales. 2 goals, 2 dropped goals, 1 try (21) to 2 tries (6), at Swansea.
1912-13—Wales. 1 goal, 1 try (8) to 0, at Inverleith.
1913-14—Wales. 2 goals, 2 dropped goals, 1 penalty goal, 1 try (24) to 1 goal (5), at Cardiff.
1919-20—Scotland. 2 penalty goals, 1 try (9) to 1 goal (5), at Inverleith.
1920-21—Scotland. 1 goal, 1 penalty goal, 2 tries (14) to 2 dropped goals (8), at Swansea.
1921-22—Drawn. Scotland 1 penalty goal, 2 tries (9); Wales 1 goal, a dropped goal (9), at Inverleith.
1922-23—Scotland. 1 goal, 2 tries(11) to 1 goal, 1 penalty goal (8), at Cardiff.
1923-24—Scotland. 4 goals, 1 penalty goal, 4 tries (35) to 2 goals (10), at Inverleith.
1924-25—Scotland. 1 goal, 1 dropped goal, 5 tries (24) to 1 goal, 1 penalty goal, 2 tries (14), at Swansea.
1925-26—Scotland. 1 goal, 1 penalty goal (8), to 1 goal (5), at Murrayfield.
1926-27—Scotland. 1 goal (5) to 0, at Cardiff.
1927-28—Wales. 2 goals, 1 try (13) to 0, at Murrayfield.
1928-29—Wales. 1 goal, 3 tries (14) to 1 dropped goal, 1 penalty goal (7), at Swansea.
1929-30—Scotland. 1 goal, 1 dropped goal, 1 try (12) to 1 goal, 1 dropped goal (9), at Murrayfield.
1930-31—Wales. 2 goals, 1 try (13) to 1 goal, 1 try (8), at Cardiff.
1931-32—Wales. 1 penalty goal, 1 try (6) to 0, at Murrayfield.
1932-33—Scotland. 1 goal, 1 penalty goal, 1 try (11) to 1 try (3), at Swansea.
1933-34—Wales. 2 goals, 1 try (13) to 1 penalty goal, 1 try (6), at Murrayfield.
1934-35—Wales. 1 dropped goal, 2 tries (10) to 2 tries (6), at Cardiff.
1935-36—Wales. 2 goals, 1 try (13) to 1 try (3), at Murrayfield.
1936-37—Scotland. 2 goals, 1 try (13) to 2 tries (6), at Swansea.
1937-38—Scotland. 1 goal, 1 penalty goal (8) to 2 tries (6), at Murrayfield.
1938-39—Wales. 1 goal, 1 penalty goal, 1 try (11) to 1 penalty goal (3), at Cardiff.
1946-47—Wales. 2 goals, 1 penalty goal, 3 tries (22) to 1 goal, 1 penalty goal (8), at Murrayfield.
1947-48—Wales. 1 goal, 1 penalty goal, 2 tries (14) to 0, at Cardiff.

## DROPPED GOAL REDUCED TO 3 POINTS

1948-49—Scotland. 2 tries (6) to 1 goal (5), at Murrayfield.
1949-50—Wales. 1 dropped goal, 1 penalty goal, 2 tries (12) to 0, at Swansea.
1950-51—Scotland. 2 goals, 1 dropped goal, 1 penalty goal, 1 try (19) to 0, at Murrayfield.
1951-52—Wales. 1 goal, 2 penalty goals (11) to 0, at Cardiff.

1952-53—Wales. 1 penalty goal, 3 tries (12) to 0, at Murrayfield.
1953-54—Wales. 1 penalty goal, 4 tries (15) to 1 try (3), at Swansea.
1954-55—Scotland. 1 goal, 1 dropped goal, 1 penalty goal, 1 try (14) to 1 goal, 1 try (8), at Murrayfield.
1955-56—Wales. 3 tries (9) to 1 penalty goal (3), at Cardiff.
1956-57—Scotland. 1 dropped goal, 1 penalty goal, 1 try (9) to 1 penalty goal, 1 try (6), at Murrayfield.
1957-58—Wales. 1 goal, 1 try (8), to 1 penalty goal (3), at Cardiff.
1958-59—Scotland. 1 penalty goal, 1 try (6) to 1 goal, (5), at Murrayfield.
1959-60—Wales. 1 goal, 1 penalty goal (8) to 0, at Cardiff.
1960-61—Scotland. 1 try (3) to 0, at Murrayfield.
1961-62—Scotland. 1 goal, 1 try (8) to 1 dropped goal (3), at Cardiff.
1962-63—Wales. 1 dropped goal, 1 penalty goal (6) to 0, at Murrayfield.
1963-64—Wales. 1 goal, 1 penalty goal, 1 try (11) to 1 try (3), at Cardiff.
1964-65—Wales. 1 goal, 2 penalty goals, 1 try (14) to 2 dropped goals, 2 penalty goals (12), at Murrayfield.
1965-66—Wales. 1 try, 1 goal (8) to 1 penalty goal (3), at Cardiff.
1966-67—Scotland. 1 goal, 1 dropped goal, 1 try (11) to 1 goal (5), at Murrayfield.
1967-68—Wales. 1 goal (5) to 0, at Cardiff.
1968-69—Wales. 1 goal, 2 penalty goals, 2 tries (17) to 1 penalty goal (3), at Murray-field.
1969-70—Wales. 3 goals, 1 try (18) to 1 dropped goal, 1 penalty goal, 1 try (9), at Cardiff.
1970-71—Wales. 2 goals, 1 penalty goal, 2 tries (19) to 4 penalty goals, 2 tries (18), at Murrayfield.

## TRY INCREASED TO 4 POINTS

1971-72—Wales. 3 goals, 3 penalty goals, 2 tries (35) to 1 goal, 2 penalty goals (12), at Cardiff.
1972-73—Scotland. 1 goal, 1 try (10) to 3 penalty goals (9), at Murrayfield.
1973-74—Wales. 1 goal (6) to 0, at Cardiff.
1974-75—Scotland. 3 penalty goals, 1 dropped goal (12) to 2 penalty goals, 1 try (10), at Murrayfield.

## SCOTLAND v FRANCE

1909-10—Scotland. 3 goals, 4 tries (27) to 0, at Inverleith.
1910-11—France. 2 goals, 2 tries (16) to 1 goal, 1 dropped goal, 2 tries (15), at Paris.
1911-12—Scotland. 5 goals, 1 penalty goal, 1 try (31) to 1 try (3), at Inverleith.
1912-13—Scotland. 3 goals, 2 tries (21) to 1 try (3), at Paris.
1913-14—No Match.
1919-20—Scotland. 1 goal (5) to 0, at Paris.
1920-21—France. 1 try (3) to 0, at Inverleith.
1921-22—Drawn. 1 try (3) each, at Paris.
1922-23—Scotland. 2 goals, 2 tries (16) to 1 goal (mark) (3), at Inverleith.
1923-24—France. 4 tries (12) to 1 dropped goal, 1 penalty goal, 1 try (10), at Paris.
1924-25—Scotland. 2 goals, 5 tries (25) to 1 dropped goal (4), at Inverleith.
1925-26—Scotland. 1 goal, 1 penalty goal, 4 tries (20) to 1 penalty goal, 1 try (6), at Paris.
1926-27—Scotland. 4 goals, 1 penalty goal (23) to 2 tries (6), at Murrayfield.
1927-28—Scotland. 5 tries (15) to 2 tries (6), at Paris.
1928-29—Scotland. 1 penalty goal, 1 try (6) to 1 try (3), at Murrayfield.
1929-30—France. 1 dropped goal, 1 try (7), to 1 try (3), at Paris.
1930-31—Scotland. 2 penalty goals (6) to 1 dropped goal (4), at Murrayfield.
1946-47—France. 1 goal, 1 try (8), to 1 penalty goal (3), at Paris.
1947-48—Scotland. 2 penalty goals, 1 try (9) to 1 goal, 1 penalty goal (8), at Murrayfield.

## DROPPED GOAL REDUCED TO 3 POINTS.

1948-49–Scotland. 1 goal, 1 try (8) to 0, at Paris.
1949-50–Scotland. 1 goal, 1 try (8) to 1 goal (5), at Murrayfield.
1950-51–France. 1 goal, 2 penalty goals, 1 try (14) to 2 penalty goals, 2 tries (12), at Paris.
1951-52–France. 2 goals, 1 penalty goal (13) to 1 goal, 2 penalty goals (11), at Murrayfield.
1952-53–France. 1 goal, 1 dropped goal, 1 penalty goal (11) to 1 goal (5), at Paris.
1953-54–France. 1 try (3) to 0, at Murrayfield.
1954-55–France. 1 penalty goal, 4 tries (15) to 0, at Paris.
1955-56–Scotland. 2 penalty goals, 2 tries (12) to 0, at Murrayfield.
1956-57–Scotland. 1 dropped goal, 1 penalty goal (6) to 0, at Paris.
1957-58–Scotland. 1 goal, 1 penalty goal, 1 try (11) to 2 penalty goals, 1 try (9), at Murrayfield.
1958-59–France. 2 dropped goals, 1 try (9) to 0, at Paris.
1959-60–France. 2 goals, 1 try (13) to 1 goal, 1 penalty goal, 1 try (11), at Murrayfield.
1960-61–France. 1 goal, 1 dropped goal, 1 penalty goal (11) to 0, at Paris.
1961-62–France. 1 goal, 2 penalty goals (11) to 1 penalty goal (3), at Murrayfield.
1962-63–Scotland. 1 goal, 1 dropped goal, 1 penalty goal (11) to 1 dropped goal, 1 penalty goal (6), at Paris.
1963-64–Scotland. 2 goals (10) to 0, at Murrayfield.
1964-65–France. 2 goals, 2 tries (16) to 1 goal, 1 try (8), at Paris.
1965-66–Drawn. Scotland 1 try (3); France 1 penalty goal (3), at Murrayfield.
1966-67–Scotland. 2 penalty goals, 1 dropped goal (9) to 1 goal, 1 try (8), at Paris.
1967-68–France. 1 goal, 1 try (8) to 1 penalty goal, 1 try (6), at Murrayfield.
1968-69–Scotland. 1 penalty goal, 1 try (6) to 1 penalty goal (3), at Paris.
1969-70–France. 1 goal, 1 dropped goal, 1 try (11) to 2 penalty goals, 1 try (9), at Murrayfield.
1970-71–France. 2 goals, 1 penalty goal (13) to 1 goal, 1 penalty goal (8), at Paris.

## TRY INCREASED TO 4 POINTS

1971-72–Scotland. 1 goal, 1 penalty goal, 1 dropped goal, 2 tries (20) to 1 goal, 1 penalty goal (9), at Murrayfield.
1972-73–France. 3 penalty goals, 1 dropped goal, 1 try (16) to 2 penalty goals, 1 dropped goal, 1 try (13), at Paris.
1973-74–Scotland. 1 goal, 3 penalty goals, 1 try (19) to 1 penalty goal, 1 dropped goal (6), at Murrayfield.
1974-75–France. 1 penalty goal, 1 dropped goal, 1 try (10) to 3 penalty goals (9), at Paris.

## IRELAND v WALES

1881-82–Wales. 2 goals, 2 tries to 0, at Dublin.
1882-82–No Match.
1883-84–Wales. 1 goal, 2 tries to 0, at Cardiff.
1884-85 and 1885-86–No Match.
1886-1887–Wales. 1 goal to 1 try, at Birkenhead.
1887-88–Ireland. 2 goals, 1 try to 0, at Dublin.
1888-89–Ireland. 2 tries to 0, at Swansea.
1889-90–Drawn. 1 goal each, at Dublin.
1890-91–Wales. 1 goal, 1 dropped goal to 1 dropped goal, 1 try, at Llanelli.
1891-92–Ireland. 1 goal, 2 tries to 0, at Dublin.
1892-93–Wales. 1 try to 0, at Llanelli.
1893-94–Ireland. 1 penalty goal to 0, at Belfast.
1894-95–Wales. 1 goal to 0, at Cardiff.
1895-96–Ireland. 1 goal, 1 try to 1 goal, at Dublin.
1896-97–No Match.
1897-98–Wales. 1 goal, 1 penalty goal, 1 try to 1 penalty goal, at Limerick.
1898-99–Ireland. 1 try to 0, at Cardiff.

J. V. Pullin (England)

D. M. D. Rollo (Scotland)

## LEADING CAP-HOLDERS

W. J. McBride (Ireland)

K. J. Jones (Wales)

P. G. Johnson (Australia)

C. E. Meads (New Zealand)

LEADING CAP-HOLDERS

F. C. H. Du Preez (South Africa)

B. Dauga (France)

The Calcutta Cup, competed
for annually between England
and Scotland

G. L. Brown (Scotland) and C. W. Ralston (England) compete for the ball in a
line-out during the 1975 Calcutta Cup match at Twickenham

The New Zealand Touring Team of 1905—probably the most famous touring side in Rugby History. Left to right (*back row*) : J. Corbett, W. Johnstone, W. Cunningham, F. Newton, G. Nicholson, C. Seeling, J. O. Sullivan, A. McDonald, D. McGregor, J. Duncan (trainer) ; (*middle row*) : E. Harper, W. J. Wallace, W. J. Stead (vice-captain), G. H. Dixon (manager), D. Gallaher (captain), J. Hunter, G. Gillett, F. Glasgow, W. Mackrell ; (*front row*) : S. Casey, H. J. Abbott, G. W. Smith, F. Roberts, H. D. Thomson, H. J. Mynott, E. E. Booth, G. Tyler, R. G. Deans

The famous Close at Rugby School where William Webb Ellis ran with the ball in his arms in direct contravention of the laws then in existence

This picture reveals the unpatterned course of a Ruby match before the great Oxford University and England pair Harry Vassall and Alan Rotherham introduced the formula of combination between backs and forwards. The "maul" as shown in this picture was the predominant feature of early Rugby, and was apt to be a lengthy thing indeed

Three of the world's most prolific points scorers. Above (*left*) Barry John (Wales 1966–72), and (*right*) Tom Kiernan (Ireland 1960–73). (*Below*) Ian Kirkpatrick (New Zealand 1967–75)

An England team of 1922, one of a number of distinguished sides of the early twenties. Left to right (*back row*): J. S. Tucker, H. L. V. Day, A. F. Blackiston, A. T. Voyce, G. S. Conway, R. Edwards, B. S. Cumberlege; (*middle row*): E. R. Gardner, W. W. Wakefield, C. N. Lowe, L. G. Brown, E. Myers, E. Hammett; (*front row*): C. A. Kershaw, V. G. Davies

The England XV that defeated the 1935–36 New Zealanders by 13–0 at Twickenham. Left to right (*back row*): P. L. Candler, E. S. Nicholson, R. A. Gerrard, E. Hamilton Hill, A. J. Clarke, A. Obolensky, H. S. Sever, P. E. Dunkley, H. G. Owen Smith, J. W. Faull (Wales, referee); (*front row*): P. Cranmer, R. J. Longland, D. A. Kendrew, B. C. Gadney (captain), C. Webb, W. H. Weston

With a career total of 3,453 points to close season 1975, Sam Doble (Moseley) seen in action left, holds the British points scoring record

Don Clarke (*right*), nicknamed "The Boot", created a world record by scoring 207 points in 31 international appearances for New Zealand 1956–64

1899-1900—Wales. 1 try to 0, at Belfast.
1900-01 —Wales. 2 goals to 3 tries, at Swansea.
1901-02—Wales, 1 goal, 1 dropped goal, 2 tries to 0, at Dublin.
1902-03—Wales. 6 tries to 0, at Cardiff.
1903-04—Ireland. 1 goal, 3 tries to 4 tries, at Belfast.
1904-05—Wales. 2 goals, to 1 try, at Swansea.

## MODERN SCORING VALUES ADOPTED

1905-06—Ireland. 1 goal, 2 tries (11) to 2 tries (6), at Belfast.
1906-07—Wales. 2 goals, 1 dropped goal, 1 penalty goal, 4 tries (29) to 0, at Cardiff.
1907-08—Wales. 1 goal, 2 tries (11) to 1 goal (5), at Belfast.
1908-09—Wales. 3 goals, 1 try (18) to 1 goal (5), at Swansea.
1909-10—Wales. 1 dropped goal, 5 tries (19) to 1 try (3), at Dublin.
1910-11—Wales. 2 goals, 1 penalty goal, 1 try (16) to 0, at Belfast.
1911-12—Ireland. 1 goal, 1 dropped goal, 1 try (12) to 1 goal (5), at Belfast.
1912-13—Wales. 2 goals, 1 penalty goal, 1 try (16) to 2 goals, 1 penalty goal (13), at Swansea.
1913-14—Wales. 1 goal, 2 tries (11) to 1 try (3), at Belfast.
1919-20—Wales. 3 goals, 1 dropped goal, 3 tries (28) to 1 dropped goal (4), at Cardiff.
1920-21—Wales. 1 penalty goal, 1 try (6) to 0, at Belfast.
1921-22—Wales. 1 goal, 2 tries (11) to 1 try (3), at Swansea.
1922-23—Ireland. 1 goal (5) to 1 dropped goal (4), at Dublin.
1923-24—Ireland. 2 goals, 1 try (13) to 1 dropped goal, 2 tries (10), at Cardiff.
1924-25—Ireland. 2 goals, 1 penalty goal, 2 tries (19) to 1 try (3), at Belfast.
1925-26—Wales. 1 goal, 2 tries (11) to 1 goal, 1 penalty goal (8), at Swansea.
1926-27—Ireland. 2 goals, 1 penalty goal, 2 tries (19) to 1 goal, 1 dropped goal (9), at Dublin.
1927-28—Ireland. 2 goals, 1 try (13) to 2 goals (10), at Cardiff.
1928-29—Drawn. 1 goal (5) each, at Belfast.
1929-30—Wales. 1 penalty goal, 3 tries (12) to 1 dropped goal, 1 penalty goal (7), at Swansea.
1930-31—Wales. 1 goal, 1 dropped goal, 2 tries (15) to 1 try (3), at Belfast.
1931-32—Ireland. 4 tries (12) to 1 dropped goal, 2 tries (10), at Cardiff.
1932-33—Ireland. 1 dropped goal, 1 penalty goal, 1 try (10), to 1 goal (5), at Belfast.
1933-34—Wales. 2 goals, 1 try (13) to 0, at Swansea.
1934-35—Ireland. 2 penalty goals, 1 try (9) to 1 penalty goal (3), at Belfast.
1935-36—Wales. 1 penalty goal (3) to 0, at Cardiff.
1936-37—Ireland. 1 goal (5) to 1 penalty goal (3), at Belfast.
1937-38—Wales. 1 goal, 1 penalty goal, 1 try (11) to 1 goal (5), at Swansea.
1938-39—Wales. 1 dropped goal, 1 try (7) to 0, at Belfast.
1946-47—Wales. 1 penalty goal, 1 try (6) to 0, at Swansea.
1947-48—Ireland. 2 tries (6) to 1 try (3), at Belfast.

## DROPPED GOAL REDUCED TO 3 POINTS

1948-49—Ireland. 1 goal (5) to 0, at Swansea.
1949-50—Wales. 2 tries (6) to 1 penalty goal (3), at Belfast.
1950-51—Drawn. Wales 1 penalty goal, (3); Ireland 1 try (3), at Cardiff.
1951-52—Wales. 1 goal, 1 penalty goal, 2 tries (14) to 1 penalty goal (3), at Dublin.
1952-53—Wales. 1 goal (5) to 1 try (3), at Swansea.
1953-54—Wales. 1 dropped goal, 3 penalty goals (12) to 2 penalty goals, 1 try (9), at Dublin.
1954-55—Wales. 3 goals, 1 penalty goal, 1 try (21) to 1 penalty goal (3), at Cardiff.
1955-56—Ireland. 1 goal, 1 dropped goal, 1 penalty goal (11) to 1 penalty goal (3), at Dublin.
1956-57—Wales. 2 penalty goals (6) to 1 goal (5), at Cardiff.
1957-58—Wales. 3 tries (9) to 1 penalty goal, 1 try (6), at Dublin.
1958-59—Wales. 1 goal, 1 try (8) to 1 penalty goal, 1 try (6), at Cardiff.

1959-60 — Wales. 2 goals (10) to 2 penalty goals, 1 try (9), at Dublin.
1960-61 — Wales. 2 penalty goals, 1 try (9) to 0, at Cardiff.
1961-62 — Drawn. Ireland 1 dropped goal (3); Wales 1 penalty goal (3), at Dublin.
        Postponed until November 18, 1962.
1962-63 — Ireland. 1 goal, 1 dropped goal, 2 penalty goals (14) to 1 dropped goal, 1
        try (6), at Cardiff.
1963-64 — Wales. 3 goals (15) to 2 penalty goals (6), at Dublin.
1964-65 — Wales. 1 goal, 1 dropped goal, 1 penalty goal, 1 try (14) to 1 goal, 1
        penalty goal (8), at Cardiff.
1965-66 — Ireland. 1 dropped goal, 1 penalty goal, 1 try (9) to 1 try, 1 penalty goal (6),
        at Dublin.
1966-67 — Ireland. 1 try (3) to 0, at Cardiff.
1967-68 — Ireland. 1 penalty goal, 1 dropped goal, 1 try (9) to 1 penalty goal, 1 dropp-
        ed goal (6) at Dublin.
1968-69 — Wales. 3 goals, 1 dropped goal, 1 penalty goal, 1 try (24) to 1 goal, 2
        penalty goals (11), at Cardiff.
1969-70 — Ireland. 1 goal, 1 dropped goal, 1 penalty goal, 1 try (14) to 0, at Dublin.
1970-71 — Wales. 1 goal, 2 penalty goals, 1 dropped goal, 3 tries (23) to 3 penalty
        goals (9), at Cardiff.

## TRY INCREASED TO 4 POINTS

1971-72 — No Match.
1972-73 — Wales. 1 goal, 2 penalty goals, 1 try (16) to 1 goal, 2 penalty goals (12), at
        Cardiff.
1973-74 — Drawn. Ireland 3 penalty goals (9) to Wales 1 goal, 1 penalty goal (9), at
        Dublin.
1974-75 — Wales. 3 goals, 2 penalty goals, 2 tries (32) to 1 try (4), at Cardiff.

## IRELAND v FRANCE

1908-09 — Ireland. 1 penalty goal, 2 goals, 2 tries (19) to 1 goal, 1 try (8), at Dublin.
1909-10 — Ireland. 1 goal, 1 try (8) to 1 try (3), at Paris.
1910-11 — Ireland. 3 goals, 1 dropped goal, 2 tries (25) to 1 goal (5), at Cork.
1911-12 — Ireland. 1 goal, 2 tries (11) to 2 tries (6), at Paris.
1912-13 — Ireland. 3 goals, 3 tries (24) to 0, at Cork.
1913-14 — Ireland. 1 goal, 1 try (8) to 2 tries (6), at Paris.
1919-20 — France. 5 tries (15) to 1 dropped goal, 1 try (7), at Dublin.
1920-21 — France. 4 goals (20) to 2 goals (10), at Paris.
1921-22 — Ireland. 1 goal, 1 penalty goal (8) to 1 try (3), at Dublin.
1922-23 — France. 1 goal, 3 tries (14) to 1 goal, 1 try (8), at Paris.
1923-24 — Ireland. 2 tries (6) to 0, at Dublin.
1924-25 — Ireland. 1 penalty goal, 2 tries (9) to 1 try (3), at Paris.
1925-26 — Ireland. 1 goal, 1 penalty goal, 1 try (11) to 0, at Belfast.
1926-27 — Ireland. 1 goal, 1 penalty goal (8) to 1 try (3), at Paris.
1927-28 — Ireland. 4 tries (12) to 1 goal, 1 try (8), at Belfast.
1928-29 — Ireland. 2 tries (6) to 0, at Paris.
1929-30 — France. 1 goal (5) to 0, at Belfast.
1930-31 — France. 1 try (3) to 0, at Paris.
1946-47 — France. 4 tries (12) to 1 goal, 1 penalty goal (8), at Dublin.
1947-48 — Ireland. 2 goals, 1 try (13) to 2 tries (6), at Paris.

## DROPPED GOAL REDUCED TO 3 POINTS

1948-49 — France. 2 goals, 2 penalty goals (16) to 3 penalty goals (9), at Dublin.
1949-50 — Drawn. France 1 dropped goal (3); Ireland 1 penalty goal (3), at Paris.
1950-51 — Ireland. 1 penalty goal, 2 tries (9) to 1 goal, 1 try (8), at Dublin.
1951-52 — Ireland. 1 goal, 1 penalty goal, 1 try (11) to 1 goal, 1 penalty goal (8), at
        Paris.
1952-53 — Ireland. 2 goals, 2 tries (16) to 1 dropped goal (3), at Belfast.
1953-54 — France. 1 goal, 1 try (8) to 0, at Paris.

1954-55—France. 1 goal, (5) to 1 penalty goal (3), at Dublin.
1955-56—France. 1 goal, 2 dropped goals, 1 try (14) to 1 goal, 1 penalty goal (8), at Paris.
1956-57—Ireland. 1 goal, 1 penalty goal, 1 try (11) to 2 penalty goals (6), at Dublin.
1957-58—France. 1 goal, 1 dropped goal, 1 penalty goal (11) to 2 penalty goals (6), at Paris.
1958-59—Ireland. 1 dropped goal, 1 penalty goal, 1 try (9) to 1 goal (5), at Dublin.
1959-60—France. 1 goal, 3 dropped goals, 3 tries (23) to 2 tries (6), at Paris.
1960-61—France. 2 dropped goals, 2 penalty goals, 1 try (15) to 1 penalty goal (3), at Dublin.
1961-62—France. 1 goal, 2 tries (11) to 0, at Paris.
1962-63—France. 3 goals, 2 dropped goals, 1 try (24) to 1 goal (5), at Dublin.
1963-64—France. 3 goals, 1 dropped goal, 3 tries (27) to 1 dropped goal, 1 try (6), at Paris.
1964-65—Drawn. 1 try each (3), at Dublin.
1965-66—France. 1 penalty goal, 1 goal, 1 try (11) to 1 dropped goal, 1 penalty goal (6), at Paris.
1966-67—France. 1 goal, 2 dropped goals (11) to 1 penalty goal, 1 try (6), at Dublin.
1967-68—France. 2 goals, 1 penalty goal, 1 dropped goal (16), to 2 penalty goals (6), at Paris.
1968-69—Ireland. 1 goal, 1 dropped goal, 3 penalty goals (17) to 2 penalty goals, 1 try (9), at Dublin.
1969-70—France. 1 goal, 1 dropped goal (8) to 0, at Paris.
1970-71—Drawn. Ireland, 2 penalty goals, 1 try (9) to France 2 penalty goals, 1 dropped goal (9), at Dublin.

## TRY INCREASED TO 4 POINTS

1971-72—Ireland. 2 penalty goals, 2 tries (14) to 1 goal, 1 penalty goal (9), at Paris.
     —Ireland. 3 goals, 2 penalty goals (24) to 1 goal, 2 tries (14), at Dublin. Not a championship match but full caps awarded.
1972-73—Ireland. 2 penalty goals (6) to 1 try (4), at Dublin.
1973-74—France. 1 goal, 1 penalty goal (9) to 2 penalty goals (6), at Paris.
1974-75—Ireland. 2 goals, 1 penalty goal, 2 dropped goals, 1 try (25) to 1 penalty goal, 1 dropped goal (6), at Dublin.

## WALES v FRANCE

1907-08—Wales. 3 goals, 1 penalty goal, 6 tries (36) to 1 dropped goal (4), at Cardiff.
1908-09—Wales. 7 goals, 4 tries (47) to 1 goal (5), at Paris.
1909-10—Wales. 8 goals, 1 penalty goal, 2 tries (49) to 1 goal, 2 penalty goals, 1 try (14), at Swansea.
1910-11—Wales. 3 goals (15) to 0, at Paris.
1911-12—Wales. 1 goal, 3 tries (14) to 1 goal, 1 try (8), at Newport.
1912-13—Wales. 1 goal, 2 tries (11) to 1 goal, 1 try (8), at Paris.
1913-14—Wales. 5 goals, 2 tries (31) to 0, at Swansea.
1919-20—Wales. 2 tries (6) to 1 goal (5), at Paris.
1920-21—Wales. 2 penalty goals, 2 tries (12) to 1 dropped goal (4), at Cardiff.
1921-22—Wales. 1 goal, 2 tries (11) to 1 try (3), at Paris.
1922-23—Wales. 2 goals, 1 penalty goal, 1 try (16) to 1 goal, 1 try (8), at Swansea.
1923-24—Wales. 1 dropped goal, 2 tries (10) to 2 tries (6), at Paris.
1924-25—Wales. 1 goal, 2 tries (11) to 1 goal (5), at Cardiff.
1925-26—Wales. 1 dropped goal, 1 try (7) to 1 try (3), at Paris.
1926-27—Wales. 2 goals, 5 tries (25) to 1 dropped goal, 1 try (7), at Swansea.
1927-28—France. 1 goal, 1 try (8) to 1 try (3), at Paris.
1928-29—Wales. 1 goal, 1 try (8) to 1 try (3), at Cardiff.
1929-30—Wales. 2 dropped goals, 1 try (11) to 0, at Paris.
1930-31—Wales. 5 goals, 1 dropped goal, 2 tries (35) to 1 try (3), at Swansea.
1946-47—Wales. 1 penalty goal (3) to 0, at Paris.
1947-48—France. 1 goal, 2 tries (11) to 1 penalty goal (3), at Swansea.

## DROPPED GOAL REDUCED TO 3 POINTS

1948-49—France. 1 goal (5) to 1 try (3), at Paris.

1949-50—Wales. 3 goals, 1 penalty goal, 1 try (21) to 0, at Cardiff.

1950-51—France. 1 goal, 1 penalty goal (8) to 1 try (3), at Paris.

1951-52—Wales. 1 dropped goal, 2 penalty goals (9) to 1 goal (5), at Swansea.

1952-53—Wales. 2 tries (6) to 1 penalty goal (3), at Paris.

1953-54—Wales. 2 goals, 3 penalty goals (19) to 2 goals, 1 penalty goal (13), at Cardiff.

1954-55—Wales. 2 penalty goals, 2 tries (16) to 1 goal, 1 dropped goal, 1 penalty goal (11), at Paris.

1955-56—Wales, 1 goal (5) to 1 try (3), at Cardiff.

1956-57—Wales. 2 goals 1 penalty goal, 2 tries (19) to 2 goals, 1 try (13), at Paris.

1957-58—France. 2 goals, 1 dropped goal, 1 penalty goal (16) to 1 goal, 1 try (8), at Cardiff.

1958-59—France. 1 goal, 1 penalty goal, 1 try (11) to 1 penalty goal (3), at Paris.

1959-60—France. 2 goals, 2 tries (16) to 1 goal, 1 penalty goal (6), at Cardiff.

1960-61—France. 1 goal, 1 try (8) to 2 tries (6), at Paris.

1961-62—Wales. 1 penalty goal (3) to 0, at Cardiff.

1962-63—France. 1 goal (5) to 1 penalty goal (3), at Paris.

1963-64—Drawn. 1 goal, 2 penalty goals (11) each, at Cardiff.

1964-65—France. 2 goals, 1 penalty goal, 1 dropped goal, 2 tries (22) to 2 goals, 1 try, (13), at Paris.

1965-66—Wales. 2 penalty goals, 1 try (9) to 1 try, 1 goal (8), at Cardiff.

1966-67—France. 1 goal, 2 dropped goals, 1 penalty goal, 2 tries (20) to 1 goal, 1 dropped goal, 2 penalty goals (14), at Paris.

1967-68—France. 1 goal, 1 penalty goal, 1 dropped goal, 1 try (14) to 2 penalty goals, 1 try (9), at Cardiff.

1968-69—Drawn. Wales 1 goal, 1 try (8) to France 1 goal, 1 penalty goal (8), at Paris.

1969-70—Wales. 1 goal, 2 penalty goals (11) to 2 tries (6), at Cardiff.

1970-71—Wales. 1 penalty goal, 2 tries (9) to 1 goal (5), at Paris.

## TRY INCREASED TO 4 POINTS

1971-72—Wales. 4 penalty goals, 2 tries (20) to 2 penalty goals (6), at Cardiff.

1972-73—France. 3 penalty goals, 1 dropped goal (12) to 1 dropped goal (3), at Paris.

1973-74—Drawn. 3 penalty goals, 1 dropped goal, 1 try (16) each.

1974-75—Wales. 1 goal, 1 penalty goal, 4 tries (25) to 2 penalty goals, 1 try (10), at Paris.

## IRISH RUGBY FOOTBALL UNION

See also INTERNATIONALS (IRELAND).

The Irish R.F.U. traces its history back to 1874, but although a Union was formed in Dublin in December of that year, largely through the initiative of members of the Dublin University Club, it was not truly representative for another five years. In January 1875 the outnumbered Ulster clubs, led by the North of Ireland Club, formed their own Northern Football Union of Ireland in Belfast, and it was not until February 1880 that these two Unions had amalgamated and the inaugural meeting of the newly formed Irish R.F.U. took place.

Nowadays the game in Ireland is administered through the four branch Unions of Ulster, Leinster, Munster, and Connaught, each of whom have their own League and Cup competitions. There is also an Inter-provinvial Championship and these games are used as "Trials" by the Irish selectors.

Irish rugby has enjoyed most of its finest spells in the period since World War II. They won the International Championship three times in four years 1948-1951 under the captaincy of Karl Mullen (Old Belvedere), the side including one of the game's all-time great fly-half Jack Kyle, whose total of 46 Internationals was, for a while, a world record. The 1947-48 team performed the "Grand Slam" for the only time in Irish history.

There was another spell of success in the period 1967-69 when the Irish side had a run of six wins in a row, beating Scotland. Wales, Australia, France, England, and Scotland (again), before losing 11—24 to Wales at Cardiff in March 1969. This team was captained by one of their most brilliant full-backs, T. J. Kiernan (University College, Cork, Cork Constitution). He captained Ireland a record 24 times and his team included another two of the outstanding players of Irish rugby history—Willie John McBride, who was to succeed Kiernan as captain, and Mike Gibson. During season 1973-74 McBride established a new world record for international appearances when he passed New Zealander, C. E. Mead's

total of 55 caps. Mike Gibson established his reputation as a fly-half before switching to the centre and taking his total of caps to over 50.

A great figure in the administrative history of Irish Rugby was R. W. Jeffares who was the Union's secretary for 26 years before being succeeded in 1964 by his son of the same initials. For the greater part of its history the Irish R.U. shared the venue of their home Internationals between Landsdowne Road, Dublin and Ravenhill, Belfast, but in 1954 the former ground became the sole venue for Internationals played in Ireland.

# JAPAN

Britishers played rugby in Yokohama as far back as 1874 but it was not until comparatively recent years that the rugby fraternity abroad has come to appreciate the rapid advance made by the game in Japan. Its development there has been largely due to the enthusiasm of the students of the Universities of Meiji, Keio, and Waseda. Keio University took up the game at the turn of the century and established a series of annual matches with Waseda in 1924.

The first representative Japanese team to tour Britain came over in 1973 (they also included France in their tour) and although they won only two of the 11 matches, they proved themselves to be one of the most disciplined and fittest teams ever to visit these islands. Dis-

playing great speed and mobility it was only lack of height and weight that prevented them from obtaining better results. Two years earlier, when the England touring team had visited Japan, they were run very close in their two games, only beating Japan 22-19 and 6-3.

In 1974 the Japanese took their dynamic brand of rugby to New Zealand and shook a few of the local stalwarts by winning five of their 11 games, including a 24-21 victory over New Zealand Universities at Wellington.

The Japanese R.F.U. was formed in 1926 and now has a membership of over 2,000 clubs although a shortage of pitches has prevented even greater expansion.

## KICKING

The longest place kick on record is credited to the South African player D. F. T. Morkel, who played for South Africa against Surrey at the Richmond Athletic Ground in 1906, kicked the ball a distance of 100 yards from kick to pitch.

Playing for South Africa against England at Twickenham in 1932 G. R. Brand dropped a goal from a distance of 90 yds.

Playing for the Royal Navy against the R.A.F. at Twickenham in 1951 B. Lewis Jones kicked an 85-yd. penalty goal.

At Ellis Park, Johannesburg, in 1938, V. G. J. Jenkins (Great Britain) kicked an 80-yd. penalty against South Africa.

D. MacNamara, playing for St. Kilda (Australia) against Geelong, in 1923, landed a penalty goal from 93 yds.

## KING COUNTRY

Founded 1922, affiliated New Zealand Rugby Union same year. Headquarters: Taumarunui. Colours: Maroon and gold hoops. The Meads brothers, C. E. and S. T. are their most famous internationals.

The giant lock-forward C. E. Meads created his country's International record with 55 appearances 1957-71 and a total of 132 games for the All Blacks, another record. Known as 'Pine Tree' Meads there has been few players in the game's history to match his play in the loose, ot his ability to win the ball in the line-out.

## KIWIS, THE

See also NEW ZEALAND and TOURS.

"The Kiwis" was the title accorded the New Zealand Army Touring team which played 27 matches in Britain and another six on the Continent during the first "peace time" season of 1945-46. The team which was drawn exclusively from personnel of the Second New Zealand Expeditionary Force based in Italy and Austria was finally selected from a field of 64 candidates including three released P. O. W.s, and was sponsored by General Sir Bernard Freyberg, V.C., managed by Colonel A. H. Andrews, O.B.E. and captained, by a former All-Black, Major Charles Saxton. The tour itself was an unqualified success, for "The Kiwis" were not only brilliantly successful in the matter of winning their matches, but in addition highly popular with British crowds who quickly recognised in their swift moving and spectacular back play much of the quality that had distinguished the play of the great New Zealand sides of the past. Winning their "Victory Internationals" against Wales, England, and France (twice), "The Kiwis" were only defeated twice in their 33 match programme in Europe, by the Scottish International side and by a Monmouthshire representative team. On their return to New Zealand they played another five matches, losing only once—to Wellington, In addition several of their members became in course of time official All-Blacks, among them R. W. H. Scott, who in many quarters, has been acclaimed as the outstanding full back of his era. Incidentally the proceeds of the "Kiwis" matches in Britain were devoted to charity, and nearly £40,000 was raised in this way.

### Record

IN BRITAIN AND FRANCE: Played 33. Won 29. Lost 2. Drawn 2. Points for 484. Points against 147.

COMPLETE RECORD: Played 38. Won 32. Lost 3. Drawn 3. Points for 712. Points against 252.

## LANDSDOWNE R.F.C.

Affiliated to the Leinster Union Landsdowne R.F.C. (founded 1872) have enjoyed a long and imposing record of successes in that Union's annual Cup Competition, and were amongst the founder members of the Irish Rugby Union in 1879. From the very beginning of Ireland's participation in International Rugby Landsdowne players have been regularly called upon by the National selectors and among the great names of both club and representative football are: W. E. Crawford, who made 30 appearances as his country's full back between 1920-27, and who has subsequently become equally famous as an Irish Rugby Union and Barbarian administrator: Eugene O'Davy (34 caps), A.T.A. Duggan (25), Rev. Robin Rowe (21), B.J. McGann (20), J.E. Arigho (16), and M.P. Crowe (13). In all they have provided Ireland with more than 60 Internationals. Colours: Red, yellow and black hoops. Ground: Landsdowne Road, Dublin.

## LAWS OF THE GAME

Although William Webb Ellis has been justly immortalised as the originator of the game of Rugby football, his act of running with the ball during the course of a Bigside Game at Rugby School in 1823, inspired though it undoubtedly was, did not as it popularly supposed, establish overnight an entirely different version of the game of Football. On the contrary there was an interval of almost fifty years before the laws of the game achieved sufficient standardisation and uniformity of usage to justify of the distinctive title "Rugby" Football. Indeed it was not until 1841 (18 years after the event) that Ellis's "innova-

tion" was legalised by his own School at Rugby, and even then "handing on," or passing was prohibited, and the ball had to be caught on the bounce. To complicate matters still further, every Public School (and they were still the main exponents of the game) had its own code of rules—usually dictated by the size and dimensions of the playing area available to them. Quite obviously the propagation of the game was virtually impossible under these circumstances, and nowhere was this more forcibly realised than at the Universities of Oxford and Cambridge, where the mixed intake from Rugby, Eton, Charterhouse, Marlborough, and other famous schools all possessed widely differing conceptions of what was permissible or non-permissible. Between 1846-63 meetings were held independently at Cambridge and London in an attempt to reach uniformity, but without success. In 1863, however, the Blackheath club, which had been formed a year earlier and which had previously conformed to a code of rules drawn up by an association of London clubs, broke away from this association after it had announced its intention to make the practice of "Hacking", i.e. the tripping of an opponent (see HACKING) illegal. This in effect represented the final cleavage between the two codes of Football, Rugby and Association, and from there it was but a short step to the formation of the Rugby Union (1871) and the drawing up of a code of laws that would consolidate the distinctive features of the Rugby game, and also ensure uniformity amongst its adherents. This task was entrusted to three Old Rugbeians—E. C. Holmes, A. E. Rutter, of the Richmond club, and L. J. Maton of Wimbledon Hornets—and naturally enough, they used as their basis the laws then operable at Rugby School. The first major changes in the code took place in 1875, and they concerned the Scoring Values (see SCORING VALUES), and was followed in 1877 by the introduction of a law that reduced the number in a team from 20 to 15. In 1886 a law was passed taking the authority for decisions out of the hands of the two opposing captains, delegating it instead equally between the referee and the umpires. Then three years later the umpiring system was abolished in favour of Touch Judges, and finally in 1893 the Referee was entrusted with complete control of the game, and at the same time allowed to utilise his discretion in respect of infringements that might be calculated to benefit the non-offending team; thus was conceived the modern "Advantage Rule." Another major change which occurred at the "Broken Time" controversy (see BROKEN TIME) was the introduction of a stringent set of rules on the subject of professionalism.

The laws of the game of Rugby Football in their present form have emerged as the result of numerous changes and amendments dictated by the demands of new and constantly altering technique, and their framing is no longer the responsibility of the Rugby Union. Instead it has been assumed by the International Board (see INTERNATIONAL BOARD) which sprang into being in 1890 simply as the arbiter of disputes arising from International games, but which nowadays exerts the function internationally.

The laws of the game as they stand in 1976 are as follows:

## Law 1. Ground

*The field-of-play is the area as shown on the plan, bounded by, but not including, the goal lines and touch lines.*

*The playing enclosure is the field-of-play, In-goal and a reasonable area surrounding them.*

The **Plan**, including all words and figures thereon, is to take effect as part of these Laws.

The **Terms** appearing on the Plan are to bear their apparent meaning and to be deemed part of the definitions as if separately included.

(1) All lines shown on the plan must be suitably marked out. The touch lines are in touch. The goal lines are in In-goal. the dead-ball line is *not* in In-goal. The touch-in-goal lines and corner posts in touch-in-goal. The goal posts are to be erected in the goal lines.

(2) The game must be played on a ground of the area (maximum) shown on the plan and marked in accordance with the plan. The surface must be grass-covered or, where this is not available, clay or sand provided the surface is not of dangerous hardness.

(3) Any objection by the visiting team about the ground or the way in which it is marked out must be made to the referee before the first kick-off.

## Law 2. Ball

(1) The ball when new shall be oval in shape, of four panels and of the following description, as far as possible:-

Length in line    ..          280-290 mm.
Circumference (end on) 760-790 mm.
Circumference ..
(in width).. ..          610-650 mm.
Weight    ..    ..    380-430 grms.

(2) Balls may be specially treated to make them resistant to mud and easier to grip. The casings need not be of leather.

## Law 3. Number of Players

(1) A match shall be played by not more than fifteen players in each team.

(2) Replacement of players shall be allowed only in

(a) recognised trial matches when replacements are allowed as determined by the Unions having jurisdiction over the match, and

(b) matches in which a national representative team is playing, and for such competition and other domestic matches as a Union gives express permission, subject to the following conditions:-

not more than two players in each team may be replaced,

a player may be replaced *only* when, in the opinion of a medical practitioner, the player is so injured that he should not continue playing in the match,

a player who has been replaced must **not** resume playing in the match.

(3) Any objection by either team as regards the number of players in a team may be made to the referee at any time but the objection shall not affect any score previously obtained.

## Law 4. Players' Dress

(1) A player must not wear dangerous projections such as buckles or rings.

(2) Shoulder pads of the "harness" type must not be worn. If the referee is satisfied that a player requires protection following an injury to a shoulder, the wearing of a pad of cottonwool, sponge rubber or similar soft material may be permitted provided the pad is attached to the body or sewn on to the jersey.

(3) Studs of a player's boots must be of leather, rubber, aluminium or any approved plastic. They must be circular, securely fastened to the boots and of the following dimensions:-

| | |
|---|---|
| Maximum length (measured from sole) | 18 mm. |
| Minimum diameter at base | 13 mm. |
| Minimum diameter at top | 10 mm. |
| Minimum diameter of washer (if separate from stud) | 20 mm. |

(4) The referee has power to decide before or during the match that any part of a player's dress is dangerous. He must then order the player to remove the dangerous part and permit him to resume playing in the match only after it has been removed.

## Law 5. Toss, Time

*No-side is the end of a match.*

(1) Before a match begins the captains shall toss for the right to kick-off or the choice of ends.

(2) The duration of play in a match shall be such time not exceeding eighty minutes as shall be directed by the Union or, in the absence of such direction, as agreed upon by the teams or, if not agreed, as fixed by the referee. In International matches two periods of forty minutes each shall be played.

(3) Play shall be divided into two halves. At half-time the teams shall change ends and there shall be an interval of not more than five minutes.

(4) A period not exceeding two minutes shall be allowed for any other permitted delay. A longer period may be allowed only if the additional time is required for the removal of an injured player from the field-of-play.

Playing time lost as a result of any such permitted delay or of delay in taking a kick at goal shall be made up in that half of the match in which the delay occurred, subject to the power vested in the referee to declare no-side before the time has expired.

## Law 6. Referee and Touch Judges.
### A. Referee

(1) There shall be a referee for every

match. He shall be appointed by or under the authority of the Union, or, in case no such authorised referee has been appointed, a referee may be mutually agreed upon between the teams or, failing such agreement, he shall be appointed by the home team.

(2) If the referee is unable to officiate for the whole period of a match a replacement shall be appointed either in such manner as may be directed by the Union, or in the absence of such direction, by the referee or, if he is unable to do so, by the home team.

(3) The referee shall keep the time and the score, and he must in every match apply fairly the Laws of the Game without any variation or omission, except only when the Union has authorised the application of an experimental law approved by the International Board.

(4) He must not give any instruction or advice to either team prior to the match. During the match he must not consult with anyone except only

(a) either or both touch judges on a point of fact relevant to their functions, or

(b) in regard to time.

(5) The referee is the sole judge of fact and of law. All his decisions are binding on the players. When he has given a decision he cannot alter it except only a decision given before he observes that the touch judge's flag remains raised.

(6) The referee must carry a whistle and must blow it

(a) to indicate the beginning of the match, half-time, resumption of play after half time, no-side, a score or a touch-down, and

(b) to stop play because of infringement or otherwise as required by the Laws.

(7) During a match no person other than the players, the referee and the touch judges may be within the playing enclosure or the field-of-play unless with the permission of the referee which shall be given only for a special and temporary purpose.

(8) (a) All players must respect the authority of the referee and they must not dispute his decisions. They must (except in the case of a kick-off) stop playing at once when

the referee has blown his whistle.

(b) A player must when so requested whether before or during the match, allow the referee to inspect his dress.

(c) A player must not leave the playing enclosure without the referee's permission. If a player retires during a match because of injury or otherwise, he must not resume playing in that match until the referee has given him permission.

*Penalty: Infringement by a player is subject to penalty as misconduct.*

## B. Touch Judges

(1) There shall be two touch judges for every match. Unless touch judges have been appointed by or under the authority of the Union, it shall be the responsibility of each team to provide a touch judge.

(2) A touch judge is under the control of the referee who may instruct him as to his duties and may over-rule any of his decisions. The referee may request that an unsatisfactory touch judge be replaced and he has power to order off and report to the Union a touch judge who in his opinion is guilty of misconduct.

(3) Each touch judge shall carry a flag (or other suitable object) to signal his decisions. There shall be one touch judge on each side of the ground and he shall remain in touch except when judging a kick at goal.

(4) He must hold up his flag when the ball or a player carrying it has gone into touch and must indicate the place of throw in [as provided in Law 23B (2)] and which team is entitled to do so. He must also signal to the referee when the ball or a player carrying it has gone into touch-in-goal.

(5) The touch judge shall lower his flag when the ball has been thrown in except on the following occasions when he must keep it raised.

(a) when the player throwing in the ball puts any part of either foot in the field-of-play.

(b) When the ball has not been thrown in by the team entitled to do so.

It is for the referee to decide whether or not the ball has been thrown in from the correct place.

(6) When a kick at goal from a try,

free kick or penalty kick is being taken both touch judges must assist the referee by signalling the result of the kick. One touch judge shall stand at or behind each of the goal posts and shall raise his flag if the ball goes over the cross bar.

## Law 7. Mode of Play

A match is started by a kick-off, after which any player who is on-side may at any time

catch or pick up the ball and run with it,

pass, throw or knock the ball to another player,

kick or otherwise propel the ball,

Tackle, push or shoulder an opponent holding the ball,

fall on the ball,

take part in scrummage, ruck, maul or line-out,

provided he does so in accordance with these Laws.

## Law 8. Advantage

(1) The referee shall not whistle for an infringement during play which is followed by an advantage gained by the non-offending team. An advantage must be either territorial or such possession of the ball as constitutes an obvious tactical advantage. A mere opportunity to gain advantage is not sufficient.

(2) The **only** occasions when advantage does not apply are:-

when, at a kick-off, the ball is not kicked from the correct place or by the correct form of kick.

when the ball emerges from either end of the tunnel at a scrummage,

when at a drop-out the kick is taken otherwise than by a drop kick,

when a free kick is void,

when the ball or a player carrying it touches the referee.

## Law 9. Ball or Player Touching Referee

(1) If the ball or a player carrying it touches the referee in the field-of-play, play shall continue unless the referee considers either team has gained an advantage in which case he shall order a scrummage. The team which last played the ball shall put it in.

(2) (a) If the ball in a player's possession or a player carrying it touches the referee in that player's In-goal, a touch-down shall be

awarded.

(b) If a player carrying the ball in his opponents' In-goal touches the referee before grounding the ball, a try shall be awarded at that place.

## Law 10. Kick-Off

*Kick-off is (a) a place kick taken from the centre of the half-way line by a team which has the right to start the resumption of play after the half-time interval or by the defending team after a goal has been scored, or (b) a drop kick taken at or from behind the centre of the half-way line by the defending team after an unconverted try.*

(1) The ball must be kicked from the correct place; otherwise it shall be kicked off again.

(2) The ball must reach the opponent's ten metres line, unless first played by an opponent; otherwise it shall be kicked off again, or a scrummage formed at the centre, at the opponents' option. If it reaches the ten metres line and is then blown back, play shall continue.

(3) If the ball pitches in touch, touch-in-goal or over or on the dead-ball line, the opposing team may accept the kick, have the ball kicked off again, or have a scrummage formed at the centre.

(4) The **kicker's team** must be behind the ball when kicked; otherwise a scrummage shall be formed at the centre.

(5) The **opposing team** must stand on or behind the ten metres line. If they are in front of that line or if they charge before the ball has been kicked, it shall be kicked off again.

## Law 11. Method of Scoring

**Try.** A try is scored by first grounding the ball in the opponents' In-goal.

A try may be awarded if one would probably have been scored but for obstruction, foul play or misconduct by the opposing team.

**Goal.** A goal is scored by kicking the ball over the opponent's cross-bar and between the goal posts from the field-of-play by any place kick or drop kick, except a kick-off or drop-out, without touching the ground or any player of the kicker's team.

A goal is scored if the ball has crossed the bar, even though it may **have** been blown backwards afterwards,

and whether it has touched the cross-bar or either goal post or not.

A goal is scored if the ball has crossed the bar notwithstanding a prior offence of the opposing team.

A goal may be awarded if the ball is illegally touched by any player of the opposing team and if the referee considers that a goal would otherwise probably have been scored.

The scoring values are as follows:-

| | |
|---|---|
| A try .. .. .. .. | 4 points |
| A goal from a try (in which case the try shall not count) .. | 6 points |
| A goal from a free kick or penalty kick .. .. | 3 points |
| A dropped goal otherwise obtained .. .. .. | 3 points |

## Law 12. Try and Touch-Down

*Grounding the ball is the act of a player who*

*(a) while holding the ball in his hand (or hands) or arm (or arms) brings the ball in contact with the ground, or*

*(b) while the ball is on the ground either*

*places his hand (or hands) or arm (or arms) on it with downward pressure, or*

*falls upon it and the ball is anywhere under the front of his body from waist to neck inclusive.*

*Picking up the ball from the ground is not grounding it.*

### A. Try

(1) A player who is on-side scores a try when

he carries the ball into his opponents' In-goal, or

the ball is in his opponents' In-goal, and he first grounds it there.

(2) The scoring of a try includes the following cases:-

(a) if a player carries, passes, knocks or kicks the ball into his In-goal and an opponent first grounds it,

(b) if, at a scrummage or ruck, a team is pushed over its goal line and before the ball has emerged it is first grounded in In-goal by an attacking player,

(c) if the momentum of a player, when held in possession of the ball, carries him into his opponents' In-goal and he first there grounds the ball, even though it touched the ground in the field-of-play.

(d) if a player first grounds the ball his opponents' goal line or if the ball is in contact with the ground and a goal post.

(3) If a player grounds the ball in his opponents' In-goal and picks it up again, a try is scored where it was first grounded.

(4) A try may be scored by a player who is in touch or in touch-in-goal provided he is not carrying the ball.

## B. Penalty Try

A penalty try shall be awarded between the posts if but for obstruction, foul play or misconduct by the defending team

a try would probably have been scored, or

it would probably have been scored in a more favourable position than that where the ball was grounded.

## C. Touch-Down

(1) A touch-down occurs when a player first grounds the ball in his In-goal.

(2) After a touch-down, play shall be restarted either by a drop-out or a scrummage, as provided in Law 14.

## D. Scrummage after Grounding in Case of Doubt

Where there is doubt as to which team first grounded the ball in In-goal a scrummage shall be formed five yards from the goal line opposite the place where the ball was grounded. The attacking team shall put in the ball.

## Law 13. Kick at Goal After A Try

(1) After a try has been scored, the scoring team has the right to take a place kick or drop kick at goal, on a line through the place where the try was scored.

If the scoring team does not take the kick, play shall be restarted by a drop kick from the centre, unless time has expired.

(2) If a kick is taken:-

(a) It must be taken without undue delay;

(b) any player including the kicker may place the ball;

(c) The kicker's team, except the placer, must be behind the ball when kicked;

(d) if the kicker kicks the ball from a placer's hands without the ball being on the ground, the kick is void;

(e) the opposing team must be behind the goal line until the kicker begins his run or offers to kick when they may charge or jump with a view to preventing a goal.

Penalty: For an infringement by the kicker's team—the kick shall be disallowed.

For an infringement by the opposing team—the charge shall be disallowed. If, however, the kick has been taken successfully, the goal shall stand. If it was unsuccessful, the kicker may take another kick under the original conditions without the charge and may change the type of kick.

*Neither the kicker nor a placer shall wilfully do anything which may lead the opposing team to charge prematurely. If either does so, the charge shall not be disallowed.*

## Law 14. In-Goal

*In-goal is the area bounded by a goal-line, touch-in-goal lines and dead-ball line. It includes the goal line and goal posts but excludes touch-in-goal lines and dead-ball line.*

*Touch-in-goal occurs when the ball touches or crosses a touch-in line or when the ball, or a player carrying it, touches a corner post, a touch-in-goal line or the ground beyond it. The flag is not part of the corner post.*

## Five Metres Scrummage

(1) If a player carrying the ball in In-goal is so held that he cannot ground the ball, a scrummage shall be formed five metres line from the goal opposite the place where he was held.

The attacking team shall put in the ball.

(2) (a) If a defending player heels, kicks, carries, passes or knocks the ball over his goal line and it there becomes dead except where

a try is scored, or

he wilfully knocks or throws the ball from the field-of-play into touch-in-goal or over his dead-ball line, or

(b) if a defending player in In-goal has his kick charged down by an attacking player after.

he carried the ball back from the field-of-play, or

a defending player put it into In-goal and the ball is then touched down or goes into touch-in-goal or over the dead-ball-line, or

(c) if a defending player carrying the ball in the field-of-play is forced into his In-goal and he then touches down, or

(d) if, at a scrummage or ruck, a defending team is pushed over its goal line and before the ball has emerged first grounds it in In-goal, a scrummage shall be formed five metres from the goal line opposite the place where the ball or a player carrying it crossed the goal line.

The attacking team shall put in the ball.

### Drop-Out

(3) Except where a try or goal is scored, if an attacking player kicks, carries, passes or knocks the ball and it travels into his opponents' In-goal either directly or after having touched a defender who does not wilfully attempt to stop, catch or kick it, and it is there

grounded by a player of **either team**, or

goes into touch-in-goal or over the dead-ball line.

a drop-out shall be awarded.

### Penalties

(a) A penalty try shall be awarded when by obstruction, foul play or misconduct in In-goal the defending team has prevented a try which otherwise would probably have been scored.

(b) A try shall be disallowed and a drop-out awarded, if a try would **probably not** have been gained but for obstruction, foul play or misconduct by the attacking team.

(c) For obstruction, foul play or misconduct in In-goal while the ball is out of play the penalty kick shall be awarded at the place where play would otherwise have restarted and, in addition, the player shall either be ordered off or cautioned that he will be sent off if he repeats the offence.

(d) For wilfully charging or obstructing in In-goal a player who has just kicked the ball the penalty shall be,

a drop-out, or, at the option of the non-offending team,

a penalty kick where the ball

alights as provided for an infringement of Law 26 (2) (d).

(e) for other infringements in In-goal, the penalty shall be:-

for an offence by the **attacking team**— a drop-out,

for an offence by the **defending team**—a scrummage five metres from the goal line opposite the place of infringement.

## Law 15. Drop-Out

*A drop-out is a drop kick awarded to the defending team.*

(1) The drop kick must be taken from anywhere on or behind the twenty-two metres line; otherwise the ball shall be dropped out again.

(2) The ball must reach the twenty-two metres line; otherwise the opposing team may have it dropped out again, or have a scrummage formed at the centre of the twenty-two metres line. If it reaches the twenty-two metres line and is then blown back, play shall continue.

(3) If the ball pitches in touch, the opposing team may accept the kick, have the ball dropped out again, or have a scrummage formed at the centre of the twenty-two metres line.

(4) The kicker's team must be behind the ball when kicked; otherwise a scrummage shall be formed at the centre of the twenty-two metres line.

(5) The opposing team must not charge over the twenty-two metres line otherwise the ball shall be dropped out again.

## Law 16. Fair-Catch (Mark) and Free Kick.

*(a) A player makes a fair-catch when being stationary he cleanly catches the ball direct from a kick, knock-on or throw-forward by one of his opponents and at the same time he exclaims, "Mark!" and has both feet on the ground.*

*A fair-catch may be obtained even though the ball on its way touches or rebounds from a goal post or crossbar and can be made in In-goal.*

*(b) A free kick is a kick-allowed for a fair-catch. It may be taken by a place kick, drop kick or punt.*

(1) The kick must be taken by the player making the fair-catch, unless he is injured in doing so. If he is unable to take the kick within two minutes a

scrummage shall be formed at the mark. His team shall put in the ball.

(2) The kick must be taken without delay.

(3) The kick must be taken behind the mark, on a line through the mark. The ball must reach a line through the mark parallel to the goal lines, unless first played by an opponent. If the mark is in In-goal, it shall be deemed to be on the goal line and the ball must cross that line unless first played by an opponent.

(4) If the kicker has indicated to the referee that he intends to attempt a kick at goal or has taken any action indicating such intention, he must not kick the ball in any other way. Any indication of intention is irrevocable.

(5) The **kicker's team,** except the placer for a place kick, must be behind the ball when kicked and may follow up.

(6) If a place kick is taken:-
the ball must not be handled by the kicker after it has been placed on the ground,
The kick is void if the ball is kicked from the placer's hands without it being on the ground.

(7) The **opposing team** may come up to, but not beyond, a line through the mark parallel to the goal lines, and may charge subject to the following conditions:-
in the case of a place kick, as soon as the ball has been placed on the ground,
in the case of a drop kick or punt, as soon as the kicker begins his run or offers to kick.
If having charged fairly, players of the opposing team prevent the kick from being taken, it is void.
Penalty:-
For a void kick or an infringement by the **kicker's team**—a scrummage at the mark and the **opposing team** shall put in the ball.
If the mark is in In-goal, the scrummage shall be awarded five yards from the goal line on a line through the mark.
For infringements by the **opposing team**—the charge shall be disallowed. If, however, the kick has been taken successfully, the goal shall stand. If it was unsuccessful, the kicker may take another kick under the original con-

ditions without the charge and may change the type of kick.

*Neither the kicker nor a placer shall wilfully do anything which may lead the opposing team to charge prematurely. If either does so, the charge shall not be disallowed.*

## Law 17. Knock-On or Throw-Forward

*A knock-on occurs when a player propels the ball with his hand or arm in the direction of his opponents' dead-ball line or when the ball after striking the hand or arm of a player travels in that direction.*

*A throw-forward occurs when a player carrying the ball throws or passes it in the direction of his opponents' dead-ball line. A throw-in from touch is not a throw-forward. If the ball is not thrown or passed forward but it bounces forward after hitting a player or the ground, it is not a throw-forward.*

(1) The knock-on or throw-forward must not be **intentional.**
**Penalty:-**Penalty kick at the place of infringement.

(2) If the knock-on or throw-forward is unintentional, a scrummage shall be formed either at the place of infringement or, if it occurs at a line-out, fifteen yards from the touch line along the line-of-touch unless:-
a fair-catch has been allowed, or
The ball is knocked on by a player who is in the act of charging down the kick of an opponent but is not attempting to catch the ball, or
the ball is knocked on one or more times by a player who is in the act of catching or picking it up and is recovered by that player before it has touched the ground or another player.

## Law 18. Tackle

A tackle occurs when a player carrying the ball in the field-of-play is held by one or more opponents so that while he is so held
The ball touches the ground, or
if he is on his feet he is unable to free himself without delay and he cannot play the ball except by releasing it.
A maul ends a tackle.
(1) A tackled player, if lying on the ground, must release the ball immediately

without **playing it in any other way** and get up or move away from it. He must not play or interfere with the ball in any way until he has got upon his feet.

(2) When a player is tackled but not brought to the ground, he must **immediately** release the ball. Another player may play the ball before it has touched the ground.

An opponent may snatch the ball from the hands of the tackled player but a prolonged struggle between the two players is not permissible.

(3) It is illegal for any player:-
to prevent a tackled player from releasing the ball, or getting up after he has released it, or
to attempt to pick up the ball before a tackled player lying on the ground has released it or to pull the ball from that player's possession.
while lying on the ground after a tackle to play or interfere with the ball in any way. Nevertheless while still lying on the ground any player may tackle or attempt to tackle an opponent carrying the ball,
**Penalty:-** Penalty kick at the place of infringement.

(4) If a player carrying the ball is thrown or knocked over but not tackled, he may pass the ball or get up and continue his run even though the ball has touched the ground.

(5) A try may be scored if the momentum of a player carries him into his opponents' In-goal even though he is held.

## Law 19. Lying On Or Near the Ball

A player who is lying on the ground and
(a) is holding the ball, or
(b) is preventing an opponent from gaining possession of it, or
(c) has fallen on or over the ball emerging from a scrummage or ruck,
must **immediately** play the ball or get up or roll away from it.
**Penalty:-** Penalty kick at the place of infringement.

## Law 20. Scrummage

*A scrummage, which can take place only in the field-of-play, is formed by players from each team closing up in readiness to allow the ball to be put on the ground between them.*

*The middle player in each front row*

*is the hooker, and the players on either side of him are the props.*

*The middle line means an imaginary line on the ground directly beneath the line formed by the junction of the shoulders of the two front rows.*

### Forming a Scrummage

(1) A team must not wilfully delay the forming of a scrummage.

(2) Every scrummage shall be formed at the place of infringement or as near thereto as is practicable within the field-of-play. It must be stationary with the middle line parallel to the goal lines until the ball has been put in.

(3) It is dangerous play for a front row to form down some distance from its opponents and rush against them.

(4) Each front row of a scrummage shall have three players in it **at all times**. Subject to this, any number of players may form a scrummage. The head of a player in a front row shall not be next to the head of a player of the same team.

(5) While a scrummage is forming and is taking place, all players in each front row must adopt a normal stance. Both feet must be on the ground, must not be crossed and must be in the position for an effective forward shove.

### Binding of Players

(6) (a) The players of each front row shall bind firmly and continuously while the ball is being put in and while it is in the scrummage.

(b) The hooker may bind either over or under the arms of his props, but in either case, he must bind firmly around their bodies at or below the level of the armpits. The props must bind the hooker similarly. The hooker must not be supported so that he is not carrying any weight on either foot.

(c) The outside arm of the near prop of the team putting in the ball shall be inside that of the near prop of the opposing team.

(d) All players in a scrummage, other than those in a front row, must bind with at least one arm and hand around the body of another player of the same team.

(e) Any outside player may hold an opponent with his outer arm but only to keep himself and the scrummage steady. He must not push or pull an opponent or his dress.

## Putting the Ball into the Scrummage

(7) The team not responsible for the stoppage of play shall put in the ball. In the event of doubts as to responsibility the ball shall be put in by the team which was moving forward prior to the stoppage or, if neither team was moving forward, by the defending team.

(8) The ball shall be put in without delay as soon as the two front rows have closed together. A team must put in the ball when ordered to do so and on the side first chosen.

(9) The player putting in the ball shall

(a) stand one metre from the scrummage and midway between the two front rows;

(b) hold the ball with both hands midway between the two front rows at a level midway between his knee and ankle;

(c) from that position put in the ball without any delay or without feint or backward movement, i.e. with a single forward movement, and

at a quick speed straight along the middle line so that it first touches the ground immediately beyond the width of the nearer prop's shoulders.

(10) If the ball is put in and it comes out at either end of the tunnel, it shall be put in again, unless a penalty kick has been awarded.

If the ball comes out otherwise than at either end of the tunnel and if a penalty kick has not been awarded play shall proceed.

## Restrictions on Front Row Players

(11) All front row players must place their feet so as to allow a clear tunnel. A player must not prevent the ball from being put into the scrummage, or from touching the ground at the required place.

(12) No front row player may raise or advance a foot until the ball has touched the ground.

(13) When the ball has touched the ground, any foot of any player in either front row may be used in an attempt to gain possession of the ball subject to the following:-

Players in the front rows must not at any time during the scrummage:-

(a) raise both feet off the ground at the same time, or

(b) wilfully adopt any position or wilfully take any action, by twisting or lowering the body or otherwise, which is likely to cause the scrummage to collapse, or

(c) Wilfully kick the ball out of the tunnel in the direction from which it is put in.

## Restrictions on Players

(14) Any player who is not in either front row must not play the ball while it is in the tunnel.

(15) A player must not:-

(a) return the ball into the scrummage, or

(b) handle the ball in the scrummage except in the act of obtaining a "push-over" try or touch-down, or

(c) pick up the ball in the scrummage by hands or legs, or

(d) wilfully collapse the scrummage, or

(e) wilfully fall or kneel in the scrummage.

(16) The player putting in the ball and his immediate opponent must not kick the ball while it is in the scrummage.

Penalty:- Penalty kick at the place of infringement.

*For Off-side at Scrummage see Law 24 B.*

## Law 21. Ruck

*A ruck, which can take place only in the field-of-play, is formed when the ball is on the ground and one or more players from each team are on their feet and in physical contact, closing around the ball between them.*

(1) A player joining a ruck must bind with at least one arm around the body of a player of his team in the ruck.

(2) A player must not:-

(a) return the ball into the ruck, or

(b) handle the ball in the ruck except in the act of securing a try or touch-down, or

(c) pick up the ball in the ruck by hands or legs, or

(d) wilfully collapse the ruck, or

(e) jump on top of other players in the ruck, or

(f) wilfully fall or kneel in the ruck, or

(g) while lying on the ground interfere in any way with the ball in or emerging from the ruck. He must do his best to roll away from it.

**Penalty:-** Penalty kick at the place of infringement.

*For Off-side Ruck see Law 24C.*

## Law 22. Maul

*A maul, which can take place only in the field-of-play, is formed by one or more players from each team on their feet and in physical contact closing round a player who is carrying the ball.*

*A maul ends when the ball is on the ground or the ball or a player carrying it emerges from the maul or when a scrummage is ordered.*

*A maul ends a tackle.*

(1) A player is not in physical contact unless he is caught in or bound to the maul and not merely alongside it.

(2) A player must not jump on top of other players in the maul.

(3) When the ball in a maul becomes unplayable a scrummage shall be ordered and the team which was moving forward immediately prior to the stoppage shall put in the ball, or if neither team was moving forward, the defending team shall put it in.

**Penalty:-** Penalty kick at the place of infringement.

*For Off-side Maul see Law 24D.*

## Law 23. Touch and Line-Out

### A. Touch

(1) The ball is in touch

When it is not being carried by a player and it touches or crosses a touch line, or

when it is being carried by a player and it or the player carrying it touches a touch line or the ground beyond it.

### Exceptions:-

If a player in the field-of-play catches the ball immediately after it has crossed the touch line it is not in touch provided the player does not go into touch.

(2) If the ball crosses a touch line and then comes back it is in touch at the place where it first crossed the line.

(3) If the ball is not in touch a player who is in touch may kick the ball or propel it with his hand but not hold it.

### B. Line-Out

*The line-of-touch is an imaginary line in the field of play at right angles to the touch line through the place where the ball is to be thrown in.*

### Formation of a Line-Out

(1) A line-out is formed by at least two players from each team lining up in single lines parallel to the line-of-touch in readiness for the ball to be thrown in between them. Players who so line up are those "in the line-out", unless excluded below.

(2) Each player in the line-out must stand at least one metre from the next player of his team in the line-out.

(3) The line-out stretches from five metres from the touch line from which the ball is being thrown in to the position at the time the line-out begins of the furthest player in the line-out of the team throwing in the ball, but the furthest player must not be more than fifteen metres from that touch line.

(4) Any player of either team who is further from the touch line than the position of the "furthest player" when the line-out begins is NOT in the line-out.

(5) A "furthest player" who fails to line up within a reasonable distance from the next player of his team in the line-out is not in the line-out unless the ball is thrown to him directly.

(6) A clear space of 500 millimetres must be left between the two lines of players.

### Throwing in the Ball

(7) When the ball is in touch the place at which it must be thrown in is as follows:-

when the ball goes into touch from a penalty kick, or from a kick within twenty-two metres of the kicker's goal line, at the place where the ball went into touch, or

when the ball pitches directly into touch after having been kicked otherwise than as stated above, opposite the place from which the ball was kicked or at the place where it went into touch if that place be nearer to the kicker's goal line, or

on all other occasions when the ball is in touch, at the place where the ball went into touch.

(8) The ball must be thrown in at the line-out by an opponent of the player whom it last touched, or by whom it was carried, before being in touch. In the

event of doubt as to which team should throw in the ball, the defending team shall do so.

(9) The player must throw in the ball at the place indicated and straight along the line-of-touch, and

so that it touches the ground or touches or is touched by a player at least five metres from the touch line, and

while throwing in the ball, he must not put any part of either foot in the field-of-play.

If any of the foregoing is infringed, the opposing team shall have the right, as its option, to throw in the ball or to take a scrummage.

If on the second occasion the ball is not thrown in correctly a scrummage shall be formed and the ball shall be put in by the team which threw it in on the first occasion.

(10) A quick throw in from touch without waiting for the lines of players to form up is permissible provided the ball that went into touch is used, it has been handled only by the players and it is thrown in correctly.

## Beginning and End of Line-Out

(11) The line-out begins when the ball leaves the hands of the player throwing it in.

(12) The line-out ends when

a ruck or maul is taking place and all feet of players in the ruck or maul have moved beyond the line-of-touch, or

a player carrying the ball leaves the line-out, or

the ball has been passed, knocked back or kicked from the line-out, or

the ball is thrown beyond the furthest player, or

the ball becomes unplayable.

## Peeling Off

*"Peeling off" occurs when a player (or players) moves from his position in the line-out for the purpose of catching the ball when it has been passed or knocked back by another of his team in the line-out.*

(13) When the ball is in touch players who approach the line-of-touch must always be presumed to do so for the purpose of forming a line-out. Except in a peeling off movement such players must not leave the line-of-touch, or the

line-out when formed, until the line-out has ended.

## Exceptions

(i) At a quick throw-in, when a player may come to the line-of-touch and retire from that position without penalty.

(ii) When the team throwing in the ball line-up less than the normal number of players, opposing players in excess of the reduced number may retire without penalty, provided they do so without delay and to their own off-side line as defined at the head of Law 24 E.

(14) A player must not begin to peel off until the ball has left the hands of the player throwing it in. He must move parallel and close to the line-out. He must keep moving until a ruck or maul is formed and he joins it or the line-out ends.

## Restrictions on Players in Line-Out

(15) Before the ball has been thrown in and has touched the ground or has touched or been touched by a player, any player in the line-out must not

(a) be off side, or

(b) push, charge, shoulder or bind with or in any way hold another player of **either** team, or

(c) use any other player as a support to enable him to jump for the ball, or

(d) stand within five metres of the touch line or prevent the ball from being thrown five metres.

(16) **After** the ball has touched the ground or touched or been touched by a player, any player in the line-out must not

(a) be off-side, or

(b) hold, push, shoulder or obstruct an opponent not holding the ball, or

(c) charge an opponent except in an attempt to tackle him or to play the ball,

(17) Except when jumping for the ball or peeling off, each player in the line-out must remain at least one yard from the next player of his team until the ball has touched or has been touched by a player or has touched the ground.

(18) Except when jumping for the ball or peeling off, a clear space of 500 millimetres must be left between the two lines of players until the ball has touched or has been touched by a player or has

touched the ground.

(19) A player in the line-out may move into the space between the touch line and the five yards mark only when the ball has been thrown beyond him and, if he does so, he must not move towards his goal line before the line-out ends, except in a peeling off movement.

(20) Until the line-out ends, no player may be or move beyond the position of the furthest player when the line-out begins except as allowed when the ball is thrown beyond that position, in accordance with the Exception Law 24E (1) (d). If the furthest player moves towards the touch line after the ball has been thrown in, other players in the line-out are not required to follow him in order to remain on-side.

## Restrictions on Players Not in the Line-Out

(21) Players of either team who are not in the line-out may not advance from behind the line-out and take the ball from the throw-in except only

a player at a quick throw-in, or

a player advancing at a long throw-in, or

a player "participating in the line-out" (as defined in Section E of Law 24) who may run into a gap in the line-out and take the ball provided he does not charge or obstruct any player in the line-out.

Penalty:- (a) For an infringement of paragraphs 3, 4, 5, 13, 14, 19, 20 or 21 a penalty kick on the offending team's off-side line (as defined in Law 24 E) opposite the place of infringement, but not less than fifteen metres from the touch line.

(b) For an infringement of paragraphs 1, 2, 6, 15, 16, 17 or 18 or any wilful infringement of any other provision of the Law, a penalty kick fifteen metres from the touch line along the line-of-touch.

Place of scrummage:-Any scrummage taken or ordered under this Law or as the result of any infringement in a line-out shall be formed fifteen metres from the touch line along the line-of-touch.

*For off-side at Line-out see Law 24 E.*

## Law 24. Off-side

*Off-side means that a player is in a position in which he is out of the game and is liable to penalty.*

In general play *the player is in an off-side position because he is in front of the ball when it has been last played by another player of his team.*

*In play at* scrummage, ruck, maul *or* line-out *the player is off-side because he remains or advances in front of the line or place stated in, or otherwise infringes, the relevent rections of this Law.*

## A. Off-Side in General Play

(1) A player is in an off-side position if the ball has been

kicked, or

touched, or

is being carried

by one of his team behind him.

(2) There is no penalty for being in an off-side position unless:-

(a) the player plays the ball or obstructs an opponent, or

(b) he approaches or remains within ten metres of an opponent waiting to play the ball.

Where no opponent is waiting to play the ball but one arrives as the ball pitches, a player in an off-side position must not obstruct or interfere with him.

## Exceptions

(a) When an off-side player cannot avoid being touched by the ball or by a player carrying it, he is "accidentally off-side". Play should be allowed to continue unless the infringing team obtains an advantage in which case a scrummage should be formed at that place.

(b) A player who receives an unintentional throw-forward is not off-side.

(c) If, because of the speed of the game, an off-side player finds himself unavoidably within ten metres of an opponent waiting to play the ball, he shall not be penalised provided he retires without delay and without interfering with the opponent.

Penalty:- Penalty kick at the place of infringement, or, at the option of the non-offending team, a scrummage at the place where the ball was last played by the offending team. If the latter place is In-goal, the scrummage shall be formed five metres from the goal line on a line through the place.

## B. Off-Side at Scrummage

*The term "off-side line" means a line parallel to the goal lines through the hindmost foot of the player's team in the scrummage.*

While a scrummage is forming or is taking place:

(1) A player is off-side if

(a) he joins it from his opponents' side, or,

(b) he not being in the scrummage nor the player of either team who puts the ball in the scrummage.

fails to retire behind the off-side line or to his goal line whichever is the nearer, or

places either foot in front of the off-side line while the ball is in the scrummage.

A player behind the ball may leave a scrummage provided he retires immediately behind the off-side line.

If he wishes to rejoin the scrummage, he must do so behind the ball.

He may not play the ball as it emerges between the feet of his front row if he is in front of the off-side line.

Exceptions:- The restrictions on leaving the scrummage in front of the off-side line do not apply to a player taking part in "wheeling" a scrummage.

(2) A player is off-side if he, being a player of either team who puts the ball in the scrummage, remains or places either foot, in front of the ball while it is in the scrummage, or if he is the immediate opponent of the player putting in the ball, takes up position on the opposite side of the scrummage in front of the off-side line.

Penalty:- Penalty kick at the place of infringement.

## C. Off-Side at Ruck

*The term "off-side line" means a line parallel to the goal lines through the hindmost foot of the player's team in the ruck.*

### (1) Ruck otherwise than a line-out

While a ruck is taking place, a player is off-side if he:-

(a) joins it from his opponents' side, or

(b) joins it if in front of the ball, or

(c) does not join the ruck but fails to retire behind the off-side line without delay, or

(d) advances beyond the off-side line

with either foot and does not join the ruck, or

(e) unbinds from the ruck and does not immediately either rejoin it behind the ball or retire behind the off-side line.

Penalty:- Penalty kick at the place of infringement.

### (2) Ruck at line-out

*The term "participating in the line-out" has the same meaning as in Section E of this Law. A player participating in the line-out is not obliged to join or remain in the ruck and if he is not in the line-out until it has ended.*

While a line-out is in progress and a ruck takes place, a player is off-side if he:

(a) joins the ruck from his opponents' side, or

(b) joins it in front of the ball, or

(c) being a player who is participating in the line-out and is not in the ruck, does not retire to and remain at the off-side line defined in this Section, or

Penalty:- Penalty kick fifteen metres from the touch line along the line of touch.

(d) being a player who is not participating in the line-out, remains or advances with either foot in front of the off-side line defined in Section E of this Law.

Penalty:- Penalty kick on the offending team's off-side line (as defined in Section E of this Law) opposite the place of infringement, but not less than fifteen metres from the touch line.

## D. Off-side at Maul

*The term "off-side line" means a line parallel to the goal lines through the hindmost foot of the player's team in the maul.*

### (1) Maul otherwise than at line-out

While a maul is taking place (including a maul which continues after a line-out has ended), a player is off-side if he:-

(a) joins it from his opponents' side,

(b) joins it in front of the ball, or

(c) does not join the maul but fails to retire behind the off-side line without delay, or

(d) advances beyond the off-side

line with either foot and does not join the maul, or

(e) leaves the maul and does not **immediately** either rejoin it behind the ball or retire behind the off-side line.

Penalty:- Penalty kick at the place of infringement.

## (2) Maul at line-out

*The term "participating in the line-out" has the same meaning as in Section E of this Law. A player participating in the line-out is not obliged to join or remain in the maul and if he is not in the maul he continues to participate in the line-out until it had ended.*

While a line-out is in progress and a maul takes place, a player is off-side of:-

(a) joins the maul from his opponents' side, or

(b) joins it in front of the ball, or

(c) being a player who is participating in the line-out and is not in the maul, does not retire to and remain at the off-side line defined in this Section, or

Penalty:- Penalty kick fifteen metres from the touch line along the line of touch.

(d) being a player who is not participating in the line-out, remains or advances with either foot in front of the off-side line defined in Section E of this Law.

Penalty:- Penalty kick on the offending team's off-side line (as defined in Section E of this Law) opposite the place of infringement, but not less than fifteen metres from the touch line.

## E. Off-side at line-out

*The term "participating in the line-out" refers exclusively to the following players:-*

*those players who are in the line-out, and*

*the player who throws in the ball, and*

*his immediate opponent who may have the option of throwing in the ball, and*

*one other player of either team who takes up position to receive the ball if it is passed or knocked back from the line-out.*

*All other players are not participating in the line-out.*

*The term "off-side line" means a line*

*ten metres behind the line-of-touch and parallel to the goal lines, or if the goal line be nearer than ten metres to the line-of-touch, the "off-side line" is the goal line.*

## Off-side while participating in line-out

(1) A participating player is off-side if:-

(a) **before** the ball has touched a player or the ground he wilfully remains or advances with either foot in front of the line-of-touch, unless he advances solely in the act of jumping for the ball, or

(b) **after** the ball has touched a player or the ground, if he is not carrying the ball, he advances with either foot in front of the ball, unless he is lawfully tackling or attempting to tackle an opponent who is participating in the line-out. Such tackle or attempt to tackle must, however, start from his side of the ball, or

Penalty:- Penalty kick fifteen metres from the touch line along the line-of-touch.

(c) in a peeling off movement he fails to keep moving close to the line-out until a ruck or maul is formed and he joins it, or the line-out ends, or

(d) before the line-out ends he moves beyond the position of the furthest player.

Exception: Players of the team throwing in the ball may move beyond the position of the furthest player for a long throw-in to them. They may do so only when the ball leaves the hands of the player throwing it in and if they do so their opponents participating in the line-out may follow them. If players so move and the ball is not thrown to or beyond them they must be penalised for off-side.

(2) The player throwing in the ball and his immediate opponent must:-

(a) remain within five metres of the touch line, or

(b) retire to the off-side line, or

(c) join the line-out after the ball has been thrown in five metres, or

(d) move into position to receive the ball if it is passed or knocked back from the line-out provided no other player is occupying that position at that line-out.

## Off-side while not participating in line-out

(3) A player who is not participating is off-side if before the line-out has ended he advanced or remains with either foot in front of the off-side line.

Exception:- Players of the team throwing in the ball who are not participating in the line-out may advance for a long throw-in to them beyond the line-out. They may do so only when the ball leaves the hand of the player throwing the ball in and, if they do, their opponents may advance to meet them. If players so advance for a long throw-in to them and the ball is not thrown to them they must be penalised for off-side.

## Players returning to "on-side" position

(4) A player is not obliged, before throwing in the ball, to wait until players of his team have returned to or behind the line-out but such players are off-side unless they return to an off-side position without delay.

Penalty:- Penalty kick on the offending team's off-side line opposite the place of infringement, but not less than fifteen metres from the touch line.

## Law 25. On-Side

*On-side means that a player is in the Game and not liable to penalty for off-side.*

### Player made on-side by action of his team

(1) Any player who is off-side in general play, including an off-side player who is within ten metres of an opponent waiting to play the ball and is retiring as required, becomes on-side as a result of any of the following actions of his team:-

when the off-side player has retired behind the player of his team who last kicked, touched or carried the ball, or

when one of his team carrying the ball has run in front of him, or

when one of his team has run in front of him after coming from the place or from behind the place where the ball was kicked.

In order to put the off-side player on-side, this, other player must be in the field-of-play or in In-goal, but he is not debarred from following up in touch or touch-in-goal.

### Player made on-side by action of opposing team

(2) Any player who is off-side in general play, except an off-side player within ten metres of an opponent waiting to play the ball, becomes on-side as a result of any of the following actions:-

when an opponent carrying the ball has run five metres, or

when an opponent kicks or passes the ball, or

when an opponent intentionally touches the ball and does not catch or gather it.

An off-side player within ten metres of an opponent waiting to play the ball cannot be put on-side by any action of his opponents. Any other off-side player in general play is always put on-side when an opponent playes the ball.

### Player retiring at scrummage, ruck, maul or line-out

(3) A player who is in an off-side position when a scrummage, ruck, maul or line-out is forming or taking place and is retiring as required by Law 24 (Off-side) becomes on-side:-

when an opponent carrying the ball has run five metres, or

when an opponent has kicked the ball.

An off-side player in this situation is not put on-side when an opponent passes the ball.

## Law 26. Obstruction, Foul Play, Misconduct, Repeated Infringements.

### Obstruction

(1) It is illegal for any player:-

(a) who is running for the ball to charge or push an opponent also running for the ball, except shoulder to shoulder.

(b) who is in an off-side position another player of his team who is carrying the ball, thereby preventing an opponent from reaching the latter player.

(c) who is carrying the ball after it come out of a scrummage, ruck, maul or line-out to attempt to force his way through the players of his team in front of him.

(d) who is an outside player in a

scrummage or ruck to prevent an opponent from advancing round the scrummage or ruck.

(e) wilfully ro knock or throw the ball from the field-of-play into touch, touch-in-goal or over his dead-ball line.

(f) wilfully to waste time or wilfully to infringe any Law for which the penalty is a scrummage.

**Penalty:-** Penalty kick at the place of infringement. A penalty try may be awarded.

## Foul Play and Misconduct

(2) It is illegal for any player:-

(a) to strike an opponent,

(b) wilfully to hack or kick an opponent or trip him with the foot,

(c) to tackle early, or late or dangerously, including the action known as "stiff arm tackle",

(d) who is not running for the ball wilfully to charge or obstruct any opponent who has just kicked the ball,

(e) to hold, push, charge, obstruct or grasp an opponent not holding the ball except in a scrummage, ruck or maul.

*(Except in a scrummage or ruck the dragging away of a player lying close to the ball is permitted. Otherwise pulling any part of the clothing of an opponent is holding.)*

(f) in the front row of a scrummage to form down some distance from the opponents and rush against them,

(g) wilfully to cause a scrummage or ruck to collapse,

(h) while the ball is out of play to molest, obstruct or in any way interfere with an opponent or be guilty of any form of misconduct.

(i) to infringe repeatedly any Law of the Game.

**Penalty:-** A player guilty of foul play or misconduct shall either be ordered off or else cautioned that he will be sent off if he repeats the offence. For a similar offence after caution, the player must be sent off.

In addition to a caution or ordering off a penalty try or a penalty kick shall be awarded as follows:

(i) If the offence prevents a try which would otherwise **probably** have been scored, a penalty try shall be awarded.

(ii) The place for a penalty kick shall be:-

(a) For offences other than under paragraphs (d) and (h), at the place of infringement.

(b) For an infringement of (d) the non-offending team shall have the option of taking the kick at the place of infringement or where the ball alights, and if the ball alights in touch the mark is fifteen metres from the touch line on a line parallel to the goal lines through the place where it crossed the touch line, or

**within fifteen metres from the touch line, it is fifteen metres from the** touch line on a line parallel to the goal lines through the place where it alighted, or

**in In-goal, touch-in-goal, or over or on the dead-ball line,** it is five metres from the goal line on a line parallel to the touch line through the place where it crossed the goal line or fifteen metres from the touch line whichever is the greater.

(c) For an offence under (h), at any place where the ball would next have been brought into play if the offence had not occurred, or, if that place is on the touch line, fifteen metres from that place, on a line parallel to the goal lines.

(iii) **For an offence in In-goal,** a penalty kick is to be awarded **only** for offences under Law 14, Penalty (d) and Law 26 (2) (h).

For an offence under Law 26 (2) (h), the penalty kick is to be taken at whichever is the place where play would restart, that is

at the twenty-two metres line (at any point the non-offending team may select), or

at the centre of the half-way line, or if a scrummage five metres from the goal line would otherwise have been awarded, at that place or fifteen metres from the touch line on a line five metres from and parallel to the goal line, whichever is the greater.

## Player Ordered Off

A player who is ordered off shall take no further part in the match. When a player is ordered off, the referee shall, as soon as possible after the match, send to the Union or other disciplinary body having jurisdiction over the match a report naming the player and describing the circumstances which necessitated the ordering off.

## Law 27. Penalty Kick

*A penalty kick is a kick awarded to the non-offending team after an infringement of the Laws. It may be taken by any player of the non-offending team and by any form of kick provided that the kicker, if holding the ball, must propel it out of his hands or, if the ball is on the ground, he must propel it a visible distance from the mark. He may keep his hand on the ball while kicking it.*

(1) The non-offending team has the option of taking a scrummage at the mark and shall put in the ball.

(2) When a penalty kick is taken the following shall apply:-

(a) The kick must be taken without undue delay.

(b) The kick must be taken at or behind the mark on a line through the mark and the kicker may place the ball for a place kick. If the place prescribed by the Laws for the award of a penalty kick is within five metres of the opponents' goal line, the mark for the penalty kick or a scrummage taken instead of it shall be five metres from the goal line on a line through that place.

(c) The kicker may kick the ball in any direction and he may place the ball again, without any restriction except:-

if the kick is taken in In-goal, neither he nor his team may next play the ball until it has travelled beyond the goal line.

if the kicker has indicated to the referee that he intends to attempt a kick at goal or has taken any action indicating such intention, he must not kick the ball in any other way. Any indication of intention is irrevocable.

(d) the **kicker's team** except the placer for a place kick must be behind the ball until it has been kicked.

(e) The **opposing team** must run without delay (and continue to do so while the kick is being taken and while the ball is being played by the kicker's team) to or behind a line parallel to the goal lines and ten metres from the mark, or to their own goal line if nearer to the mark. They

must there remain motionless with their hands by their sides until the kick has been taken.

Retiring players will not be penalised if their failure to retire ten metres is due to the rapidity with which the kick has been taken, but they may not stop retiring and enter the game until an opponent carrying the ball has run five metres.

(f) The **opposing team** must not prevent the kick or interfere with the kicker in any way. This applies to action such as wilfully carrying, throwing or kicking the ball away out of reach of the kicker.

**Penalty:-** For an infringement by the kicker's team – a scrummage at the mark.

For an infringement by the **opposing team**–a penalty kick ten metres in front of the mark or five metres from the goal line whichever is the nearer, on a line through the mark. Any player of the non-offending team may take the kick.

## LEICESTER R.F.C.

Founded in 1880 Leicester have produced many players who have worn the English jersey with fame and distinction, amongst them that very fine scrumhalf B. C. Gadney who obtained 14 caps between 1932–38, A. L. Kewney, E. J. Jackett, D. A. Kendrew, A. M. Smallwood, F. D. Prentice (later Secretary of the Rugby Union), R. Stirling, and S. H. Penny who set up a record of individual appearances for both club and County by appearing in 246 consecutive matches for the former and in 52 for the latter. In all Penny played 500 times for the Leicester club, 68 times for the Midland Counties XV, and once for England against Australia in 1908. Perennially associated too with the Leicester club are the famous Beamish brothers of Ireland, C. E. and G. R. It was George Beamish in fact who led the combined Leicester and East Midlands XV to their wonderful 30–21 victory over the 1931 South African touring side, a match which was largely dominated by another Leicester player, Charles Slow, who dropped a goal and scored two tries from the outside half positions. During one period of their history Leicester experimented with the New Zealand game of "7 forwards, 8 backs." Ground:

Welford Road. Colours Red, white and green hooped jerseys and stockings, white shorts. Hon. Secretary: J. D. Day, 3 Woodland Avenue, Leicester, LE2 3HG.

## LLANELLI R.F.C.

Llanelli, on the scores of both antiquity and their accomplishments down the years, rank with the leading clubs in the game irrespective of nationality. They were the first team to defeat the 1908 Australian team in Great Britain, and the event was celebrated with the addition of a verse to the already famous Llanelli football anthem "Sospan Fach". They were the only Welsh club to beat the Maoris in 1926, but then followed a long spell without a victory over Touring teams before October 1972 when they beat the 7th All Blacks 9–3. In British club Rugby the power and ferocity of their forward play has made them something of a by-word, and their famous players are legion. None more famous, indeed legendary, than Albert Jenkins who was surely one of the most powerful and colourful centre threequarters who ever played the Rugby Union game. On one occasion against Ireland at Cardiff in 1928 Wales fielded no fewer than seven Llanelli players for, in addition to Jenkins who won 14 caps, were David and Arthur John, Iorwerth and Ivor Jones, Ernest Finch and A. Skym. Other great players to wear the club colours have been Lewis Jones afterwards described as "The Golden Boy" of Rugby League. R. H. Williams, who went on two tours with the British Lions, and outside half, Phil Bennett, who created a Welsh International record by scoring 36 points in 5 matches in 1973–74. Llanelli too enjoy a special distinction in that in the summer of 1957 they became the first British club to play in Russia. They travelled to Moscow to participate in the Rugby Football competition sponsored by the Moscow Youth Festival, and were runners-up to Rumania in the final of the competition. Ground: Stradey Park. Colours: Scarlet jerseys, white shorts, and scarlet stockings. Their nickname is "The Scarlets." Hon Secretary: K. Jones, Homestead, 6 Ael-y-Bryn Drive, Llanelli. Dyfed.

## LONDON SCOTTISH (WELSH AND IRISH)
See EXILE CLUBS).

## MAESTEG R.F.C.

Founded in 1882 and referred to as "The Old Parish", they have had a varied existence. In the beginning they were a power in Welsh Club Rugby, but their star waned, and the club eventually disappeared into the comparative obscurity of second class Rugby. Following the 1939–45 war, however, they returned in a blaze of real glory, and season 1949–50 saw them installed as "Unofficial Welsh Champions" (the first and, so far, only time since World War II) with an invincible record. The captain on that occasion was a sturdy scrumhalf Trevor Lloyd who later played for Wales besides making club history by accompanying a British Touring side to South Africa. Other International players produced by the club include C. Pugh, W. Major, T. L. Richards and D. Watts. Colours: Black and amber jerseys and stockings, black shorts. Ground: Lynfi Road, Maesteg. Hon Secretary: B. Dixon, 30 Princess Street, Maesteg, Glam.

## MALONE R.F.C.

Another strong Ulster Senior League combination which has produced many notable Irish International players since the clubs' formation in 1892. Outstanding among them A. Tedford who gained 23 caps between 1902–08, Dr. Tom Smyth, who captained a British side in South Africa in 1910, and of more recent vintage that powerful second row forward J. E. Nelson, who made 16 appearances for Ireland, toured Australia and New Zealand in 1950, and who was a permanent fixture in Barbarian touring teams of the period. Colours: White jerseys, blue shorts, red stockings. Ground: Gibson Park Avenue, Cregagh, Belfast.

## MANAWATU RUGBY UNION

Founded 1886, founder member of New Zealand Rugby Union 1892, resigned and subsequently re-affiliated 1933. Headquarters, Palmerston North, Colours: Green with narrow white bands. Outstanding among the New Zealand Internationals produced by this Union was R. McC. McKenzie who toured the British Isles with the Third "All-Blacks".

## MANCHESTER R.F.C.

Formed in 1860, Manchester are the oldest club in the north of England. Indeed their history can be authentically traced to the year 1857, when a number of Old Rugbeians living in the town raised a side to play an "experimental match" with their counterparts in Liverpool, and the centenary of the event was marked in season 1957 with a special match between a combined Manchester and Liverpool XV, and the other antiquated combination Blackheath and Richmond. Three Manchester representatives A. S. Gibson, R. R. Osborne and H. J. C. Turner, were in the first ever England International XV which met Scotland in 1871, and since then more than 20 Manchester players have gained International honours. The best known of these perhaps are the three moderns, G. S. Conway, who was in the England pack against New Zealand in 1925, C. B. Holmes, who was an Olympic sprinter as well as an International threequarter, and T. A. Kemp, one of the finest kickers of a ball ever to occupy the stand-off half position in an England XV. Colours: Red and white hoops. Hon Secretary: A. S. Hanson, 1 Hazelbadge Road, Poynton, Stockport, Cheshire.

## MAORI

(See also NEW ZEALAND and TOURS).

Maori Rugby has existed side by side with that of New Zealand's as a whole from the beginning of the game's history in that country, and many famous players including the twin immortals George Nepia and J. B. Smith have played with distinction for New Zealand representative teams. More recently the outstanding Maori player has been S. M. Going, one of the finest scrumhalves in the world in the late sixties and early seventies. In 1922 the Maori Advisory Board was established to assist, as its title implies, the New Zealand Rugby Union in co-ordinating Maori Rugby football. In addition the Board administrated Rugby in its four affiliated districts viz.: Tai Hauuauru, Tai Tokerau, Tai Rawhiti, Te Waipounamu, and from 1928 these districts opposed each other annually in a competition for the Prince of Wales Cup. More recently however, the set-up has altered somewhat, and the districts are seldom referred to as such. Instead, since 1963, the Prince of Wales Cup has been competed for by sides representing Northern and Southern New Zealand Maoris. Famous administrators in the cause of Maori Rugby have been W. T. Parata, T. French, W. P. Barclay and P. Whaipooti.

## MARLBOROUGH RUGBY UNION

Founded 1888, founder member of New Zealand Rugby Union, 1892. Outstanding player, A. R. Sutherland, a determined lock who toured the British Isles with the Seventh All-Blacks and had one run of 124 consecutive games for the Union. Headquarters: Blenheim, South Island. Colours: Cardinal.

## MELROSE R.F.C.

Founded in 1877, when there was a split of the old Gala-Melrose club and the latter set up on their own on the Greenyards, Melrose began their history with a home victory over their greatest rivals — Hawick, and are acknowledged as one of the top three clubs in the Border tournament. The club also claims an important place in the game's history as the initiators of the first ever seven-a-side tournament staged at Greenyards in 1883. Indeed, this miniature form of rugby was "invented" by one of their players, Edward Hay. Famous internationals include former Scottish captain, Jim Telfer (25 caps), and hooker F. A. L. Laidlaw (32). Colours: Yellow and black. Ground: Greenyards, Melrose. Hon. Secretary: G. D. M. Brown, Kilmore, Douglas Road, Melrose.

## MID-CANTERBURY RUGBY UNION

Founded as Ashburton County 1904, affiliated to New Zealand Rugby Union 1927. Name changed to Mid-Canterbury, 1952. Headquarters: Ashburton, South Island. Colours: Emerald green and gold hoops. Full-back A. H. A. Smith played in over 100 games for the Union from 1957.

## MINI-RUGBY

A version of the game recently developed by the Welsh R.F.U. to encourage youngsters under 12 years of age. It is played by two teams of nine players (five backs and four forwards) across a pitch instead of lengthways, using the 22 metres line and the half-way line as touch-lines. The goals set on the touch-lines should have the bar at only 2.6 metres. There are no line-outs but when the ball goes into touch the game is restarted with a scrum 10 metres in-field. Generally the idea is to make rugby easy to learn.

## MOSELEY F.C.

The Moseley club, which has a history dating back to 1873, has both pioneered and sustained the Rugby code in a city (Birmingham) virtually dominated by the rival code of Association Football. That in itself has been a great achievement, as indeed have been several of the club's "against the odds" victories over Cardiff and other great British club sides. One of the best known of Moseley's England Internationals was that fine all round athlete Peter Cranmer, who gained 16 caps as a centre threequarter between 1934-38, in addition to captaining Warwickshire at cricket. More recently their sustained success has been due in no small part to the remarkable kicking of Sam Doble one of the most prolific points scorers of all time. Colours: Red and black hoops, navy shorts. Ground: The Reddings, Hon. Secretary: C. A. Smallwood, 26 Hartford Close, Harborne, Birmingham 17.

## NATAL

Of the really old established South African Unions, Natal (they were founded in 1890) have perhaps the least imposing record in Provincial Rugby, but the Union has nevertheless produced many fine teams and players. Perhaps the best known of all their "Springbok" representatives is the great forward P. J. Nel who captained South Africa in New Zealand and Australia in 1937, and who had also been a member of Osler's team in Britain six years earlier. Other Natal "Springboks" were W. C. Zeller, W. A. Clarkson, L. B. Seidle, A. P. Walker, P. J. Lyster, W. E. Bastard, C. J. de Nysschen and T. P. Bedford, vice-captain of their most recent tour of Britain. Union headquarters is at Durban. Colours: Black jersey with wide white band, white stockings. The club game in Natal as in all South African Provinces, is run on a competitive basis, and is administered by five sub Unions viz.: Durban, Maritzburg, Norther Districts, Southern Districts, and Zululand.

## NEATH R.F.C.

Founded in 1871, Neath have consistently been amongst the leading clubs of Britain. If they have a special claim to fame, then it lies in the traditional fire and power of their forward play, indeed it is rarely that a Welsh International pack fails to contain a Neath forward. Rhys Stephens (32 caps) and David Morris (34) are among the most capped Welsh forwards, while others who have upheld the club's reputation in this respect in International Rugby are, E. R. John (19), T. Arthur (18), and A. Lemon (13). The club colours, which incidentally earn them the title of the "Welsh All-Blacks," are black jerseys embossed with a white Maltese cross, black shorts, and black and white stockings. Ground: The Gnoll, Neath, which is also a venue for county cricket: Hon Secretary: A. Benjamin, 1 Ael-y-Bryn, School Road, Neath.

## NELSON-BAYS RUGBY UNION

Founded 1885 as Nelson, founder member of New Zealand Rugby Union 1892. The Union went through a bad patch in the sixties and amalgamated with Golden-Bay Motueka in 1969 as Nelson-Bays. Their outstanding player of recent years has been full-back T. J. Morris, capped three times against Australia in 1972. Headquarters Trafalgar Park, Nelson. Colours: Navy blue, and sky blue hoops.

## NEWBRIDGE R.F.C.

Founded as long ago as 1891, New-bridge remained a second class combination up until the outbreak of World War II, but during the war years its members revealed a quite remarkable tenacity in their efforts to keep the game going, and inevitably perhaps reaped the reward of their enterprise in the shape of a strong and cohesive combination with which to greet peacetime Rugby. Immediately they made their presence felt, and W. Gore became the first man to represent them in International football as a member of the Welsh pack in 1947. He was followed by those two superb forwards W. R. Cale, and D. J. Hayward whose efforts did so much towards Wales winning the Triple Crown in 1950. Newbridge were Welsh club champions in 1964-65. Colours: Blue jerseys, black shorts. Ground: Bridge Street, Newbridge. Hon. Secretary: B. Wellington, 11 Treowen Road, Newbridge, Gwent.

## NEWPORT R.F.C.

A name renowned throughout the world of Rugby Football, Newport, who were formed in 1874, are affiliated to both the Welsh and English Rugby Unions, and they have supplied them both with many famous players. Indeed the list of Newport players who have played International Rugby is a veritable cavalcade of Rugby greatness. The record Welsh International cap holder, K. J. Jones, played for the club throughout his career, and before him in the black and amber jersey have been such deathless names as B. V. Meredith (34 caps), B. Price (32), M. C. Thomas (27), A. J. Gould (27), George Travers (25), J. J. Hodges (23), George Boots (16), H. Uzzell (15) and C. M. Pritchard and J. C. Morely (14 apiece). All these played for Wales, whilst Reg Edwards, E.D.G. Hammett, and J.H. Hancock are among those who elected to play for England. The Newport team v Bristol in April 1921 was composed entirely of internationals. On six occasions the club have earned the rare distinction of going through a full club season undefeated, while their victory over the 1912 South African Touring team is still discussed amongst the truly famous achievements of Welsh Rugby. One of the most notable figures in British Rugby was Major T. H. Vile, a great half-back and strategist who played for Wales on eight occasions, toured New Zealand with a British team, and who when his playing days were over became one of the leading International referees, and finally assumed the Presidency of the Welsh Rugby Union. In recent years Newport have enjoyed remarkable success in the Welsh Sevens Competition, while in 1963–64 they were the only side to defeat the Fifth "All-Blacks". Colours: Black and amber jerseys and stockings, navy shorts. Ground: Rodney Parade. Hon. Secretary: R. T. Carter, 28 Firbank Crescent, Newport, Gwent.

## NEW SOUTH WALES
(See also AUSTRALIA).

A logical development of the original "Southern Rugby Union" which had been in existence since 1875, the New South Wales Union came officially into being as such in 1892, and despite intense competition from the rival Rugby League code has remained ever since, the one unassailable stronghold of the Union game in Australia. Obviously enough the game's main centre in the State is at Sydney where the Premier Competition, inaugurated in 1874, is the one that attracts most interest both from players and followers. The competition is a graded one, and since it was reorganised on a District as opposed to a Metropolitan basis in 1900, it has been largely dominated by the great combinations fielded down the years by the oldest of their clubs, Sydney University (founded 1864). The majority of New South Wales and Australian representative players have, of course, naturally enough, been drawn from the Sydney area, but in 1951 the establishment of a New South Wales Country Union ensured that both the game and its players outside the Metropolitan area are better catered for than was the case in the old days. A Sydney Rugby Union was formed in 1965 to further decentralise administration within the State.

Many times during the course of Australian Rugby history, New South Wales have taken over, sometimes (as instanced by the "Waratahs" tour of Britain and France) officially, the responsibility of representing Australia in International Rugby, and in most instances they have supplied redoubtable opposition to the visiting Touring teams. Indeed among the State's greatest exploits on the Rugby field is the overwhelming victory, on the rain soaked Sydney cricket ground, over the great South African team of 1937. The majority of Australia's leading capholders have worn the sky-blue jersey of the State, and they include: P. G. Johnson (42 caps), A. R. Miller (41), G. V. Davis, (39) J. E. Thornett (37), N. Shehadie (30), and K. W. Catchpole (27). All these men captained Australia, Thornett holding the record in this respect with 16 games.

## NEW ZEALAND
If New Zealand never sent another representative side abroad her greatness as a Rugby nation would still be universally recognised on the achievements of the two wonderful combinations which visited Great Britain in 1905 and 1924–Dave Gallaher's "Original All-Blacks," and G. G. Porter's "Invincibles." Superlatives apart, however, the standard of New Zealand Rugby both at home and in International Competition merits comparison with that exhibited by any other Rugby playing country, so that their representative side in their funeral black uniforms are both welcome and respected guests wherever they appear.

Rugby football was introduced into New Zealand in 1870 by Charles John Munroe who had learnt the game at Sherborne School in England. Munroe's sphere of influence was in and around the town of Nelson in the South Island, the club he was instrumental in forming there in 1871 is still in existence, as indeed is the Wellington club which was formed over on the North Island in the same year. The clubs met in the first season of their existence—the first recorded instance of an organised club match in New Zealand. Indeed the game's evolution in New Zealand was on similar lines to that which took place in Britain a decade earlier, for Football in the Islands varied in both laws and pattern with every locality, and indeed was probably best described as "a mixture of Association, Rugby and Australian rules." As in Britain standardisation of the rules was difficult to attain, but the die was ultimately cast in favour of Rugby when in 1876 three of the leading Provinces, Auckland, Canterbury, and Otago, adopted the laws as had been laid down by the Rugby Union in London at their meeting in 1871. This decision, together with the tremendous "propaganda" value of a tour of both Islands undertaken by Auckland in the same year undoubtedly hastened the development of the Rugby code in New Zealand. In 1879 came another important development, the formation of the Canterbury Rugby Union in the July of that year, followed in October by the establishment of a similar organisation at Wellington. Auckland followed suit in 1883. Hawke's Bay in 1884, and by 1890 New Zealand possessed no fewer than fifteen flourishing Unions responsible for the organisation of club football over a wide area. Obviously the time had now come for Rugby football to be directed at a national level, and this was achieved in 1892 with the formation of the New Zealand Rugby Union at Wellington, which city had remained its headquarters ever since. The Provincial Unions who acted as founder members of the parent body were: Auckland, Hawke's Bay, Manawatu, Marlborough, Nelson, South Canterbury, Taranaki, Wairarapa, Wanganui, Wellington, and West Coast.

Apart from visits to Australia the first major tour (see TOURS) undertaken by the newly-formed Union was that undertaken to Great Britain in 1905, and Dave Gallaher's "Original All-Blacks" have since passed into legend as one of the great touring teams of all time. Some of course have ascribed their success together with that of their successors, the 1924 "All-Blacks" to the "wing forward" (see TACTICS and EVOLUTION) which represented in its day as revolutionary an innovation as any in Rugby football history. It would however be much fairer, certainly more accurate, to ascribe New Zealand's mostly sustained success in world Rugby, to a natural aptitude for the game, the splendid physique of her forwards, and not the least to her unwavering adherence to the principles of backing up both in attack and defence. Indeed however inferior subsequent New Zealand touring sides in Great Britain, South Africa, and Australia may have appeared to be in comparison with the mighty combinations led by Gallaher and Porter their backing up of each other in every phase of the game, has remained the most conspicuous feature of their play.

As far as her participation in world Rugby is concerned, the history of New Zealand Rugby may be conveniently divided into four separate phases, viz.:

1903–1932—When with the application of the specialised "wing-forward formula," and the two man front row which allowed for it, her dominance in world Rugby was almost absolute.

1932–49—The period in which New Zealand having discarded the wing forward, adhered (with fitful success) to the principles in operation in Great Britain.

1949–1963—As a result of their disastrous experiences in South Africa—they leaned completely over to the 3–4–1 scrummage formation adopted by the South Africans, and inevitably perhaps towards the close, circumspect type of game that goes with it. They, however, earned an even greater reputation for forceful play forward. The backs were not reckoned to be as brilliant as some but the forwards were generally the most powerful in the world, and of course, it was during the later part of this period that they had fullback, D. B. Clarke, who could kick a goal from almost anywhere up to about 60 yards out.

1963—to the present—In this period the All-Blacks have completely forsaken the defensive type of Rugby which had been increasingly criticised and went over to 15-man attacking rugby amply illustrated by the Sixth All Blacks when they were undefeated on their 1967 tour of the British Isles and France. While the display of their pack in their 19—0 victory over Wales at Christchurch in 1969 has seldom been excelled.

At home of course, New Zealand Rugby is dominated by the Ranfurly Shield competition (see RANFURLY SHIELD) which was inaugurated in 1902, whilst another crowd-pulling event in their Rugby calendar is the annual Inter-Island match between North and South.

As old, indeed older, than the history of the New Zealand Rugby Union, is the tremendous influence exerted by its native population, the Maoris, who apart from the fact that thye have sent many fine touring teams overseas, have in addition provided New Zealand Rugby with some of its very greatest Internationals, including the famous George Nepia, doyen of International fullbacks. In 1922, in what has proved an altogether successful attempt to coordinate the organisation of Maoris Rugby, the Maori Advisory Board was formed at Wellington.

Their principal trophy is the Prince of Wales Cup competed for annually between representative teams from North and South New Zealand. Since 1949 they have also had the Tom French Cup awarded annually for the season's outstanding Maori player. Sid Going won this trophy six years in succession 1967—72.

## New Zealand's Record in International Rugby

*v. Great Britain.* Played 24. Won 17. Lost 4. Drawn 3.
Record victory. New Zealand 32, Great Britain 5, at Dunedin, 1908; also 29—0 at Auckland in the same year.
Record defeat. New Zealand 3, Great Britain 13, at Wellington 1971.
*v. Australia.* Played 64. Won 47. Lost 13. Drawn 4.
Record victory. New Zealand 38, Australia 3, at Auckland, 1972.
Record Defeat. New Zealand 5, Australia 20, at Wellington, 1964.
*v. South Africa.* Played 30. Won 12. Lost 16. Drawn 2.
Record Victory. New Zealand 20, South Africa 3, at Auckland, 1965.

Record Defeat. New Zealand, 0 South Africa 17, at Durban, 1928.
*v. England.* Played 10. Won 8. Lost 2. Drawn 0.
Record Victory. New Zealand 15. England 0, at Crystal Palace, 1905.
Record Defeat. New Zealand 0, England 13, at Twickenham, 1936.
*v. Wales.* Played 9. Won 6. Lost 3. Drawn 0.
Record Victory. New Zealand 33, Wales 12, at Auckland 1969.
Record Defeat. New Zealand 8, Wales 13, at Cardiff, 1953.
*v. Scotland.* Played 7. Won 6. Lost 0. Drawn 1.
Record Victory. New Zealand 24, Scotland 0, at Auckland, 1975.
*v. Ireland.* Played 7. Won 6. Lost 0. Drawn 1.
Record Victory. New Zealand 15, Ireland 0, at Dublin, 1905.
*v. France.* Played 12. Won 10. Lost 2. Drawn 0.
Record Victory. New Zealand 38, France 8, at Paris, 1905.
Record Defeat. New Zealand 6, France 13, at Paris, 1973.

*The following organisations are also affiliated to the Rugby Football Union of New Zealand.*

1. New Zealand Combined Services. Colours – Black.

2. Royal New Zealand Air Force. Colours—Dark blue with light blue and maroon hoops.

3. New Zealand Army. Colours—Maroon.

4. New Zealand Navy. Colours— Red, white and blue narrow bands.

5. Maori Advisory Board. Colours— Black.

6. New Zealand University. Colours— Black, white monogram.

7. New Zealand Railway Council.

## NORTHAMPTON R.F.C.

Founded in 1880, "The Saints," as they are universally called, have produced any number of great players to adorn the ranks of East Midland Counties and England representative sides. Among them A. F. Blakiston, who along with W. W. Wakefield and A. T. Voyce, formed the devastating England back row which virtually dominated the International scene during the middle twenties. Blakiston won 17 caps, but the Northampton club record in this respect is held by Ron Jacobs who was capped 29 times. Other famous Northampton Internationals include Eric Coley, T.W. Harries, E. R. Mobbs, H. T. Weston, W. H. Weston, R. J. Longland and Don White, whilst in R. G. Jeeps, C. R. Jacobs, J. Butterfield and L. B. Cannell, the club had no less than four representatives in the England XV which won the Triple Crown and International Championship in 1956–57. One Northampton player, the late Edgar Mobbs, who played seven times for England as a wing threequarter between 1909-10, has been immortalised by the staging of an annual encounter, "The Edgar Mobbs Memorial Match," between the Barbarians and an East Midlands Counties XV. Mobbs, who was a universally popular player and sportsman, lost his life (in the First World War) leading the Sportsmen's Battalion he himself had formed at the outbreak of war. Club colours: Black, green and gold jerseys, navy shorts. Ground: Franklyn Gardens, Hon. Secretary: R. Leslie, Meadowncroft, Tilbury Rise, East Haddon, Northampton, NN6 8BW.

## NORTH AUCKLAND RUGBY UNION

Founded 1920, affiliated to New Zealand Rugby Union the same year. Headquarters: Whangarei, North Island, Colours: Cambridge blue. Outstanding Internationals are S. M. Going, that great individualist who ranks among the worlds finest scrum-halves and has made 64 appearances for New Zealand (22 Internationals), P. F. H. Jones who made 37 papearances for New Zealand (11 Internationals) 1953-60, including British Isles tour 1953-54, and I. H. Finlayson, 36 appearances (6 Internationals) 1925-30).

## NORTHERN TRANSVAAL

Another off-shoot of the Transvaal Union, the Northern Transvaal Union was fromed as recently as 1937, even so their subsequent history has been a brilliant one, for they have gone from strength to strength in the Currie Cup Competition, first winning in 1946 and again in 1956, but thereafter gaining what is virtually a permanent hold on the trophy with five wins (one shared) in seven years 1968–74. It was Northern Transvaal too which produced two of the key players, the half backs Hannes Brewis and Fonny Du Toit, in the South African's successful tour of Britain and France in 1951, whilst another Union product, S. S. Viviers, captained his country in New Zealand and Australia in 1956. More recently another Northern Transvaal player, the great lock-forward Frik du Preez, became South Africa's record cap-holder with 38 internationals to his credit. The Union H.Q. is at Pretoria. Colours: Light blue jerseys, dark blue shorts.

## NORTH OF IRELAND R.F.C.

The North of Ireland R.F.C. founded in 1868 as the Rugby section of a Cricket club which had been in existence for eleven years, had three representatives in the first International team fielded by Ireland in 1875, and more than 70 have worn the Irish jersey in all. Competitors, and throughout their long history prominent ones, in the Ulster Senior League the N.I.F.C. have down the years been especially fortunate in that they have been able to enlist the services of so many of the great Queen's University players, Jack Kyle, G. V. Stephenson and Noel Henderson being cases in point. Jack Kyle one of Ireland's greatest fly-halfs, was the club record holder with 46 International appearances, before another of this club's world-class players, Mike Gibson, made his 47th appearance for Ireland in 1973. Ground: Shaftesbury Avenue, Belfast. Colours: Red, black and blue.

## NORTH OTAGO

Founded 1904, affiliated to New Zealand Rugby Union 1927. Headquarters: Centennial Park, Oamaru, South Island. Colours: Gold.

## NUMBERING OF PLAYERS

The first recorded instance of a Rugby Football match in which both teams were numbered was in 1897, when Queensland (Australia) met the visiting New Zealanders at Brisbane. A contemporary newspaper reported: "As an experiment to assist spectator's a number will be placed on each player's back." It was not however until season 1921-22, when England met Wales at Cardiff, that the numbering of players became an established practice in International matches, though Scotland for some time afterwards refused to come into line with the other Rugby-playing countries. At the present time all players in International Rugby are numbered, and the general custom, apart from touring teams who allot each player a permanent number throughout the tour regardless of which position he happens to be playing in, is to number the teams as follows: No 15—full-back. Nos. 11 and 14—wing threequarters; Nos. 12 and 13—centre threequarters; Nos. 9 and 10—half backs; Nos. 1, 2 and 3—front row forwards; Nos 6, 4, 5, and 7—second row forwards; No. 8, back row forward, this is in a 3—4—1—formation. Superstition, however, quite often rears its head even in Rugby Football, with the result that No. 13 is sometimes dispensed with, and No. 16 substituted.

## OLD BELVEDERE R.F.C.

Founded in 1930 by former pupils of the Jesuit College this well known Leinster club with the romantic name did not produce an Irish International player until 1947, but Irish followers in general will only be too ready to forgive them the omission for the Old Belvedere representative, K. D. (Karl) Mullen, proved himself one of the greatest leaders in history for under his captaincy Ireland won the Triple Crown in the successive winters of 1947-48 and 1948-49 – the first time they had done so since 1899. Mullen went on to win 25 consecutive caps, and alongside him in the Irish XV in those golden seasons were two other Old Belvedere players, B. T. and K. Quinn. Then in 1955 the club unearthed A. J. O'Reilly, a player of uncommon brilliance and personality. Indeed a single winter in International Rugby was sufficient to enable this strong and speedy threequarter to win a place in a British Isles team to tour South Africa, and as things turned out he was one of the outstanding successes of the tour. He subsequently brought his total of Internationals to 29, the last half-dozen while with Leicester, and only injury prevented him from adding to this figure. Ground: Anglesea Road, Ballsbridge, Dublin. Colours: Black and white hoops.

## OLD BOYS' CLUBS

There are nearly 200 Old Boys' Clubs affiliated to the Rugby Union alone and the most widely known in Great Britain are, in order of antiquity, as follows.

OLD PAULINES. Founded 1871, Colours: Red, white and black.

OLD BLUES. Founded 1873. Colours: Red, blue and gold.

OLD MILLHILLIANS. Founded 1878. Colours: Chocolate and white.

OLD MERCHANT TAYLORS. Founded 1882. Colours: White.

OLD BANCROFTIANS. Founded 1894. Colours: Royal blue, black, claret, light blue.

OLD ALLEYIANS. Founded 1898. Colours: Dark blue, light blue and black.

OLD WHITGIFTIANS. Founded 1901. Colours: Red, black and blue hoops.

OLD CRANLEIGHIANS. Founded 1919. Colours: Blue, orange and white.

OLD RUTLISHIANS. Founded 1923. Colours: Azure and gold.

The influence of the Old Boys' clubs in British club Rugby is no longer as powerful as it was in the early days of their existence, but with their bright venturesome football and traditional sporting outlook they remain an adornment to the scene. A particularly distinguished record in producing English International players is possessed by Old Merchant Taylors for headed by R. Cove-Smith, who gained 29 International caps and led a British team in South Africa, the club have produced several International players including the immortal J. E. Raphael, whose name was a by-word for grace and elusiveness during the early part of the century. Another Old Merchant Taylor to tour overseas was D.G.S. Baker, who as a full back and outside half, was a versatile and highly valued member of the British "Lions" in South Africa in 1955. The Old Millhillians too have produced some brilliant International players, none more brilliant possibly than the half back pair W. H. Sobey and R. S. Spong who, in addition to playing finely for England in Home Internationals during the thirties, were members of the team F. D. Prentice took to New Zealand in 1930. Other distinguished Old Millhillians were P. H. Howard who triumphed over an appalling leg injury to become one of the leading wing forwards of his era – the thirties, and J. E. Williams who has played at scrum-half for England, as well as for Great Britain in South Africa. Old Cranleighians too boast players of distinction in the persons of F. J. Reynolds, a South African tourist, and English Internationals R. L. S. Carr, A. Key and

M. A. McCanlis. The Old Alleyians' contribution to International Rugby came from K. J. Stark and E. C. P. Whiteley.

## OLDEST PLAYERS
See AGE.

## OLYMPIC GAMES

There are but four instances of Rugby Football being included in the list of Olympic Games events. In 1900 France, the host country won. In 1908 at the White City, London, the Rugby tournament was won by the first Australian "Wallabies" who were homeward bound from their winter's tour of Great Britain. Their opponents in only the one game played were the Cornwall County XV—Britain's representatives for the occasion, and the score was 32−3 in favour of the Australians. In 1920 at Antwerp the winners were the U.S.A. who beat France (really a Parisien XV) 14−5. Surprisingly enough the U.S.A., represented by the Stanford University team of California, again defeated France (17−3) in the Final of 1924 staged in Paris. Incidentally, this American side played three matches in Britain *en route* to France, winning one of them—against Devonport Services, and losing to Blackheath and the Harlequins.

## ORANGE FREE STATE

Founded in 1895, the Orange Free State Rugby Union have played a prominent part in the Currie Cup competition without, however, ever winning it. "Springbok" Internationals produced by the Province include—E. E. McHardy, M. G. Francis, Piet Wessels, C. F. Strydom, and P. J. F. Greyling who holds the State's record with 25 Tests to his credit. Union H.Q. is at Bloemfontein. Colours: Cream jerseys with orange collar and cuffs, blue shorts.

## ORDERED OFF

The first instance of a player being ordered off during the course of an International match took place during the England v. New Zealand match at Twickenham in 1925, when the referee, A. E. Freethy of Wales, ordered off the New Zealand breakaway forward, Cyril Brownlie, for the alleged striking of an opponent.

## ORIGINS

Rugby, as distinct from all other forms of football, was, of course, as the fact and legend of William Webb Ellis clearly substantiates, exclusively a British "invention", but like so many other facets of modern activity, it has its origins in the Roman Occupation. The Roman soldiers of the Occupation, we are reliably informed, spent much of their off duty time playing a game known as "Harpastum," a name derived from the Greek verb "to seize", thus one may reasonably deduce that tackling was one of its features. The ball used was made of cloth or leather stuffed with flock, the game being contested by opposing bands of soldiers whose objective was to seize the ball from the other and carry it over goallines marked out at the ends of the arena over which it had been agreed the game should be contested. The game became popular in Britain, and by the 12th century Fitzstephen, in his Survey of London, was able to describe its details, under the heading of "Football." Like the Roman game of "Harpastum" it was measured in miles rather than yards as today, the goal-posts were set far apart, and the participants were numbered in hundreds, all striving by a variety of devices such as carrying, kicking or hitting with sticks, to force the ball into the opponetns' goal area which could be anything from a market place to a pond or river. Chester and Derby were notoriously enthusiastic football centres during the 12th century, and equally famous and (as we shall point out) notorious, were the violent and often bloodthirsty Shrove Tuesday encounters between whole villages, and which were held at places as far apart as Cross of Scone in Scotland; Corfe Castle in Dorset; Alnwick, Northumberland; Bromfield, Cumberland, and at Midlothian where the married women played the single. Enthusiastic or not, however, the footballer's lot in those far off times was anything but a happy one, for authority frowned on their activities for a variety of reasons. The State interest in football had led to a decline in the standards of archery, the Church was against them because they played on Sundays as well as on Shrove Tuesdays, and finally the local authorities were moved to displeasure on account of the frequent damage to municipal property. Nor were the writers of the day over-friendly to the game and its adherents, as instanced by Sir Thomas Elliott, who described it as a "Friendlie fyghte rather than a play or recreation," whereas another writer with a less euphemistic approach called it a, "bloody and murthering practice." Despite official disapproval, however, and indeed despite the fact that it was actually prohibited by several Monarchs of the Realm, viz., Edward II in 1314, Edward III in 1349, and Richard II, Henry IV, Rivhard III in 1389, 1401 and 1457 respectively, football continued to enjoy a fairly widespread popularity in the villages and hamlets of England, although its actual title varied with the locality it was played in. It was known, for instance as "Hurling to Goals," or as, "Over Country" in the West Country, whereas its adherents in the Eastern parts of the country referred to it as "Camping or Campball". It is too of interest to recall that during the same period the game flourished in France under the title "La Soule" or "Chole."

In the latter part of the 18th century its hold upon the interest of the ordinary folk weakened and it was left to the great public schools of Rugby, Cheltenham and Marlborough first of all to revive, and later develop that interest These three schools pioneered what was then referred to as the "Carrying Code," whilst Charterhouse, Westminster, Eton and Harrow concentrated resolutely and conservatively on "The Kicking Code." In 1863 at the Freemasons' Tavern in London, a fateful meeting took place between the supporters of the rival codes, their objective being a compromise out of which would emerge a standardised game of football. The "Carrying Code" supporters insisted on the retention of "Hacking," "Tripping" and on carrying the ball after a fair catch or rebound, and indeed the supporters of the "Kicking Code" signified their approval of this, but as a precautionary measure first of all sought the advice of the authorities at Cambridge University who were at the time in process of drawing up a code of laws that would unify matter between themselves, Eton, Harrow, Westminster and Charterhouse. Cambridge flatly refused to compromise, and their refusal in effect opened the

way to the final and irrevocable cleavage between the two codes known henceforward as Rugby and Association Football.

## OTAGO

Founded in 1881, and affiliated to the New Zealand Rugby Union in 1895, Otago are today one of the strongest Unions in the Colony, and although they did not succeed in winning the Ranfurly Shield until the year 1936, they have held the trophy three times since. Inevitably Otago representatives have figured prominently in the lists of New Zealand Internationals, the best known being that great scrum-half Chris Laidlaw who has captained the All-Blacks in recent years. Others who have played for their country with lasting distinction: Stephen Casey, a member of the original "All-Blacks" in Britain, W. D. Duncan, R. R. Elvidge, L. S. Haig, vice-captain of the 1953 side in Britain, J. Hore, A. McDonald, J. Richardson, C. Willocks, K. L. Skinner, D. O. Oliver, and K. L. Skinner. In the seasons that followed the cessation of hostilities in 1946, the power and fire revealed by the Otago forwards in the rucks and mauls established a new phrase "Otago style rucking" in the Rugby vocabulary, and among the teams to suffer its full, and at times, awesome impact, were the 1950, 1959 and 1966 British Lions, who were overwhelmed at Dunedin. Union headquarters: Carisbrook Ground, Dunedin, South Isalnd (a Test venue). Colours: Dark blue with gold monogram.

## OXFORD UNIVERSITY

(See also CAMBRIDGE UNIVERSITY AND UNIVERSITY MATCH).

The Oxford University Rugby Football Club was formed at a meeting of Old Rugbeians held at Balliol College, Oxford, on November 2, 1869, but as was the case at Cambridge, Rugby Football had been played at the University long before that. In the early days the game was mainly confined to those undergraduates who had been at Rugby or Marlborough, and indeed the original constitution of the club demanded that both the captain and secretary and one of the three committee men be an Old Rugbeian. In 1871 came the challenge from Cambridge, and as a preparation for this first historic encounter it is recorded that the Oxonians staged a trial match between 20 Old Rugbeians and 20 from various other schools, the victory going not unexpectedly perhaps to the former who, in consequence, claimed 15 out of the 20 places in the first Oxford side that met and defeated Cambridge at the Parks on February 10, 1872. A decade later began the "Golden era" of Oxford Rugby, for it was in season 1881-82 that the legendary Harry Vassall assumed the leadership that was to steer his University through 70 matches without defeat during the following three years. A great forward in his own right, Vassall influenced not only Oxford Rugby, but even more the game at large, for it was he who first conceived the idea of the forwards playing in concert with the backs. Amid the intense individualism of his times, Vassall's theories were of course revolutionary, but put into actual practice they proved devastating, for the defences of those far off times were not attuned to the task of countering forwards whose main object was to clear the ball to their threequarters, forwards who in fact often imitated their threequarters in the speed and dexterity of their handling. His own tactical acumen, and gifts of leadership apart however, Vassall was additionally fortunate in having as his aide-de-camp, the peerless Alan Rotherham, who was without a doubt the innovator of half-back play as we know it today. Indeed between them Vassall and Rotherham revolutionised Rugby Football in the conception of their own times. It was during the Vassall era and immediately after it, that the University registered their four successive wins over Cambridge between 1882-85, but although many fine players including J. Strand-Jones, J. E. Crabbie, J. E. Raphael, A. D. Stoop, P. Munroe,

were in residence during the intervening years, it was not until season 1906-07 that the University were able to dominate as they had dominated in the heyday of Vassall. Oddly enough it was however another Vassall, H. H., a nephew of the maestro who played a leading part in the University's second "Golden Era"—that of 1907-12, during which they defeated Cambridge four times and drew the fifth. Vassall was a magnificent centre threequarter, some say, one of the greatest ever, but then for Oxford it was a period abounding with great names, R. W. Poulton (afterwards Poulton-Palmer), F. N. Tarr, W. J. Carey, L. G. Brown, to mention but a few.

Another vintage period for the University was that of 1921-25, when they won four times to Cambridge's twice. It was the era of the great Scots and Australian players, Ian Smith, G. P. S. McPherson, A. C. Wallace and T. Lawton who, aided and abetted by players of the calibre of G. C. Aitken, H. P. Jacob, H. J. Kittermaster, R. H. Bettington and J. E. Maxwell-Hyslop, made Oxford Rugby a name to conjure with. Other immortal names associated with the University are those of J. M. Bannerman, B. H. Black, P. D. Howard, H. G. Owen-Smith, V. J. G. Jenkins, P. Cranmer, H. D. Freakes, and in more modern times such as C. B. Van-Rynveld, L. B. Cannell, J. MacG. Kendall-Carpenter, D. O. Brace P. G. Robbins and C. R. Laidlaw.

Like their counterparts at Cambridge, Oxford have remained an adornment to the British club scene throughout their history, and amongst their achievements outside the field of university football, are victories over two Australian touring teams, "The Waratahs" of 1927-28, and the fourth "Wallabies" of 1957-58, and also over the "Springboks" of 1969.

## PASSING

(See also OXFORD UNIVERSITY AND TACTICS AND EVOLUTION).

In the early beginnings, i.e. in 20-a-side Rugby, the main object was for a side to force the ball through their opponents by means of a series of scrums and mauls. It was in fact the Oxford and England player, Harry Vassall, who first conceived the idea of a team making ground by passing from hand to hand, and he started (logically enough since they were the dominating force of the day) with the forwards. At Oxford with Vassall during this period (1882), was another great player and tactician—the halfback, Alan Rotherham, and between them they developed an attacking formula which had as its basis short hand to hand passing amongst the forwards with the object of clearing the ball to their threequarters who, in turn, lengthened their passes to each other in order to minimise interference from their opponents. The theory and practice of Vassall and Rotherham has, of course, subsequently remained a fundamental principle of Rugby Football.

## PENARTH R.F.C.

Founded in 1879, Penarth have had for the most part something of a struggle to maintain their first class status in face of competition from their all powerful neighbours Cardiff and Newport. They have however succeeded, and in the process produced some great players, none greater perhaps than Jack Bassett who was the acme of power and solidity as the Welsh full back in 15 Internationals. For many years Penarth languished at the foot of the unofficial Welsh Championship table but they have twice (1956 and 1960) reached the final of the Snelling Sevens Competition. A distinction the club are proud of is that of acting as "host" club to the Barbarians on the annual Easter Tour in South Wales, and the Good Friday encounter between the two clubs has become a traditional date in the Rugby calendar. When they beat the Barbarians in 1960 it was their first such victory in 40 years and their eighth over the visitors in 48 matches. Penarth repeated the victory in 1971. Colours Royal blue jerseys, blue and white stockings, white shorts. Ground: Athletic Ground, Penarth. Nickname: "Seasiders." Secretary: J. W. Musselwhite, Elm Trees, St. Ambrose Close, Sunnycroft, Dinas Powis, Glam.

## PENRYN R.F.C.

The Penryn club is one of the oldest in the West of England, having been formed in 1872, but after a successful first decade the club was forced to disband during the eighties due to the mass emigration of the local tin miners who were the club's strength. It was reformed in about 1893 by one of their former players, Billy Halls, who had returned from abroad. Halls, incidentally, won a competition run nationally by the magazine "Answers" to try and find the player with the longest kick. His winning effort measured 79 yards 30 inches. One of the first Penryn players capped for England was E. E. Richards, who like many other Cornishmen played for Plymouth Albion before gaining international honours in 1929. Best known Penryn player is probably V. G. Roberts who played 43 times for Cornwall and 17 times for England (1947-56). Ground: Memorial Ground, Penryn. Colours: White with red and black V. Hon. Secretary: M. P. Williams, Innisidgew, Boscawen Road, Falmouth.

## PENZANCE-NEWLYN R.F.C.

The original Penzance club was formed in 1876 although the game had been played in the town before that. Newlyn was formed in 1894 and intense rivalry developed between these neighbours. Despite the feeling that had built up, however, the two clubs amalgamated in 1945 and obtained a new ground—Mennaye Field, half-way between the two towns. They have since gone from strength to strength and built up a first-class fixture list. The famous England back row forward John Kendall Carpenter captained the club for a while, as did another England international, three-quarter, John Williams. But probably their most famous player is "Stack" Stevens, an England prop forward in 25 games. Ground: Mennaye Field. Colours: Black, white and red. Hon. Secretary: C. C. Ladner, Polwin House, St. Peter's Hill, Newlyn, Penzance.

## PLYMOUTH ALBION R.F.C.

This famous old club has staged a great revival in recent years. Founded in 1876 as Devon Albion they adopted their present title in 1919 following the demise of the Plymouth club which had been Albion's keenest rivals since their formation in 1895. Albion's outstanding international is Edward Stanbury who collected 16 England caps in the 1920s and later became President of both club and county. In season 1928-29 no fewer than four Albion players, appeared in the England side—E. E. Richards, E. Stanbury, R. H. W. Sparks, and C. H. A. Gummer. Ground: Beacon Park, Plymouth. Colours: Cherry, white and green. Hon. Secretary: V. Pinches, 2 Lyndhurst Close, Peverell, Plymouth.

## PONTYPOOL R.F.C.

The Pontypool Club which was founded in 1901 claim the distinction of being the first British club to have defeated two overseas touring sides in the same year. This was in 1927 when they followed up a victory over the Maoris with an even more sensational victory over the New South Wales "Waratahs" who had already defeated the Welsh International XV. Indeed any side visiting the Pontypool Park can expect the toughest of opponents for, like most of their local counterparts Pontypool are famed for the ruggedness of their forward play. Great personalities in the club history have been J. P. "Ponty" Jones who played in the Welsh threequarter line on 14 occasions besides visiting South Africa with a British representative team, whilst Rhys Thomas, C. Pritchard, C. Richards, Alun Forward, and latterly R. Prosser have all adequately upheld the club's reputation for powerful forward play in the Welsh packs of their period. R. Prosser made the club's record number of appearances

for Wales—22 (1956-61). They were Welsh unofficial Club Champions in 1958-59 and 1972-73. Colours: Red, white and black hoops, stockings of same colour, white shorts. Ground: Pontypool Park. Hon Secretary: R. Jeremiah, 138 Blaendare Road, Pontypool, Gwent.

## POVERTY BAY RUGBY UNION

Founded 1890, affiliated to the New Zealand Rugby Union 1893. Headquarters: Gisborne, North Island. Colours: Scarlet. Outstanding player, R. A. White, the 16-stone forward, who represented New Zealand in 55 matches (22 Internationals) including 25 games with the 4th "All-Blacks" in Britain 1953-54.

## PRESS

In 1926 the Scottish Rugby Union introduced a new by-law prohibiting any member of its committee, or of any club under its jurisdiction from contributing articles on Rugby football to the Press, and the Rugby Union in 1929 introduced a similar by-law but adding the modified wording "for remuneration." Today the position is that no official, committee member, referee, or player of the Rugby Union or any of its affiliated clubs can write on Rugby football matters for the Press for remuneration, unless he devotes such remuneration or material reward through his Member Union to a club or charity. The by-law of course excludes any person who happens to be a professional journalist already.

## PROFESSIONAL LAWS

Of the seven Rugby Football Unions constituting the International Board, only the Rugby Union and the Welsh Rugby Union have a definite code of laws as to Professionalism, but the other affiliated members, Ireland, Scotland, Australia, New Zealand, and South Africa, are fully "protected" by one of the Board's By-Laws which states, "No player who has transgressed the Rules as to Professionalism as laid down by any Union in membership with the Board shall be eligible to take part in any part in any game played under the jurisdiction of the Unions which constitute the Board." The Rules as to Professionalism are very strict and comprehensive, and no person can solicit or receive either directly or indirectly any monetary consideration or any benefit or reward of any kind whatsoever (including the promise of any future payment, benefit, or reward) for or arising out of the playing (or refraining from playing) managing, organising, controlling or refereeing of any type of Rugby football.

## QUEENSLAND RUGBY UNION

The most successful period in the history of the Queensland Rugby Union which dates from 1882, was the period between 1890-1900 when they defeated their traditional rivals New South Wales on 11 occasions. Other highlights of their history are the tour to New Zealand in 1896, and the defeat in 1899 of an "unofficial" British side led by the Rev. Matthew Mullineaux. In 1971 they were the only provincial side to defeat the British Lions down under. When the first representative Australian team toured Britain in 1908 it included four Queensland players in P. Carmichael, E. Parkinson, P. Flanagan and T. R. Richards. Famed too in the annals of Queensland Rugby are the McLean family for D. J. McLean who gained Australian honours in 1904 was followed by his three sons, one of whom, W. M. McLean, captained the Third "Wallabies" in Great Britain in 1947-48. Between 1919–29 apathy and lack of interest caused Rugby football to practically die out in the State, but it was eventually revived by three great enthusiasts and administrators, Messrs. D. S. Carter, T. H. Welsly and A. E. Brown. In the course of her eventful history Queensland have produced a number of the all time "greats" of Australian Rugby, these include E, T. Bonis, E. Thompson, and T. S. Lawton who is still regarded as one of the most skilful five-eights in history, and is one of only a small number of Queenslanders to captain Australia in more than a game or two. He captained the side in six tests. The Union colours are maroon, and they play their Inter-State matches at the Exhibition Ground, Brisbane.

## QUEEN'S UNIVERSITY BELFAST

If anything were needed to place the Queen's University of Belfast on the International Rugby map, then it has surely been supplied by the post-war exploits of the great outside half Jack Kyle, and his "Sancho Panza" in the centre, Noel Henderson, who between them won no fewer than 86 International caps. The truth, however, is that "Queen's" were already famous for the quality of their Rugby even before the advent of Messrs. Kyle and Henderson, for in 1930 a very fine defensive centre threequarter, G. V. Stephenson, made his 42nd appearance for Ireland, thereby setting up a world record that stood for twenty-seven years until it was beaten by K. J. Jones (Wales) in 1957. Other Queen's players who have served Ireland with particular distinction have been J. W. McKay who played on 23 occasions at wing forward, occupying as such a vital role in his country's two post-war Triple Crown victories. In addition McKay was a member of the British side that toured New Zealand in 1950. Dr. W. Tyrrel, who packed in the Irish scrum on 13 occasions between 1910-14 subsequently became the President of the Irish R.U., whilst R. B. Mayne, a magnificently energetic forward, and G. E. Cromey, an elusive stand-off half were prominent in International football during the 'thirties. More recently A. C. Pedlow has upheld the Queen's tradition in the Irish centre, while Ken Kennedy began his fine run of Internationals in 1965 while at Queen's and eventually ran up a total of 41 appearances. The club was formed in 1869. Colours: Royal blue. Ground: Upper Malone Playing Fields, Belfast.

## RANFURLY SHIELD

(See also NEW ZEALAND and Individual Clubs).

The premier New Zealand Rugby Football competition was inaugurated in 1902 when Lord Ranfurly, the then Governor of New Zealand, presented a shield as a challenge trophy open to all the Unions affiliated to the parent body. To begin with the trophy was awarded to Auckland on a merit basis, but from then onwards each holder has had to resist challenges from the other competing Unions. Auckland set up a record by holding the trophy for 9 years 1905-13, successfully defending it 23 times.

They also hold the record for the highest number of games in which they successfully resisted challenges—25, 1960-63—before losing to Wellington.

## REDRUTH R.F.C.

One of the oldest clubs in the West of England, Redruth was formed in 1875, thanks largely to the enterprise of two ex-Public schoolboys, W. M. Willmott (Marlborough) and Henry Grylls (Clifton). The first match of which a record is still in existence was that against Truro in February 1876 which Redruth won with touchdowns by Everett and Grylls. One of their stars around the turn of the century was J. Davey who later had the distinction of captaining Transvaal when they won the Currie Cup and then returned home from the South African gold mines in 1907 to captain his old club and play for Cornwall and England. When Cornwall won the County Championship in 1908 the side included, Davey and four other Redruth players. Outstanding at Redruth between the wars was Roy Jennings who toured with the British Lions team

in 1930. He made 61 appearances for Cornwall during his career with the club—1923—36. Since the war the club's fine tradition has been maintained by such stars as England captain Richard Sharp and the popular C. R. "Bonzo" Johns who played over 600 times for the "Reds". Nickname: "Reds". Ground: Recreation Ground. Hon. Secretary: T. K. Williams, The Glen, Claremont, Redruth, Cornwall.

## REFEREES

The referee today (see Law 6 under LAWS OF THE GAME) is in complete charge of every match he officiates at. It was not however always so, for in the beginnings, the opposing captains having previously decided upon the rules applicable to their own specific encounter, saw to it that they were observed by the teams they captained. Inevitably there were disagreements and this led to the appointment of two Umpires who were supplied with sticks which were raised on (and only then) appeal by one of the two captains. Since the Umpires were appointed by the opposing teams, their impartiality was often called into question by one or the other, so that in 1885 the Rugby Union called in a third arbitrator—the referee—whose only function was to give a decision when the two Umpires had failed to agree. His method of granting an appeal was a blast on the whistle provided him, but it was not until 1893 (22 years after the Rugby Union had codified their laws) that he was empowered to blow his whistle regardless of whether he had been appealed to or not. This measure in effect afforded him the complete control of the game he enjoys today, and in addition he was instructed not to stop play if an infringement was calculated to benefit the non-offending team—the birth in fact of the modern Advantage Rule. The granting of full power to the referee meant of course that the umpires reverted to flagmen, touch judges, or linesmen, we know today.

Even though vested with his vastly improved status however, the referee (In Great Britain at least) took no special pains to equip himself for the job, and indeed Dave Gallaher's original "All-Blacks" who visited Great Britain in 1905 often expressed surprise at the spectacle of referees officiating at their matches in "mufti". Things nowadays are vastly changed, however, so that the referee besides equipping himself with a uniform appropriate to the job, in the majority of cases pays assiduous attention to physical fitness, and the technical and psychological aspects of his job. No longer too are referees regarded as members of Rugby Football's lowliest estate, for in most parts of the world they are members of well ordered "Referee's Societies" who hold regular meetings, lectures, and film shows for the enlightenment of their members besides submitting recommendations of suitable candidates for the International Panels of the Unions to which they belong. As reimbursement for their contribution to the game the referee in Great Britain is allowed no more than reasonable out of pocket expenses.

Outstanding among post war referees are Kevin Kelleher and Ray Williams (Ireland), and Gwynne Walters (Wales), each of whom officiated in at least 20 internationals.

## Famous Incidents Involving Referees

In 1884 during the International between England and Scotland at Blackheath, Dr. George Scriven of Ireland made a decision which, had he but known it at the time, was destined to have far reaching consequences, including amongst other things the formation of the International Board in 1890. Dr. Scriven awarded a try to England following a "knock-back" by a Scotsman, whose colleagues thereupon disputed the award on the grounds that "knocking-back" was illegal. England on the other hand supported the referee claiming (i) that "Knocking-back" was in fact legal, and (ii) that in any case they were entitled to benefit (since no Englishman had appealed) from an infraction of the rules by an opponent. The immediate result of the dispute which ensued was Scotland's cancellation of their match with England arranged for the following winter, but more far-reaching was the referment of the case to Sir John Hay McDonald, Lord Chief Justice's Clerk of Scotland, and Major F. A. Marindin, President of the Rugby Union. This in turn led to the formation of the International Board, so out of Dr. Scriven's split second decision delivered in the heat and stress of an Anglo-Scots encounter of the long ago there emerged the vast all-embracing organisation which frames as well as arbitrates on the Laws of the Game universally.

On December 16, 1905 at the Cardiff Arms Park, J. D. Dallas, of Scotland, made the decision that cost Dave Gallaher's immortal New Zealanders an invincible record in Britain, and which has ever after remained a topic of argument and discussion wherever the game is played. Pressing hard to equalise the try scored by Teddy Morgan for Wales, the New Zealanders produced a brilliant handling movement which sent their powerful centre threequarter Deans haring for the corner flag where he was tackled by a couple of Welshmen. When Dallas reached the fateful spot, Deans was lying inches short of the line with the ball in his grasp all the while hotly maintaining that he had been tugged back by his opponents after he had grounded the ball. Deans in fact is supposed to have reiterated his claim even on his death bed years later, and to this day all New Zealand sides to Britain make a pilgrimage to the Arms Park to view the historic spot. Dallas however merely took the evidence of his own eyes, ruled "NO TRY," and thereby fired off the controversy that has become no less heated with the passage of over seventy years.

When the Fourth New Zealand Touring Team met Ireland at Landsdowne Road, Dublin, on December 7, 1935, the appointed referee, M. A. Allan, of Scotland, was unable to reach his destination owing to the stormy weather in the Irish Sea, so that his place had to be taken at the last moment by R. W. Jeffrares, the son of the Secretary of the Irish Union—the only occasion in history on which an International match has not been controlled by a neutral referee.

At Swansea in 1924, the occasion being the Wales-New Zealand match, the referee, Colonel Brunton of England, in conjunction with the two captains, rejected no fewer than four balls before deciding upon a suitable one with which to commence the match.

## REINSTATEMENT

The only case of players being reinstated as amateurs after forsaking

Rugby Union to play as professionals in the Rugby League is that of the Swansea and Wales half-back pair, the brothers David and Evan James, who joined Broughton Rangers as professionals at the turn of the present century. Following representations by the Swansea club and the Welsh Rugby Union, the brothers were reinstated at a special meeting of the Rugby Union, and were accordingly able to turn out again for Wales in International Rugby. Later the brothers returned to the professional game, this time irrevocably.

In 1949 the Bristol and Blackheath wing threequarter J. A. Gregory was suspended for three years by the Rugby Union for assisting (on his own admission) the Huddersfield Rugby League club while stationed near the town as a soldier during the war. After his reinstatement Gregory gained an England cap.

In 1949 the Rugby Union reinstated the Bridgend player Glyn John giving as their reason for doing so, the fact that he was a minor when he had signed for the Leigh Rugby club. John's father returned the £500 signing-on fee his son had received, and the player subsequently won two Welsh caps.

In 1946 the famous New Zealand full back George Nepia was reinstated by the New Zealand Union following a porfessional engagement in the North of England.

## RHODESIA

The Rhodesian Rugby Union was formed in 1899, and in 1952 was (for administrative purposes) split into sub Unions called Northern and Southern. The name of Rhodesia may not figure in the list of Currie Cup winners or very frequently in the list of Springbok representatives, but they have produced at least two brilliant Internationals in loose forward J. ("Saltie") du Rand, and the crash tackling centre, R. A. van Schoor, who rendered their country yeoman service on the 1951 Tour of Britain. Union headquarters is at Bulawayo. Colours: Green and white hooped jerseys and stockings, white shorts.

## RICHMOND F.C.

Formed in 1861 this club has played a leading role in the establishment of the game. Their founder, Edwin Ash, was also responsible for the formation of the Rugby Union and was its first secretary. Richmond also take part in the game's oldest regular inter-club fixture—that with Blackheath, which was first played in 1863. Since its formation Richmond has supplied nearly 100 Internationals. The club played its earliest games in Richmond Green but moved to the Old Deer Park in 1872, and from there to their present home—Richmond Athletic Ground, in 1899. Richmond took part in the first-ever game to be played at Twickenham, against the Harlequins, in 1909. Richmond players who have captained their country include E. Temple Gurdon, N. "Nim" M. Hall and Tony Bucknall, England; A. J. "Monkey" Gould, Wales; and Peter Kininmonth, Scotland. Colours: Old gold, red and black. Hon. Secretary: A. V. H. Skeats, 76 Westbury Road, New Malden, Surrey.

## ROSSLYN PARK R.F.C.

In view of their antiquity, they were formed in 1879 as the Rugby section of an older Cricket club at Hampstead, and their long established rating as one of the leading British clubs, it is rather surprising to note that Rosslyn Park did not get a player in an England International XV until 1937, when the strong running Army wing threequarter, E. J. Unwin, was awarded the first of his eight caps. Other Park players who have since been honoured are, B. Bobbeyer, B. A. Neale, J. V. Smith, C. E. Winn, J. A. S. Wackett, B. A. Dovey, J. M. Ranson and A. G. Ripley who is now the clubs most capped player. In addition the club have had several representatives in Irish and Scottish International XVs. The club who have enjoyed three post-war successes in the Middlesex Seven-a-side Tournament, posses another distinction in that they were the first ever British Rugby team to play in France—this occurred in 1892 when they visited Paris to play, and defeat the Stade Francais club. Associated for most of their history with the Old Deer Park at Richmond, the club moved in 1957 to new headquarters at Roehampton. Colours: Red and white hoops. Hon. Secretary: P. J. Thorley, "Spindles," Sheephouse Road, Maidenhead, Berks.

## ROYAL AIR FORCE UNION

The first truly representative R.A.F.

team included the great W. W. Wakefield, and they made a name for themselves in the Inter-Services Tournament of 1919 by gaining a surprise 7−3 win over Australia at Gloucester. They also beat Canada but lost to the Mother Country, New Zealand, and South Africa. It should be noted that although New Zealand won the trophy, they were themselves beaten by the Australians only eleven days after the R.A.F. had gained that victory at Gloucester.

The R.A.F. have been the least successful of the Services in the Triangular Tournament, winning it outright only seven times and sharing it twice with the Army. Their best period was 1958-59 when they won in successive seasons, the only time they have achieved this feat. Star of this side was Pilot Officer D. O. Brace, a Welsh International, and former Newport scrum-half and Oxford Blue.

## ROYAL HIGH R.F.C.

Until 1973 this was the Royal High School Former Pupils club, but in that year they decided to open membership to all and adopted the shorter title. Formed as early as 1868 this Edinburgh club had a representative, A. C. Buchanan in the original Scottish XV which played England in 1871. Among their finest Internationals is that great forward Mark Morrison who led the British side in South Africa in 1903, while J. P. Fisher, who captained Scotland in the 1960s, is another former pupil. Headquarters:. Jock's Lodge, Edinburgh. Colours: Black and white. Hon. Secretary: A. T. Ross, 7 Britwell Crescent, Edinburgh 7.

## ROYAL NAVY UNION

The Royal Navy was, of course, meeting the Army at Rugby long before the Triangular Tournament was begun in 1919-20. Indeed, the Navy men generally had the beating of the Army before World War I, winning the first four games in a row from 1906 onwards. The Navy played no part in the Inter-Services Tournament of 1919, a pity, because they were soon to establish such a powerful side that they might have given the fine New Zealand team a fright at that time. As it was the Royal Navy won the first three Triangular Tournaments after the war, being undefeated in all their games. Their side at that time included three England Internationals in

before World War II when they won the Triangular Tournament twice in successive seasons 1938-39. Outstanding at this time was England International forward J. K. Watkins. The Navy has won the tournament outright 13 times, being particularly strong again in recent years when they won the tournament in 1973 and 1974.

## ROYALTY

In 1886 the Prince of Wales (later King Edward VII) attended a charity match at Kennington Oval and in the following year accepted an invitation to become patron of the Rugby Union. In 1919 his son, King George V, who had shown himself an enthusiastic follower of the game, presented the King's Cup for competition in an Inter-Services tournament which was won by New Zealand, and then in 1921 unveiled a memorial at Twickenham to those Rugby players who had lost their lives in the war. King Edward VIII, and his brother King George VI were both often in attendance at Twickenham for the big matches, and Her Majesty Queen Elizabeth became patron of the Rugby Union in 1952 and the Welsh Rugby Union in 1953. There is too, an instance of a special match being played as a mark of appreciation of Royal patronage, for on the occasion of the Silver Jubilee of King George V in May, 1935, the Barbarians played a selected London XV at Twickenham. Wales, too, celebrated the occasion with a special match between their "unofficial" championship winners and runners-up, Cardiff and Aberavon.

## RUGBY SCHOOL

It was on the close at Rugby School that William Webb Ellis laid the foundation of the game of Rugby Football as we know it today by running with the ball in a Bigside game. A tablet set in the wall of the close perpetuates his memory in the following terms. "This stone commemorates the exploit of W. W. Ellis who with a fine disregard for the rules of football as played in his time, first took the ball in his arms and ran with it, thus originating the distinctive features of the Rugby game A.D. 1823." William Webb Ellis subsequently the half-backs, C. A. Kershaw and W. J. A. Davies, and the forward, T. Woods. The Navy's best spell since then was just became the incumbent of St. Clement's Dane, Strand, London, but there is no record of him ever retaining an active interest in the game he so inspiringly founded. In fact Ellis died in 1872–one year after the formation of the Rugby Union–heedless of the fact that his name was soon to echo to the most distant parts. Inevitably old Rugbeians were destined to play a leading part in the game founded on their School's playing fields, and three former pupils–E. C. Holmes, A. E. Rutter and L. J. Maton were founder members of the Rugby Union in 1871. Much earlier than that, A. Pell another former pupil, founded the first rugby club on record–at Cambridge University in 1839.

In 1923 a crowd of 2,000 one-third of them pupils at Rugby School and the remainder notabilities from the leading Rugby Football countries, watched a special "Centenary Match" played on Close between sides representing England and Wales, and those representing Scotland and Ireland. The Anglo-Welsh XV were victorious by 21–16, and as a direct result of the encounter succeeding generations of Quiz-Masters have found themselves posing the almost inevitable "catch" question, "Who were the players who have represented both England and Wales, or both Scotland and Ireland?" The answer of course being those who took part in the "Centenary Match" at Rugby Close. They were:

ENGLAND AND WALES: F. Baker, T. Johnson, R. A. Cornish (all of Wales), H. M. Locke (England), W. Rowe Harding (Wales), W. J. A. Davies, C. A. Kershaw, W. W. Wakefield, A. T. Voyce, W. E. Luddington (all England), A. Baker, T. Roberts, S. Morris, G. Michael (all Wales).

SCOTLAND AND IRELAND: W. E. Crawford, H. W. Stephenson, G. V. Stephenson (all of Ireland), A. L. Gracie (Scotland), D. J. Cussen (Ireland), J. C. Dykes, W. E. Bryce, J. Bannerman, L. M. Stuart (all of Scotland), D. S. Davies (Scotland), J. R. Lawrie (Scotland), W. P. Collopy, J. A. McClelland, R. Y. Crichton (Ireland).

Referee: V. Cartwright (England).

Touch Judges: C. F. Rutherford (France) and R. G. Waller (Ireland).

In honour of the 150th anniversary of William Webb Ellis an International Conference on the Development of Rugby Football for the Young was held at the School in December 1973. 42 delegates from 24 different countries attended.

## RUGBY UNION

The Rugby Union was formed at a meeting convened by Edwin H. Ash of Richmond at the Pall Mall Restaurant, London, on January 26, 1871, and the clubs constituting it as founder members were: Blackheath, Richmond, Wellington College. Guy's Hospital, Harlequins, King's College. St. Paul's, Civil Service (all still in existence) and Marlborough Nomads, Queen's House, West Kent, Wimbledon Hornets, Gipsies, Clapham Rovers, Flamingoes, Law, Lausanne, Addison, Mohicans, Ravenscourt Park, and Belsize Park (all of them now defunct). E. C. Holmes, of Richmond, was appointed chairman of the meeting, and the officers of the new Union were appointed as follows: President: A. E. Rutter; Secretary: Edwin H. Ash; Committee, F. Stokes, E. C. Holmes, E. Rutter, A. G. Guillemard, W. F. Eaton, L. J. Maton, F. I. Currey, F. Luscombe, R. Leigh, F. Hartley, A. J. English, I Ewart, R. H. Birkett.

The membership fee was fixed at 5/- with an annual subscription of the same sum, and a committee composed of Rutter, Holmes and Maton proceeded to draft the laws of the new Union which except for a ban on the practice of "Hacking," were substantially the same as those in operation at Rugby School. In the same year the Rugby Union took part in its first representative match when an England team captained by F. Stokes, of Blackheath, were defeated at Edinburgh by a Scottish team led by F. J. Moncrieff (Edinburgh Academicals). The teams were 20 a side. In the beginning several of the leading Scottish and Irish clubs joined the Rugby Union, but with the formation of the Scottish Union in 1873, and the Irish Union in 1879, these clubs withdrew to assume their natural allegiance. Season 1881-82 saw George (later Sir George) Rowland-Hill embark on the administrative career that was to make him one of the game's legendary figures, for it was during his tenure of office (Secretary from 1881-1904, and President from 1904-07) that the Rugby Union consolidated its humble beginnings to emerge as the game's guiding power universally. Rowland-Hill it was who presented the famous amendment to the northern clubs' "Broken Time" proposal in the dispute of 1893, and his advocacy and the sincerity underlying it on that occasion, as on many others, did much to ensure that the game of Rugby should remain amateur in the conception of its founders. As a tribute to his memory, and his services to the game, the Rowland-Hill Memorial Gates were erected at Twickenham at a cost of over £6,000 and unveiled before a special Four-country Memorial Match on the same ground on October 5, 1929.

Twickenham of course (see also TWICKENHAM) represents another great landmark in the history of the Union, and with the passing of the years the ground has come to be regarded by Rugby men with the same veneration and affection as the cricketers of Britain and the Commonwealth accord the Lord's Cricket Ground. C. J. B. Marriott, the old Blackheath and England forward who became the Union's first paid secretary in succession to Rowland-Hill in 1904, and W. Cail, the Union treasurer, who was also responsible for the drafting of the laws against Professionalism, were prominent figures in the protracted negotiations and endeavours that finally produced a vast stadium with its countless amenities, out of the derelict acreage that was once an apple and pear orchard, sometimes referred to in unflattering terms as "The cabbadge patch."

"Rugby Lodge," at Twickenham, which was originally erected to house the Union's modest staff, has nowadays of course become the very hub of the game's administration in Britain, and as the activities of the Union have increased in scope so too have the duties demanded of its secretary and his staff. Indeed the emergence of previously unheard of Sub-committees, "Overseas Liason," "Publications," and "Laws,"

to mention but a few, supply an indication of their multiplicity. For administrative purposes the Rugby Union is divided into constituent bodies each of which supply a stipulated number of representatives to the Union's General Committee. In 1975 the Constituent Bodies are as follows:

Army, Berkshire, Buckinghamshire, Central District, Cambridge University, Cheshire, Cornwall, Cumberland and Westmorland, Devon Dorset and Wiltshire, Durham, Eastern Counties, East Midlands, Gloucestershire, Hampshire, Hertfordshire, Kent, Lancashire, Leicestershire, Middlesex, North Midlands, Northumberland, Notts, Lincs and Derbyshire, Oxfordshire, Oxford University, Royal Air Force, Royal Navy and Royal Marines, Schools, Somerset, Staffordshire, Surrey, Sussex, Warwickshire, and Yorkshire.

The Rugby Union first appointed a paid Secretary in 1904 when P. Cole assumed office in succession to the great G. Rowland-Hill who had served as Hon. Secretary for 20 years. Cole's appointment lasted for the three years, 1904-07, and his successors have been C. J. B. Marriott (1907-24), S. F. Coopper (1924-33), F. D. Prentice (1933-62), and R. E. Prescott (1963-73), Air Commodore R. H. G. Weighill, C.B.E., D.F.C. (1973-). Previous to 1881 when Rowland-Hill assumed office the Secretaries were: E. H. Ash (1871-72), A. G. Guillemard (1872, '75 and '76), F. I. Currey (1873), H.J. Graham (1876-78), W. Wallace (1878-81). The Union's first Treasurer was E. H. Ash who also of course acted as Secretary, and he was succeeded by W. Slade (1875-76), H. J. Graham (1876-78), W. Wallace (1878-84), H. Vassall (1884-94), W. Cail (1894-1924), E. Prescott (1924-33), M. F. Waters (1933-47), J. R. Creasey (1947-50), W. C. Ramsay (1950-70), K. H. Chapman (1970-73), B. F. Boyden (1973-).

## PRESIDENTS OF THE UNION BETWEEN 1871 AND THE PRESENT DAY

1871-74—A. Rutter (Blackheath).
1874-75—E. Stokes (Blackheath).
1875-76—L. J. Maton (Wimbledon Hornets).
1876-77—C. D. Heatley (Richmond).
1877-78—C. D. Heatley (Richmond) (Re-elected).
1878-82—A. G. Guillemard (Kent) (re-elected).

1882-84–J. McLaren (Manchester( (Re-elected).
1884-86–F. I. Currey (Marlborough Nomads) (Re-elected).
1886-88–L. Stokes (Blackheath) (Re-elected).
1888-89–A. Budd (Blackheath).
1889-90–H. W. T. Garnett (Bradford).
1890-92–E. Temple Gurdon (Richmond) (Re-elected).
1892-94–W. Cail (Northumberland) (Re-elected).
1894-96–R. Walker (Lancashire) (Re-elected).
1896-98–R. S. Whalley (London) (Re-elected).
1898-1900–J. W. H. Thorpe (Cheshire) (Re-elected).
1900-02–F. H. Fox (Somerset) (Re-elected).
1902-04–M. Newsome (Yorkshire) (Re-elected).
1904-07–G. Rowland-Hill (London) (Re-elected).
1907-09–C. A. Crane (Midland Counties) (Re-elected).
1909-11–T. C. Pring (Devon) (Re-elected).
1911-13–A. M. Crook (Lancashire) (Re-elected).
1913-20–A. Hartley (Yorkshire) (Re-elected, also lapse owing to War).
1920-22–E. Prescott (Middlesex) (Re-elected).
1922-23–R. Henzell (Northumberland).
1923-24–M. F. Waters (Surrey).
1924-25–W. S. Donne (Somerset).
1925-26–H. E. Ferens (Durham).
1926-27–J. Baxter (Cheshire).
1927-28–Vice-Admiral P. Royds, C.B., C.M.G., R.N.
1928-29–V. H. Cartwright, D.S.O. (South Africa).
1929-32–W. T. Pearce (Gloucestershire) (Re-elected).
1932-33–A. D. Stoop, M.C. (Central District).
1933-34–R. F. Oakes (Yorkshire).
1934-35–J. Milner (Lancashire).
1935-37–J. E. Greenwood (Cambridge) (Re-elected).
1937-39–Major-General B. A. Hill, D.S.O. (Army) (Re-elected).
1939-40–G. C. Robinson (Northumberland).
1940-47–John Daniell (Somerset) (Re-elected and Wartime).
1947-48–Colonel B. C. Hartley, O.B.E. (Army).
1948-49–L. G. Brown (New South Wales).
1949-50–E. Watts Moses (Durham).
1950-51–Sir Wavell Wakefield, M.P. (Middlesex).
1951-52–H. Cleaver, O.B.E., J. P. (Warwickshire).
1952-53–P. M. Holman (Cornwall).
1953-54–J. Brunton, D.S.O., M.C. (Northumberland).
1954-55–W. C. Ramsay (Middlesex).
1955-56–W. D. Gibbs (Kent).
1956-57–Surgeon Admiral L. B. Osborne, C.B., Q.H.D.S. (Royal Navy).
1957-58–A. Marshall (East Midlands).
1958-59–Wing Commander J. L. Lawson, C. B. E. (R.A.F.).
1959-60–J. A. Tallent, O.B.E., T.D. (Central District).
1960-61–A. T. Voyce (Gloucestershire).
1961-62–Major-General R. G. S. Hobbs, C.B., D.S.O., O.B.E. (The Army).
1962-63–C. H. Gadney, M.B.E. (Middlesex).
1963-64–A. G. Butler (Oxfordshire).
1964-65–Sir Lawrie Edwards, K.B.E., D.L., J.P. (Northumberland).
1965-66–Air Marshall Sir Augustus Walker, K.C.B., C.B.E., D.S.O., D.F.C., A.F.C.
            (R.A.F.).
1966-67–D. H. Harrison (Dorset and Wiltshire)
1967-68–J. R. Locker (Lancashire).
1968-69–J. T. W. Berry (Leicestershire).
1969-70–D. T. Kemp, T.D. (Hampshire).
1970-71–Sir William Clark Ramsay, C.B.E. (Past President).
1971-72–Dr. T. A. Kemp (Cambridge University).

1972-73 – R. M. A. Kingswell (Yorkshire).
1973-74 – M. R. Steele-Bodger (Central District).
1974-75 – K. H. Chapman (Middlesex).
1975-76 – G. T. Bainbridge (Durham).

## RULES OF RUGBY
(See LAWS OF THE GAME).

## RUMANIA

Rugby football is reputed to have been introduced into Rumania well in advance of World War I, but it was not until the autumn of 1954 when the Welsh club, Swansea, accepted an invitation to journey to Bucharest where they met the Rumanian club champions, Locomatavia, that the Western world was vouchsafed an opportunity of studying its conduct at first hand. Heading the Swansea party was Judge W. Rowe Harding, a famous Cambridge University and British International threequarter of the nineteen-twenties, and he and his fellow officials brought back with them a report that told of sweeping enthusiasm for the game (especially in the Bucharest area), of a standard of play not very far removed from the best British standards and of an attention to technical detail that rivalled in its thoroughness that associated with South African Rugby. The following autumn British followers had the opportunity of seeing these things for themselves when a Rumanian representative side paid a return visit embracing fixtures with four of the leading British club sides, Swansea, Cardiff, Bristol, and Harlequins in that order. Swansea were overwhelmed, a full strength Cardiff XV held to a 3 points margin in a hard and bitter forward struggle, Bristol defeated, and the Harlequins held to an exciting draw at Twickenham. British followers were, to say the least, impressed with the speed and skill of the visitors, and in a hardly lesser degree, with their *approach* to the game which was sporting, and where circumstances permitted, adventurous. Both Cardiff, and the Harlequins paid a return visit to Rumania in succeeding summers, but neither was able to avoid defeat at the hands of a representative Bucharest XV playing before a wildly partisan home crowd. In the summer of 1957, the Welsh club Llanelli, containing several Internationals, encountered Rumania in the finals of the Rugby competition organised in Moscow under the auspices of the Russian Youth Festival and after a bitterly contested drawn game were defeated in the replay. In the same year Rumania Rugby faced its major test to date, when the full strength French International team were met at Bucharest in a game that was advertised as for the Continental Championship, 95,000 people were reported to have watched the game, and it ended in an 18–15 victory for France, but only after a gloriously fluctuating struggle that was throughout gladiatorial in its intensity. What was probably an accurate commentary on the standards of Rumanian Rugby was supplied afterwards by the vastly experienced French captain, Gerrad Dufau who said, "The Rumanians were in superb condition, and their pack which played a British type game, seemed of International standard." Since then Rumania have become a force in International Rugby, although their entry into the International Championship may conceivably be delayed until the International Board have completely satisfied themselves that the game behind the "Iron Curtain" is being conducted to the letter and spirit of the amateur code. Meanwhile Rumania may be considered the leading Rugby nation outside the International Championship and the Commonwealth. They are members of the European Federation Internationale de Rugby Amateur.

in his first International. P. H. Davies (1927) was the first of Sale's International players. Ground: Brooklands, Colours: Blue and white. Hon. Secretary: J. F. Hornbrook, 17 Barlow Moor Court, West Didsbury, Manchester, M20 844.

## SALE R.F.C.

Claiming 1861, as the date of its foundation the Sale club has throughout its history been regarded as one of the strongest in the North of England. If the club ever struck a truly purple patch then it was probably during the mid-thirties when they were able to command the regular assistance of such renowned International players as H. S. Sever (England), Claude Davey and W. Wooller (Wales), and K. C. Fyfe, of Scotland. The club's record cap holder is Eric Evans (30) whose skilful hooking allied to truly inspiring leadership had much to do with his country's splendid success around 1957-58. Evans incidentally set up a unique record by captaining his country against Australia 10 years after he had played against the same country

## SCHOOL RUGBY

As even the most perfunctory scrutiny of the game's history will quickly reveal, the influence of the schools on Rugby football in Great Britain, both in its formative stages and subsequent development, has been tremendous. Indeed St. Paul's School was actually amongst the founder members of the Rugby Union, Rugby and Marlborough being important influences in the game's evolution, whilst all through history the Public Schools of England, Scotland, Ireland and Wales together with their Grammar and Primary School counterparts have been serving the formative needs of the International of tomorrow.

The English Schools' R.F.U. was formed in 1904. Since 1970 it has been known as The Rugby Football Schools' Union and has a membership of over 1,000. It is a constituent part of the R.F.U. and is divided into eight areas. The leading schools sides in Great Britain are:-

## ENGLAND

ALL HALLOWS SCHOOL—Colours: Magenta and black.
AMPLEFORTH COLLEGE—Colours: Red and black.
BEAUMONT COLLEGE—Colours: Dark blue, Eton blue and chocolate.
BEDFORD SCHOOL—Colours: Red jersey with Eagle in dark blue.
BLUNDELL'S SCHOOL—Colours: White, red stockings, black tops.
BROMSGROVE SCHOOL—Colours: Maroon and silver.
CHELTENHAM COLLEGE—Colours: Black and red.
CITY OF LONDON SCHOOL—
CRANLEIGH SCHOOL—Colours: White, old gold crest and collar, black and old gold stockings.
CRANBROOK SCHOOL—Colours: Maroon and black.
CLIFTON COLLEGE—Colours: White.
DENSTONE COLLEGE—Colours: White with red trimmings.
DOUAI SCHOOL—Colours: Red, blue and gold.
DOVER COLLEGE—Colours: Black and white.
DOWNSIDE SCHOOL—Colours: Red and gold.
DULWICH COLLEGE—Colours: Blue and black.
DURHAM SCHOOL—Colours: Green and white.
EASTBOURNE COLLEGE—Colours: Blue and white squares, stag's head badge.
ELLESMERE COLLEGE—Colours: Black and white.
EPSOM COLLEGE—Colours: Blue and white.
ETON COLLEGE—Colours: White jersey with fleur-de-lis, blue and black quartered stockings.

FELSTED SCHOOL—Colours: Blue and white.
FRAMLINGHAM COLLEGE—Colours: Chocolate and light blue.
GIGGLESWICK SCHOOL—Colours: Red and black.
GRESHAM'S SCHOOL—Colours: Black and white hoops.
HABERDASHER'S ASKEY'S SCHOOL—Colours: Blue and white hoops.
HAILEBURY COLLEGE—Colours: Magenta and white.
HARROW SCHOOL—Colours: Blue jersey, silver lion badge.
HURSTPIERPOINT COLLEGE—Colours: Red and white.
KING EDWARD'S SCHOOL, BIRMINGHAM—Colours: Dark blue, and thin light
    blue hoops.
KING'S SCHOOL, CANTERBURY—Colours: Blue and white.
KING'S SCHOOL, ROCHESTER—Colours: Blue and black.
KING WILLIAM'S COLLEGE, I.O.M.—Colours: Black jerseys and shorts, magenta
    rings on black stockings.
LEIGHTON PARK SCHOOL—Colours: Chocolate, yellow and blue.
LEY'S SCHOOL—Colours: Blue and white.
MARLBOROUGH COLLEGE—Colours: Blue and white.
MERCHANT TAYLOR'S SCHOOL—Colours: All white.
MILL HILL SCHOOL—Colours: Chocolate and white.
MONKTON COMBE SCHOOL—Colours: Navy blue and white.
MOUNT ST. MARY'S COLLEGE—Colours: Royal blue, sky blue, old gold.
NAUTICAL COLLEGE, PANGBOURNE—Colours: Red, white and blue jerseys.
OAKHAM SCHOOL—Colours: Black, red collars and cuffs.
OUNDLE SCHOOL—Colours: White jersey, blue collar, and School crest, white shorts,
    blue stockings with red tops.
PERSE SCHOOL—Colours: Purple, black and white.
RADLEY COLLEGE—Colours: Cerise and white.
RATCLIFFE COLLEGE—Colours: Royal blue and white.
ROSSALL SCHOOL—Colours: Red and white.
RUGBY SCHOOL—Colours: White jersey, light and dark blue stockings.
ST. ALBAN'S SCHOOL—Colours: Red, yellow, blue and black.
ST. BEE'S SCHOOL—Colours: Blue, red collar, red stockings, white shorts.
ST. EDWARD'S SCHOOL, OXFORD—Colours: Red and dark blue.
ST. PETER'S SCHOOL, YORK—Colours: Chocolate and white.
ST. PAUL'S SCHOOL—
SEDBERGH SCHOOL—Colours: Brown and gold.
SHERBORNE SCHOOL—Colours: Royal blue, yellow badge.
STONEHURST COLLEGE—Colours: Maroon and white.
STOWE SCHOOL—Colours: Royal blue and gold.
SUTTON VALENCE SCHOOL—Colours: Light and dark blue rings.
TAUNTON SCHOOL—Colours: Royal blue and dark blue.
TONBRIDGE SCHOOL—Colours: Black and white.
TRENT COLLEGE—Colours: Blue and white.
UPPINGHAM SCHOOL—Colours: White and royal blue.
WELLINGTON COLLEGE—Colours: Black and orange hoops.
WEST BUCKLAND SCHOOL—Colours: Red and black.
WHITGIFT SCHOOL—
WORKSOP COLLEGE—Colours: Blue and white rings.
WREKIN COLLEGE—Colours: Dark blue and light blue.

## SCOTLAND

EDINBURGH ACADEMY—Colours: Blue and white.
FETTE'S COLLEGE—Colours: Magenta and chocolate.
GEORGE WATSON'S COLLEGE, EDINBURGH—Colours: Maroon and white.
MERCHISTON CASTLE SCHOOL—Colours: Navy blue.
DOLLAR ACADEMY—
GLASGOW ACADEMY—
GLENALMOND (TRINITY COLLEGE)—

GEORGE HERIOT'S SCHOOL—
LORRETTO SCHOOL—
DANIEL STEWART'S COLLEGE—

## WALES

LLANDOVERY COLLEGE—Colours: White jerseys, blue cuffs, navy shorts, scarlet
   stockings.
CHRIST COLLEGE, BRECON—Colours: Green and gold.
GOWERTON—Colours: Navy and red.
NEATH GRAMMAR SCHOOL—Colours: Navy and gold.
AMMAN VALLEY GRAMMAR SCHOOL—Colours: Brown and yellow.
CARDIFF HIGH SCHOOL—
PONTARDAWE GRAMMAR SCHOOL—Colours: Red and navy.
YSTALYFERA GRAMMAR SCHOOL—Colours: Navy and light blue.

## IRELAND

ARMAGH ROYAL SCHOOL—Colours: Maroon and blue.
BELFAST R.A.I.—Colours: Yellow and black.
BLACKROCK COLLEGE—Colours: Blue and white.
CAMPBELL COLLEGE—Colours: Black and white.
CLONGOWES SCHOOL—Colours: White with purple badge.
FOYLE COLLEGE—Colours: White jerseys and shorts, black, red and yellow
   stockings.
PORTORA ROYAL SCHOOL—Colours: Black and yellow.
WESLEY COLLEGE, DUBLIN—Colours:

## SCORING

The Modern Scoring values which were adopted in 1906, viz.: Converted goal=5 points, try=3 points, penalty goal=3 points, dropped goal=4 points, goal from a mark=3 points, remained unchanged right up to the season 1948-49 when the value of the dropped goal was reduced from 4 to 3 points. In an effort to encourage more open rugby a further alteration was made in 1971 when the value of a try was increased from 3 to 4 points. In the game's earliest beginnings matches were decided purely by goals, a try, or rouge or touchdown, as they were then referred to, having no scoring significance unless it was converted into a goal. Indeed the rouge or touchdown was looked upon merely as the opportunity to kick at goal. In 1875, however, the try did achieve something akin to recognition in that 3 touchdowns or rouges were adjudged as equal to a try, three tries in turn counted as one goal. It was not, however, until 1887, that the adoption of the rules prevailing at Cheltenham College saw the try accorded a definite numerical value. It now counted 1 point, but was still inferior to the goal which counted three. This was varied somewhat in 1889 when the Rugby Union decreed

that the value of a penalty goal be reduced to 2 points, but the ruling differed from that of the International Board's which affixed the scoring values for International matches as follows: Goal from a try=4 points, dropped goal or goal from a mark=3 points, try=2 points, with the reservation that when a goal was kicked from a try only the goal counted.

## SCORING FEATS
### (Individuals)

Scores are arranged in order of contemporary value but where significant the modern equivalent value is given in brackets.

### International Games

Phil Bennett (Llanelli) created the world record when he scored 26 points (2 tries, 9 conversions) for Wales v. Japan, Cardiff, October 1973.

The record for games between members of the International Board was created at Auckland in June 1969 when W. Fergie McCormick scored 24 points (1 dropped goal, 3 conversions, and 5 penalty goals) for New Zealand v. Wales.

Although his total of 22 at the time, if updated then D. Lambert's points for

England (5 conversions, 2 tries, 2 penalty goals) v. France, Twickenham, January 1911, would equal McCormick's score mentioned above.

22 points—G. Bosch, 6 penalty goals, 2 conversions, v. France, Pretoria, June 1975.

19 points (20 today)—K. Jarrett (Wales), 5 conversions, 2 penalty goals, 1 try, v. England, Cardiff, April 1967. Jarrett was making his international debut.

19 points—J. Bancroft (Wales), 8 conversions, 1 penalty goal, v. France, Swansea, January 1910.

18 points—D. B. Clarke (New Zealand), 6 penalty goals, v. British Isles, Dunedin, July 1959.

17 points—T. J. Kiernan (British Isles), 5 penalty goals, 1 conversion, v. South Africa, Pretoria, June 1968.

17 points—G. Camberabero (France), 4 penalty goals, 1 dropped goal, 1 conversion, v. Australia, Paris, February 1967.

17 points—D. B. Clarke (New Zealand), 4 conversions, 3 penalty goals, v. France, Christchurch 1961.

17 points—A. Old (England), 5 penalty goals, 1 conversion, v. Ireland, Twickenham, 1974.

16 points (17 today)—B. Lewis Jones (British Isles), 1 dropped goal, 2 penalty goals, 2 conversions, 1 try, v. Australia, Sydney, August 1950.

16 points—K. Oxlee (South Africa), 5 conversions, 2 penalty goals, v. British Isles, Bloemfontein 1962.

It is also worth noting that D. S. Maré scored 22 points for South Africa against France in Paris in 1907 although this is not always considered to have been a full international, and G. Camberero scored 27 points for France v. Italy at Toulon in 1967.

## Other Games

44 points—Tommy Yssel (Diggers), 2 tries, 18 conversions, v. Alberton Johannesburg, September 2, 1972.

41 points—J. F. Karam (New Zealanders), 2 tries, 15 conversions, 1 penalty goal, v. S. Australia, Adelaide, May 1, 1974.

40 points—Ben Erwee (Springs) v. Vrede, Eastern Transvaal 1945.

38 points—R. A. Jarden (New Zealanders), 6 tries, 10 conversions, v. Central West Australia, Parkes, 1952. (44

points today).

37 points—J. L. Graham (Counties Union), 14 conversions, 3 penalty goals, v. West Coast, Pukekohe, New Zealand, September 26, 1972.

37 points—Alan Old (British Lions), v. South-West District, Mossel Bay, May 29, 1974.

36 points—Gerald Bosch (Transvaal), 13 conversions, 2 dropped goals, 1 try, v. Far Northern Transvaal, Johannesburg, July 1973.

35 points—J. Dowse (Wallabies), v. Western Australia, Perth, July 22, 1961.

34 points—G. F. Kember (New Zealanders), 14 conversions, 2 penalty goals, v. N. E. Cape, Burgersdorp, 1970.

## Points on Tour

W. J. Wallace (Wellington) scored a total of 230 points (251 today) while on tour with the first New Zealand team in Great Britain in 1905, 23 tries, 72 conversions, 3 penalty goals, 2 dropped goals. Wallace added a further 16 points (20 today), 4 tries, 2 conversions, to this total in two games in California on the way home.

In New Zealand and Australia in 1937, G. H. Brand of Western Province and South Africa, scored 209 points made up of, 77 conversions, 17 penalty goals, 1 dropped goal (208 today).

Barry John scored 191 points (7 tries, 31 conversions, 8 dropped goals, 28 penalty goals) (198 points today) in British Lions tour of New Zealand in 1971.

D. B. Clarke (Waikato) in South Africa in 1960, scored 175 (176) points for New Zealand—32 conversions, 32 penalty goals, 4 dropped goals, and 1 try. In Australia in 1956, scored 163 points (167) for New Zealand—44 conversions, 20 penalty goals, 1 goal from mark, 4 tries. In the British Isles and France with the 5th "All-Blacks" 1963-64 Clarke scored 136 points (137)—32 conversions, 18 penalty goals, 5 dropped goals, 1 try.

A. Irvine scored 156 points, 5 tries, 26 conversions, 27 penalty goals, 1 dropped goal, for the British Lions in South Africa in 1974.

J. F. Karam scored 145 points on the Seventh "All-Blacks" 1972-73 tour of Great Britain, France, Canada and U.S.A. 2 tries, 31 conversions, 25 penalty goals. In 1974 he scored 139 points, 3 tries, 38 conversions, 15 penalty goals, 2 dropped goals, with the "All-Blacks" in Australia and Fiji.

On tour with the New Zealand Services team in Britain and France in 1945, H. E. Cooke totalled 129 points, made up of 34 conversions, 18 penalty goals, 1 dropped goal (125).

In New Zealand and Australia in 1937 F. G. Turner of Transvaal and South Africa registered 125 points made up as follows: 17 tries, 29 conversions, 4 penalty goals, 1 dropped goal (141).

P. Carmichael (Queensland) scored 122 points for Australia in Britain in 1908 viz.—52 conversions, 5 penalty goals, 1 goal from a mark.

J. F. Byrne scored 120 points (120) with the British team in South Africa in 1896, 5 tries, 29 conversions, 9 penalty and 5 dropped goals.

In Great Britain and France in 1935-36 G. Gilbert, of West Coast and New Zealand, scored 118 points as follows: 29 conversions, 16 penalty goals, 3 dropped goals (115).

In Great Britain in 1905, J. Hunter of Taranaki and New Zealand, scored 117 points—all tries (156).

In 1927-28 T. S. Lawton, of West Suburbs and Australia, scored 104 points while on tour of Britain and France with a New South Wales representative team. His total was made up of 47 conversions, 2 penalty goals, 1 dropped goal (103).

P. Bennett scored 103 points, 1 try, 15 conversions, 21 penalty goals and 2 dropped goals, in South Africa in 1974 with the British Lions.

In Great Britain and France in 1924 M. F. Nicholls (Wellington and New Zealand) scored 103 points made up of 1 try, 35 conversions, 6 penalty goals, 3 dropped goals. (101).

In Great Britain and France with the 1945 New Zealand Services team R. W. H. Scott of Auckland, scored 99 points, viz., 33 conversions, 11 penalty goals (105).

In 1950 M. C. Thomas of Newport, playing for Great Britain in New Zealand and Australia, scored 96 points made up of 9 tries, 18 conversions, 11 penalty goals.

In New Zealand and Australia in 1950, B. Lewis Jones (Devonport Services) scored 92 points (94) for Great Britain, made up of 22 conversions, 13

penalty goals, 1 dropped goal, 2 tries. Jones, incidentally, was only flown out as a replacement for the injured Irish full-back George Norton, so that his appearances were restricted to seven matches.

## Points in a Season

Sam Doble (Moseley) created a world record by scoring 581 points in season 1971-72. His total included 47 points in 5 matches for England in South Africa.

In 1973-74 Peter Butler scored 574 points including 488 for his own club—Gloucester.

Robin Williams scored 561 points in season 1974-75, including 517 for Pontypool.

Alan Pearn's total for Bristol in 1972-73 was 557 points.

Malcolm Young (Gosforth) totalled 480 points in 1972-73.

## Most Points in International Career

D. B. Clarke, 207 points in 31 appearances for New Zealand.

T. J. Kiernan, 158 points in 54 appearances for Ireland plus another 35 points in Tests against South Africa with the British Lions.

R. B. Hiller (Harlequins) scored 138 points in 19 appearances for England.

## Points in a Career

At the end of season 1974-75 Sam Doble (Moseley) had taken his career total to 3,453 points, thus beating the previous British record held by George Cole (Coventry) with 3,393.

To end of season 1974 in New Zealand, W. F. McCormick had scored a record total of 2013 points, most of them for Canterbury.

So he has surpassed the previous record created by another New Zealander, D. B. Clarke (Waikato), who scored 1,851 points (todays value 1,853) 1951-61. Clarke's total included a record 207 points in Internationals.

## Tries on Tour

The record number of tries scored by a player on tour belongs to J. Hunter, the Taranaki threequarter, who scored 42 for New Zealand in Britain in 1905.

Next highest is that of R. L. Aston

(Blackheath and England) who scored 30 with the 1891 British representative team in South Africa. Tries in those days, however, only counted a single point.

Other notable try scoring achievements on tour were:-

24 Tries—J. Lubster (Wesern Province) for South Africa in Great Britain, 1906; C. Russell (Newtown) for Australia in Britain, 1908.

23 Tries—W. J. Wallace (Wellington) for New Zealand in Great Britain, 1905.

21 Tries—A. J. F. O'Reilly (Old Belvedere and Leicester) for Great Britain in Australia and New Zealand 1959.

20 Tries—A. H. Hart (Taranaki) for New Zealand in Britain and France, 1924.

J. P. Engelbrecht (Western Province) for South Africa in Australia and New Zealand, 1965.

19 Tries—G. W. Smith and A. E. Cooke (both of Auckland) for New Zealand in Britain and France in 1905 and 1924 respectively; M. J. Dick for Fifth "All-Blacks" 1963-64; P. B. Jackson for Great Britain in Australia and New Zealand, 1959.

18 Tries—E. E. McHardy (Orange Free State) for South Africa in Great Britain, 1912; A. Stegman (Western Province) for South Africa in Britain, 1906; A. L. Novis (Blackheath and England) for Great Britain in New Zealand and Australia, 1930.

17 Tries—F. Turner (Transvaal) for South Africa in New Zealand and Australia, 1937; E. E. Ford (Glebe-Balmain) for New South Wales in Great Britain and France, 1927-28; A. Asher (Auckland) for New Zealand in Australia 1903; R. Watt (Otago) for New Zealand in Australia, 1956; G. S. Thorne (Auckland) for New Zealand in South Africa, 1970.

16 Tries—D. O. Williams (Western Province) for South Africa in New Zealand and Australia, 1937; L. Babrow (Western Province) for South Africa on same tour; K. J. Jones (Newport and Wales) for Great Britain in New Zealand and Australia, 1950; A. J. O'Reilly (Old Belvedere and Ireland) for Great Britain in South Africa, 1955, J. T. Viljoen (Natal) for South Africa in Australia 1971.

15 Tries—P. Lyster (Natal) for South Africa in New Zealand and Australia, 1937; C. Towers (Randwick) for New South Wales in Great Britain and France, 1927-28; J. K. Osche (Western Province) for South Africa in Great Britain, 1951.

14 Tries—M. Zimmerman (Western Province) for South Africa in Great Britain and France, 1931; H. Wilkinson (Halifax and England) for Great Britain in New Zealand Australia, 1930; T. H. Caughey (Auckland) for New Zealand in Great Britain, 1935; G. R. Horsley (Queensland) for Australia in South Africa, 1953; R. W. Caulton for New Zealand in Great Britain, 1963-64; M. J. Antelme for South Africa in Great Britain, 1960-61.

## Tries in a Match

The record for most tries in an International is five; shared by two players —G. Lindsay for Scotland v. Wales, 1887, and D. Lambert for England v. France, 1907.

The following are among the best in important matches other than Internationals: 8 tries—T. R. Heeps, New Zealanders v. Northern N.S.W., 1962.

6 tries—R. G. Dryburgh, South Africans v. Queensland, 1956; R. A. Jarden, New Zealanders v. Central West Australia, 1951; J. S. Boyce, Australians v. Wairarapa (New Zealand), 1962.

## Tries in a Season

Dan Jones scored 85 tries (63 for Neath) in season 1927-28. This is a British first-class Rugby Union record.

Here are a few of the best records of recent years:

Chris Scotford scored 60 tries for Solihull in season 1970-71. This was the season in which their 1st XV created a record with a total of 247 tries.

D. Hoyland, 52 tries for Morley, 1973-74; A. J. Morley, 45 tries, 1973-74, including 28 for Bristol; B. Fishwick, 44 tries for Orrell, 1973-74.

## SCORING FEATS
### (Teams)

For highest victories and defeats in Internationals see under INTERNATIONALS, and also under AUSTRALIA, NEW ZEALAND, and SOUTH AFRICA.

The highest scoring under modern scoring values—Queen's College, Taunton 171, Huish Grammar School 0, 1920. H. G. Reason scored 7 tries and made 10 conversions, total 41 points.

## Most Points in a Season

Morley 1,223 points in 42 games, 1973-74.

Bristol 1,138 points in 48 games, 1971-72.

Orrell 1,124 points in 49 games, 1971-72.

St. Lukes College 1,082 points in 42 games 1953-54.

Solihull 1,072 points in 39 games 1970-71.

Kingston Park 1,061 points in 31 games, 1971-72.

Pontypool 1,061 points in 50 games, 1974-75.

## Heavy scoring by teams on tour

### GREAT BRITAIN

IN SOUTH AFRICA: 97−0 against South Western Districts, in 1974.

IN NEW ZEALAND: 64−5 against Combined Marlborough-Nelson, Golden Bay, Motueka XV in 1959.

IN AUSTRALIA: 71−3 against Western Australia in 1930.

### SOUTH AFRICA

IN AUSTRALIA: 63−0 against Western Districts in 1937.

IN NEW ZEALAND: 55−11 against N.Z. Universities, Auckland, 1965.

IN BRITAIN: 44−0 against Northumberland in 1906; repeated against Scotland in 1951.

IN FRANCE: 36−9 against Coast of Basque, 1961.

### NEW ZEALAND

IN SOUTH AFRICA: 85−0 against N.E. Cape, 1970.

IN BRITAIN: 55−0 against Devon in 1905.

IN AUSTRALIA: 117−6 against South Australia, Adelaide, 1974.

### AUSTRALIA

IN SOUTH AFRICA: 50−12 against Western Transvaal in 1953.

IN NEW ZEALAND: 41−6 against Combined Golden Bay Motueka-Nelson in 1955.

IN BRITAIN: 49−0 against Northumberland and Durham in 1947.

IN FRANCE: 28−12 against Lille, 1971.

### ENGLAND

IN SOUTH AFRICA: 97−0 against South Western Districts, Mossel Bay, 1974.

IN NEW ZEALAND: 16−10 against New Zealand, 1973.

IN AUSTRALIA: 64−3 against Western Australia, Perth, 1975.

### FRANCE

IN SOUTH AFRICA: 50−0 against Western Transvaal, 1971.

IN AUSTRALIA: 45−12 against Tasmania, 1972.

IN NEW ZEALAND: 23−9 against King Country, 1968.

## Tries

The New Zealanders scored 22 tries when beating Northern New South Wales 103−0, at Quirindi in 1962.

When the Diggers beat Alberton 124−0 in Transvaal Grand Challenge, September, 1972, they also scored 22 tries.

## SCOTTISH RUGBY UNION

The fact that the Scottish Rugby Union (1873) was formed two years later than the Rugby Union is apt to mislead many followers to believing that the development of Rugby Football in Scotland lagged behind that of its English counterpart. In actual fact, however, there is ample evidence to support Scottish claims that the game flourished in their country even when it was in its embryonic stages elsewhere. To begin with Edinburgh Academicals and West of Scotland rank with any on the score of antiquity, and then the fact must not be overlooked that it was these two clubs with St. Andrew's University and Royal High, who took the initiative in issuing the challenge that led to the playing of the first Scotland-England encounter at Edinburgh in 1871. As recorded elsewhere (see INTERNATIONALS) Scotland's success on this occasion influenced them to emulate their English rivals by organising their Rugby on a national basis, and thus it came about that the Scottish Union came into being at Edinburgh in 1873. As a result several of the leading clubs who had affiliated themselves to the Rugby Union, withdrew from that body, and transferred their allegiance to where it quite rightly belonged.

The Union was originally formed by these six clubs—Edinburgh Academicals, Glasgow Academicals, West of Scotland, Royal High School F.P., Merchistonians, and Edinburgh University.

Prominent in the vital consolidatory period of the Union's existence was the famous J. Aikman-Smith, who acted as Secretary from 1890 to 1914, and then again from 1919-20 after his successor, A. D. Flett, had been killed in action during World War I. In 1920 H. M. Simson was appointed Secretary, and remained in office until 1953 when he was succeeded by John Law, who nowadays combines the office with that of Treasurer.

From 1871 to 1899, the Scottish Rugby Union played its Home Internationals at venues such as Raeburn Place, Edinburgh, Old Anniesland, Glasgow, and Powderhall, but in 1899-1900 Inverleith (Edinburgh) became the permanent ground, and it remained so until 1924-25, when the great stadium, Murrayfield, became the headquarters of the game in Scotland.

The constitution of the Union at the present time allows for six special representatives and nine District representatives reposnsible for the five districts into which the Union is divided viz., two each from Edinburgh, Glasgow, and Southern Districts, and one each from the Midlands, Northern and London districts.

The Secretary and Treasurer is John Law, Murrayfield, Edinburgh, EH12 5PJ.

See also under INTERNATIONALS (SCOTLAND).

## SCRUM FORMATIONS

(See also under TACTICS AND EVOLUTION and LAWS OF THE GAME).

Although New Zealand teams between 1930-32 adopted a "2-3-2" scrummaging formation in order to accommodate the inclusion of a "roving" or winging-forward, the two main scrummaging formations throughout the history of the game in its 15-a-side version have been:-

(a) The traditional British formation of "3-2-3".

(b) The "3-4-1" formation originally favoured by South Africa, and which has subsequently achieved universal popularity.

Positionally the only difference between the two formations is that the two flank or winging-forwards as they are called in the back row of an orthodox "3-2-3" scrum move up to become the flank men in the four-man second row of a "3-4-1" scrum—the function of the middle man in the back row i.e. the lock remaining the same in either formation. Advantages claimed for the "3-4-1" formation over its "3-2-3" counterpart are:-

(1) A quicker heel in that the ball has only to pass through two rows of feet against three in the "3-2-3" scrum.

(2) It facilitates the spoiling activities of the wing forwards in that they are brought positionally nearer to the opposing half-backs. In addition they (the wing forwards) are afforded a clearer and earlier sight of the ball than they are allowed in the 3-row scrum, which in turn enables them to reach an instantaneous decision on the question of whether to break in pursuit of the opposing backs, or of retreating to assist the defence of their own. Against these advantages however there is the consideration—as it happens a practical one—that a "3-4-1" scrum tends to be lop-sided and slovenly in action unless it is manned by experts in the eight specialist positions, and moreover practically excludes the use of "the wheel" as part of the strategy of scrummaging.

From a technical viewpoint the main difference between the two formations is that whereas in the traditional "3-2-3" scrum the "shove" is directed squarely against the whole opposition front row in the "3-4-1" version it is concentrated at an angle which serves to make the opposing "hooker" its focal point. Under both formations however the sought-after millenium is the concentrated shove the moment the ball is in the scrum, and this can only be achieved by perfect binding and muscular coordination between the eight pack members.

## SEVEN-A-SIDE RUGBY

In Britain more especially, seven-a-side Rugby has gained great popularity as an end of season diversion from the dourer and sterner stuff that provides the bulk of a normal season's watching. The composition of a sevens team called for four backs and three forwards, and speed and handling ability are the main qualities demanded of the participants. Inevitably the Rugby is open and spectacular and the pace is such that all matches are curtailed to a duration of 14-20 minutes.

Seven-a-side Rugby was first introduced on a proper competitive basis in Scotland where it was "invented" by Edward Haig, a quarter-back with Melrose R.F.C. In 1883, when the club was seeking a solution to their financial problems, Haig suggested this abbreviated form of Rugby as an entertaining crowd-puller and the first competition was held at Greenyards with Melrose being the winners. Today the Melrose competition is considered by many—and certainly by the Scots—to be the premier seven-a-side competition despite the claims of the Middlesex Sevens.

Edward Haig's gravestone at Melrose bears this inscription: "Edward 'Ned' Haig. Born Jedburgh 7th December, 1858. Died Melrose 29th March, 1939. Erected by the Border Rugby Clubs in memory of the originator of Seven-a-side Rugby."

The major tournament staged in England is the Middlesex Sevens Competition which was inaugurated in 1926 and attracts an increasingly large entry as the years go by. The preliminary rounds of the competition which is staged wholly for charity, are played on a variety of London grounds, with the 16 surviving clubs contesting the final rounds at Twickenham on the first Saturday in May, the successful finalists receiving the Russell-Cargill trophy. Harlequins, who won the cup in the first season of the competition, have in all seven successes to their credit a record for the competition. A pleasing innovation .which was introduced in 1934 saw the Barbarians invited to compete as a guest club, and the custom was subsequently maintained with invitations to several of the famous clubs of Scotland, Wales and the North of England. Guest teams who have actually won the competition are Barbarians, Cardiff, Sale, and Heriots F.P.

## SOUTH AFRICA

A form of rugby was introduced to South Africa as far back as 1861 by the Rev. Canon George Ogilvie who had migrated to that country after playing football at Winchester College. His version of the game, however, was a mixture of rugby and soccer and it was probably this mixed style of play which was adopted when the Military met the Civilians on the Green Point Common, Cape Town, August 23rd, 1862. The game was nicknamed 'Gog's Game' after the instigator and although we are left in some doubt as to the style of play in 1862 we do know that the first club to adopt rugby proper was Hamilton in Cape Town. This club was formed in 1875 and turned over to Rugby in 1878, closely followed by the Villager R.F.C.

With the game taking such a firm hold in Cape Town it is not surprising that the first Union formed in this part of the African continent was the Western Province in 1883, and from there the game spread so quickly that the South African Rugby Board was formed in 1889. Two years later, in 1891, the South Africans received their first visit from a British team led by the Scottish International and Edinburgh Academicals player, W. E. Maclagan, but they proved no match for their opponents who won all their 19 matches, including three "Tests". By 1896, however, the standard of South African Rugby had improved sufficiently to enable them to win one of the three Tests against a reasonably strong British touring side captained by J. Hammond, of Cambridge University, and then seven years later they actually had the better of a series with a fully representative British side led by the Scotsman, Mark Morrison. Three matches were played, South Africa winning one, with the other two drawn. It was not until 1906 however that the Rugby world at large came to a full realisation of the now formidable strength of South African Rugby, for the team led by Paul Roos—the first ever to leave the Union for a tour abroad—played 28 matches in Great Britain, winning 25 of them, and suffered only two defeats, one at the hands of the full Scottish International side, and the other at the hands of a near International standard Cardiff XV in a game played on a surface far removed from the bonehard grounds they were accustomed to play on in their own country. Indeed it speaks much for the achievements of Paul Roos and his men that they were acclaimed in Great Britain as an even greater combination than Dave Gallaher's "All-Blacks" who had toured there a year earlier. South African Rugby was now recognised as a major force in world Rugby, and so indeed it proved, for in 1910 a British team led by Dr. T. Smyth, of Ireland, were defeated in eight of the twenty-four matches they played in the Union, and were in addition beaten 2−1 in the Test series. Then in 1912 came a return visit to Great Britain from a team led by W. A. Millar, which actually went one better than its 1906 predecessors by winning all five of their Internationals. In all, Millar's team were successful in 24 of their 27 engagements two of their three defeats being sustained in Wales against Newport and Swansea respectively, and the other by a London Counties XV.

In 1921 South Africa broke new ground by sending a team to Australia and New Zealand under the leadership of Theo Pienaar, and in addition to drawing a Test series in the latter country, won 20 of the 24 matches played on the entire tour, their two defeats being inflicted by Canterbury and the New Zealand representative side. In 1924 they were once again the hosts to a British team led by R. Cove-Smith, and were easy 3−0 victors in the Test series. Then in 1928−the occasion being the visit of Maurice Brownlee's New Zealanders−South African Rugby faced what was to date, undoubtedly, its greatest Test, for Brownlee's team containing as it did, many of the team which had gone invincible in Great Britain in 1924, was probably one of the strongest which had visited South Africa up until that time. As it turned out indeed not unexpectedly, the honours were even, each country winning two Tests, although on the entire tour the New Zealanders were defeated on five occasions. The next South African venture abroad took place in 1931, when B. L. Osler's team played 26 matches in Great Britain, losing only one of them−a 21−30 defeat at the hands of a combined Leicester and Midland Counties XV. Back at home in 1933, South Africa won their Test series with A. W. Ross's Australian team 3−2, and then in 1937 travelled to Australia and New Zealand

under the captaincy of P. J. Nel, and suffered but two defeats against New Zealand, and New South Wales, during a 28 match itinerary in the two countries. South African Rugby had by now fully established itself as the most powerful instrument of its kind in world sport, and in 1938, yet another successful Test series was contested with a British touring side led by the Irishman, Sam Walker. Following the Second World War, South Africa once again re-established her domination in world Rugby, and in 1949 they defeated Fred Allan's visiting New Zealand side in all four of the Test matches played, and followed this up with a tour of Great Britain under Basil Kenyon in 1951, where they were successful in 30 of their 31 matches, losing only to a London Counties XV. Back once again at home in opposition to an Australian team led by John Solomon in 1953, they were easy 3−1 victors in the Tests−by which time people were becoming to accept South African domination as one of the inevitabilities of International sport. Such then was the position when a British side led by Robin Thompson, of Ireland, visited the Union in 1955, and they in fact were to achieve what was generally regarded as next to the impossible by holding their hosts to a 2−2 draw in the Test series. Thus for the first time in 27 years had South Africa failed to win outright a Test series in her own country, and indeed there were further disasters immediately ahead, for in 1956 S. S. Vivier's team were defeated in six of the twenty-three matches they played in New Zealand and in addition lost the Test "Rubber" 1−3.

South Africa had another shock in 1958 when the first French representative side to pay them a visit won one of the two Tests and drew the other. But after beating the first Scottish International side to appear in South Africa (1960) thoughts that the Springboks were on the wane were at least temporarily dispelled by the Fifth Springboks tour of Britain and France in 1960-61. The complete masters up front this side gave a great exhibition of "power Rugby," winning all but three of their 34 matches and losing only once. Their tactics met with plenty of criticism but they made an almost clean sweep in the five Tests, only France being able to hold them to a draw.

The South Africans' dour style of play, however, was not popular about this period of their history. The Barbarians beat them by playing them at their own game and although the South Africans subsequently defeated the visiting British Lions in 1962, defeats by France, New Zealand and Australia in the mid-sixties led to some deep thinking at home and proposals for sharpening domestic competition, particularly the Currie Cup.

In the late sixties South Africa was again dominant. Their comparatively poor record in Britain in 1969-70 could be largely ignored for it was obvious that the anti-apartheid demonstrations must have unnerved them, besides which it was only a few months later back home that almost the same players beat an All-Blacks side that had enjoyed a run of 17 consecutive Test victories.

If proof was needed that South African rugby was not what it used to be, however, this came with England's surprise victory there in 1972. And when, in 1974, the British Lions swept all before them in their glorious undefeated tour the South African Rugby Board began an investigation into the improvement of their game.

So much for the factual record. The successful part of their history has been founded mainly in the tradition of great heavy, albeit, highly skilful forward apotheosised by such as A. S. Knight, M. M. ("Boy") Louw, P. J. Mostert, P. J. Nel, Chris Koch, and Hennie Muller who have rucked and scrummaged their opponents almost literally into the ground, before bringing their own backs into the game as an attacking force. This of course, was not in the original South African tradition, for the earlier teams, notably Paul Roos's 1906 team with its brilliant All-Stellenboch University three-quarter line, achieved their success on the basis of swift and fluent back play. As the years however brought their new techniques, including the use of the back row forwards as spoilers pure and simple, the South Africans, who have always been the astutest of tacticians, were quick to perceive that success in Test Rugby invariably went to the side which made the fewest errors the opposition could capitalise on. Thus was introduced the technique which B. L.

Osler brought to a pitch of nearly complete, if unspectacular, perfection in Great Britain in 1931, the technique which had its basis in a powerful pack of forwards as the main striking force, with the backs as "support troops" kicking accurately to touch until they had gained enough ground to handle with comparative impunity. "Attack only within sight of your opponent's goal-posts," was the principle that Osler and his men never lost sight of, and even though the spectacle was often dreary there could be no cavilling at the results it produced, for the team suffered but one defeat in their 26 matches, and that in a high scoring match in which they lacked the services of Osler, the arch strategist.

When Dr. Danie Craven (Osler's scrum-half partner on the 1931 tour of Great Britain) assumed what was virtually complete responsibility for his country's Test Rugby after the Second World War, he adhered closely to the principles established by Osler, and indeed concentrated even more closely on reducing the game to a science which would admit to the least possible number of errors. Perhaps not surprisingly South African Rugby continued to remain the least attractive to watch, but as with the Osler regime there was no denying either its power or effect. It was perhaps the visit of the 1955 British "Lions" with their magnificently open and spectacular back play that caused many followers and critics in the Union to experience a feeling of revulsion from the dour and circumspect pattern of their own country's Rugby. As already mentioned, more recent results have done little to relieve a feeling of anxiety, but there can be no possible doubt (in view of her past record) that South Africa will solve her Rugby Football problems in a manner that will allow her to continue as one of the leading Rugby nations.

## Record in Test Rugby

v. *Great Britain.* Played 36. Won 17. Lost 13. Drawn 6.
Biggest Win. 34–14, Bloemfontein, 1962.
Biggest Defeat. 9–28 Pretoria, 1974.

v. *New Zealand.* Played 30. Won 16. Lost 12. Drawn 2.
Biggest Win. 17–0, Durban, 1928.
Biggest Defeat. 3–20, Auckland, 1965.

*v. Australia.* Played 28. Won 21. Lost 7. Drawn 0.

Biggest Win, 28–3, Johannesburg, 1961.

Biggest Defeat. 6–21, Durban, 1933.

*v. England.* Played 7. Won 4. Lost 2. Drawn 1.

Biggest Win. 7–0, Twickenham, 1932.

Biggest Defeat. 9–18, Johannesburg, 1972.

*v. Scotland.* Played 8. Won 5. Lost 3. Drawn 0.

Biggest Win. 44–0, Murrayfield, 1951.

Biggest Defeat. 0–6, Glasgow, 1906.

*v. Wales.* Played 7. Won 6. Lost 0. Drawn 1.

Biggest Win. 24–3, Durban, 1964.

*v. Ireland.* Played 8. Won 6. Lost 1. Drawn 1.

Biggest Win, 38–0, Dublin, 1912.

*v. France.* Played 19. Won 12. Lost 3. Drawn 4.

Biggest Win. 55–6, Paris, 1906.

Biggest Defeat. 14–19, Johannesburg, 1967.

## SOUTH CANTERBURY RUGBY UNION

Founded 1888, affiliated to New Zealand Rugby Union 1892. Headquarters: Timaru, South Island. Colours: Green and black hoops. Outstanding player, R. T. Stewart, who appeared in 39 of New Zealand's presentative game's including 5 Internationals, 1923-30.

## SOUTHLAND RUGBY UNION

Founded in 1887, and affiliated to the New Zealand Rugby Union in 1894. Southland's players have been representing New Zealand from the beginning of history, and among those who have distinguished themselves are J. W. Stead and R. T. Glasgow, two of the indomitable 1st "All-Blacks" 1905-06. John Richardson, 2nd "All-Blacks" 1924-25. N. A. Mitchell, 3rd "All-Blacks" 1935-36, W. A. McCaw, 4th "All-Blacks" 1953-54 and E. J. Hazlett, 6th "All-Blacks" 1967-68. Union Headquarters: Invercargill, South Island. Colours: Maroon.

## SOUTH WESTERN DISTRICTS RUGBY UNION

Founded in 1899, South Western Districts have never perhaps loomed large in South African Rugby affairs, but

they have produced a number of famous Springbok Internationals including P. K. Albertyn and the great W. F. (Ferdie) Bergh who gained 17 caps for South Africa. Union H.Q. is at Mossell Bay.

## ST. ANDREW'S UNIVERSITY

Next to Edinburgh, St. Andrew's have produced more Scottish Internationals than any of the other Universities. P. Munroe and A. C. Ross were in the first Scottish team that met England at Raeburn Place in 1871, whilst of the subsequent representatives none achieved greater distinction than D. J. Macrae, a truly gifted centre three-quarter who played a brilliant part in his country's Triple Crown and Championship successes of 1937-38, besides touring South Africa as a member of the 1938, British team led by Sam Walker.

## ST. LUKE'S COLLEGE R.F.C.

This Exeter College's Rugby club achieved first-class recognition soon after World War II and in 1953-54 they became the first ever side to score more than 1,000 points in a season. Their remarkable record was Played 42, Won 39, Drawn 2, Lost 1; Points For 1082, Points Against 121. That solitary defeat was against Peter Evans' International XV, 6–11. A year later they first reached the finals of the Middlesex Sevens and in 1957 they won this competition by beating the holders, London Welsh, 18–5. Their second success in this competition came in 1969. Their 20 or so internationals have included such talented players as B. V. Meredith, G. Griffiths, and B. Sparks. The first Devon side to win the County Championship for 45 years, that of 1957, included four men from St. Luke's. Colours: Light and dark blue.

## ST. MARY'S HOSPITAL R.F.C.

Founded in 1864, St. Mary's have won the Hospital's Cup on 18 occasions five of these successes being gained during the 'thirties when that brilliant all-round South African athlete, H. G. Owen-Smith, was in residence. Another splendid run of success was experienced during the 1940s and 1950s when the side could call on English Internationals of the calibre of L. B. Cannell, N. M. Hall, E. K. Scott and N. O. Bennett. St. Mary's, too have figured prominently in the Middlesex "Sevens" at Twickenham with five victories to show for their endeavours. Colours: Navy with white fleur-de-lys. Hon Secretary: J. L. K. Bankes, F.R.C.S., 27 Hartley Street, London, WIN 1DA.

## "SPRINGBOK HEAD"

Every South African side visiting Great Britain bring with them a mounted "Springbok Head" which they award to the first team to defeat them, or otherwise to the team that provides them with their hardest match. The original was presented to the Welsh club, Newport, who defeated W. A. Millar's second South African side in 1912. Subsequent British combinations to achieve the honour were: Leicestershire and East Midlands (1931), London Counties (1951) the Barbarians (1961) and Oxford University (1969). The Cardiff club, although they failed to defeat Basil Kenyon's 1951 side, were nevertheless presented with a head on the merit of a fine display against them.

## SUBSTITUTES

Although substitutes had been used for many years in domestic matches in New Zealand there was generally resistance to the spread of this practice, except in trial games. The New Zealanders, however, campaigned for a number of years to persuade the International Board to allow substitutes, and in this campaign they were supported by the South Africans.

The break came at the meeting of the International Board in March 1968 when it was decided to allow up to two substitutes each side for injured players in tour and international matches, and the first to be so allowed was F. P. K. Bresnihan (U. C. Dublin) who came on for the injured C. M. H. Gibson (N.I.F. C.) in the British Isles team v. Western Transvaal, Potchefstroom, May, 18, 1968. Gibson was himself the first substitute in a full international nearly four weeks later at Pretoria, July 13, when he replaced Barry John (Cardiff) in the first Test against South Africa.

## SWANSEA R.F.C.

Swansea Rugby Football Club, formed 1873, rank with the very greatest in Rugby Football. Among their achievements are an invincible season in 1901, and victories over the three major touring teams to visit Great Britain: Australia (1908, 1966), South Africa (1912) and New Zealand (1935), whilst in addition they held the 1953 New Zealand touring side to a draw. Many of the immortals amongst Welsh players have worn the club colours, among them R. M. Owen who, with 35 caps, was the Welsh record holder until overhauled by K. J. Jones a generation later, D. I. Bebb, 34 caps and the finest Welsh wing of the 1960s, W. J. Bancroft, who gained 33 consecutive caps as the Welsh full-back, W. J. Trew, reckoned the most graceful and versatile of all quarter and half-backs, the famous crash-tackling Claude Davey, and the schoolboy half-backs Haydn Tanner and W. H. T. Davies, who earned world-wide renown by encompassing the defeat of a New Zealand touring side while they were still pupils at a local grammar school. Swansea too are famous as pioneers of the game in distant parts, for they were the first British club side to visit France, and since the last war the club have fulfilled similar missions in Rumania and Italy. The club play at the St. Helen's ground, which has had long and mostly illustrious association with both International Rugby and County cricket. Colours: White jerseys, white shorts and black and white stockings, giving them the nickname of "All-Whites." Secretary D. P. Price, The Pavilion, St. Helen's Ground, Swansea.

## TACTICS AND TEAM EVOLUTION

Up until 1875 Rugby Football was played by teams of 20-a-side, their positional composition being as follows: 13 forwards, 3 half-backs, 1 threequarter back, 3 full-backs. Inevitably the emphasis in those early beginnings was on individuality, consequently what little combination there was between back and forwards emerged more by accident than design. In 1875, however, largely at the instigation of the University clubs of Oxford and Cambridge, teams were reduced to 15 in number, which had the effect, of course of giving the game the discernible pattern it had lacked previously. There was still however little or no uniformity concerning the individual positions, for although the majority of teams might have employed a "eight forwards, seven backs formation", they continued to exercise practically unlimited choice as to their dispositions behind the scrum. Some teams, for instance, played three full-backs, two threequarters, and two half-backs, whilst others preferred to play an extra threequarter at the expense of one of the full-backs. It was in fact Scotland who pioneered the "three threequarter game"—they did so against Ireland at Belfast in 1881—and when England and Wales both followed suit a year later the position seemed to have become standardised. It was around this same period that the Oxford University, Richmond and England half-back, Alan Rotherham, conceived and implemented the idea of the half-back as the vital link in the chain of combination between forwards and backs, so that altogether the game of Rugby had reached a stage in its evolution not so very far removed from modern conceptions. Indeed the final process in the transition from "ancient" to "modern" might be said to have been effected by the Cardiff club which, in 1885, under the captaincy of F. E. Hancock, introduced a fourth threequarter to their line up behind the scrum. Wales, inevitably, with her traditional galaxy of fast elusive backs, immediately adopted the system, and although the actual results they obtained with it in International matches between 1886-93 did not suggest any match winning innovations, it was adopted by England, Scotland and Ireland in 1894, and with "fractional" diversions by Australia and New Zealand, has remained an established feature of the Rugby game ever since. The New Zealanders, of course, and to a lesser degree, the Australian's have forsworn the four threequarter game in favour of their own modified "five-eighths" game which in effect means that they employ two stand-off halves (the five-eighths), and one centre threequarters. In actual practice though this formation is only distinguishable from the traditional four threequarter game, in that the centre is *always* the last man to hand the ball on to the wings irrespective of whether the attack develops to right or left. If indeed there is any advantage claimed for this system over the traditional method, then it is the hardly discernible one of a closer understanding between the mid-field backs.

Once uniformity had been achieved in respect of the positions, it was of course, but a short step to the allocation of specific functions of the players occupying them, thus emerged the clear pattern of team combination through the forwards to the threequarters via the half-backs. Thus broadly speaking the period 1894-1905, in Great Britain at least was the era of swift spectacular back play in which forwards in the main concentrated their efforts on solid scrummaging with the object of setting their backs in motion with the minimum of delay. Inevitably it was an era that produced a whole crop of talented half-backs and threequarters, and Wales in particular, with such as Trew, Bush, Owen and the immortal line of Llewelyn, Nicholls, Gabe and Morgan, might be said to have produced more than her

Her Majesty the Queen is introduced to members of The President's Overseas XV when they met England at Twickenham in April 1971 as part of the Rugby Union's Centenary celebrations. Her Majesty is shaking hands with the great South African lock, F. C. H. Du Preez

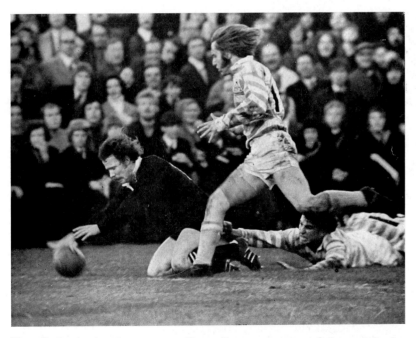

New Zealand wing-three-quarter Grant Batty scores one of the 21 tries he obtained with the Seventh All Blacks 1972–73. This one was against Cambridge University

Two all-time greats whose careers coincided in the 1920s. (*Above*) W. W. Wakefield, England's famous back-row forward (pictured in 1923), and (*left*) John MacDonald Bannerman, Scotland's lock-forward who enjoyed a run of 37 consecutive internationals

John Dawes (left) known to his teammates as "Sid", was the first Welshman to captain a full British Lions team when he led them through one of their most successful tours down under in 1971

Mike Campbell-Lamerton led the British Lions down under in 1966. Standing 6ft 4½in and weighing over 17 stone he was a powerful lock-forward and one of Scotland's most regular internationals of the 1960s

Wilson Whineray (*left*), one of the finest captains the game has ever known. New Zealand lost only 5 of the 30 Internationals in which he led the side 1958–65

Hennie Muller who captained South Africa during the 1950s is regarded as one of the finest, fittest and fastest No. 8 forwards the game has ever produced. He is seen (*right*) leading the Springboks out against Scotland in 1952

With over 2,000 points to his credit, W. F. "Fergie" McCormick (Canterbury and New Zealand) (*left*) is one of the game's most prolific scorers. His total of 443 for the All Blacks is second only to Don Clarke

John Thornett (*right*) who led the Australians to some of their finest victories in the early 1960s, including an 18–9 victory over England, a 20–5 win over New Zealand, and a 9–5 victory against the Springboks

The England team which beat Wales 17–9 at Swansea in 1924. (*Left to right standing*): H. C. Clatheside, B. S. Chantrill, H. P. Jacob, R. Cove-Smith, A. F. Blakiston, H. M. Locke, Ref. A. W. Angers; (*seated*): G. S. Conway, R. Edwards, A. T. Voyce, W. W. Wakefield, E. Myers, L. J. Corbett, and W. G. E. Luddington; (*on ground*): A. Robson and A. F. Young

The Welsh team which beat England 28–6 at Cardiff in 1922. (*Left to right standing*) (*players only*): D. Hiddlestone, Rev. J. T. Stephens, T. Roberts, S. Morris, T. Whitfield, W. Cummings; (*centre row*): C. Richards, J. Rees, B. Evans, T. Parker, T. Jones, I. Evans, F. Palmer; (*on ground*): W. Bowen, W. Delahay

The Irish team beaten 11–8 by Wales at Swansea in 1926. (*Left to right, back row*):
W. R. Brown, J. Farrell, A. Buchanan, J. McVickers, S. J. Cagney, M. J.
Bradley; (*middle row*): J. Crage, C. Hanrahan, J. D. Clinch, W. E. Crawford,
D. J. Cussen, G. V. Stephenson, T. Hewitt; (*sitting*): M. Sugden, E. Davey

England v Scotland 1975. M. A. Biggar (Scotland) passes back to scrum-half
D. W. Morgan

During the classic match between the Barbarians and the All Blacks at Cardiff in January 1973, Bryan Williams beats Mike Gibson before putting in Grant Batty (*extreme right*) for a try. David Duckham is second from right

R. M. Uttley feeds the ball back from a line-out during England's disappointing display at Cardiff in February 1975. Wales won 20–4

quota, whilst Ireland with Basil Maclear and J. C. Parke, Scotland with the McLeod brothers and L. L. Grieg and England with her Gents, Jagos and Raphaels, hardly lagged behind.

In 1905 with the visit to Great Britain of the first New Zealand team led by Dave Gallaher, came the first major revolution (see FLANKER) In Rugby Football conceptions, for Gallaher's team reversed the current conception by playing a seven forwards eight backs game in which the extra back who was termed a "Wing Forward" put the ball into the scrummage, and in the event of his own side heeling, acted as a stationary shield for his own scrum-half, and after that as an "Extra" three-quarter in the cause of securing the overlap. Inevitably there was great controversy over the legality of this new position created by the New Zealanders, but it took 27 years in the course of which the All-Blacks achieved yet another overwhelmingly successful tour of Great Britain, before the roving wing forward was obliged by legislation to pack down in the scrummage like the rest.

Although the winging forward system as employed by the New Zealanders had been declared illegal, it had nevertheless, far reaching consequences in that its use undoubtedly added impetus to the quest for new tactical devices by which the forwards could arrest the supremacy of the outside players. In consequence there emerged in ever-growing numbers the type of forward who by virtue of his great speed, finely developed sense of anticipation, and all round football acumen, could make it his own special function to harry and if possible destroy the opposing attack at its point of instigation. In the beginnings forwards of this type often revealed and indeed exploited a constructive bent, as instanced by the methods of "originals" such as Pillman of England and Ivór Morgan of Wales, but by the mid-twenties their mission had become predominantly destructive, and the wing forward in thé new British mode, had become both a menace and a deterrent to the classical back play that had flourished right up to the outbreak of World War I.

As happens in all revolutions, there was counter revolution, which logically enough, inasmuch as they were the main targets of the winging forward's depredations, commenced with the half-backs. In the old era where the emphasis had been on solid scrummaging, and a brisk clearance to attack-minded backs, the half-backs had been usually players of small physique who were deft and elusive around the scrummage, and who in most cases conducted their joint operations but a short way away from it. With the intensification of spoiling tactics around the skirt of the scrum and line-out however, the traditional "small box of tricks" type scrum-half was in the main superseded by the player who possessed a physique strong and powerful enough to withstand the buffettings of the wing forwards, and who was able at the same time, to throw out a pass long enough to enable his partner the stand-off to receive the ball unimpeded by the attentions of the open side wing forward. The Guardsman W. C. Powell, who played 27 times for Wales between 1926-35 was perhaps the prototype of the species, whilst his successors in Welsh XVs, Tanner and Willis, Logan (Scotland), Gadney (England), and Craven (South Africa) were all outstanding exponents of the new, and (as was thought) necessitous, mode in half-back play.

While it cannot perhaps be claimed that the new technique in half-back play was the complete answer to the winging forward, it did in fact contain the marauder sufficiently to enable classical back play to remain a feature of the game, though on a far more restricted basis than in the past. Indeed the considerable degree of success obtained by backs of the calibre of Wooller, C. W. Jones, W. H. T. Davies (Wales), Dick, Macrae, Wilson-Shaw (Scotland), Cranmer, Reynolds (England), during the middle thirties when winging forward play was supposedly at its destructive zenith, presented a sound argument in favour of the long passing scrum-half.

At this juncture however it is advisable, indeed imperative, to discuss the visit to Great Britain of the third South African side led by B. L. Osler in 1931, for their influence on the future trend of world Rugby was to prove even more far reaching and wide embracing than that of their New Zealand predecessors of 1905. South Africa of course had already sent touring teams abroad, to

Britain in 1906, and 1912, and to Australia and New Zealand in 1921, and in each instance had impressed with the quality and power of their forward play in general, and (using the 3-4-1 formation) with the solidity and compactness of their scrummaging in particular, Osler's team were no exception in this respect, but in contrast to their predecessors who had in the main utilised their scrummaging efficiency to provide opportunities for backs who ran and passed in the old classical vein, the 1931 "Springboks" utilised it as the corner stone of a strategy that sought in effect to reduce the game of Rugby to an exact science with the margin of error reduced in consequence, to an absolute minimum. To begin with the formidable South African scrummaging machine, was directed with two objectives:-

(1) To wear down the opposition with its sheer concentrated weight and shoving power.

(2) To establish an out and out ascendancy in the matter of possession from the earliest possible moment.

Once his forwards had attained these objectives, the main part of the strategy was implemented by Osler himself with accurate and remorseless touch kicking which worked his side up-field into a position from which they could attack with little anxiety of committing an error on which the opposition might capitalise. Indeed Osler who operated from the stand-off half position rarely trusted his outside men, even when the side had penetrated their opponents' twenty-five preferring in most cases one of three alternatives, viz., a drop at goal, or a diagonal kick ahead to his supporting wings, or on-rushing forwards. Needless to say these tactics almost ruined the game as a spectacle, but they were highly effective, indeed (as the results of the tour showed) match winning tactics, and implemented as they were with a calculating preciseness, they were almost the complete answer to the winging forward whose mission it was to harass the mid-field backs to errors that could be capitalised on.

Universally condemned at the time, and indeed for long afterwards, the tactics adopted by the 1931 South African team in Britain, have nevertheless lived on to become the basis of what

is now so often referred to as "modern Rugby." In South Africa, Dr. Danie Craven, who was Osler's scrum-half partner on the 1931 tour, developed them to a pitch of perfection never perhaps visualised even by Osler himself, and South Africa's success in world Rugby had inevitably dictated the employment of similar tactics in New Zealand, Great Britain and France. Thus the wheel has turned full circle, for just as they were in Rugby's 20-a-side beginnings, the forwards are once again the dominating force in the game. Unlike the rugged individualists of old, however, the modern forward, highly mobile, and tactically minded, hunts in concert with his fellows, and their objective—complete ascendancy in all phases of forward play before bringing their own backs into the game, is sought with a ruthlessness and intelligence of purpose that has denuded the game of much of its enjoyment as a spectacle. Back play has inevitably suffered, and where once elusive skill and audacity were the hall marks of a great mid-field player, accuracy and the tactical bent became the more desirable attributes of the game in the 1950s.

Critics and followers alike bemoaned the uniform drabness of post-war Rugby, and indeed as a direct result of the widespread dissatisfaction expressed, a British team travelled to South Africa in 1955 self dedicated to an attempt at reviving the glories of classical back play, and indeed to a large extent succeeded. A year later, however, New Zealand succeeded in wresting the mythical World Championship from South Africa, and inasmuch as that success was achieved on the merit of a diligent application of the modern formula, it seemed that (failing the *emergence* of some new and revolutionary genius) the major countries would continue to pin their faith in the only type of game that appeared to offer any hope of sustained success in International Rugby.

In recent years, however, there have been more widespread attempts to improve back play. The Laws have been altered in order to encourage the game to flow and the half-backs and threequarters have been given more room, while the destructive flanker now has less opportunity to destroy.

The attacking full-back is a must in any successful team nowadays and J. P.

R. Williams is one of the finest examples on the present international scene.

Stars among modern threequarters are limited, Gerald Davies, David Duckham, John Dawes have the right qualifications, but many teams find it difficult to beat the organised system where forward domination is given first priority together with a reliance on the opposition's mistakes and occasional attacking threequarter plays. Successful county side, Gloucestershire, and the 1974 British Lions in South Africa used these tactics.

It could be that Wales, under the enlightened coaching of John Dawes, may find the method and the means leading to consistently exciting back play. Their success in 1975 gave promising indications.

## TARANAKI RUGBY UNION

Founded 1889, affiliated to the New Zealand Union on its formation in 1892, Taranaki is another household name in New Zealand history. Indeed many of the Colony's greatest players have also represented the Union. They include, H. J. Mynott, J. Hunter, F. T. Glasgow, J. J. O'sullivan, K. C. Briscoe, R. H. Brown, M. Cain, and B. L. Muller. Headquarters: New Plymouth, North Island. Colours: Amber and black hoops. W. J. Orr made a record number of 68 consecutive appearances for the Union 1953-58.

## "TERRIBLE EIGHT"

Title bestowed on the Welsh pack which played against Ireland in Belfast in 1914, in what is generally regarded as the roughest International match in British Rugby history before World War II. Led by the Rev. J. Alban Davies of Swansea, its members were: Percy Jones, H. Uzzell (Newport), J. Bedwellty Jones (Abertillery), Edgar Morgan (Swansea), D. Watts (Maesteg), T. C. Lloyd (Neath), W. H. Evans (Llwynypia).

## THAMES VALLEY RUGBY UNION

Founded 1922, affiliated to New Zealand Union same year. Among their outstanding players of recent years are R. C. Kerby who played 101 games for the Union to 1964 and J. R. Hodge who has also made over 100 appearances. Headquarters: Paeroa, Colours: Gold with scarlet band, collar and cuffs.

## TICKETS

Rugby Football in common with most sports experienced a terrific boom following World War II, with the result that for the first time in history International matches in Britain were made "All-Tickets" affairs. This of course imposed enormous administrative burdens on the four Home Unions, and the officials of the affiliated clubs through whom the tickets are in every case distributed. The allocation to each club or organisation affiliated to each of the parent Unions is of course dependent upon membership which inevitably means that the first class clubs receive a far larger allocation than their second class or junior counterparts. The system is probably the fairest that can be devised, but it has nevertheless caused much acrimony and heartburning, particularly in Wales where the ground capacity is small, and the demand overwhelming. The system of complimentary tickets is more or less standardised throughout the four Unions and amongst the recipients of these are former Internationals, club secretaries, and selected players and reserves. In addition to a complimentary ticket the latter are entitled to a grandstand ticket at purchase price. The shortage of tickets on big match days in Britain has inevitably produced many queer incidents—the queerest of all perhaps, the one that befell the chosen Welsh captain, Bleddyn Williams, at Twickenham, in 1953. Williams as one might expect, had presented his complimentary tickets to members of his family beforehand, so that when a last minute injury forced him to withdraw from the side he found himself ticketless. Nor was he able to obtain a ticket through official channels; in fact it was only by the intervention of a friend, that Bleddyn Williams was able to see the match he should have been playing in.

## TONGA

Comparatively new to the international scene the Tongans play a style of game in keeping with the name of their home—the Friendly Isles. They are unorthodox but full of enthusiasm and when they were first given Test match status by Australia in 1973 they proceeded to shock the rugby world by winning one of their two Tests on that tour—beating Australia 16 (4 tries) to

11 (2 tries, 1 penalty goal), at Brisbane.

A Rugby Union was formed in Tonga as long ago as 1923 after the game had been developed by students returning from colleges in New Zealand and Australia.

# TOURS

See also under CASUALTIES for instances of players killed or injured on tour.

The first tour abroad by a representative national team was that of New Zealand who visited Australia in 1884 and played seven matches. It should be mentioned, however, that New South Wales had previously sent a team to New Zealand in 1882.

The first tour arranged by a team from the British Isles was the direct outcome of an England cricket team's winter tour of Australia. This took place in the winter of 1887-88 and two of its members, the famous Nottingham and England cricketers Albert Shaw and Arthur Shrewsbury, conceived the idea of taking a Rugby Football side out to play in what were then known as the Southern colonies. Shaw and Shrewsbury applied for and obtained the consent though not the patronage of the Rugby Union, with the result that a party managed by them and captained by the Swinton and England forward R. L. Seddon played a total of 35 matches in New Zealand and Australia, winning 27, losing 2, with 6 being left drawn. Successful however as the tour had been from a playing point of view it was yet marred by the tragic death of the British captain, R. L. Seddon, who was drowned whilst bathing in the Hunter River, New South Wales. In the following season, that of 1888-89, the process was reversed with the visit to Great Britain of a New Zealand Maori team captained by Joe Warbrick, of Auckland, who was one of five brothers in the team. This tour was important in that it was the forerunner of the visit of the full New Zealand representative party led by Dave Gallaher in 1905, which in turn was the starting point of the series that saw subsequent New Zealand sides visit Britain in 1924, 1935, 1953, 1963, 1967 and 1972, with reciprocal visits by British teams to New Zealand in 1904, 1908, 1930, 1950, 1959, 1966 and 1971. An England team (as distinct from British

Isles team) first toured New Zealand in 1963.

South Africa were the next country to enter the International arena, and they did so as hosts to British teams which visited them first of all in 1891 under the captaincy of W. E. Maclagan, and again in 1896, and 1903 respectively. It was not until 1906 however that South African teams ventured out of the Union, and the first to do so was Paul Roos's first Springboks who followed hard on the heels in Great Britain of Gallaher's immortal New Zealanders, and what is more, suffered no wit in comparison. South Africa had a reciprocal visit from a British side in 1910, toured themselves in Britain in 1912, and then 19 years later came again under B. L. Osler. In the meantime they had entertained Cove-Smith's British side in 1924, and before the second World War interrupted the proceedings in 1939 received yet another visit from a team captained by Sam Walker. Since the war South Africa has visited Britain in 1951, 1960, 1965 (Scotland and Ireland only) and 1969, while British Isles have toured South Africa, 1955, 1962 and 1968. In addition Scotland (1960), Ireland (1961), Wales (1964), and England (1972), have also visited South Africa.

It was perhaps the visit of Staff-Sergeant C. Brown's New Zealand Services to their country that first opened South African eyes to the possibilities of exchange visits between the two countries. In 1921 leastways, a South African side led by Theo Pienaar broke new and indeed wider ground with a tour to New Zealand and Australia. The New Zealanders responded with a return visit in 1928, and since then have made additional visits in 1949, 1960 and 1970, whilst South Africa have toured in New Zealand and Australia four times in 1937, 1956, 1965, and 1971 (Australia only), since the original visit of Pienaar's pioneer's. Australia who had already formed a mutual "touring trust" beginning in 1884, with their nearest neighbours New Zealand, sailed for fresh horizons with a tour of Britain in 1908, sent a New South Wales team there in 1927, and official "Wallaby" teams in 1947, 1957, 1966, 1968 and 1973. In addition, in 1939 there was the visit of the ill starred second "Wallabies", whose arrival in Britain coincided with the outbreak of war, and who consequently had to return home without playing a match. In 1933 Australia made the first of her five visits to South Africa, and has herself received visits from all the major Rugby nations as well as the colourful representative teams of the Fiji Islands, and the Maoris of New Zealand. Below in chronological order as they affect the individual countries are set forth the complete records of all International tours.

## Tours in Great Britain and France

1888-89–Joe Warbrick's MAORIS
RECORD–Played 74. Won 49. Lost 20. Drew 5. Points for 394. Against 188.
INTERNATIONAL MATCHES–Played 3. Won 1. Lost 2. Beat Ireland 13–4. Lost to Wales 0–5. Lost to England 0–7.
DEFEATS APART FROM INTERNATIONALS.
  –Lost to: Moseley, Burton-on-Trent, Middlesex, Hull, Wakefield Trinity, Halifax, Free Wanderers, Swinton, Lancashire, Llanelli, Yorkshire, Cambridge, Leigh, Oldham, Barrow.
PLAYERS:
  *Backs*–W. Elliott, D. R. Gage, E. Ihimaira, P. Keogh, H. H. Lee, C. Mardigan, E. McCausland, Frederick Warbrick, Joe Warbrick, William Warbrick, H. J. Wynard, W. T. Wynard.
  *Forwards*–T. R. Ellison, Wi Karauria, W. Anderson, R. Maynard, Wiri Nehua, T. Rene, D. Stewart, R. G. Taiaroa, Alfred Warbrick, Arthur Warbrick, A. Webster, G. Wynyard, G. A. Williams.
  *Joint Managers*–J. R. Scott and T. Eyon.

1905–Dave Gallaher's New Zealand Team.
RECORD–Played 33. Won 32. Lost 1. Drawn 0. Points for 868. Against 47.
INTERNATIONAL MATCHES–Played 5. Won 4. Lost 1. Drawn 0. Beat Scotland at Inverleith 12–7. Beat Ireland at Dublin 15–0. Beat England at Crystal Palace 15–0. Lost to Wales at Cardiff 0–3. Beat France in Paris 38–8.
PLAYERS:
  *Full-backs*–W. J. Wallace, G. Gillett.
  *Threequarters*–G. W. Smith, R. G. Deans, J. W. Stead, J. Hunter, D. Mc-

Gregor, H. J. Mynott, H. D. Thompson, E. E. Booth.
  *Half-back*–F. Roberts.
  *Forwards*–D. Gallaher, C. Seeling, J. Corbett, F. Newton, S. Casey, A. McDonald, G. W. Nicholson, J. O'Sullivan, G. A. Tyler, F. Glasgow, W. Cunningham, W. Johnston, H. J. Abbott, E. Harper, W. Mackrell.
  *Manager*–G. H. Dixon.

1906–Paul Roos's South African Team
RECORD–Played 28. Won 25. Lost 2. Drawn 1. Points for 533. Against 79.
INTERNATIONAL MATCHES–Played 4. Won 2. Lost 1. Drawn 1. Lost to Scotland at Glasgow 0–6. Beat Ireland at Belfast 15–12. Beat Wales at Swansea 11–0. Drew with England at Crystal Palace 3–3. Beat France 55–6 in unofficial match in Auteuil.
DEFEATS APART FROM INTERNATIONALS
  –Lost 0–17 to Cardiff.
PLAYERS:
  *Full-backs*–A. F. W. Marsberg. A. R. Burmeister, Steve Joubert (Sent over as a replacement for the injured Burmeister).
  *Threequarters*–J. A. Loubser, A. C. Stegmann, J. S. le Roux, Andrew Morkel, J. D. Krige, H. A. de Villiers, S. C. de Melker, J. G. Hirsch.
  *Half-backs*–F. J. Bobbin, H. W. Carolin, D. C. Jackson, Dietlof Mare.
  *Forwards*–Paul Roos, D. J. Brink, P. A. le Roux, A. F. Burdett, H. C. Daneel, J. W. E. Raaff, W. C. Martheze, D. F. T. Morkel, W. S. Morkel, H. G. Reid, W. A. Millar, W. A. Burger, D. S. Brooks, W. A. Neill.
  *Manager*–J. C. Carden.

1908–Dr. H. M. Moran's Australian Team (First "Wallabies")
RECORD–Played 31. Won 25. Lost 5. Drawn 1. Points for 438. Against 146.
INTERNATIONAL MATCHES–Played 2. Won 1. Lost 1. Lost to Wales at Cardiff 6–9. Beat England at Blackheath 9–3.
DEFEATS APART FROM INTERNATIONALS
  –Lost 3–8 to Llanelli. 5–16 to Combined Midlands and East Midlands XV. 0–6 to Swansea. 8–24 to Cardiff.
PLAYERS:

*Full-back*—P. Carmichael.
*Threequarters*—C. Russell, E. Mandible, J. Hickey, D. B. Carroll, W. Dix, A. J. McCabe, E. Parkinson, F. B. Smith, H. Daly.
*Half-backs*—C. H. McKivatt, Ward Prentice.
*Forwards*—Dr. H. M. Moran, T. J. Richards, J. T. Barnett, S. A. Middleton, P. McCue, C. A. Hammond, A. B. Burge, R. Craig, T. Griffin, M. McArthur, N. E. Row, F. Wood, P. Flanagan, P. H. Burge, K. Gavin, C. E. Murnin.
*Manager*—S. Wickham.

1912—W. A. Millar's South African Team (Second "Springboks").
RECORD—Played 27. Won 24. Lost 3. Drawn 0. Points for 441. Against 101.
INTERNATIONAL MATCHES—Played 5. Won 5. Lost 0. Beat Scotland at Inverleith 16—0. Beat Ireland in Dublin 38—0. Beat Wales at Cardiff 3—0. Beat England at Twickenham 9—3. Beat France at Bordeaux 38—5.
DEFEATS APART FROM INTERNATIONALS
—Lost 3—9 to Newport. Lost 8—10 to London. Lost 0—3 to Swansea.
PLAYERS:
*Full-backs*—P. Gerhard Morkel, J. J. Meintjies.
*Threequarters*—J. A. Stegmann, E. E. McHardy, W. J. Mills, A. de la Ray, A. van der Hoff, R. R. Luyt, J. W. Morkel, W. A. Krige, G. M. Wrentmore.
*Half-backs*—F. J. Dobbin, F. P. Luyt, J. D. McCulloch, H. J. Immelman.
*Forwards*—W. A. Millar, G. Thompson, L. H. Louw, W. H. Morkel, D. F. T. Morkel, A. S. Knight, E. H. Shum, J. A. J. Francis, S. N. Cronje, T. van Vuuren, J. S. Braine, S. H. Ledger, E. T. Delaney, J. D. Luyt.
*Manager*—Max Honnet.

1924—C. G. Porter's New Zealand Team (Second "All-Blacks").
RECORD—Played 30. Won 30. Lost 0. Drawn 0. Points for 721. Against 112.
INTERNATIONAL MATCHES—Played 4. Won 4. Beat Ireland in Dublin 6—0. Beat Wales at Swansea 19—0. Beat England at Twickenham 17—11. Beat France at Toulouse 30—6.
PLAYERS:
*Full-back*—George Nepia.
*Threequarters*—K. Svenson, F. Lucas,

A. H. Hart, J. Steel, H. W. Brown, A. C. C. Robilliard.
*Five-Eighths*—M. F. Nicholls, A. E. Cooke, N. P. McGregor, C. E. O. Badeley, L. Paewai.
*Half-backs*—J. Mill, W. C. Dalley.
*Forwards*—C. G. Porter, M. J. Brownlie, C. J. Brownlie, J. Parker, W. Irvine, Q. Donald, J. Richardson, R. R. Masters, L. F. Cupples, A. H. White, I. H. Harvey, A. H. West, B. V. McCleary, R. F. Stewart, H. G. Munroe.
*Manager*—S. S. Dean.

1926-27 W. Barclay's MAORIS.
RECORD—Played 31. Won 22. Lost 7. Drew 2. Points for 457. Against 194.
INTERNATIONAL MATCHES—Beat France 12—3 at Colombes in the only one played.
DEFEATS APART FROM INTERNATIONALS
—Lost to Harlequins 5—11. Lost to Devon 0—20. Lost to Gloucester 0—3. Lost to Llanelli 0—3. Lost to Cornwall 3—6. Lost to a Paris XV 9—11.
PLAYERS:
*Full-backs*—D. Pelham, J. McDonald,
*Threequarters*—A. Falwasser, H. Phillips, P. Potaka, T. P. Robinson, L. R. Grace. W. Lockwood, W. Barclay.
*Five-Eighths*—R. J. Bell, E. G. Love, D. Wi Nena.
*Half-backs*—W. Shortland, H. Kingi, W. Mete.
*Forwards*—O. Olsen, J. Stewart, J. Mannihera, A. Crawford, T. Dennis, W. Rika, T. Manning, S. Gemmell, P. Haupapa, D. Tatana, Rev. P. Matene, W. Wilson, J. Gemmell.
*Manager*—W. T. Parata.

1927—28—A. C. Wallace's New South Wales Team ("The Waratahs").
RECORD—Played 31. Won 24. Lost 5. Drew 2. Points for 432. Against 207.
INTERNATIONAL MATCHES—Played 5. Won 3. Lost 2. Beat Ireland in Dublin 5—3. Beat Wales at Cardiff 18—8. Lost to Scotland at Murrayfield 8—10. Lost to England at Twickenham 8—18. Beat France at Colombes 11—8.
DEFEATS APART FROM INTERNATIONALS
—Lost to Oxford University 0—3. Lost to Pontypool 3—6. Lost to South-West of France 10—19.

PLAYERS:

*Full-back*–A. W. Ross.

*Threequarters*–E. E. Ford, A. C. Wallace, A. J. Bowers, G. C. Gordon, W. H. Mann, C. H. Towers, W. B. J. Sheean, S. C. King, J. B. Egan.

*Half-backs*–A. T. Lawton, S. J. Malcolm, F. W. Meagher, J. L. Duncan.

*Forwards*–J. A. Ford, A. J. Tancred, J. W. Breckenridge, E. N. Greatorex, A. N. Finlay, G. P. Storey, G. Bland, E. J. Thorn, C. L. Fox, B. Judd, M. R. Blair, J. G. Blackwood, H. F. Woods, K. Tarleton, J. L. Tancred.

*Manager*–E. Gordon Shaw.

1931-32–B. L. Osler's South African Team (The Third "Springboks").
RECORD–Played 26. Won 23. Lost 1. Drew 2. Points for 407. Against 124.
INTERNATIONAL MATCHES–Played 4. Won 4. Beat Wales at Swansea 8–3. Beat Ireland in Dublin 8–3. Beat England at Twickenham 7–0. Beat Scotland at Murrayfield 6–3.
DEFEATS APART FROM INTERNATIONALS
   –Lost to Leicester and East Midland Counties 21–30.
PLAYERS:

*Full-backs*–G. H. Brand, J. C. Tindall.

*Threequarters*–M. Zimmerman, F. D. Venter, J. A. van Niekerk, J. H. van der Westhuizen, D. Owen Williams, J. C. van der Westhuizen, B. G. Gray, F. W. Waring, J. White.

*Half-backs*–B. L. Osler, M. G. Francis, P. de Villiers, D. H. Craven.

*Forwards*–P. J. Mostert, M. M. Louw, S. C. Louw, A. J. van der Merwe, S. R. du Toit, J. A. J. Macdonald, L. C. Strachan, J. N. Bierman, G. M. Daneel, V. Geere, H. M. Forrest, H. G. Kipling, P. J. Nel, F. Bergh, J. B. Dold.

*Manager*–Theo B. Pienaar.

1935-36–J. E. Manchester's New Zealand Team (the Third "All-Blacks").
RECORD–Played 28. Won 24. Lost 3. Drew 1. Points for 431. Against 180.
INTERNATIONAL MATCHES–Played 4. Won 2. Lost 2. Beat Scotland at Murrayfield 18–8. Beat Ireland in Dublin 17–9. Lost to England at Twickenham 0–13. Lost to Wales at Cardiff 12–13.
DEFEATS APART FROM INTERNATIONALS

   –Lost to Swansea 3–11.
PLAYERS:

*Full-back*–G. Gilbert.

*Threequarters*–N. Ball, H. M. Brown, G. F. Hart, N. A. Mitchell, C. J. Oliver, T. C. H. Caughey.

*Five-Eighths*–J. L. Griffiths, J. R. Page, D. Solomon, E. W. Tindill, M. M. N. Corner, B. S. Sadler.

*Forwards*–A. Mahoney, H. F. McClean, J. J. Best, W. R. Collins, R. R. King. J. E. Manchester, R. M. McKenzie, S. T. Reid, F. H. Yorrath, J. G. Wynyard, G. T. Adkins, D. Dalton, W. E. Hadley, J. Hore, A. Lambourne, C. S. Pepper.

*Manager*–V. R. S. Meredith.

1947-48–W. M. McLean's Australian Team (Third "Wallabies").
RECORD–Played 35. Won 29. Lost 6. Drawn 0. Points for 500. Against 243.
INTERNATIONAL MATCHES–Played 5. Won 3. Lost 2. Beat Scotland at Murrayfield 16–7. Beat Ireland in Dublin 16–3. Lost to Wales at Cardiff 0–6. Beat England at Twickenham 11–0. Lost to France at Colombes 6–13.
DEFEATS APART FROM INTERNATIONALS
   –Lost to Lancashire and Cheshire at Manchester 8–9. Lost to London Counties at Twickenham 8–14. Lost to Cardiff at Cardiff 3–11. Lost to Barbarians at Cardiff 6–9.
PLAYERS:

*Full-backs*–B. J. Piper, Dr. C. J. Windsor.

*Threequarters*–C. C. Eastes, A. E. J. Tonkin, J. W. T. MacBride, T. K. Bourke, T. Allan, M. L. Howell, A. K. Walker.

*Five-Eighths*–J. F. Cremin, N. A. Emery, E. G. Broad.

*Half-backs*–C. T. Burke, R. M. Cawsey.

*Forwards*–W. M. McLean, A. J. Buchan, C. J. Windon, J. O. Stenmark, K. C. Winning, J. G. Fuller, G. M. Cooke, Dr. P. A. Hardcastle, D. F. Kraefft, N. Shehadie, R. E. McMaster, E. Tweedale, Dr. D. H. Keller, E. H. Davies, K. H. Kearney, W. L. Dawson.

*Manager*–A. J. Tancred.

1951-52–Basil Kenyon's South African Team (Fourth "Springboks").

RECORD—Played 31. Won 30. Lost 1.
Drawn 0. Points for 562. Against 167.
INTERNATIONAL MATCHES—Played
5. Won 5. Beat Scotland at Murray-
field 44—0. Beat Ireland at Dublin
17—5. Beat Wales at Cardiff 6—3.
Beat England at Twickenham 8—3.
Beat France at Colombes 25—3.
DEFEATS APART FROM INTER-
NATIONALS
    —Lost to London Counties at
Twickenham 9—11.
PLAYERS:
    *Full-backs*—J. Buchler, A. C. Keevy.
    *Threequarters*—J. K. Osche, F. P.
Marais, M. J. Saunders, P. Johnstone,
M. T. Lategan, R. A. van Schoor, D.
Sinclair, S. S. Viviers.
    *Half-backs*—J. D. Brewis, D. J. Fry,
J. S. Oelosfe, P. A. du Toit.
    *Forwards*—P. W. Wessels, W. H. Del-
port, C. Koch, A. Geffin, H. J. Bekker,
F. van der Ryst, E. E. Dinklemann, J. A.
Pickard, G. Dannhauser, W. H. Barnard,
S. P. Fry, C. J. van Wyk, B. Myburgh,
J. du Rand, B. J. Kenyon, H. S. Muller.
    *Manager*—Frank Mellish.

1953-54—R. S. Stuart's New Zealand
Team (Fourth "All-Blacks").
RECORD—Played 30. Won 24. Lost 4.
Drawn 2. Points for 425. Against 116.
INTERNATIONAL MATCHES—Played
5. Won 3. Lost 2. Lost to Wales at
Cardiff 8—13. Beat Ireland at Dublin
14—3. Beat England at Twickenham
5—0. Beat Scotland at Murrayfield
3—0. Lost to France at Colombes
0—3.
DEFEATS APART FROM INTER-
NATIONALS
    —Lost to Cardiff at Cardiff 3—8.
Lost to South Western France at
Bordeaux 8—11.
PLAYERS:
    *Full-backs*—R. W. H. Scott, J. W.
Kelly.
    *Threequarters*—R. A. Jarden, M. J.
Dixon, W. S. S. Freebairn, A. E. G.
Elsom, J. T. Fitzgerald, J. M. Tanner.
    *Five-Eighths*—D. D. Wilson, B. B. J.
Fitzpatrick, C. J. Loader, L. S. Haig, R.
G. Bowers.
    *Half-backs*—V. D. Bevan, K. Davis,
    *Forwards*—W. A. McGaw, R. C.
Stuart, P. F. Jones, W. H. Clark, D. O.
Oliver, R. J. O'Dea, R. A. White, G. N.
Dalzell, K. P. Bagley, K. L. Skinner,
H. L. White, P. Eastgate, I. J. Clarke,

R. C. Hemi, C. A. Woods.
    *Joint Managers*—N. Millard and A.
Marslin.

1957-58—R. L. Davidson's Australian
Team.
RECORD: Played 30. Won 14. Lost 13.
Drew 3. Points for 248. Against 203.
INTERNATIONAL MATCHES—Played
5. Lost 5. Lost to Wales 3—9. Lost to
Ireland 6—9. Lost to England 6—9.
Lost to Scotland 8—12. Lost to
France 0—19.
DEFEATS APART FROM INTER-
NATIONALS
    —Lost to Oxford University 6—12,
to Cambridge University 3—13, to
Newport 0—11, to Cardiff 11—14, to
Western Counties 8—9, to Combined
Abertillery and Ebbw Vale XV 5—6,
to North Western Counties 3—6, to
Barbarians 9—11, to Midland Coun-
ties 5—6.
PLAYERS:
    *Full-backs*—T. Curley, J. Lenehan.
    *Threequarters*—K. G. Donald, R.
Phelps, A. R. Morton, O. G. Fox, J. A.
Phipps, G. D. Bailey, J. M. Potts, S. W.
White.
    *Half-backs*—R. Harvey, A. Summons
D. Logan, D. M. O'Connors.
    *Forwards*—R. L. Davidson, P. Fen-
wicke, N. M. Hughes, W. J. Gunther,
J. E. Thornett, K. Yanz, E. M. Purkiss,
R. A. Miller, A. S. Cameron, D.
Emmanuel, S. Scotts, N. Shehadie, G.
N. Vaughan, K. J. Ryan, J. V. Brown,
R. Meadows.
    *Manager*—T. H. McClenaughan (N.S.
W.).
    *Asst. Manager*—D. L. Cowper (Vic-
toria).

1960-61—A. S. Malan's South African
Team (Fifth "Springboks").
RECORD—Played 34. Won 31. Lost 1.
Drawn 2. Points for 567. Against 129
INTERNATIONAL MATCHES—Played
5. Won 4. Lost 0. Drawn 1. Beat
Wales at Cardiff 3—0. Beat Ireland
at Dublin 8—3. Beat England at
Twickenham 5—0. Beat Scotland at
Murrayfield 12—5. Drew with France
at Colombes 0—0.
DEFEATS APART FROM INTER-
NATIONALS
    —Lost to Barbarians, at Cardiff 0—6.
PLAYERS:
    *Full-backs*—L. G. Wilson, G. J. Wen-
tzel.

*Threequarters*—H. J. van Zyl, M. J. G. Antelme, F. Roux, J. P. Engelbrecht, A. I. Kirkpatrick, B. B. van Niekerk, D. A. Stewart, J. L. Gainsford, B. P. van Zyl.

*Half-backs*—C. Nimb, K. Oxlee, R. J. Lockyear, P. de W. Uys.

*Forwards*—G. F. Malan, P. S. du Toit, R. A. Hill, S. P. Kuhn, J. L. Myburgh, D. N. Holton, A. S. Malan, P. J. van Zyl, G. H. van Zyl, J. T. Claasen, H. S. van der Merwe, H. J. M. Pelser, J. P. F. Botha, D. J. Hopwood, F. C. du Preez, A. P. Baard, R. Johns.

*Manager*—F. Bergh.

1963-64—W. J. Whineray's New Zealand Team (Fifth "All-Blacks").
RECORD—Played 34. Won 32. Lost 1. Drawn 1. Points for 568. Against 153.
INTERNATIONAL MATCHES—Played 5. Won 4. Lost 0. Drawn 1. Beat Ireland at Dublin 6–5. Beat Wales at Cardiff 6–0. Beat England at Twickenham 14–0. Drew with Scotland at Murrayfield 0–0. Beat France at Colombes 12–3.
DEFEATS APART FROM INTERNATIONALS
—Lost to Newport at Newport 0–3.
PLAYERS:
*Full-back*—D. B. Clarke.
*Threequarters*—P. F. Little, R. W. Caulton, W. L. Davis, M. J. Dick, I. R. Macrae.
*Five-Eighths*—D. A. Arnold, P. T. Walsh, M. A. Herewini, E. W. Kirton, B. A. Watt.
*Half-backs*—K. C. Briscoe, C. R. Laidlaw.
*Forwards*—W. J. Whineray, I. J. Clarke, K. F. Cray, J. M. Le Lievre, D. Young, J. Major, C. E. Meads, A. J. Stewart, R. H. Horsley, S. T. Meads, K. E. Barry, W. J. Nathan, K. R. Tremain, D. J. Graham, B. J. Lochore, K. A. Nelson.
*Manager*—F. D. Kilby.

1964-65—A. S. Malan's South African Team's five match tour of Ireland and Scotland.
RECORD—Played 5. Won 0. Lost 5. Points for 22. Against 53.
INTERNATIONAL MATCHES—Played 2. Lost 2. Lost to Ireland, at Dublin 6–9. Lost to Scotland at Murrayfield 5–8.
DEFEATS APART FROM INTERNATIONALS

—Lost to Combined Provinces at Belfast 3–8. Lost to Combined Universities P. & P. at Limerick 10–12. Lost to Scottish District XV at Hawick 8–16.
PLAYERS:
*Full-back*—L. G. Wilson.
*Threequarters*—J. P. Engelbrecht, J. L. Gainsford, W. J. Mans, C. W. Dirksen, D. A. Stewart, G. D. Cilliers.
*Half-backs*—D. J. de Vos, J. H. Barnard, K. A. Oxlee, J. de Villiers.
*Forwards*—S. P. Kuhn, D. C. Walton, J. F. K. Marais, A. S. Malan, G. Carelse, J. A. Schoeman, F. du Preez, T. P. Bedford, J. B. Neethling, A. W. Wessels, M. R. Suter, D. J. Hopwood.

1966-67—J. E. Thornett's Australian team.
RECORD—Played 34. Won 16. Lost 15. Drawn 3. Points for 348. Against 324.
INTERNATIONAL MATCHES—Played 5. Won 2. Lost 3. Beat Wales, at Cardiff 14–11, England at Twickenham 23–11. Lost to Scotland at Murrayfield 5–11. Lost to Ireland at Dublin 8–15. Lost to France at Paris 14–20.
DEFEATS APART FROM INTERNATIONALS
—Lost to N. E. Counties, at Gosport 14–17, Cardiff 8–14, London Counties, at Twickenham 9–14, South of Scotland at Hawick 0–13, Swansea 8–9, Pontypool-Cross Keys-Newbridge at Pontypool 3–12, N. W. Counties, at Manchester 3–8, West Midlands at Coventry 9–17, Western Counties at Bristol 0–9, Llanelli 0–11, Munster, at Cork 8–11, S. W. France 9–11.
PLAYERS:
*Full-backs*—P. F. Ryan, J. K. Lenehan.
*Threequarters*—P. F. Smith, E. S. Boyce, J. E. Brass, R. Webb, R. J. Marks, A. M. Cardy, J. A. Francis.
*Five-eighths*—P. R. Gibbs, A. M. C. Moore, P. F. Hawthorne.
*Scrum-halves*—K. W. Catchpole, J. N. B. Hipwell.
*Forwards*—J. E. Thornett, R. G. Teitzel, R. J. Heming, R. D. Tulloch, R. B. Prosser, R. Cullen, J. O'Gorman, G. V. Davis, A. D. Taylor, A. R. Miller, P. C. Crittle, P. G. Johnson, J. M. Miller, D. A. O'Callaghan, M. P. Purcell, J. Guerassimoff.

1967–B. J. Lochore's New Zealand Team (Sixth "All-Blacks").
RECORD–Played 15. Won 14. Lost 0. Drawn 1. Points for 294. Against 129.
INTERNATIONAL MATCHES–Played 4. Won 4. Beat England, at Twickenham 23–11. Beat Wales at Cardiff 13–6. Beat France, at Colombes 21–15. Beat Scotland, at Murrayfield 14–3.
PLAYERS:
*Full-back*–W. F. McCormick.
*Threequarters*–W. M. Birtwistle, P. H. Clarke, M. J. Dick, G. S. Thorne, A. G. Steel, W. L. Davis.
*Five-eighths*–M. A. Herewini, W. D. Cottrell, I. R. Macrae, E. W. Kirton, G. F. Kember.
*Scrum-halves*–C. R. Laidlaw, S. M. Going.
*Forwards*–E. J. Hazlett, S. C. Strahan, B. J. Lochore, I. A. Kirkpatrick, B. L. Muller, A. E. Smith, K. R. Tremain, G. C. Williams, M. C. Wills, A. G. Jennings, C. E. Meads, A. E. Hopkinson, K. F. Gray, J. Major, B. E. McLeod.

1968–P. G. Johnson's Australian team to Ireland and Scotland only.
RECORD–Played 5. Won 2. Lost 3. Drawn 0. Points for 38. Against 40.
INTERNATIONAL MATCHES–Played 2. Lost 2. Lost to Ireland, at Dublin 3–10. Lost to Scotland, at Murrayfield 3–9.
DEFEATS APART FROM INTERNATIONALS
–Lost to Combined Provinces, at Belfast 3–9.
PLAYERS:
*Full-back*–A. N. McGill.
*Threequarters*–B. D. Honan, P. V. Smith, R. P. Batterham, T. R. Forman, W. Cole, A. M. Pope, P. V. Smith.
*Five-eighth*–J. P. Ballesty.
*Scrum-halves*–M. J. Barry, J. Hipwell.
*Forwards*–A. J. Skinner, R. V. Turnbull, P. Darveniza, P. G. Johnson, P. N. P. Reilly, R. B. Prosser, K. R. Bell, S. C. Gregory, D. A. Taylor, H. A. Rose, G. V. Davis.

1968–D. J. de Villier's South African team to France.
RECORD–Played 6. Won 5. Lost 1.

Drawn 0. Points for 84. Against 43.
INTERNATIONAL MATCHES–Played 2. Won 2. Beat France 12–9 at Bordeaux and 16–11 at Paris.
DEFEAT–Lost to S. W. France, at Toulouse 3–11.
PLAYERS:
*Full-backs*–H. O. de Villiers, R. L. Gould.
*Threequarters*–S. H. Nomis, J. P. Engelbrecht, E. Olivier, O. A. Roux, F. de T. Roux.
*Half-backs*–D. J. de Villiers, M. A. Menter, P. J. Visagie, P. de W. Uys.
*Forwards*–G. Carelse, J. B. Neethling, J. F. K. Marais, J. L. Myburgh, G. Pitzer, F. C. H. de Preez, D. C. Walton, J. P. Naude, T. P. Bedford, M. J. Lourens, P. J. F. Greyling, J. H. Ellis.

1969-70–D. J. de Villiers' South African team to British Isles only.
RECORD–Played 25. Won 16. Lost 5. Drawn 4. Points for 345. Against 163.
INTERNATIONAL MATCHES–Played 4. Lost 2. Drawn 2. Drew with Ireland at Dublin, 8–8, and with Wales, at Cardiff 6–6. Lost to Scotland, at Murrayfield 3–6. Lost to England, at Twickenham 8–11.
DEFEATS APART FROM INTERNATIONALS
–Lost to Oxford University, at Twickenham 3–6; Newport 6–11; Gwent at Ebbw Vale 8–14.
PLAYERS:
*Full-backs*–H. O. de Villiers, P. J. Durand.
*Threequarters*–G. H. Muller, S. H. Nomis, R. N. Grobler, A. E. van der Watt, E. Olivier, O. A. Roux, P. J. van der Schyff, J. V. van der Merwe, F. du T. Roux.
*Half-backs*–D. J. de Villiers, P. J. Visagie, M. J. Lawless, D. J. de Vos.
*Forwards*–M. W. Jennings, J. H. Ellis, J. B. Neethling, J. F. K. Marias, J. L. Myburgh, F. C. H. du Preze, R. Potgeiter, A. E. de Wet, G. Pitzer, P. I. van Deventer, G. Carelse, D. C. Walton, A. J. Bates, M. C. J. van Rensburg, T. P. Bedford, P. J. F. Greyling, I. J. de Klerk, C. H. Cockrell, R. Barnard.

1971–G. V. Davis's Australian team to France only.
RECORD–Played 8. Won 4. Lost 4. Drawn 0. Points for 110 Against 101.

INTERNATIONAL MATCHES–Played 2. Won 1. Lost 1. Beat France, at Toulouse 13–11. Lost to France, at Paris 9–18.

PLAYERS:

*Full-back*– A. N. McGill.

*Threequarters*– J. W. Cole, D. Rathie, R. D. L'Estrange, L. Monaghan, P. R. Batterham, G. Shaw, J. McLean.

*Half-backs*– G. Richardson, J. N. B. Hipwell, G. Grey, R. Fairfax.

*Forwards*– M. Flynn, O. Butler, R. McLean, R. Smith, B. Stumbles, G. V. Davis, P. Sullivan, D. Dunworth, S. Gregory, P. G. Johnson, R. B. Prosser, B. Brown, R. Thompson.

1972-73–I. A. Kirkpatrick's New Zealand Team (Seventh "All-Blacks").

RECORD–Played 30. Won 23. Lost 5. Drawn 2. Points for 568. Against 254.

INTERNATIONAL MATCHES–Played 5. Won 3. Lost 1. Drawn 1. Beat Wales, at Cardiff 19–16. Beat Scotland, at Murrayfield 14–9. Beat England, at Twickenham 9–0. Drew with Ireland, at Dublin 10–10. Lost to France, at Paris 6–13.

DEFEATS APART FROM INTERNATIONALS

–Lost to Llanelli 3–9; N. W. Counties, at Workington 14–16; Midland Counties (West), at Moseley 8–16; Barbarians, at Cardiff 11–23.

PLAYERS:

*Full-backs*– J. F. Karam, T. J. Morris.

*Threequarters*– B. J. Robertson, G. B. Batty, B. G. Williams, D. A. Hales, G. R. Skudder, I. A. Hurst.

*Five-eighths*– R. E. Burgess, M. Sayers, R. M. Parkinson, I. N. Stevens.

*Scrum-halves*– S. M. Going, G. L. Colling.

*Forwards*– A. J. Wyllie, I. A. Kirkpatrick, R. A. Urlich, A. R. Sutherland, B. Holmes, A. I. Scown, K. W. Stewart, P. J. Whiting, J. D. Matheson, H. H. Macdonald, I. M. Eliason, A. M. Haden, K. Murdoch, K. K. Lambert, R. W. Norton, G. J. Whiting, A. L. R. McNichol, L. A. Clark.

1973–P. D. Sullivan's Australian team to England and Wales only.

RECORD–Played 8. Won 2. Lost 5. Drawn 1. Points for 85. Against 131.

INTERNATIONAL MATCHES–Played 2. Lost 2. Lost to Wales, at Cardiff 0–24, and to England, at Twickenham 3–20.

DEFEATS APART FROM INTERNATIONALS

–Lost to South and South-West Counties, at Bath 14–15; East Wales, at Newport 11–19; Northern Counties, at Gosforth, 13–16.

PLAYERS:

*Full-backs*– A. N. McGill, R. L. Fairfax.

*Threequarters*– J. J. McLean, L. E. Monaghan, O. Stephens, G. A. Shaw, D. R. Burnet, R. D. L'Estrange.

*Half-backs*– G. C. Richardson, J. N. B. Hipwell, P. G. Rowles, R. G. Hauser.

*Forwards*– P. D. Sullivan, K. G. McCurrach, B. R. Battishall, A. A. Shaw, G. Fay, M. R. Cocks, J. L. Howard, S. C. Gregory, R. A. Smith, R. Graham, S. G. MacDougall, C. M. Carberry, M. E. Freney.

1974–H. Marais's South African team to France only.

RECORD–Played 9. Won 8. Lost 1. Points for 170. Against 74.

INTERNATIONAL MATCHES–Played 2. Won 2. Won 13–14 at Toulouse, 10–8 in Paris.

DEFEAT–4–7 v. French Selection at Angouleme.

PLAYERS:

*Full-backs*– D. Snyman, I. Robertson.

*Threequarters*– W. Stapelberg, J. Oosthuizen, C. Fourie, C. Pope.

*Half-backs*– R. McCallum, G. Bosch, P. Bayvel, J. A. van Standen, P. Whipp.

*Forwards*– K. de Klerk, M. du Plessis, J. Kritzinger, J. L. van Heerden, J. Williams, J. Ellis, R. Cockrell, J. F. K. Marais, N. Bezuidenhout, J. Snyman, D. van den Berg, J. C. J. Stander, A. Bestier, T. T. Fourie, C. J. Grobler, J. de Bruyn.

1974–A. R. Leslie's New Zealand team to Ireland, Wales and England.

RECORD–Played 8. Won 7. Drawn 1. Points for 127. Against 50.

INTERNATIONAL MATCH–Beat Ireland 15–6 at Dublin.

PLAYERS:

*Full-backs*– J. F. Karam, K. T. Going.

*Threequarters*– G. B. Batty, B. G. Williams, B. J. Robertson, T. W. Mitchell, I. A. Hurst, J. E. Morgan, G. N. Kane.

*Half-backs*– D. J. Robertson, O. D.

Bruce, S. M. Going, I. N. Stevens.

*Forwards*—A. R. Leslie, K. W. Stewart, K. A. Eveleigh, G. M. Crossman, I. A. Kirkpatrick, I. G. Knight, P. J. Whiting, J. A. Callesen, H. H. Macdonald, K. K. Lambert, K. J. Tanner, A. J. Gardiner, W. K. Bush, R. W. Norton.

## Tours in New Zealand

1888—R. L. Seddon's British Team.
RECORD—Played 19. Won 13. Lost 2. Drawn 4. Points for 82. Against 33.
NO TEST MATCHES PLAYED.
DEFEATS—Lost to Taranaki 0-1, Auckland 0—4.
PLAYERS:
*Full-backs*—J. T. Haslam, A. Paul.
*Threequarters*—H. C. Speakman, Dr. H. Brooks, J. Auderton, A. E. Stoddart.
*Half-backs*—W. Bumby, J. Nolan. W. Burnett.
*Forwards*—R. L. Seddon, S. Williams, T. Banks, H. Eagles, T. Kent, C. Mathers, A. J. Stuart, J. P. Clowes, W. H. Thomas, A. P. Pinketh, Dr. D. J. Smith, R. Burnett, A. J. Lang.
*Managers*—Albert Shaw and Arthur Shrewsbury.

1904—D. R. Bedell-Sivright's British Team.
RECORD—Played 5. Won 2. Lost 2. Drawn 1. Points for 22. Against 33.
TEST MATCHES—Played 1. Lost 1. Score 3—9.
DEFEATS APART FROM TESTS—Lost 0—13 to Auckland. In addition this team were defeated 6—8 by the Maoris in an "unofficial" game.
PLAYERS:
*Full-back*—C. F. Stranger—Leathes.
*Threequarters*—J. L. Fisher, R. T. Gabe, W. F. Jowett, W. M. Llewelyn, E. T. Morgan, P. F. McEvedy, A. B. O'-Brien.
*Half-backs*—P. F. Bush, F. C. Hume, T. H. Vile.
*Forwards*—D. R. Bedell-Sivright, T. S. Bevan, S. N. Crowther, J. T. Sharland, D. D. Dobson, C. D. Paterson, J. Edwards, A. F. Harding, B. F. Massey, R. J. Rogers, S. McK. Saunders, D. H. Traill, B. I. Swannell.
*Manager*—Dr. A. B. O'Brien.

1905—S. Wickham's Australian Team.
RECORD—Played 7. Won 3. Lost 4. Drawn 0. Points for 51. Against 83.
TEST MATCHES—Played 1. Lost 1. Lost

to New Zealand 3—14 at Dunedin.
DEFEATS APART FROM TESTS—Lost 7—23 to Wellington. Lost 3—12 to Combined Marlborough, Buller, Nelson, and West Coast Unions. Lost 3—8 to Canterbury.
PLAYERS:
*Full-back*—P. Carmichael.
*Threequarters*—S. Wickham, A. P. Penman, C. Russell, F. B. Smith, L. M. Smith, D. J. McLean.
*Five-eighths*—M. Dore, A. E. Anlezark.
*Half-back*—F. Wood.
*Forwards*—A. Burdon, P. H. Burge, J. Clarken, W. Hirschberg, H. A. Judd, C. E. Murnin, B. I. Swannell, T. Colton, B. Lucas, F. Nicholson, E. O'Brien, A. Oxlade, E. W. Richards.
*Manager*—J. Henderson.

1908—A. F. Hardings British Team.
RECORD—Played 17. Won 9. Lost 7. Drawn 1. Points for 184. Against 153.
TEST MATCHES—Played 3. Lost 2. Drawn 1. Scores: 5—32, 3—3, 0—29.
DEFEATS APART FROM TESTS—Lost 13—19 to Wellington, 6—9 to Otago, 8—13 to Canterbury, 0—5 to Taranaki, 0—11 to Auckland.
PLAYERS:
*Full-backs*—J. C. M. Dyke, E. J. Jackett.
*Threequarters*—F. E. Chapman, R. A. Gibbs, J. L. Williams, R. B. Griffiths, J. P. (Ponty) Jones, J. P. (Tuan) Jones, Dr. P. F. McEvedy, H. H. Vassall.
*Half-backs*—W. J. Davey, H. Laxon, W. L. Morgan, G. L. Williams.
*Forwards*—A. F. Harding, R. Dibble, H. A. Archer, P. J. Down, G. V. Kyrke, R. K. Green, Edgar Morgan, L. S. Thomas, J. F. Williams, G. R. Hind, F. Jackson W. L. Oldham, J. A. S. Ritson, T. W. Smith.
*Manager*—G. H. Harnett.

1913—L. J. Dwyer's Australian Team.
RECORD—Played 9. Won 4. Lost 5. Drawn 0. Points for 118. Against 114.
TEST MATCHES—Played 3. Won 1. Lost 2. Lost to New Zealand 5—30 at Wellington, 13—25 at Dunedin. Beat New Zealand 16—3 at Christchurch.
DEFEATS APART FROM TESTS—Lost 13—15 to Auckland. Lost 6—11 to Wanganui. Lost 8—13 to Southland.

PLAYERS:
*Full-backs*–L. J. Dwyer, M. J. Mc-
Mahon.
*Threequarters*–E. T. Carr, H. Jones,
R. Simpson, D. Suttor, L. W. Wogan,
P. J. Flynn, L. Meibusch.
*Five-eighth*–W. G. Tasker.
*Half-back*–F. Wood.
*Forwards*–H. George, C. O'Donnell,
W. T. Watson, E. J. Fahey, E. W. Cody,
C. Wallach, B. D. Hughes, R. Roberts,
Ralph Hill, A. Horodan, P. Murphy, F.
Thompson, D. Williams.
*Manager*–C. E. Morgan.

1921–Theo Pienaar's South African
Team.
RECORD–Played 17. Won 15. Lost 2.
Drawn 0. Points for 244. Against
81.
TEST MATCHES–Played 3. Won 1. Lost
1. Drawn 1. Scores: 5–13, 9–5, 0–0.
DEFEATS APART FROM TESTS–Lost
4–6 to Canterbury.
PLAYERS:
*Full-backs*–P. G. Morkel, I. D. de
Villiers.
*Threequarters*–A. J. van Heerden,
W. C. Zeller, H. W. Morkel, C. du Meyer,
S. S. F. Strauss, W. D. Sendin, W. A.
Clarkson, J. S. Weepener.
*Half-backs*–J. P. Michau, J. S. de
Kock, J. C. Tindall, W. H. Townsend.
*Forwards*–Theo B. Pienaar, Royal
Morkel, Harry Morkel, F. W. Mellish,
H. Scholtz, P. J. Mostert, J. S. Oliver
J. M. Michau, M. Ellis, T. L. Kruger,
G. W. van Rooyen, W. H. (Boy) Morkel,
N. du Plessis, A. P. Walker, L. B. Siedle.
*Manager*–H. C. Bennett.

1930–F. D. Prentice's British Team.
RECORD–Played 21. Won 15. Lost 6.
Drawn 0. Points for 420. Against
205.
TEST MATCHES–Played 4. Won 1. Lost
3. Scores: 6–3, 10–13, 10–15, 8–
22.
DEFEATS APART FROM TESTS–Lost
8–12 to Wellington, 8–14 to Can-
terbury, 6–19 to Auckland.
PLAYERS:
*Full-backs*–J. Bassett, G. M. Bonner.
*Threequarters*–C. D. Aarvold, J. S.
R. Reeve, J. C. Morley, A. L. Novis, R.
Jennings, H. M. Bowcott, T. E. Jones-
Davies.
*Half-backs*–R. S. Spong, W. H. Sobey,
T. P. Murray, T. C. Knowles, H. Poole.
*Forwards*–F. D. Prentice, H. Rew, D.

Parker, W. B. Welsh, B. H. Black, M. J.
Dunne, G. R. Beamish, J. L. Farrell, J.
McD. Hodgson, H. O'H. O'Neil, Ivor
Jones, H. Wilkinson, S. A. Martindale,
D. A. Kendrew, H. C. S. Jones.
*Manager*–James Baxter.

1931–S. J. Malcolm's Australian Team.
RECORD–Played 10. Won 3. Lost 6.
Drawn 1. Points for 131. Against
115.
TEST MATCHES–Played 1. Lost to
New Zealand 13–20 at Auckland.
DEFEATS APART FROM TESTS– Lost
8–12 to Southland, 13–16 to Can-
terbury, 5–14 to Combined Nelson,
West Coast, Golden Bay and Buller
Unions, 8–15 to Wellington, 10–11
to Taranadi, Drew 3–3 with Otago.
PLAYERS:
*Full-backs*–A. W. Ross, J. C. Steg-
gall.
*Threequarters*–C. H. T. Towers, G.
T. B. Palmer, H. A. Tolhurst, W. H.
Hemingway, H. V. Herd, D. L. Cowper.
*Five-eighths*–H. E. Primrose, P. A.
Clark.
*Half-bakcs*–S. J. Malcolm, W. G.
Bennett.
*Forwards*–W. H. Cerutti, P. B. Judd,
T. D. Perrin, J. R. Palfreyman, M. R.
Blair, E. W. Love, O. L. Bridle, F. J.
Whyatt, E. T. Bonis, J. F. Reville, W.
Ritter, M. C. White, J. Clark.
*Manager*–T. C. Davis.

1936–E. S. Haye's Australian Team.
RECORD–Played 10. Won 3. Lost 7.
Drawn 0. Points for 144. Against
160.
TEST MATCHES–Played 3. Won 1.
Lost 2. Lost to New Zealand 6–11
at Wellington, 13–38 at Dunedin.
Beat Maoris 31–6.
DEFEATS APART FROM TESTS–Lost
5–8 to Auckland, 14–20 to Hawkes
Bay, 13–19 to Wairarapa and Bush
Districts, 6–14 to Southland, 18–19
to Canterbury.
PLAYERS:
*Full-back*–K. P. Storey.
*Threequarters*–J. D. Keleher, A. D.
McLean, R. E. M. McLaughlin, B. C.
Egan, R. Rankin, E. S. Hayes, R. W. Dorr.
*Five-eighths*–L. S. Lewis, J. D. C.
Hammon.
*Half-backs*–E. de C. Gibbons, V.
Richards.
*Forwards*–T. P. Pauling, R. L. F.

Kelly, A. J. Hodgson, K. S. Windon, K. Mack Ramsay, F. E. Hutchinson, W. G. S. White, R. J. Walden, J. H. Malone, A. H. Stone, W. H. Cerutti, O. L. Bridle, E. T. Bonis.
*Manager*—E. G. Shaw.

**1937**—P. J. Nel's South African Team.
RECORD—Played 17. Won 16. Lost 1. Drawn 0. Points for 411. Against 104.
TEST MATCHES—Played 3. Won 2. Lost 1. Scores: 7–13, 13–6, 17–6.
PLAYERS:
*Full-backs*—G. H. Brand, F. G. Turner.
*Threequarters*—J. A. Broodryk, A. D. Lawton, P. J. Lyster, D. O. Williams, L. Babrow, J. Bester, S. R. Hofmeyer, J. White.
*Half-backs*—T. A. Harris, G. P. Lochner, D. F. van der Vyver, D. H. Craven, P. de Villiers.
*Forwards*—M. M. Louw, S. C. Louw, J. W. Lotz, C. B. Jennings, P. J. Nel, H. J. Martin, H. H. Watt, W. E. Bastard, W. F. Bergh, W. A. du Toit, A. R. Sheriff, L. C. Strachan, M. A. van der Berg, G. L. van Reenen.
*Manager*—P. W. Day.

**1946**—W. M. McLean's Australian Team.
RECORD—Played 12. Won 5. Lost 7. Drawn 0. Points for 139. Against 207.
TEST MATCHES—Played 2. Lost 2. Scores: 8–31 and 10–14. Also lost 0–20 to Maori Rep. Team.
DEFEATS APART FROM TESTS—Lost 19–32 to North Auckland, 11–20 to Canterbury, 9–21 to Combined South Canterbury, North Otago XV, 6–9 to Southland.
PLAYERS:
*Full-back*—B. J. Piper.
*Threequarters*—C. C. Eastes, J. M. Stone, J. R. McLean, A. P. Johnson, J. W. T. MacBride, T. Allan, M. L. Howell.
*Five-eighths*—J. F. Cremin, D. P. Bannon.
*Half-backs*—C. T. Burke, B. G. Schulte.
*Forwards*—K. S. Windon, C. J. Windon, A. E. Livermoie, G. A. Gourlay, A. J. Buchan, P. A. Hardcastle, G. M. Cooke, W. M. McLean, E. Tweedale, E. Freeman, R. E. McMaster, W. L. Dawson, K. J. Hodda, D. C. Furness, B. G. Hamilton.

*Manager*—Dr. W. H. Ward.

**1949**—T. Allan's Australian Team.
RECORD—Played 12. Won 11. Lost 1. Drawn 0. Points for 228. Against 108.
TEST MATCHES—Played 2. Won 2. Scores: Beat New Zealand 11–6 at Wellington, 16–9 at Auckland.
DEFEATS APART FROM TESTS—Lost 15–17 to West Coast and Buller Unions.
PLAYERS:
*Full-back*—B. J. C. Piper.
*Threequarters*—J. R. Fogarty, R. L. Garner, H. J. Solomon, J. Blomley, T. Allan, A. Ware, C. C. Davis.
*Five-eighths*—N. A. Emery, E. G. Broad.
*Half-backs*—C. T. Burke, R. M. Cawsey.
*Forwards*—A. J. Baxter, N. T. Betts, F. J. C. McCarthy, B. J. Wilson, K. M. Gordon, R. P. Mossop, N. Shehadie, D. C. Furness, N. V. Cottrell, C. J. Windon, J. D. Brockhoff, R. G. W. Cornforth, K. A. Cross.
*Managers*—W. H. Cerutti and R. J. Walden.

**1950**—K. D. Mullen's British Team.
RECORD—Played 23. Won 17. Lost 5. Drawn 1. Points for 420. Against 162.
TEST MATCHES—Played 4. Won 0. Lost 3. Drawn 1. Scores: 9–9, 0–8, 3–6, 8–11.
DEFEATS APART FROM TESTS—Lost 9–23 to Otago, 0–11 to Southland.
PLAYERS:
*Full-backs*—G. W. Norton, W. B. Cleaver.
*Threequarters*—D. V. C. Smith, Lewis Jones, Ken Jones, M. F. Lane, M. C. Thomas, B. L. Williams, J. Matthews, N. J. Henderson, R. McDonald.
*Half-backs*—Rex Willis, A. W. Black, G. Rimmer, I. P. Reece, J. W. Kyle.
*Forwards*—K. D. Mullen, D. M. Davies, G. M. Budge, C. Davies, T. Clifford, J. D. Robins, D. J. Hayward, J. E. Nelson, R. John, J. R. G. Stephens, V. G. Roberts, P. W. Kininmonth, J. W. McKay, R. T. Evans, J. S. McCarthy.
*Manager*—Surgeon-Captain L. B. Osborne.

**1952**—H. J. Solomon's Australian Team
RECORD—Played 10. Won 8. Lost 2.

Drawn 0. Points for 155. Against 120.

TEST MATCHES—Played 2. Won 1. Lost 1. Scores: Beat New Zealand 14—9 at Christchurch. Lost 8—15 at Wellington.

DEFEATS APART FROM TESTS—Lost 9—24 to Southland.

PLAYERS:
*Full-back*—R. Colbert.
*Threequarters*—E. T. Stapleton, G. G. Jones, H. J. Solomon, H. Barker, J. M. O'Neill, J. A. Phipps, L. Johnson.
*Five-eighths*—M. J. Tate, S. W. Brown.
*Half-backs*—C. T. Burke, B. P. Cox.
*Forwards*—A. R. Miller, K. A. Cross, B. B. Johnson, C. J. Windon, J. C. Carroll, N. Shehadie, A. S. Cameron, N. V. Cottrell, J. Walsh, A. J. Baxter, R. A. L. Davidson, F. M. Elliott, C. F. Forbes.
*Co-Managers*—J. E. Blackwood and T. B. McCormack.

1955—H. J. Solomon's Australian Team.
RECORD—Played 13. Won 10. Lost 3. Drawn 0. Points for 219. Against 106.

TEST MATCHES—Played 3. Won 1. Lost 2. Scores: Lost to New Zealand 8—16 at Wellington. Lost 0—8 at Dunedin. Won 8—3 at Auckland.

DEFEATS APART FROM TESTS—Lost 11—14 to Hawkes Bay.

PLAYERS:
*Full-back*—R. M. Tooth.
*Threequarters*—E. T. Stapleton, R. Phelps, G. W. G. Davis, B. T. Roberts, J. A. Phipps, P. J. Phipps, B. A. Wright, G. G. Jones.
*Five-eighths*—H. J. Solomon.
*Half-backs*—B. P. Cox, C. T. Burke.
*Forwards*—J. E. Thornett, N. McL. Hughes, J. J. Pashley, K. A. Cross, B. B. Johnson, A. S. Cameron, A. R. Miller, D. M. Emanuel, N. Shehadie, D. J. Strachan, N. Adams, J. R. Cross, T. P. Mooney.
*Co-Managers*—J. W. Breckenridge and W. H. Cerutti.

1956—S. S. Vivier's South African Team.
RECORD—Played 23. Won 16. Lost 6. Drawn 1. Points for 370. Against 177.

TEST MATCHES—Played 4. Won 1. Lost 3. Scores:6—10 at Dunedin, 8—3 at Wellington, 10—17 at Christchurch, 5—11 at Auckland.

DEFEATS APART FROM TESTS—Lost 10—13 to Waikato, 6—9 to Canterbury, 15—22 to New Zealand Universities. Also drew 3—3 with Taranaki.

PLAYERS:
*Full-backs*—J. Buchler, S. S. Viviers.
*Threequarters*—K. T. van Vollenhoven, P. G. Johnstone, R. G. Dryburgh, J. du Preez, P. E. Montini, J. J. Nel, A. I. Kirkpatrick, W. Rosenberg, T. Briers.
*Half-backs*—C. A. Ulyate, B. F. Howe, B. D. Pfaff, T. A. Gentles, C. F. Strydom.
*Forwards*—H. P. J. Bekker, A. C. Koch, P. du Toit, H. Newton-Walker, A. J. van der Merwe, M. Hanekom, J. T. Claasen, J. du Rand, C. J. de Nysschen, J. A. J. Pickard, C. J. van Wyk, C. J. de Wilzem, D. S. P. Ackermann, G. P. Lochner, D. F. Retief, J. J. Starke.
*Manager*—Dr. D. H. Craven.

1958—C. Wilson's Australian Team.
RECORD—Played 13, Won 6. Lost 6. Drawn 1. Points for 139. Against 154;

TEST MATCHES—Played 3. Won 1. Lost 2. Scores: 3—25 at Wellington, 6—3 at Christchurch, 8—17 at Auckland.

DEFEATS APART FROM TESTS—Lost 6—8 to Hawkes Bay, 8—26 to Southland, 6—12 to Manawatu, 8—9 to North Auckland.

PLAYERS:
*Full-back*—T. Curley.
*Threequarters*—A. Morton, E. Stapleton, T. Baxter, R. Phelps, B. Ellwood, A. Kay, J. Lenehan.
*Five-eighths*—H. Roberts, A. Summons.
*Half-backs*—J. Cocks, D. Connor.
*Forwards*—K. Ryan, M. van Gelder, J. Thornett, D. Lowth, C. Wilson, J. Carroll, G. McLean, P. Dunn, J. White, L. Forbes, K. Ellis, R. Meadows, P. Johnson.
*Manager*—C. Blunt.

1959—A. R. Dawson's British Team.
RECORD—Played 25. Won 20. Lost 5. Drawn 0. Points for 582. Against 266.

TEST MATCHES—Played 4. Won 1. Lost 3. Scores:17—18 at Dunedin, 8—11 at Wellington, 8—22 at Christchurch, 9—6 at Auckland.

DEFEATS APART FROM TESTS—Lost to Otago 8—26, Lost to Canterbury

14–20.
PLAYERS:
*Full-backs*–T. E. Davies, K. J. F. Scotland.
*Threequarters*–J. R. C. Young, P. B. Jackson, A. J. F. O'Reilly, N. H. Brophy, M. J. Price, W. M. Patterson, D. Hewitt, J. Butterfield, M. C. Thomas, G. H. Waddell.
*Half-backs*–J. P. Horrocks-Taylor, A. B. W. Risman, M. A. F. English, R. E. G. Jeeps, S. Coughtrie, A. A. Mulligan.
*Forwards*–B. V. Meredith, R. Prosser, A. R. Dawson, H. F. McLeod, G. K. Smith, S. Millar, B. G. M. Wood, R. H. Williams, W. A. Mulcahy, W. R. Evans, R. W. D. Marques, A. Ashcroft, N. A. Murphy, H. J. Morgan, J. Faull.
*Manager*–A. W. Wilson.

1961–F. Moncla's French Team.
RECORD–Played 13. Won 6. Lost 7. Drawn 0. Points for 150 Against. 149.
TEST MATCHES–Played 3. Lost 3. Scores:6–13 at Auckland, 3–5 at Wellington, 3–32 at Christchurch.
DEFEATS APART FROM TESTS–Lost to Waikato 3–22, North Auckland 6–8, N. Z. Maoris 3–5, and South Canterbury 14–17.
PLAYERS:
*Full-backs*–M. Vannier, J. Meynard.
*Threequarters*–S. Plantey, F. Boniface, H. Rancoule, J. Dupuy, G. Calvo, J. Pique, J. Bouquet.
*Five-eighths*–C. Lacaze, G. Camberabero, P. Albaladejo.
*Half-backs*–P. Lacoix, L. Camberabero, J. Serin.
*Forwards*–M. Celaya, S. Meyer, R. Lefevre, M. Crauste, F. Moncla, C. Vidal, M. Cassiede, J. Saux, A. Domenach, A. Bianco, G. Bouguyon, P. Cazals, J. Laudouar, J. Rollet.
*Managers*–M. Laurent, G. Basquet.

1962–J. Thornett's Australian Team.
RECORD–Played 13. Won 6. Lost 6. Drawn 1. Points for 218. Against 211.
TEST MATCHES–Played 3. Won 0. Lost 2. Drawn 1. Scores: 9–9 at Wellington, 0–3 at Dunedin, 8–16 at Auckland.
DEFEATS APART FROM TESTS–Lost to Canterbury 3–5, North Otago 13–14, Southland 0–3, Thames Valley 14–16.

PLAYERS:
*Full-backs*–J. Lenehan, S. Spence.
*Threequarters*–J. Boyce, J. Douglas, K. Walsham, B. Harland, R. Marks.
*Five-eighths*–P. Hawthorne, A. Town.
*Half-backs*–K. Catchpole, K. McMullen.
*Forwards*–R. Heming, E. Heinrich, P. Crittle, G. Chapman, D. O'Neill, J. Thornett, R. Thornett, A. Evans, J. White, J. Freedman, R. Prosser, P. Johnson, A. Laurie.
*Manager*–J. McLean.

1963–M. P. Weston's England Team.
RECORD–Played 5. Won 1. Lost 4. Drawn 0. Points for 45. Against 73.
TEST MATCHES–Played 2. Lost 2. Scores: 11–21 at Auckland, 6–9 at Christchurch.
DEFEATS APART FROM TESTS–Lost to Otago 9–14, Hawke's Bay 5–20.
PLAYERS:
*Full-back*–R. W. Hosen.
*Threequarters*–M. S. Phillips, F. D. Sykes, M. P. Weston, G. C. Gibson, J. M. Ranson, J. M. Dee.
*Half-backs*–T. C. Wintle, J. P. Horrocks-Taylor, R. F. Read, S. J. S. Clarke.
*Forwards*–P. E. Judd, J. E. Highton, C. R. Jacobs, H. O. Godwin, J. D. Thorne, J. E. Owen, T. A. Pargetter, A. M. Davis, D. P. Rogers, D. G. Perry, B. J. Wightman, V. R. Marriott.
*Manager*–J. T. W. Berry.

1964–J. Thornett's Australian Team.
RECORD–Played 8. Won 4. Lost 4. Drawn 0. Points for 109. Against 80.
TEST MATCHES–Played 3. Won 1. Lost 2. Scores: 9–14 at Dunedin, 3–18 at Christchurch, 20–5 at Wellington.
DEFEATS APART FROM TESTS–Lost to Auckland 6–11, Mid-Canterbury 10–16.
PLAYERS:
*Full-back*–T. Casey.
*Threequarters*–J. Boyce, S. Boyce, D. Grimmond, B. Ellwood, R. Honan, R. Marks.
*Five-eighths*–P. Hawthorne, R. Trivett.
*Half-backs*–K. Catchpole, L. Lawrence.
*Forwards*–J. Guerassimøff, E. Heinrich, D. Shepherd, G. Davis, P. Crittle, R. Heming, J. Thornett, J. White, L. Austin, P. Johnson, A. Laurie.

*Managers*—J. French and A. Roper.

**1965**—D. J. de Villier's South African Team.
RECORD—Played 24. Won 19. Lost 5. Drawn 0. Points for 485. Against 232.
TEST MATCHES—Played 4. Won 1. Lost 3. Scores: 3—6 at Wellington, 0—13 at Dunedin, 19—16 at Christchurch, and 3—20 at Auckland.
DEFEATS APART FROM TESTS—Lost to Wellington 6—23.
PLAYERS:
*Full-backs*—L. G. Wilson, C. G. Mulder.
*Threequarters*—J. P. Engelbrecht, F. de T. Roux, J. L. Gainsford, E. Oliver, G. Brynard, J. T. Truter, S. H. Nomis, W. J. Mans, C. J. C. Cronje.
*Five-eighths*—K. A. Oxlee, J. H. Banard.
*Half-backs*—D. J. de Villiers, C. M. Smith.
*Forwards*—D. Hopwood, J. Nel, J. Schoeman, F. du Preez, J. Naude, J. H. Ellis, A. Macdonald, G. F. Malan, C. P. van Zyl, D. C. Walton, C. Goosen, T. P. Bedford, L. J. Slabber, P. H. Botha, A. Janson, W. H. Parker, J. F. Marais.
*Manager*—K. Louw.

**1966**—M. J. Campbell-Lamerton's British Team.
RECORD—Played 25. Won 15. Lost 8. Drawn 2. Points for 300. Against 281.
TEST MATCHES—Played 4. Lost 4. Scores: 3—20 at Dunedin, 12—16 at Wellington, 6—19 at Christchurch, 11—24 at Auckland.
DEFEATS APART FROM TESTS—Lost 8—14 to Southland, 9—17 to Otago, 6—20 Wellington, 6—12 Wanganui—King Country.
PLAYERS:
*Full-backs*—D. Rutherford, S. Wilson, T. Price.
*Threequarters*—D. I. E. Bebb, A. J. W. Hinshelwood, K. Savage, S. Watkins, D. K. Jones, F. P. Bresnihan, M. P. Weston, C. W. McFadyean.
*Half-backs*—C. M. H. Gibson, D. Watkins, A. R. Lewis, R. H. Young.
*Forwards*—R. Lamont, A. Pask, N. A. Murphy, D. Grant, G. Prothero, J. Telfer, W. J. McBride, M. J. Campbell-Lamerton, W. Thomas, B. Price, R. McLoughlin, D. Powell, H. Norris, D.

Williams, K. W. Kennedy, F. A. Laidlaw.
*Manager*—D. J. O'Brien.

**1968**—C. Carrére's French team.
RECORD—Played 12. Won 8. Lost 4. Drawn 0. Points for 154. Against 120.
INTERNATIONAL MATCHES—Played 3. Won 0. Lost 3. Lost to New Zealand, at Christchurch 9—12; at Wellington 3—9; at Auckland 12—19.
DEFEAT OTHER THAN INTERNATIONAL—Lost to Marlborough, at Blenheim, 19—24.
PLAYERS:
*Full-backs*—P. Villepreux, C. Lacaze.
*Threequarters*—A. Piazza, A. Campaes, P. Besson, J. M. Bonal, C. Dourthe, J. P. Lux, J. Trillo, J. Maso.
*Half-backs*—J. Andrieu, J. L. Berot, C. Boujet.
*Forwards*—W. Spanghero, M. Billiere, J. Salut, B. Dutin, M. Greffe, C. Carrère, B. Dauga, C. Chenevay, A. Plantefol, J. M. Esponda, E. Cester, J. C. Noble, M. Lasserre, M. Yachvili, J. Iraçabal.

**1969**—B. Price's Welsh team.
RECORD—Played 5. Won 2. Lost 2. Drawn 1. Points for 62. Against 76.
INTERNATIONAL MATCHES—Played 2. Lost 2. Lost to New Zealand at, Christchurch 0—19, and at Auckland 12—33.
PLAYERS:
*Full-back*—J. P. R. Williams.
*Threequarters*—A. P. Skirving, S. J. Dawes, S. J. Watkins, M. R. C. Richards, K. S. Jarrett, T. G. R. Davies.
*Half-backs*—B. John, G. O. Edwards, P. Bennett, R. Hopkins.
*Forwards*—T. M. Davies, W. D. Morris, J. Taylor, D. Hughes, N. R. Gale, B. Price, W. D. Thomas, B. E. Thomas, D. B. Llewelyn, D. J. Lloyd, D. Williams, J. Young, V. C. Perrins.

**1971**—S. J. Dawe's British team.
RECORD—Played 24. Won 22. Lost 1. Drawn 1. Points for 555. Against 204.
INTERNATIONAL MATCHES—Played 4. Won 2. Lost 1. Drawn 1. Beat New Zealand, at Dunedin 9—3, and 13—3 at Wellington. Lost 12—22 at Christchurch and drew 14—14 at Auckland.
PLAYERS:

*Full-backs*–R. B. Hiller, J. P. R. Williams.

*Threequarters*–A. G. Biggar, J. C. Bevan, D. J. Duckham, T. G. R. Davies, A. J. L. Lewis, S. J. Dawes, J. S. Spencer, C. W. W. Rea.

*Half-backs*–B. John, C. M. H. Gibson, G. O. Edwards, R. Hopkins.

*Forwards*–J. F. Slatery, D. L. Quinnell, T. M. Davies, W. D. Thomas, P. J. Dixon, J. Taylor, M. L. Hipwell, W. J. McBride, M. G. Roberts, G. L. Brown, R. J. Arneil, T. G. Evans, A. B. Carmichael, R. J. McLoughlin, J. M. McLauchlan, J. V. Pullin, J. F. Lynch, F. A. Laidlaw, C. B. Stevens.

1972–G. V. Davis's Australian team
RECORD–Played 13. Won 5. Drawn 1. Lost 7. Points for 208. Against 244.
INTERNATIONAL MATCHES–Played 3. Lost 3. Lost 6–29 at Wellington, 17–30 at Christchurch, and 3–38 at Auckland.
DEFEATS OTHER THAN INTERNATIONALS–Lost to Otago, at Dunedin 0–26; to West Coast-Buller, at Westport 10–15; Hawke's Bay, at Napier 14–15; Waikato, at Hamilton 24–26.
PLAYERS:
*Full-back*–A. N. McGill.
*Threequarters*–J. W. Cole, J. J. McLean, J. I. Taylor, D. R. Burnet, D. L'Estrange, D. S. Rathie, P. Rowles.
*Half-backs*–G. C. Richardson, G. O. Gray, R. L. Fairfax, J. R. Cornes.
*Forwards*–R. B. Prosser, J. L. Howard, M. E. Frency, B. R. Brown, G. Fay, R. J. Thompson, R. A. Smith, B. D. Stumbles, G. V. Davis, P. D. Sullivan, R. N. Wood, M. R. Cocks, A. M. Gelling.
1973–J. V. Pullin's England team.
RECORD–Played 4. Won 1. Lost 3. Drawn 0. Points for 47. Against 60.
INTERNATIONAL MATCH–Beat New Zealand, at Auckland 16–10.
DEFEATS–Lost to Taranaki, at New Plymouth 3–6; to Wellington, at Wellington 16–25, and to Canterbury, at Christchurch 12–19.
PLAYERS:
*Full-backs*–P. A. Rossborough, A. M. Jorden.
*Threequarters*–D. J. Duckham, P. J. Squires, P. M. Knight, J. P. A. G. Janion, G. W. Evans, P. S. Preece.
*Half-backs*–A. G. B. Old, M. J. Cooper, S. J. Smith, J. G. Webster.

*Forwards*–C. B. Stevens, F. E. Cotton, J. V. Pullin, M. A. Burton, C. W. Ralston, J. White, N. O. Martin, R. M. Wilkinson, R. M. Uttley, P. J. Hendy, J. A. Watkins, A. Neary, A. G. Ripley.

N.B. This team also played one game in Fiji beating a Fijian representative side 13–12 in Suva.

1975–J. M. McLaughlan's Scotland Team
RECORD–Played 7. Won 4. Lost 3. Points for 157. Against 100.
INTERNATIONAL MATCH–Lost 0–24 at Auckland.
DEFEATS APART FROM TEST–15-19 v. Otago, 9-20 v. Canterbury.
PLAYERS:
*Full-backs*–A. R. Irvine, B. Hay.
*Three-quarters*–W. C. C. Steele, J. M. Renwick, J. N. M. Frame, L. G. Dick, I. R. McGeechan, D. L. Bell, G. A. Birkett.
*Half-backs*–C. M. Telfer, A. J. M. Lawson, D. W. Morgan.
*Forwards*–D. J. Leslie, G. Y. Mackie, W. Lauder, W. S. Watson, A. F. McHarg, A. J. Tomes, I. A. Barnes, N. E. K. Pender, M. A. Biggar, A. B. Carmichael, D. F. Madsen, J. M. McLauchlan, C. D. Fisher.

## Tours in Australia
1884–W. V. Milton's New Zealand Team.
RECORD–Played 8. Won 8. Lost 0. Drawn 0. Points for 167. Against 17.
REPRESENTATIVE MATCHES WITH SOUTH WALES–Played 3. Won 3. Scores: 11–0, 21–2, 16–0.
PLAYERS:
*Backs*–T. Ryan, J. A. Warbrick, E. Davy, J. Dumbell, H. Roberts, G. H. Helmore, H. Y. Braddon, J. Taiaroa.
*Forwards*–G. Carter, J. Lecky, T. B. O'Connor, H. Udy, P. P. Webb, E. B. Milton, W. V. Milton, R. J. Wilson, James Allan, J. O'Donnell, G. S. Robertson.
*Manager*–S. E. Sleigh.

1888–R. L. Seddon's British Team.
RECORD–Played 16. Won 14. Lost 0. Drawn 2. Points for 218. Against 68.
RECORD IN THE THREE REPRESENTATIVE MATCHES WITH NEW SOUTH WALES–Played 3. Won 3. Scores: 18–2, 18–6, 16–2, (A try counted 2 points).

PLAYERS:

*Full-backs*—J. T. Haslam, A. Paul.

*Threequarters*—H. C. Speakman, Dr.
H. Brooks, J. Auderton, A. E. Stoddart.

*Half-backs*—W. Bumby, J. Nolan, W.
Burnett.

*Forwards*—R. L. Seddon, S. Williams,
T. Banks, H. Eagles, T. Kent, C. Mathers,
A. J. Stuart, J. P. Clowes, W. H. Thomas,
A. P. Pinketh, Dr. D. J. Smith, R.
Burnett, A. J. Laing.

*Managers*—Alfred Shaw and Arthur
Shrewsbury.

1889—J. Warbrick's Maoris Team.
RECORD—Played 15. Won 15. Lost 0.
Drawn 0. Points for 258. Against
60.
No representative Matches played.
PLAYERS:

*Backs*—W. Elliott, E. Madigan, E.
McCausland, F. Warbrick, Joe Warbrick,
W. Warbrick, W. T. Warbrick, Taare, P.
Keogh, H. Lee.

*Forwards*—W. Anderson, R. Maynard,
D. Stewart, Alf Warbrick, Arthur War-
brick, G. Wynyard, W. Nehua, T. R.
Ellison, G. Williams, T. Rene, R. Taiaroa.

*Manager*—G. Scott.

1893—T. R. Ellison's New Zealand Team.
RECORD—Played 10. Won 9. Lost 1.
Drawn 0. Points for 168. Against 44.
REPRESENTATIVE MATCHES WITH
NEW SOUTH WALES—Played 3.
Won 2. Lost 1. Scores:17—8, 3—25,
16—0.
PLAYERS:

*Full-backs*—A. E. d'Arcy, H. C.
Wilson.

*Threequarters*—A. Bayly, H. Good,
F. M. Jervis, W. F. Winward.

*Half-backs*—H. Butland, D. R. Gage,
G. Shannon, G. Harper.

*Forwards*—F. S. Murray, R. H. Mc-
Kenzie, C. Speight, J. Lambie, T. Hiroa,
S. Cockcroft, J. Mowlem, R. Gray, W.
McKenzie, W. Watson, T. R. Ellison, R.
Oliphant, W. Pringle, A. J. Stuart, J. H.
Gardiner, C. N. McIntosh.

*Manager*—Col. G. F. Campbell.

1897—A. Bayly's New Zealand Team.
RECORD—Played 10. Won 9. Lost 1.
Drawn 0. Points for 228. Against 73.
REPRESENTATIVE MATCHES WITH
NEW SOUTH WALES—Played 3.
Won 2. Lost 1. Scores: 13—8, 8—27,
26—3.

PLAYERS:

*Full-backs*—S. Orchard, G. W. Smith.

*Threequarters*—W. Roberts, A. Bayly,
L. Allan, A. M. Armitt.

*Half-backs*—J. Duncan, E. Glennie,
A. L. Humphries.

*Forwards*—R. A. Handcock, F. S.
Murray, Alec Wilson, H. Mills, W. Wells,
J. Blair, J. Calnan, W. Hardcastle, W.
McKenzie, T. Pauling, F. J. Brooker, W.
Harris.

*Manager*—J. Hyams.

1899—Rev. M. Mullineaux's British
Team.
RECORD—Played 21. Won 18. Lost 3.
Drawn 0. Points for 333. Against
90.
TEST MATCHES—Played 4. Won 3.
Lost 1. Scores: 3—13, 11—0, 11—10,
13—0.
DEFEATS APART FROM TESTS—Lost
3—11 to Queensland, and 5—8 to
Sydney Metropolitan.
PLAYERS:

*Full-backs*—E. Martelli, C. E. K.
Thompson.

*Threequarters*—A. B. Timms, E. T.
Nicholson, A. M. Bucher, E. Gwynne
Nicholls, G. P. Doran.

*Half-backs*—Rev. M. Mullineaux, C.
Y. Adamson, G. Cookson.

*Forwards*—F. M. Stout, G. R. Gibson,
W. Judkins, B. I. Swannell, F. C. Belson,
J. W. Jarman, T. M. McGown, A. Ayre-
Smith, G. V. Evers, J. S. Francombe,
H. G. S. Gray.

*Manager*—Rev. M. Mullineaux.

1903—J. Duncan's New Zealand Team.
RECORD—Played 10. Won 10. Lost 0.
Drawn 0. Points for 276. Against 13.
TEST MATCHES—Played 1. Won 1.
Beat Australia 22—3 at Sydney Cri-
cket Ground.
PLAYERS:

*Full-back*—W. J. Wallace.

*Threequarters*—A. Asher, R. Mc-
Gregor, D. McGregor, J. Stalker.

*Five-eighths*—M. E. Wood, J. W.
Stead, J. Duncan.

*Half-backs*—H. Kiernan, A. L.
Humphries.

*Forwards*—L. Armstrong, H. G.
Porteous, D. Gallaher, A. J. Long, G. W.
Nicholson, G. A. Taylor, A. McMinn,
D. Udy, J. Spencer, B. J. Fanning,
R. J. Cooke, F. Given.

*Manager*—A. C. Norris.

1904–D. R. Bedell-Sivright's British Team.
RECORD–Played 14. Won 14. Lost 0. Drawn 0. Points for 265. Against 51.
TEST MATCHES–Played 3. Won 3. Lost 0. Drawn 0. Scores: 17–0, 17–3, 16–0.
PLAYERS:
*Full-back*–C. F. Stanger-Leathes.
*Threequarters*–J. L. Fisher, R. T. Gabe, W. F. Jowett, W. M. Llewelyn, E. T. Morgan, P. F. McEvedy, A. B. O'Brien.
*Half-backs*–P. F. Bush, F. C. Hulme, T. H. Vile.
*Forwards*–D. R. Bedell-Sivright, T. S. Bevan, S. N. Crowther, J. T. Sharland, D. D. Dobson, C. D. Patterson, J. Edwards, A. F. Harding, B. F. Massey, R. J. Rogers, S. McK. Saunders, D. H. Traill, B. I. Swannell.
*Manager*–Dr. A. B. O'Brien.

1905–J. Hunter's New Zealand Team.
RECORD–Played 3. Won 2. Lost 0. Drawn 1. Points for 49. Against 11.
REPRESENTATIVE MATCHES WITH NEW SOUTH WALES–Played 2. Won 1. Lost 0. Drawn 1. Scores: 19–0, 8–8.
PLAYERS:
*Full-backs*–W. J. Wallace, G. A. Gillet.
*Threequarters*–G. W. Smith, H. D. Thomson, D. McGregor, E. E. Booth.
*Five-eighths*–J. Hunter, H. J. Mynott
*Half-back*–F. Roberts.
*Forwards*–C. E. Seeling, G. W. Nicholson, F. T. Glasgow, W. S. Glenn, J. J. O'Sullivan, F. Newton, S. Casey, A. McDonald, J. Corbett, W. Johnston.
*Manager*–N. Galbraith.
(The above team was a portion of the party which were about to embark on the historic tour of Great Britain under the leadership of the immortal Dave Gallaher).

1907–J. Hunter's New Zealand Team.
RECORD–Played 7. Won 5. Lost 1. Drawn 1. Points for 96. Against 47.
TEST MATCHES–Played 3. Won 2. Lost 0. Drawn 1. Beat Australia 26–6 at Sydney, 14–5 at Brisbane, and drew 5–5 at Sydney.
DEFEATS APART FROM TESTS–Lost 0–14 to New South Wales at Sydney.
PLAYERS:

*Full-back*–G. Spencer.
*Threequarters*–W. J. Wallace, F. Mitchinson, F. C. Fryer, E. E. Booth.
*Five-eighths*–J. Hunter, H. J. Mynott, A. E. Eckhold.
*Half-backs*–J. D. Colman, F. Roberts.
*Forwards*–G. A. Gillet, W. Cunningham, A. H. Francis, G. W. Nicholson, C. E. Seeling, J. J. O'Sullivan, J. Hogan, J. Spencer, S. Casey, W. Johnston, A. McDonald, H. Paton, E. E. Hughes.
*Manager*–E. Wylie.

1908–A. F. Harding's British Team.
RECORD–Played 9. Won 7. Lost 2. Drawn 0. Points for 139. Against 48. No Tests played. Lost to Western Districts 10–15, and to New South Wales 3–6.
PLAYERS:
*Full-backs*–J. C. M. Dyke, E. J. Jackett.
*Threequarters*–F. E. Chapman, R. A. Gibbs, J. L. Williams, R. B. Griffiths, J. P. "Ponty" Jones, J. P. "Tuan" Jones, Dr. F. P. McEvedy, H. H. Vassall.
*Half-backs*–W. J. Davey, H. Laxon, W. L. Morgan, G. L. Williams.
*Forwards*–H. A. Archer, R. Dibble, P. J. Down, G. V. Kyrke, R. K. Green, E. Morgan, L. S. Thomas, A. F. Harding, J. F. Williams, G. R. Hind, F. Jackson, W. L. Oldham, J. A. S. Ritson, T. W. Smith.
*Manager*–G. H. Harnett.

1910–A. Takarangi's Maori Team.
RECORD–Played 11. Won 7. Lost 2. Drawn 2. Points for 207. Against 99. No Representative Matches played.
DEFEATS–Lost 0–11 and 13–27 to New South Wales.
PLAYERS:
*Full-backs*–H. Martin, A. Takarangi.
*Threequarters*–C. Ryland, M. Winiata, R. Dansey, G. Rogers, H. Rawhiri.
*Five-eighths*–W. T. Stead, A. Kaipara, P. Warbrick.
*Half-back*–S. M. Piki.
*Forwards*–H. Poanga, C. Lipene, C. Sellars, H. Tamu, W. Cunningham, W. Winiata, J. Hall, D. Small, W. Burnett, J. Martin, M. Paratena, R. Pitchirs, J. Hiahia, H. Hamson.
*Manager*–W. T. Parata.

1910–F. Roberts's New Zealand Team.
RECORD–Played 7. Won 6. Lost 1.

Drawn 0. Points for 112. Against 61.
TEST MATCHES–Played 3. Won 2.
Lost 1. Beat Australia 6–0 at Sydney. Lost 0–11 at Sydney. Won
28–13 at Sydney.
PLAYERS:
*Full-backs*–J. O'Leary, J. Ryan.
*Threequarters*–F. R. Wilson, P. J.
Burns, W. J. Mitchell, F. Mitchinson, J.
Stohr.
*Five-eighths*–H. J. Mynott, W. B.
Fuller.
*Half-back*–F. Roberts.
*Forwards*–G. McKellar, A. H. Francis, J. Maguire, D. Evans, H. E. Avery,
"Ranji" Wilson, A. Budd, F. E. B.
Ivimney, H. Paton, A. Patterson, J.
Ridland, S. Bligh.
*Manager*–V. R. Meredith.

1913–A. Takarangi's Maoris Team.
RECORD–Played 8. Won 5. Lost 3.
Drawn 0. Points for 107. Against 69.
REPRESENTATIVE MATCHES–Played
2 (both with N. S. W.). Lost 2.
Scores: 3–15, 5–16.
ADDITIONAL DEFEAT–Lost to
Queensland 9–19.
PLAYERS:
*Full-back*–N. Pakakura.
*Threequarters*–C. Ryland, T. M.
Grace, M. Winiata, Ru Kingi, H. Leaf.
*Five-eighths*–P. Blake, Paki, C. Woods.
*Half-backs*–S. M. Piki, C. Montgomery.
*Forwards*–J. Hiahia, T. Tresize, A.
Takarangi, H. Tapsell, J. Martin, C.
Jacobs, J. Rogers, J. Hikatarewa, S.
French, Te Wahie, Kauka.
*Manager*–W. T. Parata.

1914–R. W. Roberts' New Zealand Team.
RECORD–Played 10. Won 10. Lost 0.
Drawn 0. Points for 246. Against 50.
TEST MATCHES–Played 3. Won 3.
Beat Australia 5–0 at Sydney, 17–
0 at Brisbane, 22–7 at Sydney.
PLAYERS:
*Full-backs*–J. G. O'Brien, E. A. Cockcroft.
*Threequarters*–L. Weston, T. W.
Lynch, R. W. Roberts, G. Loveridge, H.
M. Taylor.
*Five-eighths*–R. S. Black, James
Ryan, J. R. McKenzie.
*Half-back*–E. J. Roberts.
*Forwards*–J. Barrett, J. A. Bruce,
A. J. Downing, M. Cain, W. Francis,
"Ranji" Wilson, H. V. Murray, J. B.

Graham, J. C. Irvine, W. G. Lindsay,
J. McNeece, T. Fisher.
*Manager*–R. M. Isaacs.

1920–J. Tilyard's New Zealand Team.
RECORD–Played 7. Won 7. Lost 0.
Drawn 0. Points for 264. Against 77.
REPRESENTATIVE MATCHES WITH
NEW SOUTH WALES–Played 3.
Won 3. Scores:26–15, 14–6, 24–
13.
PLAYERS:
*Full-back*–J. G. O'Brien.
*Threequarters*–P. W. Storey, B. Algar,
J. Steel, V. W. Wilson.
*Five-eighths*–C. E. O. Badeley, J.
T. Tilyard, E. J. Roberts.
*Half-back*–C. Brown.
*Forwards*–J. G. Donald, W. D.
Duncan, A. Carroll, E. W. Hasell, J.
E. Moffitt, J. D. Shearer, A. H. West,
D. L. Baird, E. A. Belliss, C. Fletcher,
J. Jacobs, C. McLean.
*Manager*–T. Jones.

1921–T. B. Pienaar's South African
Team.
RECORD–Played 5. Won 5. Lost 0.
Drawn 0. Points for 134. Against 38.
REPRESENTATIVE MATCHES WITH
NEW SOUTH WALES–Played 3.
Won 3. Scores: 25–10, 16–11, 28–
9.
PLAYERS:
*Full-backs*–P. Gerhard Morkel, I. D.
de Villiers.
*Threequarters*–A. J. van Heerden,
W. C. Zeller, Henry W. Morkel, C. du
P. Meyer, S. S. F. Strauss, W. D. Sendin,
W. A. Clarkson, J. S. Weepener.
*Half-backs*–J. P. Michau, J. S. de
Kock, J. C. Tindall, W. H. Townsend.
*Forwards*–Theo B. Pienaar, Royal
Morkel, Harry Morkel, F. W. Mellish,
H. Scholtz, P. J. Mostert, J. S. Olivier,
J. M. Michau, M. Ellis, T. L. Kruger,
G. W. van Rooyen, W. H. (Boy) Morkel,
N. du Plessis, A. P. Walker, L. B. Siedle.
*Manager*–H. C. Bennett.

1922–E. Bellis's New Zealand Team.
RECORD–Played 5. Won 3. Lost 2.
Drawn 0. Points for 120. Against 66.
REPRESENTATIVE MATCHES WITH
NEW SOUTH WALES–Played 3.
Won 1. Lost 2. Scores: 26–19, 8–
14, 6–8.
PLAYERS:
*Full-back*–R. Bell.

*Threequarters*–J. Steel, C. Fitzgerald, W. A. Ford, P. H. Hickey, K. S. Svenson.
*Five-eighths*–M. F. Nicholls, G. Dickinson, R. Mathieson, V. Badeley.
*Half-back*–H. E. Nicholls.
*Forwards*–A. E. Bellis, J. O'Brien, L. Cupples, F. H. Masters, M. J. Brownlie, J. G. Donald, U. P. Calcinai, S. D. Shearer, F. Smyth, L. Peterson, J. Richardson, L. Williams, A. White.
*Manager*–S. S. Dean.

1922–H. Jacobs Maoris Team.
RECORD–Played 6. Won 5. Lost 1. Drawn 0. Points for 169. Against 96.
REPRESENTATIVE MATCHES WITH NEW SOUTH WALES–Played 3. Won 2. Lost 1. Scores: 25–22, 13–28, 23–22.
PLAYERS:
*Full-back*–Matui.
*Threequarters*–H. Phillip, W. Barclay, W. R. Akuira, J. M. Blake, T. Tate.
*Five-eighths*–Peina K. Taituha, W. Potaka, N. F. Stead.
*Half-back*–J. Mill.
*Forwards*–T. Tangitu, H. R. Bevan, S. Gemmell, R. Brougon, J. C. McGregor, S. Parakuka, H. Jacobs, M. Love, Pini Taiapa, R. Park, F. L. Tresize, T. Barclay.
*Manager*–W. T. Parata.

1922–H. Jacobs' Maoris Team.
RECORD–Played 4. Won 0. Lost 3. Drawn 1. Points for 67. Against 78.
REPRESENTATIVE MATCHES WITH NEW SOUTH WALES–Played 3. Lost 3. Scores: 23–27, 16–21, 12–14.
PLAYERS:
*Full-back*–M. McGregor.
*Threequarters*–Kingston, W. Potaka, W. Barclay, Haka Pupini.
*Five-eighths*–Peina, J. Tureia, L. Pai Wai.
*Half-backs*–J. Mill, Poi.
*Forwards*–A. Keppa, W. Kane, J. Bannister, P. Taiapa, T. Walker, S. Gemmell, Pai Heta, H. R. Bevan, K. Black, R. George, R. J. Bell, T. Winiata.
*Manager*–W. T. Parata.

1924–C. E. Badeley's New Zealand Team.
RECORD–Played 4. Won 3. Lost 1. Drawn 0. Points for 113. Against 38.
REPRESENTATIVE MATCHES WITH

NEW SOUTH WALES–Played 3. Won 2. Lost 1. Scores: 16–20, 21–5, 38–8.
PLAYERS:
*Full-back*–G. Nepia.
*Threequarters*–F. W. Lucas, A. H. Hart, H. W. Brown, K. S. Svenson.
*Five-eighths*–A. E. Cooke, C. E. Badeley, M. Nicholls, N. P. McGregor.
*Half-backs*–W. C. Dalley, J. Mill.
*Forwards*–C. G. Porter, J. H. Parker, L. F. Cupples, A. White, J. Richardson, M. Brownlie, C. Brownlie, W. R. Irvine, R. R. Masters, B. B. McLeary, I. H. Harvey, H. G. Munro.
*Manager*–E. A. Little.
This team was a section of the party that later went on to Great Britain to achieve an invincible record.

1925–J. Donald's New Zealand Team.
RECORD–Played 6. Won 5. Lost 1. Drawn 0. Points for 101. Against 46.
REPRESENTATIVE MATCHES WITH NEW SOUTH WALES–Played 3. Won 3. Scores: 26–3, 4–0, 11–3.
DEFEATS APART FROM REPRESENTATIVE MATCHES–Lost to New South Wales 2nd XV: 16–18.
PLAYERS:
*Full-back*–J. Harris.
*Threequarters*–W. Elvey, J. Blake, G. D. Wise, A. D. Law.
*Five-eighths*–D. Johnson, A. Matson, L. Johnson.
*Half-backs*–D. Wright, J. P. Lawson.
*Forwards*–A. Lomas, J. Donald, L. Righton, L. Knight, A. Kirkpatrick, J. McNab, A. McCormack, J. Waters, D. Dickson, B. Finlayson, A. Thomas, J. Archer.
*Manager*–E. McKenzie.

1926–C. G. Porter's New Zealand Team.
RECORD–Played 5. Won 4. Lost 1. Drawn 0. Points for 104. Against 67.
REPRESENTATIVE MATCHES WITH NEW SOUTH WALES–Played 4. Won 3. Lost 1. Scores: 20–26, 11–6, 14–0, 28–21.
PLAYERS:
*Full-backs*–H. W. Brown, D. M. Stevenson.
*Threequarters*–J. Blake, A. E. Cooke, A. C. Robilliard, W. Elvey, K. S. Svenson.
*Five-eighths*–M. Nicholls, T. R. Sheen, J. Mill.
*Half-back*–W. C. Dalley.

*Forwards*—C. G. Porter, A. Knight, A. Finlayson, I. H. Harvey, W. Hazlett, G. Alley, W. R. Irvine, C. Brownlie, M. Brownlie, A. Kirkpatrick, R. Stewart.
*Manager*—H. S. Leith.

1929—C. G. Porter's New Zealand Team
RECORD—Played 10. Won 6. Lost 3. Drawn 1. Points for 186. Against 80.
TEST MATCHES—Played 3. Won 0. Lost 3. Lost to Australia at Sydney 8—9. Lost to Australia at Brisbane 9—17. Lost to Australia at Sydney 13—15.
PLAYERS:
*Full-back*—G. Nepia.
*Threequarters*—B. Grenside, W. Waterman, J. A. Geddes, S. R. Colston, C. Stringfellow.
*Five-eighths*—H. Lilburne, C. Oliver, R. Cundy, L. Hook.
*Half-backs*—W. C. Dalley, J. M. Tuck, E. T. C. Leys.
*Forwards*—C. G. Porter, B. Palmer, R. G. McWilliams, A. Cottrell, R. Souter, C. Sontagg, E. R. Steere, A. Kivell, W. Rika, M. Reside, A. K. Reid, A. Mahoney, E. M. Snow.
*Manager*—Jas. McLeod.

1930—F. D. Prentice's British Team.
RECORD—Played 7. Won 5. Lost 2. Drawn 0. Points for 204. Against 113.
TEST MATCHES—Played 1. Lost 1. Lost to Australia 5—6 at Sydney.
DEFEATS APART FROM TESTS—Lost to New South Wales 3—28 at Sydney.
PLAYERS:
*Full-backs*—J. Bassett, G. M. Bonner.
*Threequarters*—C. D. Aavold, J. S. R. Reeve, J. C. Morley, A. L. Novis, R. Jennings, H. M. Bowcott, T. Jones-Davies.
*Half-backs*—R. S. Spong, W. H. Sobey, T. P. Murray, T. C. Knowles, H. Poole.
*Forwards*—F. D. Prentice, H. Rew, D. Parker, W. B. Welsh, B. H. Black, M. J. Dunne, G. R. Beamish, J. L. Farrell, J. McD. Hodgson, H. O'H. O'Neil, Ivor Jones, H. Wilkinson, S. A. Martindale, D. A. Kendrew, H. C. S. Jones.
*Manager*—James Baxter.

1932—F. D. Kilby's New Zealand Team.
RECORD—Played 10. Won 9. Lost 1. Drawn 0. Points for 308. Against 99.
TEST MATCHES—Played 3. Won 2. Lost 1. Lost to Australia at Sydney 17—22. Beat Australia at Brisbane 21—3. Beat Australia at Sydney 21—13.
PLAYERS:
*Full-back*—A. Collins.
*Threequarters*—A. C. Proctor, G. A. Bullock-Douglas, J. R. Page, N. Ball, F. C. Holder, T. H. C. Caughey.
*Five-eighths*—H. R. Pollock, H. T. Lilburne, G. D. Innes.
*Half-backs*—F. D. Kilby, M. M. N. Corner.
*Forwards*—E. F. Barry, H. F. McLean, E. M. Jessop, G. W. Purdue, T. C. Metcalfe, F. Solomon, B. P. Palmer, E. R. G. Steere, R. Clarke, J. Hore, A. I. Cottrell, J. E. Manchester, D. Max.
*Manager*—W. J. Wallace.

1934—F. D. Kilby's New Zealand Team.
RECORD—Played 8. Won 6. Lost 1. Drawn 1. Points for 176. Against 90.
TEST MATCHES—Played 2. Won 0. Lost 1. Drawn 1. Lost to Australia 11—25, and drew with Australia 3—3, both at Sydney.
PLAYERS:
*Full-back*—A. Collins.
*Threequarters*—G. A. Bullock-Douglas, G. F. Hart, E. C. Holder, T. H. Caughey, C. H. Smith.
*Five-eighths*—J. R. Page, H. T. Lilburne, J. L. Griffiths, C. J. Oliver.
*Half-backs*—F. D. Kilby, M. M. N. Corner.
*Forwards*—W. E. Hadley, A. Knight, H. F. McLean, A. Lambourn, E. F. Barry, J. Hore, R. M. McKenzie, D. S. Max, J. E. Manchester, A. Mahoney, R. King, J. Leson, H. Maitara.
*Manager*—A. J. Geddes.

1935—G. Nepia's Maori Team.
RECORD—Played 11. Won 9. Lost 2. Drawn 0. Points for 256. Against 132.
REPRESENTATIVE MATCHES WITH NEW SOUTH WALES—Played 3. Won 2. Lost 1. Scores: 6—5, 13—20, 14—5.
DEFEATS APART FROM REPRESENTATIVE MATCHES—Lost 22—39 to Queensland.
PLAYERS:

Full-back—George Nepia.

Threequarters—C. Smith, W. J. Phillips, J. McDonald, J. Hemi, T. Ngaia.

Five-eighths—T. Chase, N. Kotua, J. C. Reedy.

Half-backs—H. Harrison, C. Mellish.

Forwards—H. Whiu, W. Cooper, K. Reedy, J. Kershaw, G. Harrison, H. Maitara, J. Greening, P. Smith, P. Parata, B. Rogers, R. Mitchell, L. Kawe, T. Whiteley, J. Broderick.

Co-Managers—Kingi Tahiwi and W. J. Wallace.

1937—P. J. Nel's South African Team.

RECORD—Played 11. Won 10. Lost 1. Drawn 0. Points for 444. Against 76.

TEST MATCHES—Played 2. Won 2. Scores: 9–5, 26–17.

DEFEATS APART FROM TESTS—Lost 6–17 to New South Wales at Sydney.

PLAYERS:

Full-backs—G. H. Brand, F. G. Turner.

Threequarters—J. A. Broodryk, A. D. Lawton, P. J. Lyster, D. O. Williams, L. Babrow, J. Bester, S. R. Hofmeyer, J. White.

Half-backs—T. A. Harris, G. P. Lochner, D. F. van der Vyver, D. H. Craven, P. de Villiers.

Forwards—M. M. Louw, S. C. Louw, J. W. Lotz, C. B. Jennings, P. J. Nel, H. J. Martin, H. H. Watt. W. E. Bastard, W. F. Bergh, W. A. du Toit, A. R. Sherriff, L. C. Strachan, M. A. van der Berg, G. L. van Reenen.

Manager—P. W. Day.

1938—N. A. Mitchell's New Zealand Team.

RECORD—Played 9. Won 9. Lost 0. Drawn 0. Points for 279. Against 73.

TEST RECORD—Played 3. Won 3. Beat Australia 24–9 and 20–14 at Sydney, and by 14–6 at Brisbane.

PLAYERS:

Full-back—J. M. Taylor.

Threequarters—J. Dick, W. J. Phillips, T. C. Morrison, N. A. Mitchell, A. W. Wesney, J. L. Sullivan, J. A. Hooper, A. Wright.

Five-eighths—T. Berghan, J. L. Griffiths.

Half-backs—C. K. Saxton, E. W. Tindill.

Forwards—E. S. Jackson, D. Dalton, A. W. Bowman, C. E. Quaid, A. A.

Parkhill, L. George, H. M. Milliken, C. W. Williams, R. M. McKenzie, R. R. King, J. G. Wynyard, W. N. Carson, A. Lambourn.

Managers—Dr. G. J. Adams and A. McDonald.

1947—F. Allen's New Zealand Team.

RECORD—Played 9. Won 8. Lost 1. Drawn 0. Points for 260. Against 99.

TEST MATCHES—Played 2. Won 2. Beat Australia 27–14 at Sydney, and by 13–5 at Brisbane.

DEFEATS APART FROM TESTS—Lost 9–12 to New South Wales at Sydney.

PLAYERS:

Full-backs—R. W. H. Scott, T. R. D. Webster.

Threequarters—W. G. Argus, J. K. McKean, D. F. Mason, M. P. Goddard, J. B. Smith, P. Smith.

Five-eighths—F. Allen, J. C. Kearney, M. B. Couch.

Half-backs—P. L. Tetzlaff, V. D. Bevan.

Forwards—E. H. Catley, K. D. Arnold, J. McCormick, H. F. Frazer, J. G. Simpson, R. A. Dalton, R. M. White, N. H. Thornton, C. Willocks, F. G. Hobbs, L. S. Connolly, L. A. Grant.

Managers—H. Strang and N. McKenzie.

1949—A. J. West's Maori Team.

RECORD—Played 11. Won 9. Lost 1. Drawn 1. Points for 258. Against 86.

TEST MATCHES v. AUSTRALIA—Played 3. Won 1. Lost 1. Drawn 1. Scores: 12–3, 8–8 and 3–18.

PLAYERS:

Full-back—H. W. Kenny.

Threequarters—N. P. Cherrington, W. Lanigan, R. McKinley, W. H. Taylor, M. E. Delamere.

Five-eighths—P. Smith, B. W. Beazley, M. B. Couch, T. D. Kipa.

Half-back—L. Raueti.

Forwards—K. Matthewson, A. W. Blake, C. S. Parahi, S. T. Reid, W. Carrington, L. W. Hohaia, A. J. West, R. Hohaia, S. Heperi, C. W. Shirling, J. Marriner, R. F. Bryers,

Manager—T. A. French.

1950—Dr. Karl Mullen's British Team.

RECORD—Played 6. Won 5. Lost 1. Drawn 0. Points for 150. Against 52.

TEST MATCHES—Played 2. Won 2.

Scores: 19–6, 24–3.
DEFEATS APART FROM TESTS–Lost
to New South Wales at Sydney 12–
17.
PLAYERS:
*Full-backs*–G. V. Norton, W. ·B.
Cleaver, B. Lewis Jones.
*Threequarters*–D. V. C. Smith, Ken
Jones,. M. F. Lane, M. C. Thomas, B.
L. Williams, J. Matthews, N. J. Henderson, R. Macdonald.
*Half-backs*–J. W. Kyle, I. Preece,
R. Willis, A. W. Black, G. Rimmer.
*Forwards*–K. D. Mullen, D. M.
Davies, G. M. Budge, C. Davies, T.
Clifford, J. D. Robins, D. J. Hayward,
J. E. Nelson, R. John, V. G. Roberts,
P. W. Kininmonth, R. Stephens, J. W.
McKay, R. T. Evans, J. S. McCarthy.
*Manager*–Surgeon-Captain L. B.
Osborne.

1951–P. Johnstone's New Zealand
Team.
RECORD–Played 12. Won 12. Lost 0.
Drawn 0. Points for 366. Against 83.
TEST MATCHES–Played 3. Won 3.
Beat Australia 8–0 and 17–11 at
Sydney, 16–6 at Brisbane.
PLAYERS:
*Full-back*–M. S. Cockerill.
*Threequarters*–R. A. Jarden, R. H.
Bell, P. Erceg, D. R. Wightman, J. M.
Tanner, N. P. Cherrington, T. W. Lynch,
B. J. Fitzpatrick.
*Five-eighths*–L. S. Haig, A. L. Wilson.
*Half-backs*–L. B. Steele, A. R. Reid.
*Forwards*–P. Johnstone, N. L. Wilson, K. I. Skinner, H. W. Wilson, G.
Mexted, L. E. Robinson, W. A. McCaw, L. A. Grant, R. A. White, R. H.
Duff, P. S. Burke, I. A. Hammond.
*Managers*–R. W. S. Botting and L.
Clode.

1956–S. S. Viviers' South African Team.
RECORD–Played 6. Won 6. Lost 0.
Drawn 0. Points for 150. Against 26.
TEST MATCHES–Played 2. Won 2.
Scores: 9–0 at Sydney, 9–0 at Brisbane.
PLAYERS:
*Full-backs*–J. Buchler, S. S. Viviers.
*Threequarters*–K. T. von Vollenhoven, P. G. Johnstone, R. G. Dryburgh,
J. du Preez, P. E. Montini, J. J. Nel, A. I.
Kirkpatrick, W. Rosenberg, T. Briers.
*Half-backs*–C. A. Ulyate, B. F. Howe,

B. D. Pfaff, T. A. Gentles, C. F. Strydom.
*Forwards*–H. P. J. Bekker, A. C.
Koch, P. du Toit, H. Newton-Walker,
M. Hanekom, J. T. Claassen, J. du Rand,
C. J. de Nysschen, J. A. J. Pickard, C. J.
van Wyk, C. J. de Wilzem, D. S. P.
Ackermann, G. P. Lochner, D. F. Retief,
J. Starke.
*Manager*–D. H. Craven.

1957–A. R. Reid's New Zealand Team.
RECORD–Played 14. Won 14. Lost 0.
Drawn 0. Points for 500. Against 86.
TEST MATCHES–Played 2. Won 2.
Scores: 25–11 and 38–14.
PLAYERS:
*Full-back*–D. B. Clarke.
*Threequarters*–M. J. Dixon, R. F.
McMullen, P. T. Walsh, J. R. Watt.
*Five-eighths*–W. R. Archer, Ross H.
Brown, W. N. Gray, H. J. Leiver, T. R.
Lineen.
*Half-backs*–B. P. J. Molloy, A. R.
Reid.
*Forwards*–P. S. Burke, L. J. Clarke,
W. D. Gillespie, R. C. Hemi, S/Sgt. S. F.
Hill, J. N. MacEwan, F. S. McAtamney,
D. N. McIntosh, C. E. Meads, E. A. R.
Pickering, A. J. Soper, W. J. Whineray,
D. Young.
*Manager*–W. A. G. Craddock, J.P.

1959–A. R. Dawson's British Team.
RECORD–Played 6. Won 5. Lost 1.
Points for 174. Against 70.
TEST MATCHES–Played 2. Won 2.
Scores: 17–6 at Brisbane, 24–3 at
Sydney.
DEFEATS APART FROM TESTS–Lost
to New South Wales at Sydney 14–
18.
PLAYERS:
See under TOURS IN NEW ZEALAND in this section.
*Manager*–A. W. Wilson.

1960–W. Whineray's New Zealand Team.
RECORD–Played 5. Won 5. Points for
184. Against 15.
TEST MATCHES–None.
DEFEATS–None.
PLAYERS:
*Full-backs*–D. B. Clarke, W. A. Davies.
*Threequarters*–R. W. Caulton, J. R.
Watt, R. F. McMullen, D. H. Cameron,
T. P. O'Sullivan, K. F. Laidlaw, T. R.
Lineen.
*Five-eighths*–S. G. Bremner, A. H.

Clarke, S. R. Nesbit.
*Half-backs*–K. C. Briscow, R. J. Urbahn.
*Forwards*–D. J. Graham, E. A. R. Pickering, R. J. Conway, K. R. Tremain, W. D. Gillespie, P. F. H. Jones, I. N. MacEwan, R. H. Horsley, C. E. Meads, M. W. Irwin, I. J. Clarke, E. J. Anderson, R. C. Hemi, D. Young, R. Boon.
*Manager*–T. Pearce.

1961–F. Moncia's French Team.
RECORD–Played 2. Won 2. Points for 30. Against 20.
TEST MATCH–Played 1. Won 1. Score: 15–8 at Sydney.
PLAYERS:
See under TOURS IN NEW ZEALAND in this section.
*Manager*–M. Laurent, G. Basquet.

1963–M. P. Weston's England Team.
RECORD–Played 1. Lost 1.
TEST MATCH–Played 1. Lost 1. Score: 9–18 at Sydney.
PLAYERS:
See under TOURS IN NEW ZEALAND in this section.
*Manager*–J. T. W. Berry.

1965–D. J. de Villiers' South African Team.
RECORD–Played 6. Won 3. Lost 3. Points for 184. Against 53.
TEST MATCHES–Played 2. Lost 2. Scores: 11–18 and 8–12.
DEFEATS APART FROM TESTS–Lost to New South Wales 3–12.
PLAYERS:
See under TOURS IN NEW ZEALAND in this section.
*Manager*–K. Louw.

1966–M. J. Campbell-Lamerton's British Team.
RECORD–Played 8. Won 7. Lost 0. Drawn 1. Points for 202. Against 48.
TEST MATCHES–Played 2. Won 2. Scores: 11–8 at Sydney, 31–0 at Brisbane.
DEFEATS–None
PLAYERS:
*Full-backs*–D. Rutherford, S. Wilson.
*Threequarters*–D. I. E. Bebb, A. J. W. Hinshelwood, K. Savage, S. Watkins, D. K. Jones, J. Walsh, M. P. Weston, C. W. McFadyean.
*Half-backs*–C. M. H. Gibson, D. Watkins, A. R. Lewis, R. H. Young.

*Forwards*–R. Lamont, A. Pask, N. A. Murphy, D. Grant, G. Prothero, J. Telfer, W. J. McBride, M. J. Campbell-Lamerton, W. Thomas, B. Price, R. McLoughlin, D. Powell, H. Norris, D. Williams, H. W. Kennedy, F. A. Laidlaw.
*Manager*–D. J. O'Brien.

1967–T. J. Kierman's Ireland Team.
RECORD–Played 6. Won 4. Lost 2. Drawn 0. Points for 119. Against 80.
INTERNATIONAL MATCH–Beat Australia, at Sydney 11–5.
DEFEATS–Lost to N. S. W., at Sydney, 9–21, and to Sydney 8–30.
PLAYERS:
*Full-back*–T. J. Kiernan.
*Threequarters*–A. T. A. Duggan, J. C. Walsh, M. H. Brophy, F. P. K. Bresnihan, J. B. Murray, P. J. McGrath.
*Half-backs*–B. F. Sherry, C. M. H. Gibson, L. Hall.
*Forwards*–K. W. Kennedy, S. MacHale, S. A. Hutton, P. O'Callaghan, M. G. Molloy, K. G. Goodall, W. J. McBride, T. A. Moore, L. G. Butler, J. M. Flynn, M. G. Doyle, D. J. Hickie.

1968–B. J. Lochore's New Zealand Team.
RECORD–Played 11. Won 11. Points for 427. Against 60.
INTERNATIONAL MATCHES–Played 2. Won 2. Beat Australia, at Sydney 27–11, and at Brisbane 19–18.
PLAYERS:
*Full-backs*–W. F. McCormick, P. A. Johns.
*Threequarters*–M. Knight, W. L. Davis, W. D. Cottrell, W. D. R. Currey, A. G. Steel, G. S. Thorne, T. N. Wolfe.
*Half-backs*–S. M. Going, E. W. Kirton, K. F. Laidlaw.
*Forwards*–B. J. Lochore, G. C. Williams, A. G. Sutherland, C. E. Meads, T. N. Lister, B. E. McLeod, T. M. McCashin, A. E. Hopkinson, I. A. Kirkpatrick, S. C. Strahan, K. R. Tremain, K. F. Gray, A. J. Kreft, B. L. Muller.

1968–C. Carrère's French Team.
RECORD–Played 2. Won 1. Lost 1. Points for 43. Against 22.
INTERNATIONAL MATCH–Lost to Australia at Sydney 10–11.
PLAYERS:
See under teams to NEW ZEALAND.

1969–B. Price's Welsh Team to Australia. (See also under New Zealand).

RECORD—Played 1. Won 1. Points for 19. Against 16.
INTERNATIONAL MATCH—Beat Australia at Sydney 19—16.
PLAYERS:
See under teams to New Zealand.

**1970—F. A. L. Laidlaw's Scottish Team.**
RECORD—Played 6. Won 3. Lost 3. Points for 109. Against 94.
INTERNATIONAL MATCH—Lost to Australia at Sydney 3—23.
DEFEATS OTHER THAN INTERNATIONALS—
—Lost to N.S.W. at Sydney 14—28, and to Queensland, at Brisbane 13—16.
PLAYERS:
*Full-back*—L. S. G. Smith.
*Threequarters*—M. A. Smith, A. D. Gill, A. G. Biggar, J. N. M. Frame, C. W. Rea, J. W. C. Turner.
*Forwards*—F. A. L. Laidlaw, N. Suddon, A. B. Carmichael, D. T. Deans, J. McLauchlan, P. K. Stagg, G. L. Brown, P. C. Brown, T. G. Elliot, G. K. Oliver, W. Lauder, R. J. Arneil.

**1971—S. J. Dawes' British Team.**
RECORD—Played 2. Won 1. Lost 1. Points for 25. Against 27.
INTERNATIONAL MATCH—Nil
DEFEAT—Lost to Queensland, at Brisbane 11—15.
PLAYERS:
See under teams to New Zealand.

**1971—J. F. K. Marais's South African Team.**
RECORD—Played 13. Won 13. Points for 396. Against 102.
INTERNATIONAL MATCHES—Played 3. Won 3. Beat Australia at Sydney 19—11, at Brisbane 14—6 and at Sydney 18—6.
PLAYERS:
*Full-backs*—I. D. McCallum, O. A. Roux.
*Threequarters*—G. H. Muller, J. T. Viljoen, S. H. Nomis, J. S. Jansen, P. S. Swanson, A. E. van der Watt, P. A. Cronje.
*Half-backs*—P. J. Visagie, J. F. Viljoen, D. S. L. Snyman, D. J. J. de Vos.
*Forwards*—J. F. K. Mariais, J. T. Sauermann, J. F. B. van Wyk, R. W. Barnard, F. C. H. du Preez, J. G. Williams, J. H. Ellis, M. J. Lourens, M. J. Louw, J. Spies, P. J. F. Greyling, T. P. Bedford, M. du Plessis, A. J. Bates.

**1972—W. Spanghero's French Team.**
RECORD—Played 9. Won 8. Lost 0. Drawn 1. Points for 254. Against 122.
INTERNATIONAL MATCHES—Played 2. Won 1. Drawn 1. Drew with Australia at Sydney 14—14. Beat Australia at Brisbane 16—15.
PLAYERS:
*Full-backs*—P. Villepreux, H. Cabrol.
*Threequarters*—B. Duprat, J. Trillo, C. Dourthe, J. Cantoni, G. Lavagne, J. P. Lux, J. Maso.
*Half-backs*—A. Marot, M. Barrau, J. L. Berot, J. Fouroux.
*Forwards*—J. C. Skrela, W. Spanghero, J. P. Bastiat, P. Biemouret, O. Saisset, B. Vinsonneaux, C. Spanghero, A. Vaquerin, J. L. Azarète, J. C. Rossignol, A. Lubrano, R. Bénésis, A. Estéve, J. Iraçabal.

**1974—A. R. Leslie's New Zealand Team.**
RECORD—Played 12. Won 11. Drawn 1. Points for 423. Against 60.
INTERNATIONAL MATCHES—Played 3. Won 2. Drawn 1. Beat Australia at Sydney 11—6. Drew with Australia at Brisbane 16—16. Beat Australia at Sydney 16—6.
PLAYERS:
*Full-back*—J. F. Karam.
*Threequarters*—B. G. Williams, G. B. Batty, J. S. McLachlan, G. N. Kane, J. E. Morgan, B. J. Robertson, I. A. Hurst.
*Half-backs*—D. J. Robertson, O. D. Bruce, B. M. Gemmell, I. N. Stevens.
*Forwards*—A. R. Leslie, R. A. Barber, L. G. Knight, K. W. Stewart, I. A. Kirkpatrick, K. A. Eveleigh, P. J. Whiting, J. A. Callesen, W. K. Bush, A. J. Gardiner, K. J. Tanner, R. W. Norton, G. E. Crossman.

**1975—A. Neary's England team.**
RECORD—Played 8. Won 4. Lost 4. Points for 217. Against 106.
INTERNATIONAL MATCHES—Played 2. Lost 2. 9—16 at Sydney, and 21—30 at Brisbane.
DEFEATS APART FROM TESTS—10-14 v. Sydney, 13-14 v. N.S.W. Country.
PLAYERS:
*Full-backs*—A. Hignell, P. E. Butler.
*Threequarters*—D. Wyatt, P. J. Squires, K. Smith, P. S. Preece, A. W. Maxwell, A. J. Morley, J. P. A. G. Janion.
*Half-backs*—A. J. Wordsworth, W. N. Bennett, B. Ashton, P. Kingston, I. Orum.

A. G. B. Old.

*Forwards*—A. G. Ripley, R. M. Uttley, W. Beaumont, D. M. Rollitt, N. D. Mantell, R. Wilkinson, S. Callum, A. Neary, M. A. Burton, P. Blakeway, J. V. Pullin, F. E. Cotton, J. A. G. D. Raphael, B. G. Nelmes, P. J. Dixon.

## Tours in South Africa

1891—W. E. MacLagan's British Team.
RECORD—Played 19. Won 19. Lost 0. Drawn 0. Points for 223. Against 1.
TEST MATCHES—Played 3. Won 3. Scores: 4—0, 3—0 and 4—0.
PLAYERS:
*Full-backs*—W. G. Mitchell, E. Bromet.
*Threequarters*—W. E. MacLagan, P. R. Clauss, R. L. Aston.
*Half-backs*—W. Wotherspoon, A. Rotherham, H. Marshall, B. G. Roscoe,
*Forwards*—John Hammond, W. E. Bromet, R. G. M'Millan, P. Frouden-Hancock, G. H. Gould, W. Jackson, W. E. Mayfield, C. Simpson, W. H. Thorman, A. A. Surtees, T. Whittaker, R. Thompson.
*Manager*—Edward Ash.

1896—John Hammond's British Team.
RECORD—Played 21. Won 19. Lost 1. Drawn 1. Points for 320. Against 45.
TEST MATCHES—Played 4. Won 3. Lost 1. Scores: 8—0, 17—8, 9—3 and 0—5.
PLAYERS:
*Full-back*—J. F. Byrne.
*Threequarters*—L. O. Bulger, C. O. Robinson, J. T. Magee, C. A. Boyd, O. G. Mackie.
*Half-backs*—L. M. Magee, S. P. Bell, M. Mullineaux.
*Forwards*—John Hammond, T. J. Crean, R. Johnstone, J. Sealey, P. F. Hancock, A. F. Todd, A. D. Clinch, W. Mortimer, R. C. Mullins, A. D. Meares, G. W. Lee, W. G. Carey.
*Manager*—Roger Walker.

1903—Mark Morrison's British Team.
RECORD—Played 22. Won 11. Lost 8. Drawn 3. Points for 229. Against 138.
TEST MATCHES—Played 3. Won 0. Lost 1. Drawn 2. Scores: 10—10, 0—0 and 0—8.
DEFEATS APART FROM TESTS—Lost 7—13 to Western Province (Country). Lost 3—12 to Western Province,

(Town). Lost 4—8 to Western Province. Lost 0—11 to Griqualand West. Lost 6—8 to Griqualand West. Lost 3—12 to Transvaal. Lost 4—14 to Transvaal.
PLAYERS:
*Full-back*—E. M. Harrison.
*Threequarters*—A. E. Hind, G. F. Collett, I. G. Davidson, R. T. Skrimshire, E. F. Walker.
*Half-backs*—L. L. Greig, J. I. Gillespie, R. M. Neill, P. S. Hancock.
*Forwards*—Mark Morrison, W. P. Scott, D. R. Bedell-Sivright, F. M. Stout, A. Tedford, R. S. Smyth, J. Wallace, James Wallace, W. T. Cave, T. A. Gibson, J. C. Hosack.
*Manager*—John Hammond.

1910—Tom Smythe's British Team.
RECORD—Played 24. Won 13. Lost 8. Drawn 3. Points for 226. Against 290.
TEST MATCHES—Played 3. Won 1. Lost 2. Scores: 10—14, 8—3, 5—21.
DEFEATS APART FROM TESTS—Lost 0—3 to Griqualand West, 8—27 to Transvaal, 6—13 to Transvaal, 3—9 to Griqualand West, 0—19 to Cape Colony, 0—8 to Western Province.
PLAYERS:
*Full-back*—S. H. Williams.
*Threequarters*—A. M. Baker, R. C. S. Plummer, J. P. ("Ponty") Jones, M. E. Neale, A. R. Foster, C. J. Timms, K. B. Wood, Jack Spoors.
*Half-backs*—A. N. M'Clinton, E. Milroy, N. F. Humphrey, G. A. M. Isherwood.
*Forwards*—Dr. Tom Smyth, O. J. S. Piper, W. H. Tyrell, C. H. Pillman, D. F. Smith, E. O'D. Crean, H. Jarman, P. D. Waller, W. Ashley, R. Stevenson, W. A. Robertson, J. Webb, T. J. Richards, F. G. Handford, J. Reid-Kerr, L. M. Spiers.
*Joint-Managers*—William Cail and Walter Rees.

1924—R. Cove-Smith's British Team.
RECORD—Played 21. Won 9. Lost 9. Drawn 3. Points for 175. Against 155.
TEST MATCHES—Played 4. Lost 3. Drawn 1. Scores: 3—7, 0—17, 3—3 and 9—16.
DEFEATS APART FROM TESTS—Lost 6—7 to Western Province (Town and Country), 0—6 to Orange Free State (Country), 3—6 to Orange Free State,

6–10 to Witwatersrand, 0–6 to Pretoria, 6–14 to Eastern Province.

PLAYERS:

*Full-backs*–D. Drysdale, W. F. Gaisford.

*Threequarters*–Rowe Harding, Ian Smith, S. W. Harris, W. Wallace, T. E. Holliday, R. N. Kinnear, J. H. Bordass, R. B. Maxwell.

*Half-backs*–V. M. Griffiths, H. Waddle, W. Cunningham, A. T. Young, H. Whitley.

*Forwards*–Dr. R. Cove-Smith, A. T. Voyce, A. F. Blakiston, R. Gordon Henderson, D. Marsden-Jones, D. S. Davies, N. McPherson, K. G. P. Hendrie, A. Ross, R. A. Howie, Dr. W. G. Roche, J. M. McVicker, M. G. Bradley, T. N. Brand, H. Davies, J. D. Clinch.

*Manager*–Harry Packer.

1928–M. Brownlie's New Zealand Team.

RECORD–Played 22. Won 16. Lost 5. Drawn 1. Points for 339. Against 144.

TEST MATCHES–Played 4. Lost 2. Scores: 0–17, 7–6, 6–11 and 13–5.

DEFEATS APART FROM TESTS–Lost to Cape Combined Town 3–7. Lost to Transvaal 0–6. Lost to Western Province 3–10.

PLAYERS:

*Full-back*–H. Lilburne.

*Threequarters*–S. R. Carleton, C. A. Rushbrook, T. R. Sheen, D. F. Linsay, A. C. C. Robilliard, F. W. Lucas, B. A. Grenside.

*Half-backs*–F. D. Kilby, W. C. Dalley, L. M. Johnson, W. A. Strang, M. F. Nicholls, N. P. McGregor.

*Forwards*–M. Brownlie, J. P. Swain, J. Hore, S. Hadley, W. E. Hazlett, R. T. Stewart, J. T. Burrows, I. H. Finlayson, C. J. Brownlie, I. H. Harvey, R. G. Mc-Williams, P. E. Ward, E. M. Snow, G. Scrimshaw, G. T. Alley.

*Manager*–W. F. Hornig.

1933–A. W. Ross's Australian Team.

RECORD–Played 23. Won 12. Lost 10. Drawn 1. Points for 299. Against 195.

TEST MATCHES–Played 5. Won 2. Lost 3. Scores: 3–17, 21–6, 3–12, 0–11 and 15–4.

DEFEATS APART FROM TESTS–Lost 6–13 to Johannesburg Reef Country, 8–13 to Combined Pretoria,

9–14 to Griqualand West, 8–16 to Northern Provinces, 9–13 to Western Provinces, 9–11 to Transvaal, 0–4 to Western Province (Town and Country).

PLAYERS:

*Full-backs*–Dr. A. W. Ross, F. G. McPhillips.

*Threequarters*–B. A. Grace, J. D. Kelaher, A. D. McLean, W. J. Warlow, J. C. Steggall, J. Young, D. L. Cowper, Dr. G. S. Sturtridge.

*Half-backs*–R. R. Billmann, C. N. Campbell, S. J. Malcolm, W. G. Bennett.

*Forwards*–O. L. Bridle, J. C. Clarke, R. B. Loudon, W. A. R. Mackney, M. C. White, A. J. Hodgson, G. M. Cooke, W. S. G. White, G. V. Bland, E. W. Love, W. Ritter, J. B. T. Doneley, E. T. Bonis, M. F. Norton, W. H. Cerutti.

*Manager*–Dr. W. F. Matthews.

1938–Sam Walker's British Team.

RECORD–Played 23. Won 17. Lost 6. Drawn 0. Points for 407. Against 272.

TEST MATCHES–Played 3. Won 1. Lost 2. Scores: 12–26, 3–19 and 21–16.

DEFEATS APART FROM TESTS–Lost to Western Province (Town and Country) 8–11. Lost to Western Province 11–21. Lost to Reef 9–16. Lost to Northern Provinces 8–26.

PLAYERS:

*Full-backs*–V. G. J. Jenkins, C. F. Grieves.

*Threequarters*–E. J. Unwin, W. H. Clement, C. V. Boyle, E. L. W. Jones, B. E. Nicholson, D. J. Macrae, R. Leyland, H. R. McKibbin.

*Half-backs*–F. J. Reynolds, G. E. Cromey, J. L. Giles, H. Tanner, G. T. Morgan.

*Forwards*–S. Walker, M. E. Morgan, W. H. Travers, C. R. Graves, R. B. Mayne, S. R. Couchman, J. A. Waters, P. L. Duff, Ivor Williams, A. R. Taylor, R. Alexander, G. T. Dancer, A. H. G. Purchase, W. G. Howard.

*Manager*–Major B. C. Hartley.

1949–Fred Allen's New Zealand Team.

RECORD–Played 24. Won 14. Lost 7. Drawn 3. Points for 230. Against 143.

TEST MATCHES–Played 4. Lost 4. Scores: 11–16, 6–12, 3–9 and 8–11.

DEFEATS APART FROM TESTS–Lost 0–9 to Border, 5–6 to Eastern Transvaal, 8–10 to Rhodesia.

PLAYERS:

*Full-backs*–R. W. H. Scott, J. W. Goddard.

*Threequarters*–P. Henderson, E. Boggs, W. A. Meates, I. J. Botting, R. Elvidge, F. R. Allen, M. P. Goddard, N. W. Black.

*Half-backs*–J. C. Kearney, J. G. Delamore, K. E. Gudsell, L. T. Savage, W. J. M. Conrad.

*Forwards*–J. G. Simpson, K. L. Skinner, E. H. Catley, N. L. Wilson, R. A. Dalton, C. Willocks, D. L. Christian, H. F. Frazer, M. J. McHugh, L. H. Harvey, J. R. MacNab, L. A. Grant, P. J. Crowley, P. Johnstone, N. H. Thornton.

*Manager*–J. H. Parker.


1953–John Solomon's Australian Team.

RECORD–Played 27. Won 16. Lost 10. Drawn 1. Points for 450. Against 416.

TEST MATCHES–Played 4. Won 1. Lost 3. Scores: 3–25, 18–14, 8–18, and 9–22.

DEFEATS APART FROM TESTS–Lost 14–15 to Natal, 3–28 to Orange Free State, 14–20 to Transvaal, 3–13 to Griqualand West, 11–27 to Northern Transvaal, 5–24 to Western Province Universities, 13–23 to Orange Free State.

PLAYERS:

*Full-backs*–T. Sweeney, R. Colbert.

*Threequarters*–E. Stapleton, G. G. Jones, H. J. Solomon, H. S. Barker, J. Blomley, G. R. Horsley, J. A. Phipps, S W. White.

*Half-backs*–S. W. Brown, M. Tate, C. T. Burke, J. M. Bosler.

*Forwards*–C. F. Forbes, R. A. L Davidson, N. Shehadie, J. C. Carroll, F. M. Elliott, J. J. Walsh, E. Morey, J. Bain, A. S. Cameron, A. R. Miller, N. M. Hughes, B. V. Johnson, D. Brockhoff, K. A. Cross, C. J. Windon, R. Outterside.

*Manager*–J. W. Brenckenridge.


1955–Robin Thompson's British Team.

RECORD–Played 24. Won 18. Lost 5. Drawn 1. Points for 418. Against 271.

TEST MATCHES–Played 4. Won 2. Lost 2. Scores: 23–22, 9–25, 9–6, and 8–22.


DEFEATS APART FROM TESTS–Lost 6–9 to Western Transvaal, 0–20 to Eastern Province, 12–14 to Border.

PLAYERS:

*Full-backs*–A. Cameron, Alun Thomas.

*Threequarters*–A. R. Smith, F. D. Sykes, H. Morris, A. C. Pedlow, J. Butterfield, W. P. C. Davies, A. J. O'Reilly, J. P. Quinn, Gareth Griffiths.

*Half-backs*–C. I. Morgan, D. G. S. Baker, J. E. Williams, R. E. G. Jeeps, T. Lloyd.

*Forwards*–R. H. Thompson, C. Meredith, B. V. Meredith, A. M. McLeod, W. O. Williams, R. Roe, T. Elliott, E. J. S. Michie, T. E. Reid, R. H. Williams, J. T. Greenwood, R. J. Robins, R. Higgins, D. S. Wilson, R. C. C. Thomas.

*Manager*–J. A. E. Siggins.

*Secretary*–D. E. Davies.


1958–M. Celaya's French Team.

RECORD–Played 10. Won 5. Lost 3. Drawn 2. Points for 137. Against 124.

TEST MATCHES–Played 2. Won 1. Drawn 1. Scores: 3–3 at Cape Town, 9–5 at Johannesburg.

DEFEATS APART FROM TESTS–Lost to Northern and Western Transvaal 18–19, Western Province, S.W. Districts and Boland 8–38, Junior Springboks 5–9.

PLAYERS:

*Full-backs*–M. Vannier, P. Lacaze.

*Threequarters*–J. Dupuy, H. Rancouie, J. Lepatey, L. Roge, G. Stener, A. Marquesuzaa.

*Five-eighths*–R. Martine, A. Haget,

*Half-backs*–P. Lacroux, P. Danos,

*Forwards*–M. Celaya, J. Barthe, J. Carrere, L. Mias, B. Mommejat, R. Baulon, F. Moncia, L. Echava, A. Roques, R. Barriere, A. Quaglio, L. Casaux, R. Vigier, A. Fremeaux, J. De Gregorio.

*Manager*–S. Saulnier.


1960–W. Whineray's New Zealand Team.

RECORD–Played 26. Won 20. Lost 4. Drawn 2. Points for 441. Against 164.

TEST MATCHES–Played 4. Won 1. Lost 2. Drawn 1. Scores: 0–13 at Johannesburg, 11–3 at Cape Town, 11–11 at Bloemfontein, 3–8 at Port Elizabeth.

PLAYERS:

See under TOURS IN AUSTRALIA

(1960) in this section.
*Manager*-T. H. Pearce.

**1960**-G. H. Waddell's Scottish Team.
RECORD-Played 3. Won 2. Lost 1.
Points for 61. Against 45.
TEST MATCH-Played 1. Lost 1. Score:
10-18 at Port Elizabeth.
PLAYERS:
*Full-back*-R. W. T. Chisholm.
*Threequarters*-A. R. Smith, G. D.
Stevenson, R. H. Thompson.
*Half-backs*-G. H. Waddell, R. B.
Shillinglaw, T. McClung, R. Cowan, A. J.
Hastie, P. J. Burnet.
*Forwards*-N. S. Bruce, D. B. Edwards, J. W. Y. Kemp, W. Hart, T. O.
Grant, H. F. McLeod, J. B. Neill, D. M.
D. Rollo, C. E. B. Stewart, F. H. ten
Bos, R. M. Tollervey.
*Managers*-R. W. Shaw, and C. W.
Drummond.

**1961**-A. R. Dawson's Irish Team.
RECORD-Played 4. Won 3. Lost 1.
Points for 59. Against 36.
TEST MATCH-Played 1. Lost 8-24 at
Cape Town.
PLAYERS:
*Full-back*-T. J. Kiernan.
*Threequarters*-A. J. F. O'Reilly, J.
C. Walsh, K. N. Houston, W. J. Hewitt,
N. H. Brophy, J. F. Dooley, W. J.
Tormey, T. G. Cleary.
*Half-backs*-D. C. Glass, A. A. Mulligan.
*Forwards*-T. McGrath, J. R. Kavanagh, D. Scott, G. J. Dick, W. A. Mulcahy, B. G. Wood, A. R. Dawson, S.
Millar, J. S. Dick, J. N. Thomas, M. G.
Culliton, N. A. A. Murphy.
*Manager*-Noel Murphy.

**1961**-K. Catchpole's Australian Team.
RECORD-Played 6. Won 3. Lost 2.
Drawn 1. Points for 90. Against 80.
TEST MATCHES-Played 2. Lost 2.
Scores: 3-28 at Johannesburg, 11-23 at Port Elizabeth.
PLAYERS:
*Full-back*-J. Lenehan.
*Threequarters*-M. Cleary, E. Magrath, R. Phelps, B. Ellwood, J. Lisle.
*Five-eighths*-J. Dowse, H. Roberts,
*Half-backs*-O. Edwards, .K. Catchpole.
*Forwards*-T. Reid, E. Heinrich, J.
O'Gorman, R. Heming, J. Thornett, R.
Thornett, G. Macdougall, A. Miller, J.

White, D. McDeed, P. Johnson.
*Manager*-B. J. Halvorsen.

**1962**-A. R. Smith's British Team.
RECORD-Played 24. Won 15. Lost 5.
Drawn 4. Points for 351. Against
208.
TEST MATCHES-Played 4. Won 0.
Lost 3. Drawn 1. Scores: 3-3 at
Johannesburg, 0-3 at Durban, 3-8
at Cape Town, 14-34 at Bloemfontein.
DEFEATS APART FROM TESTS-Lost
to Northern Transvaal 6-14, Eastern
Transvaal 16-19.
PLAYERS:
*Full-backs*-T. J. Kiernan, J. G. Willcox.
*Threequarters*-N. R. Brophy, D. I.
E. Bebb, R. C. Cowan, A. R. Smith.
*Half-backs*-R. A. W. Sharp, R. E. G.
Jeeps, G. H. Waddell, A. O'Connor, H.
J. C. Brown.
*Forwards*-S. Millar, K. D. Jones, D.
M. D. Rollo, P. T. Wright, B. V. Meredith, S. A. M. Hodgson, M. J. Campbell-Lamerton, W. J. McBride, W. A. Mulcahy, K. A. Rowlands, H. J. Morgan, D.
P. Rogers, J. Douglas, D. Nash, H. O. Godwin, G. D. Davidge.
*Manager*-Instructor-Commander D.
B. Vaughan, R.N.

**1963**-J. Thornett's Australian Team.
RECORD-Played 24. Won 15. Lost 8.
Drawn 1. Points for 303. Against
227.
TEST MATCHES-Played 4. Won 2.
Lost 2. Scores: 3-14 at Pretoria,
9-5 at Cape Town, 11-3 at Johannesburg, 6-22 at Port Elizabeth.
DEFEATS APART FROM TESTS-Lost
9-11 to Southern Universities, 13-14 to Natal, 9-15 to Northern Universities, 5-12 to Junior Springboks,
6-12 to Western Provinces, 8-14
to Orange Free State.
PLAYERS:
*Full-backs*-T. Casey, P. Ryan.
*Threequarters*-K. Walsham, J. Williams, J. Boyce, J. Wolfe, R. Marks, I.
Moutray, P. Jones, B. Ellwood.
*Five-eighths*-P. Hawthorne, J. Klem.
*Half-backs*-K. Catchpole, K. McMullen.
*Forwards*-J. Guerassimoff, D. O'-Neill, G. Davis, D. Shepherd, E. Heinrich, J. O'Gorman, R. Heming, J. Miller,
P. Crittle, J. Thornett, J. White, L.

Austin, J. Freedman, B. Bailey, P. Johnson, M. Jenkinson.

*Manager*–R. E. M. McLaughlin.

**1964**–D. C. T. Rowland's Welsh Team.
RECORD–Played 4. Won 2. Lost 2. Points for 43. Against 58.
TEST MATCH–Played 1. Lost 1. Score: 3–24 at Durban.
DEFEATS APART FROM TESTS–Lost to Northern Transvaal 9–22.
PLAYERS:
*Full-backs*–H. J. Davies, G. T. R. Hodgson.
*Threequarters*–K. Bradshaw, J. Dawes, D. I. Bebb, D. K. Jones, S. J. Watkins.
*Half-backs*–A. Lewis, D. C. T. Rowlands, D. Watkins, M. Young.
*Forwards*–N. R. Gale, L. J. Cunningham, R. Waldron, J. Isaacs, D. Williams, J. Mantle, B. E. V. Price, B. E. Thomas, D. J. Hayward, H. J. Morgan, A. I. E. Pask, G. J. Prothero.
*Manager*–D. J. Phillips.

**1964**–M. Crauste's French Team.
RECORD–Played 6. Won 5. Lost 1. Points for 117. Against 55.
TEST MATCH–Played 1. Won 1. Score: 8–6 at Springs.
DEFEATS APART FROM TESTS–Lost to Western Province 11–20.
PLAYERS:
*Full-back*–P. Dedieu.
*Threequarters*–J. Gachassin, C. Darrouy, A. Boniface, G. Boniface, J. Dupuy, J. Pique.
*Half-backs*–P. Albaladejo, J. Capdouze, J. Claude.
*Forwards*–C. Laborde, M. Crauste, M. Lira, M. Sitjar, J. Fabre, B. Dauga, E. Cester, A. Herrero, A. Gruarin, J. C. Berejnoi, M. Etcheverry, Y. Menthillier, J. M. Cabanier.
*Manager*–Serge Saulnier.

**1967**–C. Darrouy's French Team.
RECORD–Played 13. Won 8. Lost 4. Drawn 1. Points for 209. Against 161.
INTERNATIONAL MATCHES–Played 4. Won 1. Lost 2. Drawn 1. Lost 3–26 at Durban, 3–16 at Bloemfontein, Won 19–14 at Johannesburg. Drew 6–6 at Cape Town.
DEFEATS OTHER THAN INTERNATIONALS.
–Lost to Griqualand West 14–20 at

Kimberley, Northern Transvaal 5–19 at Pretoria.
PLAYERS:
*Full-backs*–P. Villepreux, C. Lacaze, J. Crampagne.
*Threequarters*–C. Darrouy, B. Duprat, J. Londois, J. P. Lux, J. Trillo, C. Dourthe, J. Saby, J. P. Mir.
*Half-backs*–J. C. Roques, G. Camberaro, M. Puget, J. L. Dehez, G. Sutra.
*Forwards*–J. M. Esponda, M. Lassere, A. Abadie, J. M. Cabanier, B. Cardebat, J. C. Malbet, B. Dauga, W. Spanghero, A. Plantefol, J. Fort, C. Carrère, G. Viard, A. Quilis, M. Sitjar.

**1968**–T. J. Kiernan's British Isles Team.
RECORD–Played 20. Won 15. Lost 4. Drawn 1. Points for 377. Against 181.
INTERNATIONAL MATCHES–Played 4. Won 0. Lost 3. Drawn 1. Lost 20–25 at Pretoria, 6–11 at Cape Town, 6–19 at Johannesburg. Drew 6–6 at Port Elizabeth.
DEFEAT OTHER THAN INTERNATIONALS–Lost to Transvaal 6–14 at Johannesburg.
PLAYERS:
*Full-backs*–T. J. Kiernan, R. B. Hiller.
*Threequarters*–A. J. W. Hinshelwood, M. C. R. Richards, W. K. Jones, K. F. Savage, T. G. R. Davies, W. H. Raybould, F. P. K. Bresnihan, K. S. Jarrett, J. W. C. Turner.
*Half-backs*–G. O. Edwards, C. M. H. Gibson, B. John, R. M. Young, G. C. Connell.
*Forwards*–M. J. Coulman, A. L. Horton, J. P. O'Shea, P. J. Larter, S. Millar, W. J. McBride, W. D. Thomas, J. V. Pullin, P. K. Stagg, J. Young, J. Taylor, M. G. Doyle, K. C. Goodall, R. J. Arneil, R. B. Taylor, J. W. Telfer, B. R. West.

**1969**–J. V. Davis's Australian Team.
RECORD–Played 26. Won 15. Lost 11. Drawn 0. Points for 465. Against 353.
INTERNATIONAL MATCHES–Played 4. Won 0. Lost 4. Lost 11–30 at Johannesburg, 9–16 at Durban, 3–11 at Cape Town, 8–19 at Bloemfontein.
PLAYERS:
*Full-backs*–A. N. McGill, B. A. Weir.
*Threequarters*–T. R. Forman, J. W. Cole, R. P. Batterham, P. D. Moore, S. O.

Knight, B. D. Honan, P. V. Smith, G. A. Shaw.

*Forwards*—J. R. Roxburgh, J. L. Howard, R. B. Prosser, S. S. Sullivan, P. Darveniza, B. S. Taafe, S. C. Gregory, A. M. Abrahams, N. P. Reilly, G. V. Davis, O. F. Butler, M. R. Cocks, B. McDonald, R. J. Kelleher, H. A. Rose, A. J. Skinner, R. Wood.

1970—B. J. Lochore's New Zealand Team.
RECORD—Played 24. Won 21. Lost 3. Drawn 0. Points for 687. Against 228.
INTERNATIONAL MATCHES—Played 4. Won 1. Lost 3. Lost 6—17 at Pretoria, 3—14 at Port Elizabeth, 17—20 at Johannesburg. Won 9—8 at Cape Town.
PLAYERS:
*Full-back*—W. F. McCormick.
*Threequarters*—M. J. Dick, B. A. Hunter, G. S. Thorne, B. G. Williams, W. L. Davis, H. P. Milner.
*Half-backs*—W. D. Cottrell, I. R. MacRae, E. W. Kirton, B. D. M. Furlong, G. F. Kember, C. R. Laidlaw, S. M. Going.
*Forwards*—A. R. Sutherland, B. J. Lochore, I. A. Kirkpatrick, A. J. Wyllie, T. N. Lister, B. Holmes, C. E. Meads, A. E. Smith, S. C. Strahan, J. F. Burns, K. Murdoch, B. L. Muller, A. E. Hopkinson, B. E. McLeod, N. W. Thimbleby, R. A. Urlich.

1971— C. Carrère's French Team.
RECORD—Played 9. Won 7. Lost 1. Drawn 1. Points for 228. Against 92.
INTERNATIONAL MATCHES—Played 2. Lost 1. Drawn 1. Lost 9—22 at Bloemfontein. Drew 8—8 at Durban.
PLAYERS:
*Full-back*—P. Villepreux.
*Threequarters*—R. Bertranne, R. Bourgarel, J. Cantoni, C. Dourthe, J. Maso, A. Marot.
*Half-backs*—M. Barrau, J. L. Berot, M. Pebeyre, G. Pardiès.
*Forwards*—J. P. Bastiat, J. L. Azarete, P. Biemouret, C. Carrère, B. Dauga, A. Estève, M. Etcheverry, J. Iracabel, M. Lasserre, J. le Droff, C. Spanghero, J. C. Skrela, W. Spanghero, C. Swierczinski, M. Yachvili.

1972—J. V. Pullin's English Team.
RECORD—Played 7. Won 6. Lost 0. Drawn 1.

INTERNATIONAL MATCHES—Played 1. Won 1. Won 18—9 at Johannesburg.
PLAYERS:
*Full-backs*—S. A. Doble, D. F. Whibley.
*Threequarters*—P. M. Knight, J. P. A. G. Janion, A. A. Richards, A. J. Morley, J. S. Spencer, P. S. Preece.
*Half-backs*—A. G. B. Old, T. Palmer, J. G. Webster, L. E. Weston, S. Smith,
*Forwards*—F. E. Cotton, M. A. Burton, C. B. Stevens, J. V. Pullin, A. V. Boddy, P. J. Larter, D. E. J. Watts, C. W. Ralston, T. A. Cowell, A. Neary, J. A. Watkins, J. Barton, A. G. Ripley.

1974—W. J. McBride's British Isles Team.
RECORD—Played 22. Won 21. Lost 0. Drawn 1. Points for 729. Against 203.
INTERNATIONAL MATCHES—Played 4. Won 3. Drawn 1. Won 12—3 at Cape Town, 28—9 at Pretoria, 26—9 at Port Elizabeth, and drew 13—13 at Johannesburg.
PLAYERS:
*Full-backs*—A. Irvine, J. P. R. Williams.
*Threequarters*—W. Steele, C. Rees, R. Bergiers, I. McGeechan, G. Evans, J. J. Williams, R. Milliken, A. Morley, T. Grace.
*Half-backs*—P. Bennett, G. Edwards, A. G. B. Old, A. Irvine, J. Moloney, M. Gibson.
*Forwards*—T. M. Davies, R. Uttley, G. Brown, W. J. McBride, F. Slattery, F. Cotton, R. Windsor, I. McLauchlan, S. McKinney, C. Ralston, M. Burton, K. Kennedy, A. Ripley, A. Neary, A. Carmichael, T. David.

1975—J. Fouroux and R. Astre's French Team.
RECORD—Played 11. Won 6. Lost 4. Drawn 1.
INTERNATIONAL MATCHES—Played 2. Lost 2, 25—38 at Bloemfontein, and 18—33 at Pretoria.
DEFEAT APART FROM TESTS—3—18 v. S. A. Invitation XV, Cape Town.
PLAYERS:
*full-backs*—M. Droitecourt, J—M. Aguirre.
*Threequarters*—J—C. Amade, C. Badin, J—M. Etchnique, J—L. Averous, F. Sangalli, R. Bertranne, D. Harize, J.

Decrae, J–C. Joinel, J. P. Romeu.

*Half-backs*–J–P. Peteil, R. Astre, J. Fouroux, S. Lassoujade.

*Forwards*–R. Paparemborde, D. Revallier, B. Forestier, P. Peron, M. Rousset, J–C. Skrela, A. Guilbert, M. Palmir, Y. Brunet, G. Cholley, M. Yachvili.

## TRANSVAAL RUGBY UNION

Although they have only won the coveted Currie Cup on six occasions, in their history as against Western Provinces 21 successes, Transvaal have always been, both statistically and in actual fact the Province's most feared rivals. Indeed it is possible that the Transvaal Union would have achieved even more imposing successes had not the formation of the Western, Northern and Eastern Transvaal Unions in 1920, 1939 and 1938 respectively, had the effect of deploying their resources. Even with their strength distributed, however, the Transvaal have been a match for most, indeed more often than not, rather more of a match, as may be gathered from their record against the various touring teams to visit South Africa, which includes victories over the following: Mark Morrison's 1903 British team (twice), Tom Smythe's 1910 British team (twice), M. Brownlie's 1928 New Zealand team, A. W. Ross's 1933 Australian team, John Solomon's 1953 Australian team and T. J. Kiernan's British team 1968. Inevitably the Union's contribution to South African Test teams has been a large one, in which respect the names of the following Transvaal players will find ready response in the memories of Rugby followers the world over–J. A. Stegmann, A. J. van Heerdon, J. M. Michau, G. W. van Rooyen, L. C. Strachan, A. S. Knight, F. G. Turner, T. A. Harris, J. W. Lotz, W. F. Bergh, J. Buchler, A. Geffin, C. J. van Wyk, H. S. Muller, S. H. Nomis, and A. S. Malan who became South Africa's youngest captain in 1960 (v. New Zealand) and a few months later led them on their spectacular tour of the British Isles. The Union colours are red and white hooped jerseys and stockings, and black shorts. Their ground, a South African Test venue, is Ellis Park, Johannesburg.

## TRIPLE CROWN

The entirely mythical award which goes to the country which defeats all three of the opposing Home Countries during the course of any one International season, France being excluded from this rather private competition. Mythical though the Crown may be, however, it has inspired tremendous rivalry between the countries competing. England with .13 victories, viz. 1883–84, 1891-92, 1912-13, 1913-14, 1920-21, 1922-23, 1923-24, 1927-28, 1933-34, 1936-37, 1953-54, 1956-57 and 1959-60, have won the honour on most occasions. They are followed by Wales with twelve victories in seasons 1892-93, 1899-1900, 1901-02, 1904-05, 1907-08, 1908-09, 1910-11, 1949-50, 1951-52, 1964-65, 1968-69 and 1970-71. Next are Scotland who have won it on eight occasions, viz. 1890-91, 1894-95, 1900-01, 1902-03, 1906-07, 1924-25, 1932-33, and 1937-38, and finally Ireland who were successful on four occasions–1893-94, 1898-99, 1947-48, and 1948-49.

No country has succeeded in winning the Crown three times in succession, but England (1912-13 and 1913-14, 1922-23, and 1923-24) have twice won it in successive years, whilst Wales (1907-08 and 1908-09) and Ireland (1947-48 and 1948-49) have performed the same feat once.

## TRY

See SCORING FEATS.

## TWICKENHAM

Twickenham has long since established itself not only as the Headquarters of the Rugby Union in Britain, but as a kind of "Mecca Locarno" for Rugby men the world over. The site was selected in 1907 by the late Billy Williams, whose photograph hangs in a place of honour in the administrative block, and was subsequently purchased by the Rugby Union for the sum of £5,572 12s. 6d. the original 10¼ acres having been gradually extended to its present area of 30 acres. The first match staged at Twickenham was that between The Harlequins and Richmond on October 2, 1909, and then in the January of 1910, 18,000 spectators saw England beat Wales in the ground's first ever International. In December, 1921, the first Oxford v. Cambridge match was played there, and the ground's capacity was gradually increased to its present capacity of 72,000 (seating capacity 32,500). In actual fact though this figure was exceeded when Wales played England there in January 1950, for 75,000 watched the match-an all time record. Not only is Twickenham the venue of all the Rugby Union's Home International matches, but it is in addition the game's administrative centre. Twickenham has always been looked upon as a lucky ground for England, indeed Wales's failure to win a match there from their first attempt in 1910 to 1933 gave rise to the term, "The Twickenham Bogey".    Specially impressive features of this vast and finely appoin-

ted stadium are the beautifully furnished Royal Retiring Room, the cost of which was defrayed by the Shanghai R.F.C., and the "Rowland Hill Memorial Gates" which were erected to the memory of one of the Rugby Union's most famous administrators.

## First Try at Twickenham

The first try at Twickenham in an International match was scored direct from the kick-off in the England v. Wales match of Janaury, 1910, and the scorer was the England wing three-quarter, F. E. Chapman, of Westoe, Hartlepools Rovers and Durham County.

## U.A.U.

The abbreviation which covers organised Rugby Football in the provincial Universities. The U.A.U. was founded in 1920 with nine universities in membership. Today it has grown to 38 and administers nearly 30 different sports. An annual competition, the U.A.U. Rugby Championship, is conducted on an area basis, and the U.A.U. representative team fulfils fixtures with some of the leading first class clubs and county organisations.

Some of the game's greatest player's have worn the dark blue jersey of the U.A.U.

## UNDEFEATED

The outstanding record among teams that have enjoyed a season in which they remained invincible is, of course, that of C. G. Porter's New Zealand team, the Second "All-Blacks", who toured Britain and France in 1924-25 with the following results—Played 30, Won 30. Points for 721, against 112.

B. J. Lochore's Sixth "All-Blacks" were also undefeated in Britain and France in 1967, but they played 15 games.

After losing 4—0 to Auckland in their first tour of 1888 the British Isles were not defeated until losing 5—0 to South Africa at Cape Town in the final game of their third tour (1896). Between these they were undefeated in 65 games, 26 in Australia and New Zealand and 39 in South Africa.

The British Isles team captained by W. J. McBride were unbeaten in their 1974 tour of South Africa, winning 21 out of 22 games.

Other national representative teams which have completed an overseas tour without defeat are as follows:—

*In Australia*—W. V. Milton's New Zealand team 1884, Played 8. Won 8; R. L. Seddon's British team 1888, Played 16, Won 14, Drew 2; J. Warbrick's Maoris 1889, Played 15, Won 15; J. Duncan's New Zealand team 1903, Played 10, Won 10; D. R. Bedell-Sivright's British team 1904, Played 14, Won 14; J. Hunter's New Zealand team 1905, Played 3. Won 2, Drew 1; R. W. Robert's New Zealand team 1914, Played 10, Won 10; J. Tilyard's New Zealand team 1920, Played 7, Won 7; T. B. Pienaar's South African team 1921, Played 5, Won 5; N. A. Mitchell's New Zealand team 1938, Played 9, Won 9; P. Johnstone's New Zealand team 1951, Played 12, Won 12; S. S. Viviers' South African team 1956, Played 6, Won 6; A. R. Reid's New Zealand team 1957, Played 14, Won 14; W. Whineray's New Zealand team 1960, Played 5. Won 5; M. J. Campbell-Lamerton's British team 1966, Played 8, Won 7, Drew 1; B. J. Lochore's New Zealand team 1968, Played 11, Won 11; J. F. K. Marais's 1971 South African team, Played 13, Won 13; W. Spanghero's 1972 French team, Played 9, Won 8, Drew 1; A. R. Leslie's 1974 New Zealand team, Played 12, Won 11, Drew 1.

*In South Africa*—W. E. Maclagan's British team 1891, Played 19, Won 19. J. V. Pullin's 1972 England team, Played 7, Won 6, Drew 1.

Newport have been undefeated in six of their playing seasons. The best record being that of 1922-23 when they won 35 games and drew 4. Points for 462, against 112.

Another Welsh club, Maesteg, were undefeated in season 1949-50 when their record read Played 43, Won 37, Drew 6. Points for 426, against 110.

Coventry enjoyed a fine run during the Second World War, when they actually won all of their 72 games between December 1941 and January 1945.

## UNIVERSITY MATCH

(See also under OXFORD AND CAMBRIDGE).

The first University match, played at the Parks, Oxford, on February 10, 1872, was the direct outcome of a meeting which took place at Oxford a month or two previously between two distinguished athletes and scholars, H. A. Hamilton, later Canon Douglas-Hamilton of Cambridge, and C. W. L. Bulpett of Oxford. Cambridge, attired for the occasion in pink-coloured jerseys, were defeated by a goal and a try to nil, the teams being: –

OXFORD–W. O. Moberley (capt.), T. S. Pearson, A. T. Michell (backs); C. K. Francis, K. R. Fletcher, E. A. Deacon (Half-backs); A. G. S. Botfield, H. Brierly C. W. L. Bulpett, H. B. Carlyon, F. G. Cholmondeley, E. M. R. Edgell, W. R. B. Fletcher, J. W. Gardner, F. W. Isherwood, A. Macgregor, H. W. Peake, J. Sayer, E. R. Still, J. W. Weston (forwards).

CAMBRIDGE–J. M. Batten, H. A. Hamilton, R. P. Luscombe (backs); I. C. Lambert (capt.), H. Riley, C. E. Lyon (half-backs); G. W. Agnew, F. F. Black, R. Baxter, T. Colin, J. E. Deakin, R. F. Dudgeon, F. M. Hull, A. Macdonald, R. Margerison, E. St. J. Morse, Hon. M. F. Napier, J. P. Sisson, A. Sprot, W. Y. Winthrop (forwards).

The second match in the series was played at Parker's Piece the following year, and resulted in a win for Cambridge, and one of its aftermaths was the decision to play all future encounters on a neutral ground–Kennington Oval being the venue decided upon. In 1874 Oxford tried vainly as it happened, to persuade Cambridge to play them "15-a-side", but were successful in the following season, the formation being: 2 backs, 1 threequarter, 2 half-backs, and 10 forwards. In 1876 Cambridge discarded their original pink jerseys in favour of blue and white stripes, whilst Oxford turned out in white. In 1880 and in an effort to create a more enthusiastic following, the match venue was transferred to the well-established Rugby centre at Blackheath, where (shades of Twickenham) the teams changed at a hostelry, "The Princess of Wales", sited on Blackheath Common, and walked the two miles to the actual arena. Blackheath remained the venue from 1880-87, when it was discarded in favour of the Queen's Club, West Kensington, where the attendance at the first time of asking soared to (the then) unprecedented figure of 5,000. Fresh history was made in season 1893-94, when both Universities employed the four three-quarter formation. In 1921 came the move to Twickenham, and the beginnings of the saga which amongst other things has served to install the second Tuesday in December as one of the most important and crowd-pulling dates in the Rugby Calender. Here are the teams which contested the first Inter-Varsity match ever held at Rugby's Headquarters:

OXFORD–H. H. Forsyth, E. F. van der Riet, V. R. Price, A. M. David, I. J. Pitman, E. Campbell, T. Lawton, J. E. Maxwell-Hyslop, J. C. Chambers, H. P. Marshall, H. L. Price, J. W. Robertson, A. W. L. Rowe, C. A. Siepmann, B. G. Scholfield.

CAMBRIDGE–F. A. Gardiner, D. D. B. Cook, S. Cook, R. H. Hamilton-Wickes, E. R. H. Seddon, K. R. J. Saxon, H. B. Style, R. Cove-Smith, G. S. Conway, W. W. Wakefield, R. R. Stones, D. J. MacMyn, A. Carnegie-Brown, D. C. D. Ryder, T. R. K. Jones.

On this occasion Oxford rather unexpectedly, in view of the vaunted power and reputation of the Cambridge pack, ran out thoroughly-deserved winners by 11–5.

Although both Universities have enjoyed their periods of sustained success over the whole series the tide of battle has flowed surprisingly evenly. Cambridge for instance won four successive victories between 1886-89, and again between 1926-29, only for Oxford to achieve a similar domination between the years 1882-85, and 1949-52. Then, after Oxford had won a record 35–3 victory in season 1909-10, Cambridge exacted ample revenge with a 33–3 victory at Twickenham 16 years later. More recently Cambridge enjoyed another run of four wins 1961-64, but Oxford are still slightly ahead on the total of wins. Up to and including season 1974-75 the Universities have met on 93 occasions, with Oxford boasting 41 victories to Cambridge's 39. 13 matches have been drawn.

## Blues

"Blues" were first awarded for Rugby Football at Oxford University in the Michaelmas term of 1882, thus bringing the sport into line with rowing, cricket and athletics. At Cambridge, however, there was to be much bickering and controversy before the Rugby players were granted equality with the rest. Indeed the "Blues" Committee's response to the Rugbymen's application made in 1883, was to suggest a compromise whereby a stipulated number of "Blues" were to be divided between the Rugby and

Association teams. This suggestion so incensed the Rugby men that they took the law into their own hands, so that on December 10, 1884, they turned up at Blackheath for the match with Oxford wearing the coveted Blue coats. This, of course, was a direct challenge to the authority of the "Blues" Committee, and as a result the following motion was debated on the packed floor of the Union—"That this meeting regrets the resolution of the authorities of the C.U.R.U.F.C. and the C.U.A.F.C. to adopt the full Blue against the decision of the committee to whom they had submitted the question, and trusts they will yet find it possible to bring themselves into harmony with those unwritten laws by which the social relations of this University are governed". The house divided after the impassioned orators on both sides had stated their cases, and returned to find that the motion had been defeated by the over-whelming majority of 707 votes to 446. Thus it was that in the Lent term of 1885 a "Blue" for Rugby Football gained official approval at the University.

## Appearances In

The record number of appearances in the University match is the six to the credit of the Cambridge forward and captain, H. G. Fuller, who later played for both Bath and England. Fuller's six appearances spanned the years 1879-83, J. E. Greenwood, of Cambridge, made five appearances, viz. 1910-11-12-13 and 1919, but his fifth and last was only made by special dispensation of the Oxford authorities for he was not officially in residence at his University at the time. He was in fact permitted to play only because the war years had denuded the Cambridge ranks of all their experienced players.

Oxford have had 40 players, with four appearances, and Cambridge have had 39. They are:—

OXFORD—G. E. B. Abell, A. G. G. Asher, D. McL. Bain, E. M. Baker, C. T. Bloxham, W. J. Carey, V. H. Cartwright, J. E. Crabbie, J. D. Currie, C. J. N. Fleming, E. C. Fraser, E. J. H. Gould, R. G. Grellett, T. W. Gubb, A. H. Heath, H. A. Hodges, W. W. Hoskin, F. Kershaw, R. C. M. Kitto, F. H. Knott, F. H. Lee, C. G. Lindsay, A. T. Michell, E. S. Nicholson, C. Phillips, M. S. Phillips, F.

O. Poole, J. E. Raphael, P. G. D. Robbins, W. Roberts, H. Russell, A. R. Smith, J. F. A. Swanston, H. A. Tudor, H. Vassall, A. C. Wallace, J. G. Willcox, R. S. Wix.

CAMBRIDGE—C. D. Aarvold, C. S. Barlow, J. M. Batten, D. R. Bedell-Sivright, J. V. Bedell-Sivright, P. C. B. Blair, P. W. P. Brook, B. S. Cumberlege, W. J. Downey, P. T. Finch, T. E. S. Francis, K. C. Fyfe, J. R. C. Greenlees, R. H. Hamilton-Wickes, W. Rowe-Harding, W. W. A. Jones, H. M. Kimberley, C. D. Laborde, W. J. Leather, G. A. Lewis, R. P. Luscombe, K. G. McLeod, D. J. MacMyn, H. Mainprice, R. W. D. Marques, D. M. Marr, W. G. Morgan, P. H. Morrison, C. B. Nicholl, G. W. Parker, B. I. Rees, R. W. Smeddle, H. Y. L. Smith, J. W. P. Storey, A. R. Smith, W. E. Tucker, M. R. Wade, C. P. Wilson, P. T. Wrigley.

Seven Americans have played in the University Match, strangely enough all seven for Oxford. They are:—

D. G. Herring, Princeton University 1909.

A. C. Valentine, Pennsylvania, 1923-24-25.

F. L. Hovde, University of Minnesota, 1931.

V. W. Jones, Dartmouth, 1954.

P. M. Dawkins, West Point Military Academy, 1959-60-61.

T. B. Neville, Yale, 1971-72.

R. D. Love, Sewanee, 1972.

In 1931 Oxford's threequarter line consisted of an American (F. L. Hovde), a South African (S. G. Osler), a Welshman (V. G. J. Jenkins), and a New Zealander (P. C. Minns).

In 1928 two brothers played on opposite sides, they were J. Roberts (Cardiff High School) playing at fullback for Cambridge, and W. Roberts (Cardiff High School) at stand-off half for Oxford.

## U.S.A.

Although the early history of football in the U.S.A. is somewhat confused between Rugby and the Association game it seems likely that the handling code was first introduced into this country by McGill University of Montreal when they challenged Harvard to "a game of Rugby Football" in May 1874. This game was played at Cambridge, Mass., and ended in a draw 0—0.

The following year Harvard first met Yale at "Rugby" and it was not until after this game that the two college converted Rutgers, Princeton, and Columbia from soccer and formed the American Intercollegiate Football Association.

Their early games were played under only slightly modified Rugby rules, but since then, as mentioned in this Encyclopaedia under AMERICAN FOOTBALL, these colleges so changed the rules that their game soon became something quite different and with these changes we lose sight of the Rugby game in the U.S.A. before the turn of the century.

Rugby Union football in the U.S.A. has attained its maximum popularity in the State of California, where the University teams have for a long while now, aspired to a standard far higher than one might expect from the resources and amenities available to them. The origins of the game in the State are doubtful, but what is known is that by the outbreak of World War I, Californian Rugby was of a high enough standard to entertain a visit from a stronger New Zealand representative side–the logical sequence perhaps to the visit Dave Gallaher's original "All-Blacks" had made to San Francisco to play two games against a side from British Columbia when homeward bound from the tour of Britain in 1905. The 1913 New Zealand team played 12 matches in California, their opponents being: Olympic Club, Barbarian Club, Leland, Stanford University (2), University of Santa Clara (2),University of California (3), University of Southern California, All American XV, and St. Mary's College, Oakland. They also met the University of Nevada, at Reno. Then, as further evidence of the growing strength of Californian University Rugby, we have the unique achievement of the Stanford University team who at Paris in 1924, defeated the full French National XV by 17–3, in the Final of the Olympic Games Rugby Football competition. They also visited England, beating Devonport Services but losing to Blackheath and the Harlequins.

An Australian team toured the U.S.A. as far back as 1912 and among their 8 games was a "Test" which the visitors only won by 12–8 after being 8–0 down until near the end.

In the 'thirties a strenuous attempt was made to popularise the Union game in New York, and towards this end the New York club obtained affiliation with the Rugby Union in London. Indeed in the beginnings it looked as though the game might make headway even in competition with the established code of American football, for it was adopted in the Universities (though not to the exclusion of American football) of Yale, Harvard, Princeton, and Pennsylvania. Further impetus to the drive was forthcoming from the 1935 visit of the Cambridge University team who played brilliant and spectacular football to defeat Harvard (41–19), Princeton (40–10), Yale (32–5), and Eastern Universities (23–9). Even this however proved insufficient to induce the Americans to adopt the Union game in sufficient numbers to make their country serious competitors in world Rugby, although the spread continues. There is a U.S. National Knock-out tournament and the U.S. Rugby Union was formed in 1968.

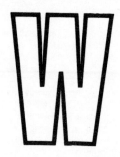

## WAIKATO RUGBY UNION

Founded as South Auckland in 1909, the Union was renamed Waikato in 1921, and during the post-war period have developed into one of the strongest provincial combinations in New Zealand. In 1956 they joined Canterbury in the distinction of being the only provincial teams to defeat the South African touring team, and indeed in that season Waikato players did much to ensure their country's triumph in the Test series, for the brothers D. B. and I. J. Clarke, at full-back and prop forward, respectively, A. R. Reid, at scrum-half, and R. C. Hemi, as hooker, were all dominating personalities in the series. Indeed, the Clarke family, six of whose sons have played for the Kereone Club in recent years, provided the Waikato Union with two of New Zealand's greatest personalities in full-back D. B. and "prop" forward I. J. Clarke, Colours: Red, yellow and black. Ground: Rugby Park, Hamilton, North Island.

## WAIRARAPA-BUSH RUGBY UNION

The separate Wairarapa and Bush Unions were both founded in 1886. The former was among the founder members of the New Zealand Rugby Union in 1892, while Bush affiliated the following year. The two Unions amalgamated in 1971. Colours: Green with scarlet collar. Headquarters: Masterton. Oustanding international is B. J. Lochore the brilliant back-row forward who captained the sixth "All-Blacks" and in all made 25 appearances for New Zealand.

## WANDERERS R.F.C. (DUBLIN)

The Wanderers Club, Dublin was formed in 1870, largely on the initiative of Mr. Richard Milliken Peter who became the first Treasurer of the Irish Rugby Union, and three of their members played in the first Ireland-England International at the Oval in 1875. Famous players who have worn their jersey include the 30 times capped Mark Sudgen, J. D. Clinch, P. F. Murray, and the moderns, J. R. Kavanagh who has been capped 35 times, and A. R. Dawson, capped 27 times and skipper of the British Lions of 1959. The club are members of the Leinster Senior League. Colours: Blue, black and white. Ground: Lansdowne Road, Dublin 4.

## WANGANUI RUGBY UNION

Founded 1888, affiliated to New Zealand Rugby Union 1892, Headquarters: Wanganui, North Island. Colours: Blue and black hoops with narrow white band.

## WASPS R.F.C.

Founded in 1867, largely by students of University College Hospital, the Wasps have throughout their entire history been regarded amongst the corps d'elite of British Rugby, but they have never ceased to regret the fact that an administrative misunderstanding excluded them from a place in history amongst the founder-members of the Rugby Union in 1871. Oddly enough, in view of their great tradition and antiquity, the Wasps did not have a player capped for England before the Second World War. Since then however, they have had many. R. V. Stirling leads the way with 18 caps. The Wasps have won the Middlesex "Sevens" tourney twice, and throughout their history have remained one of the main sources of supply for the Middlesex County team. Colours: Black jerseys with gold wasp on left breast, black shorts, gold and black stockings. Ground: Sudbury. Hon Secretary: I. A. Montlake, Burghside, Brighton Road, Banstead, Surrey, SM7 1BB.

## WATERLOO R.F.C.

Formed in 1882, Waterloo have produced many famous Internationals, none possibly with a fame more unique than that of that great scrummaging forward, H. G. Periton, who earned 21 England caps between 1925-30, and in addition, a niche in the archives of "the unusual", as the only Irishman to have captained England against his native land on the Rugby field. Other notable Waterloo players have been J. Heaton, R. Leyland, H. B. Toft, R. H. Guest, and R. C. Bazeley, whilst a record the club are especially proud of is the fact that during a period of 37 years, 1923-60, they always had at least one player in an International side. Club colours: Green, red and white. Ground: Blundellsands. Hon. Secretary: J. A. Carter, 1 Rosehay Close, Formby, Liverpool.

## WATSONIANS

Another of the well known Scottish clubs, perhaps more widely known than most for the Watsonians (Old Boys of Watson's School, Edinburgh) have for years now, made a Christmastide tour to South Wales, a traditional item in their fixture card. Since J. Tod was capped for Scotland against England in 1884, the club have produced more than 40 Internationals, the leading cap holder being J. C. McCallum with 26, whilst other distinguished Watsonians in Scottish XVs were: A. W. Angus (18), E. Milroy (12), A. C. Gillies (12), H. O. Smith (11), D. M. Bertram (11). Another Watsonian International, J. D. Dallas, earned even greater fame or (according to national viewpoints) notoriety, as referee of the controversial Wales v. New Zealand game at Cardiff in 1905. Club colours: Maroon and white hoops. Ground: Myreside, Edinburgh. Secretary: D. D. Carmichael, 1 Royal Terrace, Edinburgh. EH7 5AB.

## WEIGHT

Among the heaviest men ever to play rugby at international level are J. L. Myburgh (South Africa) 19st. 4 lbs. (270 lbs.), P. F. Hancock (England) 17st. 9 lbs. (247 lbs.), G. Fay (Australia) 17st. 8 lbs. (246 lbs.), M. J. Campbell-Lamerton (Scotland) 17st. 8 lbs. (246 lbs.), P. J. Whiting (New Zealand) 17st. 8 lbs. (246 lbs)

Among the lightest rugby internationals are the New Zealanders, M. N. Corner, 9st. 6 lbs. (132 lbs.), and A. E. Cooke, 9st. 12 lbs. (138 lbs.).

## WELLINGTON RUGBY UNION

Founded in 1879 and affiliated to the New Zealand Rugby Union in 1892, Wellington have been among the most successful Ranfurly Shield competitors. Famous players in the Union's history include the versatile and spectacular W. J. Wallace, who was a member of Gallaher's original All-Blacks, M. F. Nicholls, one of the shining lights in Porter's "Invincibles", F. Roberts, greatest of half-backs, B. S. Sadler, A. Lambourn, R. A. Jarden, W. H. Clarke and, more recently, I. N. MacEwan, capped 20 times, and prop K. F. Gray capped 24 times. It is, too, an historical fact that the Wellington club affiliated to the parent Union took part in the first inter-club game ever staged in New Zealand, this was in 1881, their opponents being the Nelson R. F. C. Colours: Black with gold monogram. Ground: Athletic Park, Wellington, North Island.

## WELSH RUGBY UNION

The Welsh Rugby Union, which stemmed from the old South Wales Rugby Union, was formed at a meeting convened at the Castle Hotel, Neath, in March 1881. The 11 pioneer clubs were Bangor, Brecon, Cardiff, Lampeter, Llandeilo, Llandovery, Llanelli, Merthyr, Newport, Pontypool, and Swansea. Prominent administrators in the early days of the Union's existence were R. Mullock, of Newport (the first Secretary), and Sir J. T. D. Llewelyn, M.P., who acted as President from 1895-1906. Then in 1906 Horace Lyne, M.B.E., of Newport, a former Welsh International player, embarked on a tenure of the Presidency that was to last 42 years. He was succeeded in 1947 by another famous figure, Sir David Rocyn Jones, C.B.E., K.St.J., D.L., J.P. Other famous administrators in the Union's history include Humphrey Leyshon and W. R. Thomas (Aberavon), A. E. Freethy (Neath), Ernest Davies, J.P. (Swansea), J. Lot Thorn (Penarth), W. J. Llewelyn (Bridgend), and T. D. Schofield (Bridgend).

In 1953, Ernest Davies, J.P., of Swansea, succeeded to the Presidency of the Union on the death of Sir David Rocyn Jones, and his election marked a departure from a tradition that had lasted almost 60 years, for the Union decided that henceforward their President would be appointed on an annual basis only.

In all respects the Welsh Rugby Union have been long and faithfully served by its officials, and in this respect it is noteworthy to point out that in the 95 years of its existence the Union have only had five secretaries. The original secretary, R. Mullock, presided until 1892, when he handed the post over to W. H. Gwynn, of Swansea, whose services spanned the years 1892-96. Then in 1896 Capt. Walter Rees, of Neath, assumed the office he was to hold for over half a century. In 1948 Capt. Rees was succeeded by Eric Evans, who was already well known to Rugby people as the founder and secretary of the Welsh Secondary School's Union. Evans held office until his premature death in 1954; and was succeeded by W. H. Clement, M.C. T.D., the former Wales and Great Britain wing threequarter.

There are 178 clubs affiliated to the W.R.U., and the traditional resistance to official recognition of competitive rugby was broken in 1971 with the launching of the W.R.U. Challenge Cup, the inaugural tournament being won by Neath. For administrative purposes the Union is divided into nine districts. In addition, the following bodies are represented on the Union committee: Welsh Secondary School's R.U., Welsh Youth Union, Welsh Schools' R.U., Welsh Junior R.U., and London Welsh. Finally there are five Vice-Presidents chosen by ballot at the Union's annual meeting.

Address: Royal London House, 28-31 St. Mary Street, Cardiff.

See also under INTERNATIONALS (Wales.).

## WEST COAST

Founded in 1890, affiliated to New Zealand Rugby Union 1893. Headquarters: Greymouth, South Island. Colours: Red and white hoops. Outstanding player, R. R. King who was capped 13 times in the 1930s.

## WESTERN PROVINCE

Founded in 1883, Western Province are the oldest of the Provincial Rugby Unions of South Africa, and if one is to judge from their accomplishments throughout the intervening years, then they must be esteemed the greatest as well Indeed the Province have virtually dominated the Currie Cup competition for out of the 36 occasions on which the trophy has been up for competition since 1889, they can show no fewer than 19 outright wins, whilst on another two

occasions—in 1932 and 1934—they shared the Cup with Border. Inevitably Western Province has contributed heavily, and indeed near luminously, to the triumphal progress of South Africa in the field of Test Rugby, and amongst those who have worn the famous blue and white jersey of the Province are many of the legendary figures of "Springbok" history, including the fabulous Morkel family, seven of whose members have played for South Africa. Other Western Provinces immortals include: Paul Roos, the Steggmann brothers, W. A. Millar, G. H. Brand, M. Zimmermann, D. O. Williams, B. L. Osler, D. H. Craven, the brothers "Boy" and "Fanie" Louw, P. J. Mostert, J. K. Osche, and Stephen Fry. More recently they have produced such brilliant Internationals as full-back L. G. Wilson, wing-threequarter J. P. Engelbrecht and centre threequarter J. L. Gainsford. Within the Union club Rugby is organised on a strictly competitive basis, with the Western Province Grand Challenge Cup the incentive to success in the Province's Senior Log (League) competition.

The ancestral home of Western Province Rugby is the Newlands Ground at Cape Town, the venue of so many historic Test and Currie Cup encounters.

## WESTERN TRANSVAAL

Formed in 1920 when they first participated in the Currie Cup, Western Transvaal have produced a number of Springbok International players including: J. Aucamp, N. J. du Plessis, A. Myburgh, H. Newton-Walker, and more recently J. T. Claassen, certainly one of South Africa's finest ever lock-forwards capped 28 times. Union headquarters is at Potchefstroom. Colours: Green jersey with red band, white shorts, green stockings with red band.

## WEST OF SCOTLAND R.F.C.

West of Scotland R.F.C. are one of the oldest clubs in Scotland—and in the early days of their existence—one of the most powerful. Together with Edinburgh Academicals they were prime movers in the "Challenge" that resulted in the first ever International match between Scotland and England. One of the club's members A. H. Robertson, played in that encounter, and by 1914 the club had supplied no fewer than 42 players for the Scottish national side, among them the famous Neilson brothers, J. D. Boswell, W. P. Scott and W. Wotherspoon. Between the wars the club had a long spell out of the limelight but the 1960s brought something of a revival and they shared the unofficial Scottish club championship with Hawick in 1964-65, and were then runners-up on four occasions before winning the title in 1970-71. In 1973-74 they were only beaten on points difference (by Hawick) for the championship of the new national league. Colours: Red and yellow. Ground: Burnbrae, Glasgow Road, Milngavie, Glasgow. Hon. Secretary: J. M. McGill, 12 Woodside Place, Glasgow, G3 7QN.

## WEST WALES RUGBY UNION

The West Wales Rugby Union which is in effect a Union within a Union (it is affiliated to, and represented on the parent body, the Welsh Rugby Union) has its origins in the period of industrial depression that affected South Wales so badly during the early and middle 'thirties. Indeed so poor was the support accorded the second class clubs of the West Wales coalfield during the period that many of them were threatened with extinction. In an effort to stimulate enthusiasm, Mr. F. G. Phillips, who was at the time a prominent referee, got a number of clubs to agree to the introduction of competitive Rugby run on the lines of the Cup and Championship competition favoured by the Rugby League

in the North of England. This came into being in 1930, the West Wales Rugby League with its knock-out cup and championship competition which created widespread enthusiasm, besides restoring to solvency many clubs who were on the verge of bankruptcy. It was the West Wales Rugby League, whose title was later changed to the West Wales Rugby Union, which played the main part in the repelling of the "Rugby League" invasion of West Wales in 1949. Colours: Red, black and amber, Secretary: S. G. Thorn, 14 Gors Road, Burry Port, Dyfed.

## WING FORWARD
See under FLANKER.

## WOODEN SPOON

The entirely mythical award made to the bottom team in the International Championship in Great Britain and France. In season 1956-57, however, when France lost all her International Championship matches, a disappointed supporter was moved to make the award tangible, and accordingly presented Jean Prat, one of his country's greatest players and captains, with a 6ft. long spoon boasting a business end that could absorb 3½ pints of any sorrow-drowning liquid the recipient cared to choose. Prat, it should be pointed out, was not a member of the French side which suffered these indignities for he had retired the previous season.

**YOUNGEST PLAYER**
See AGE.

# INDEX

NOTES

# INDEX